Contents

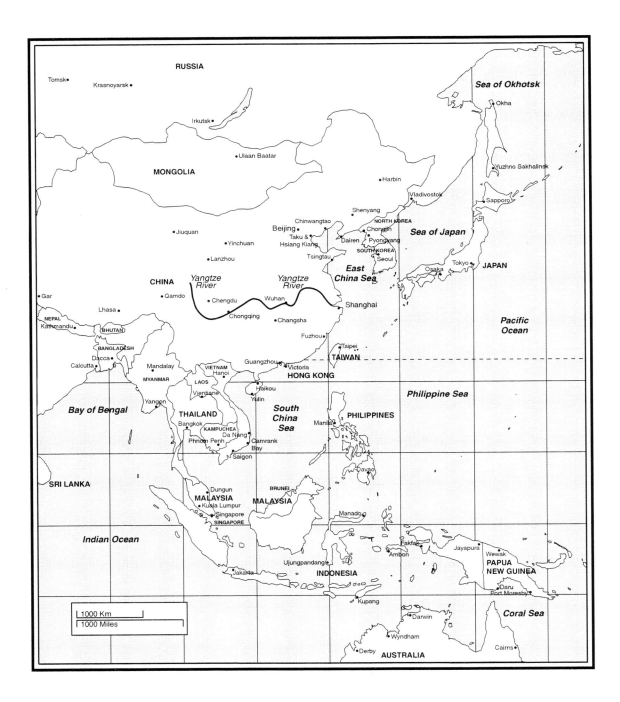

Foreword

The Society for Nautical Research is international in both its membership and its research in maritime history, as can be seen by any study of papers published in its journal, *The Mariner's Mirror*. The pages of '*MM*', as the journal is familiarly known, demonstrate a long and continuing interest in Chinese trade, shipbuilding and navigation, and the history of European, particularly British, contacts is evident annually in our publications. The China Seas have a prominent place in British maritime history and it is appropriate that a conference in Liverpool should take this as its theme, beginning with trade in the seventeenth century by the East India Company and broadening to encompass a whole range of enterprises owned by different businesses. The British share in this trade is not often taken in context and the thriving maritime traffic, which had its origin long before foreign intrusion, was shared with the coasters and vessels of Asian or other European nations.

The papers presented at the conference provide an overview which is often missing. Their content takes account both of British interest in the region and the foreign, European and American, contribution, bringing the history of these contacts down to the modern era of container shipping. The strategic implications for the Royal Navy were important throughout this history, particularly after Britain acquired a base in Hong Kong, and the advantages this brought to British shipping for safe navigation and political protection are clearly set out in this volume. Neither is the human element neglected. One highlight of the conference was the personal reminiscences of those who had experienced the China Seas at first hand during the twentieth century, and the roles of British and Chinese crews in local shipping were described by seveal contributors. The overseas links created by Chinese comminities established in Britain as a result of trade with China remain a familiar and now long-established feature of some British cities.

The success of the Conference in Liverpool can be judged from the papers published in this volume, and it was fortunate to draw support from many quarters. The conference was hosted by the Merseyside Maritime Museum and benefited from the generous financial help of two charitable trusts, the Swire Charitable Trust and the P. H. Holt Trust, and the Society for Nautical Research also provided a grant. The planning for the conference was shared by the Soociety, led by Professor Sarah Palmer as Chairman of the Research and Programme Committee, and National Museums Liverpool, where Dr Adrian Jarvis shouldered the burden. Both would wish me to say, however, how much is owed to Dr Ann Shirley and Captain Roger Parry, whose inspiration and enthusiasm secured the success of a meeting notable not only for distinguished contributors but for the lively and busy discussions that accompanied each session. I am delighted to have had the opportunity to furnish the foreword to this book, with its comprehensive modern review of British shipping in the China Seas, where the real credit for the stimulating papers belongs to the contributors who researched and presented the scholarly proceedings published in this volume.

Alan Aberg,
Chairman,
Society for Nautical Research.

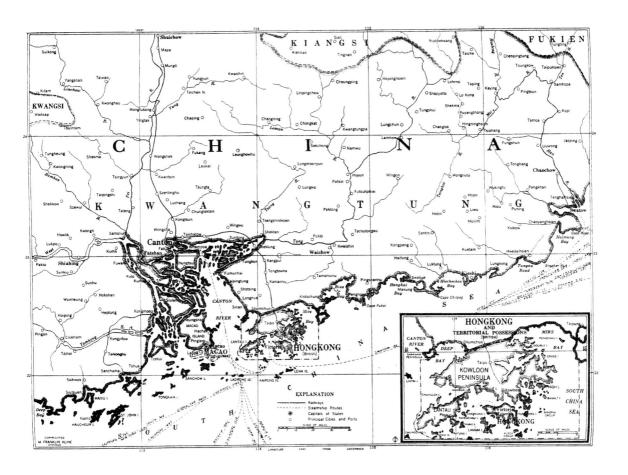

The Century of the China Station: the Royal Navy in Chinese Waters, 1842-1942

Eric Grove

Between the beginning of the 1840s and the anti-western Japanese offensive a century later Chinese waters were a major area of deployment for the Royal Navy. After the so called Opium War of 1839-42 Chinese waters were elevated to the status of a fully fledged 'Station' based at Hong Kong, a status it kept until the Japanese took Hong Kong at the end of 1941. This paper seeks briefly to summarise the story of this important naval command that for a century was the lynchpin of the British Empire's strategic position in the Western Pacific.

1842 saw the signature of the Treaty of Nanking in the cabin of the 72 gun ship of the line *Cornwallis*, flagship of Vice Admiral Sir William Parker, 'Commander of Her Majesty's Ships and Vessels in the East Indies and in the Seas Adjacent'. This was at the end of an increasingly aggressive maritime and riverine campaign that had begun in 1839. Usually called the Opium War, because of the exports the British were trying to force on China (but perhaps better called the 'Tea War' after the commodity that caused the trade imbalance corrected by the drug), operations had been carried out by a major force of sailing warships of the Royal Navy and paddle steamers of the Indian Navy and Bengal Marine. A major prize for the British was the island of Hong Kong.[1]

By 1844 the need to protect British trade from both official and unofficial threats led to the splitting of the East Indies Station into two administrative parts, one being based in Hong Kong as a 'China Station'. Thus Rear Admiral Sir Thomas Cochrane became the first Commander of the East Indies and China Stations. He had one ship of the line *Agincourt*, six frigates, five sloops and three steamers to cover the two parts of his command.[2]

In 1848 Australia became a third part of the 'East Indies, China and Australia' command.

During the Russian War, the Russian ships in the Far East were dealt with by the ships of the Pacific Station based on the other side of the Pacific rather than the ships based to the southwest. At this time the station deployed two 50 gun frigates, two 40 gun frigates, a 26 gun frigate, the 14 gun steam screw frigate *Encounter*, two steamers (one paddle and one screw) and four sailing sloops. Two hulks, *Minden* and *Calcutta*, supported the fleet at Hong Kong and the *Sappho* at Trincomalee. One of the 50s was replaced by an 84 gun liner (HMS *Calcutta*) by June. The Australian part of the station was maintained by a single small frigate and a survey cutter.[3]

In the context of the Second China War (the 'Arrow War') further reorganisation took place and Australia was hived off as a completely separate command in 1859. The war clearly made the China Station dominate over the East Indies, especially as the Treaty of Peking led to the need for gunboats to police extraterritorial rights on rivers. The war had seen a large force of gun vessels and gunboats arrive, eleven of which were used in the unsuccessful attack on the Peiho Forts in 1859.[4]

In 1863 the Station was involved in the armed coercion of Japanese factions. Vice Admiral Kuper initially deployed a screw frigate *Eyryalus*, a screw corvette, a screw sloop, a paddle sloop, a new screw gun vessel and a gunboat. The following year the station's screw liner, the 78 gun *Conqueror*, helped an international squadron force the straits of Shimonoseki, although as much as a troop transport as for her firepower.[5] She was, however, the last British 'wooden wall' to fire her guns in anger.[6]

The following year, 1864, the East Indies became a separate Flag Officer's command and the China Station (for a time 'The China and Japan Station') emerged as the largest single station in the Royal Navy in terms of numbers of ships. In August 1866 there were 36 ships of 26,639 tons manned by 3966 personnel. The flagship was the 73 gun screw liner *Princess Royal* and the other major combatants were three screw corvettes of 17-21 guns, two paddle sloops, three screw sloops, five gun vessels and no less than fourteen gunboats with a fifteenth being used as a tender. There were eight smaller vessels in order to have one at each consular port. *Princess Charlotte* was the receiving ship and there were hospital ships at both Hong Kong and Shanghai.

The station began in the west from 95 degrees East longitude in the latitude of 8 degrees North, east along that parallel to the West coast of Malaya and south down 95 degrees longitude to 10 degrees South. It originally went east at that latitude until it struck 170 degrees which it then followed to the Bering Straits. The southern corner was soon removed, however, to place Papua New Guinea and the Carolines on the Australia station. The new south eastern corner of the China Station was at longitude 130 and it ran up that line to 12 degrees north when it went east to meet 170 degrees as before.[7]

The Station was divided into four Divisions, South China, North China (with a senior officer at Shanghai), Japan (SO Yokohama) and Straits of Malacca (SO Singapore). There was a coaling station at Singapore, a coal store at Kowloon and coaling facilities at Swatow, Amoy and Foochow.[8]

In 1867 Admiral Sir Henry Keppel requested an ironclad to reinforce his new flagship, the last operational wooden liner, the 78 gun *Rodney*, which came home to pay off in 1870. The wooden ironclad *Ocean* duly made her passage east in 1867, largely under sail and became flagship when *Rodney* came home in 1870. The small centre battery ironclad *Vanguard*, one of the *Audacious* class specially built for foreign stations replaced *Ocean* in 1872. *Iron Duke* and *Audacious* alternated as flagships until 1889.[9]

Iron Duke led a major demonstration to overawe the Sultan of Selangor at the beginning of 1874. It was accompanied by the

corvette *Thalia*, sloop *Rinaldo* and gun vessels *Frolic*, *Avon* and *Midge*, as well the despatch paddle steamer *Salamis* and a colonial steamer. Units of the station were also involved in subsequent operations asserting British control in Malaya in 1874-6. Naval personnel also served with distinction ashore.

By 1876 the first modern screw corvette *Modeste* had appeared and another, *Juno* (a partial troop carrier) was replacing three smaller vessels. Another new cruiser was the screw sloop *Egeria*. Fifteen gun vessels and gunboats provided the backbone of the Squadron although numbers were coming down. The new receiving ship was the former steam liner HMS *Victor Emmanuel*, fresh from her activities as depot ship in the Ashanti Wars. In 1869 the station had been reduced to 25 units. By 1876 it had shrunk to only 20 combatant ships and 2724 men, although the number of gunboats still made it the largest foreign station.

In order to supplement the ironclad flagship, the turret ram HMS *Wivern* was sent to Hong Kong in 1880. She was one of the 'Laird rams' taken over in the American Civil war to stop them being acquired by their Confederate owners. She was placed in reserve there and remained as a mobilisable reserve until 1898 when she was hulked.

Two years later Vice Admiral Sir George Willes (an old China hand with bitter experience of the Peiho Forts) reported back to London on the state of his Station which he had commanded for a year. He had been asked by the Admiralty to report on 'the amount of naval force maintained on the China Station as well as the type of ship, in view of the possible contingency of war.[10] He first drew attention to the amount of British trade in the area. In 1880 British ships had made almost 12,400 entries and clearances at China ports carrying over 9.6 million tons of trade. The total value of foreign and coastal trade carried in British vessels was over £665 million This, plus the 'large number of foreign ships of war now within the limits of this command' prevented him acquiescing in any reduction of units, that now numbered only seventeen combatants (leaving out his despatch vessel and the *Victor Emmanuel*).

He was dissatisfied with his flagship *Iron Duke* about which he had grumbled since his arrival. She was slow, had no sailing ability and could not make passage to Singapore or Nagasaki against the Monsoon. Willes wanted the new centre battery armoured cruiser *Nelson* that had just gone to the Australia Station. With his flag in that ship the Commander in Chief could proceed from one distant part of his command to the other without exhausting his supply of fuel – a point vital in the event of hostilities.[11]

Willes was happy with the steel corvettes *Cleopatra*, *Curacoa* and *Comus* but less so with the screw sloop *Pegasus* that neither sailed nor steamed well. He was also pleased with the *Ariel* class composite gunboats *Zephyr* and *Mosquito* and the *Forester* class composite gunboat *Foxhound* which were 'well suited to both river and sea service'. The older composite gun vessels *Fly* and *Midge* were however 'quite out of date'. The old paddle steamer *Vigilant* was still giving good service as a despatch vessel along with the gun vessel *Swift* and the C-in-C made the case for maintaining two such shallow draft ships, one with a flag officer's accommodation, the other for more general service. The flatiron gunboats *Esk* and *Tweed* he did not consider generally useful in Chinese conditions although they would be useful in Malaya. He therefore kept them with false keels so they could be deployed there. The C-in-C still considered *Wivern* to be 'a most useful and efficient ship for the protection of Hong Kong, and under certain circumstances for service elsewhere on the station'. He planned to man her with the ship's company of his least efficient cruiser.

He put the requirements of the station as a better ironclad, four 'C' class corvettes, six improved *Pegasus* class sloops, five *Zephyr/Foxhound* gun vessels, two despatch vessels and *Wivern*. This would however be *utterly inadequate* for war. He recommended therefore stockpiling equipment to convert 12-15 fast and long range merchant steamers better able

than contemporary warships to cope with Chinese conditions of monsoons, currents and heavy seas.

Willes did not get his way. *Iron Duke* was replaced not by *Nelson* (or her sister *Northampton*) but by *Audacious* in 1883. The latter ironclad was still there in 1887 by which time the station had lost its pre-eminence in operational units to the Mediterranean.[12] The crisis with Russia had just caused the station to be reinforced by another acquired vessel, the ram *Orion* bought during the previous Russian scare of 1878. *Orion* was kept at Singapore until 1890. The cruising force had however been maintained at more or less the level for which Willes had asked, indeed it had been strengthened in quality As well as three remaining 'C's, two having just gone home, there was the fine new steel protected cruiser *Leander* and the older corvette *Sapphire* . The recently built large sloops/small corvettes *Satellite* and *Heroine* were also deployed to the station along with the smaller sloops *Mutine* and *Wanderer*. *Linnet* had been joined by her more combatant sister *Swift* to maintain gun vessel/gunboat strength at six. *Forester* had gone but her sister *Firebrand* was on station There was a sister of *Zephyr*, *Merlin*, and still newer gunboats were deployed in the shape of *Wasp*, *Cockchafer* and *Espoir*. A new purpose-built despatch vessel was available to the C-in-C, HMS *Alacrity*, but *Victor Emmanuel* was still there, despite Willes' request to have her replaced by a shore establishment. In 1898 she was replaced by the former troopship *Tamar* that would last out the Station.

The flagship ironclad (from October 1887 a 'battleship') was replaced by the second class battleship *Centurion* in 1894, *Centurion* was another type specially built for distant stations with long range and shallow draught. Her armament of 10-in and 4.7-in quick firing guns made her quite a formidable ship given the gunnery techniques of the day that emphasised quantity of fire rather than accuracy.

1895 saw the defeat of China by Japan and the beginnings of a scramble for Chinese territory by the major powers. Worries were expressed in London about British strength in the region in the new competitive atmosphere. Britain, however, still had almost a two power standard in the area over France and Russia; 26 ships against 29.[13] It was hoped to remain on good terms with Japan which was building a most impressive fleet largely in British yards. To increase combat power rapidly three *Orlando* class armoured cruisers were sent out in 1895 and plans made to build a new class of less well armoured, slightly smaller, but faster, first class battleship with 6-in and 12-in guns that would be suitable to pass through the Suez canal. The design was approved at the end of the year and the first two *Canopus* class ships were laid down the following year.[14]

In 1897 the Germans occupied Kiaochow and the Russians Port Arthur. Early in 1898 *Centurion*'s sister ship *Barfleur* was sent to join her along with the larger *Majestic* class battleship *Victorious* (the deep draught vessel grounding in the Suez canal). This gave Britain parity in battleships with Japan and superiority over the other powers. The British were also provoked by the Russian lease on Port Arthur to demand a similar lease on Wei-hai-wei which became British on its evacuation by the Japanese in May. The port and the island of Liu Kun were occupied in a major operation in May and this base became the China Station's second home.

In 1897 there were eight unarmoured cruisers with the China Station, four protected cruisers built under the Naval Defence Act, one first class and three second, a former torpedo cruiser and two new and one older sloops. *Swift* and *Linnet* were still on station as was *Alacrity*. Five first class gunboats of relatively recent build together with the older *Firebrand* and a flatiron vessel made up the gunboat flotilla. Willes had asked for torpedo craft as available and the 1880s had seen the deployment at Hong Kong of four of the earliest torpedo boats TBs *8-11*. By 1897 they had been joined by a couple of new destroyers, *Hardy* and *Hart*.

Two more armoured cruisers were added to the Station in 1899 but the coming of the *Canopus* class led to the build up of a powerful battleship squadron in Chinese waters. *Goliath* replaced *Victorious* in 1900, *Glory* commissioned as flagship at the end of the same year and *Ocean* and *Albion* came out in 1901. *Centurion* returned to the Station in 1903 in which year *Vengeance* replaced *Goliath*.[15] Thus by 1904 there were five battleships on station, four first class and one second.

The five older and smaller armoured cruisers had gone home to be replaced by the large and impressive *Leviathan*, the smaller *Cressy* and the only slightly smaller first class protected cruisers *Andromeda* and *Amphitrite*. There were four second class cruisers, an older third class (former torpedo) cruiser and six modern sloops. There was an old composite gunboat, a newer steel gunboat and a 'flatiron' but the gunboat flotilla had been transformed by the arrival from 1898 of the small specialist river gunboats or 'shallow draught steamers' of 85-180 tons, seven of which were in commission, together with a larger purchased paddler, *Kinsha*. The destroyer flotilla had increased to five units.

The radical First Sea Lord, Admiral Sir John Fisher, who came into office in 1904, planned major changes on the China Station. He wished to prune older obsolete vessels and replace the battleships with faster armoured cruisers. Then in 1905 the strategic situation suddenly changed with the defeat of the Russians by Britain's Japanese ally. Not only did this wipe out the Russians but the French and Americans recalled their heavy units also. With a radical cost-cutting Liberal government in power at home and no strategic threat the Station was run down.[16] The battleships came home in 1905 but there was no increase in first class cruisers.

By 1906 there were still only four such ships, three armoured (a large *Drake* and two smaller *Monmouths*) and a large protected cruiser. The smaller cruiser force was reduced to two *Astreas*. There were five modern first class gunboats (all three *Brambles* and two re-rated *Cadmus* class sloops). The river gunboat flotilla had expanded to ten and the destroyer flotilla to six.

As Nicholas Lambert has shown, British control of coal supplies made operations by numbers of hostile large armoured ships in the Pacific very difficult. The Admiralty maintained an infrastructure to fight in the Pacific (including a massive coal stock at Hong Kong), but did not feel the need to deploy a large fleet. Extra armoured cruisers could be sent East if required to confront an enemy *guerre de course*.

At the beginning of 1909 the C-in-C China, Vice Admiral Hedworth Lambton, set the cat among the pigeons by complaining to the Governor General of Hong Kong that the base's defences were too weak, that Britain had 'lost command of the sea in Far Eastern waters'.[17] The Admiralty, in accordance with its idea of flotilla defence, thought a few submarines could protect the Colony quite satisfactorily. When Lambton's complaints were discussed in the Committee of Imperial Defence the Government was assured that the Mediterranean Fleet could reinforce the Far East in just over three weeks; that a massive fleet of twenty battleships could be sent East even in the case of war with Germany; and that, anyway, the Japanese Alliance made the Empire in the Far East secure. Members of the Committee expressed doubts, however, about the long term survival of the Alliance and called for the strengthening of Britain's stationed forces.

The result was the concept of 'fleet units' each based around one of the new battlecruisers, three light cruisers, six destroyers and three submarines. There were to be four in the Pacific at Sydney (Australian), Vancouver (Canadian), Singapore and Hong Kong. The Hong Kong unit would be British but partly subsidised by New Zealand. Only the Australian unit was formed, as the scheme foundered on Churchill's desire to concentrate maximum strength in European waters. HMS *Indomitable*, about to be deployed to Hong Kong stayed at home and HMS *New Zealand* was earmarked for home waters after an Imperial cruise.

In 1910 the Admiralty had deployed two of its newest amd most powerful armoured cruisers, *Defence* and *Minotaur* to Hong Kong.[18]

These outclassed the two German cruisers *Scharnhorst* and *Gneisenau* the core of the German Asiatic Squadron.[19] In 1912 the less powerful *Hampshire* relieved *Defence* and the following year the relatively fast pre-Dreadnought HMS *Triumph* was sent to back up the Station's cruisers, that also included the two modern light cruisers *Newcastle* and *Yarmouth*. There were still five gunboat/sloops and ten 'shallow draught steamers'. The torpedo defences had been strengthened with five active destroyers, with three more and four torpedo boats in reserve. A new departure however were the submarines *C36, 37* and *38* with their depot ship *Rosario* which had duly arrived to reinforce Hong Kong's defences in 1911.

The creation of the Australian Fleet Unit in 1913 did more to restore the balance in the Pacific than the arrival of *Triumph*, that was refitted and maintained in reserve with a nucleus crew. Paul Halpern correctly assesses that, even with this reinforcement, the superiority of the China Station over its German counterpart was 'questionable'.[20] A French armoured cruiser arrived at Hong Kong on 5 August, restoring the balance a little. Luckily the largest German ships were far away, cruising around Germany's Pacific possessions. Vice Admiral Martyn Jerram's plans to deploy his squadron against Tsingtao were thrown into confusion by Admiralty orders to concentrate on Hong Kong, Churchill being anxious that Jerram had *Triumph* with him before he gave battle. This assisted German shipping, including the light cruiser *Emden*, to escape.

Triumph was reactivated using the crews of most of the shallow draught steamers and naval reservists, but there were not enough and locally based soldiers volunteered. She was ready for sea by 6 August. Four armed merchant cruisers were also fitted out in August at Hong Kong, *Himalaya*, and the *Empresses of Asia, Japan* and *Russia*. The personnel problem led to the armed merchant cruisers (AMCs) having to use British and Indian Army troops and *Empress of Russia* had a miscellaneous and possibly unique crew made up of Chinese from her original crew; volunteers from shore; Royal Marines; and French sailors from their river gunboats.[21] *Triumph* and the destroyer *Usk* assisted the Japanese at Tsingtao while the cruisers and AMCs, with Allied support, hunted for the *Emden* in the Bay of Bengal. *Minotaur* helped escort the Australian troop convoys but was detached to the Cape in case the German Asiatic Squadron tried to break back across the Pacific to South West Africa after its victory at Coronel.

The Japanese Navy dominated the area for the Allies and the Station rapidly became a backwater. In 1918, its equipment was obsolete. The armoured cruiser *Suffolk* was at Vladivostok and her sister *Kent* at Hong Kong along with the sloop *Cadmus* and the old destroyer *Virago*. The destroyer *Fame* was at Amoy and *Whiting* at Singapore. The river flotilla had been re-activated, the construction of vessels for operations on the Danube in the war providing a source of new and improved 'China gunboats' as they had been called to disguise their original purpose. The new 6-in gun armed *Insect* class *Tarantula* was at Hong Kong by the war's end with *Bee*, *Scarab* and *Gnat* on the lower Yangtse. The other six operational river gunboats were the old shallow draught steamers.[22] Four of the latter in reserve were soon sold for scrap, although one recommissioned. The submarine flotilla was also sold for scrap in 1919 as were the four old torpedo boats.

The end of the war transformed the strategic situation. After a brief period of planning against the United States as the primary enemy, the loss of the Japanese Alliance in the Washington Treaty in 1922 made the British Empire's erstwhile ally her most plausible enemy. A battlefleet could not be based in Chinese waters but a substantial force of smaller vessels was required on station in China to maintain British presence, and act if necessary as a defensive screen before the main fleet arrived at the planned-for base at Singapore. Britain offered to hand back Wei hai wei in 1922 but conditions in China prevented

the conclusion of a suitable agreement and it was not until April 1930 that the situation was regularised with the signing of a ten year lease with the Nationalist government running from October of that year.[23]

By 1922 the Station had a modernised cruiser force in the shape of the First Light Cruiser Squadron of three 'C' class ships and one 'D'. Submarines were now a more important part of the forces deployed, with the Fourth Submarine Flotilla and its six operational and six reserve boats, all of the modern and capable 'L' class. Four wartime sloops provided a modernised large gunboat force and there were fourteen gunboats on the rivers, over half of them *Insects*.

In 1924 a new capability came out to the China Station , the newly created Fleet Air Arm. The aircraft tender *Pegasus* was transferred to the station in April and stayed for almost a year. She was replaced by the first British purpose built aircraft carrier *Hermes* that joined the station in July 1925. After a brief return to the Mediterranean in 1926 and trips home to refit and recommission *Hermes* was a feature of the China seas until the end of 1936. When she went home in 1927 the pioneer carrier *Argus* replaced *Hermes* and in 1933 it was *Eagle* that filled the gap. *Eagle* also replaced *Hermes* when she finally went home and she provided the China Station's carrier until 1939. The carriers proved effective means of countering Chinese pirates as well as increasing the reach of British naval power on the station.[24]

Under stress of Japanese competition the British cruiser force on the China Station was increased in power and size. By 1925 as well as a 'C' and three 'D's there were two 7.5-in *Hawkins* class ships and an Australian light cruiser. The advent of the 8-in *County* class cruisers transformed the situation further and by 1930 there were five of these impressive ships on station, *Kent*, *Cumberland*, *Cornwall*, *Berwick* and *Suffolk*. There was also a destroyer flotilla, the 8th, with eight 'S' class units of end of war vintage. The river gunboat flotilla was also being modernised with the first two new *Tern* class vessels with better accommodation adding to a flotilla that now comprised 17 vessels, four in the West river and the rest in the Yangtse.

1930 saw a hiatus in that the 'L' class submarines were withdrawn by May. They were, however, replaced by bigger and better submarines specially built for reconnaissance and screening missions in the theatre. There were no less than twelve new 'O', 'P' and 'R' class submarines by the beginning of 1935. These boats were specially built for operations off Japan. A 'C' class cruiser was supplementing five *Counties* and the 8th Destroyer Flotilla had been re-equipped with nine modern 'D' class fleet destroyers. The minelayer *Adventure* was also on station along with six new sloops.[25] Modernisation of the 18 strong river gunboat flotilla had also continued with five new vessels launched between 1927 and 1934.[26] Thirteen were on the Yangtse and five on the West River.

Singapore was to be the main base for the Royal Navy in war with Japan as Hong Kong was deemed to be indefensible but there were hopes that the colony could, in certain circumstances, provide a forward base. Indeed, at the end of 1928, Admiral Sir Richard Tyrwhitt, the C-in-C, thought that:

> …no enemy (and most assuredly not the cautious and slow moving Nation against whose aggression our plans are assuredly made) would ever attempt to capture Singapore without first reducing Hong Kong.[27]

It was decided therefore to order the China Fleet to concentrate on Hong Kong. During the 1930s Singapore became once more the major concentration point, but the Fleet's second duty after securing Malaya was the relief of Hong Kong, that would assist in the blockade of Japan. The hope of hanging on to Hong Kong became even more distant when the Japanese occupied its hinterland in 1938 but it was still intended to defend Hong Kong as 'an outpost…for as long as possible in order to deny the use of the anchorage to the enemy'.[28] Some of the first motor torpedo boats, 7-12, were based at Hong Kong for local defence.

In 1938 the cruiser squadron received the latest of the new large 6-in gun *Southampton* Class, HMS *Birmingham*. In the summer of that year the 'China Fleet' still made a fine sight at Wei-hai-wei with the cruisers *Cumberland*, *Suffolk* and *Birmingham*, the 'D' class fleet destroyers and the submarine depot ship *Medway* with her flotilla of large and impressive submarines.[29]

The outbreak of war in Europe in which, contrary to pre-war fears, Japan did not intervene, inevitably saw a run down of the China Station The fleet destroyer flotilla, now numbered the 21st, went to the Mediterranean. Five old 'S' class destroyers were retained as a local defence flotilla for Hong Kong and Singapore. *Eagle* and the *County* class cruisers disappeared to search for raiders and were replaced by three 'D' class light cruisers and two armed merchant cruisers. *Birmingham* remained to be joined by *Liverpool* in November 1939 but the two modern cruisers were soon redeployed to the Mediterranean in 1940, the first to refit at Malta before joining the Home Fleet and the second to fight the Italians.[30] The sloop force was increased to eight units with the arrival of a New Zealand detachment. The opening of the new base at Singapore in 1939 had made the latter base more important even before the war began and the dozen submarines of the Fourth Flotilla were based there in late 1939, the 'O', 'P' and 'R' class boats being reinforced by a pair of *Grampus* class minelayers. There were eleven operational river gunboats on the Yangtse including the new specially built flagship *Scorpion* and five on the West River.

The strains of the naval war, greatly increased by Italy's entry into it, saw further run down of the Station, including the loss of the submarines and as war clouds gathered with Japan the main force of the Station were the cruisers *Danae*, *Dauntless*, *Dragon* and *Durban*. None were at Hong Kong when the Japanese attacked in December 1941 and two of the three destroyers were also ordered to Singapore leaving only *Thracian* (with mines). The MTBs were also available, the original five having been reinforced by two MTBs acquired from China and numbered 26 and 27. There were three river gunboats , one in dry dock, a boom defence vessel, eight auxiliary patrol vessels and two minelayers (by this time there were only four river gunboats in commission in Chinese waters, with three more laid up).

The ships gave what support they could although the Chinese crews of the auxiliaries had all deserted by 17 December. *Thracian* sank two ferry boats containing Japanese troops but was seriously damaged and her ships company were used ashore. As the Japanese crossed to Hong Kong island they were attacked by MTBs which had some success taking the Japanese by surprise. Two boats taking part in a later attack were, however both sunk. The river gunboat *Cicala* having done much with her two 6-in guns was bombed and sunk on 21 December. When the end came on Christmas Day the last active gunboat *Robin* was scuttled as were the remaining five MTBs, their crews, together with the Chinese Naval mission, making their way overland to Burma. Symbolically, the old depot ship *Tamar* had also been scuttled.[31]

It was the end of the old China Station. Those gunboats that survived on Chinese rivers were transferred to the Chinese and extraterritorial rights given up in 1943. Yet, when the Royal Navy came back in 1945 it looked as if business as usual was being restored. The headquarters of the 'British Pacific Fleet' moved initially to Hong Kong and there were even preparations to reconstitute a Yangtse Flotilla. The fleet itself had a remarkably familiar look to it : in 1947 two small carriers, three large cruisers (*Sussex*, *Belfast* and *Gambia*), flotillas of destroyers and submarines and six sloops. With China in the throes of civil war, British ships still saw action one last time on the Yangtse and major maritime intervention was threatened when the Chinese Nationalists took action against British shipping. British warships could still act in traditional ways, as when in 1950 the captain of the frigate HMS *Cardigan Bay* informed the commanding officer of a

Nationalist warship that there was no point in hanging onto a detained Red Ensign merchantman against the will of 'the ubiquitous British Navy'. The ship was duly returned.[32] Nevertheless times had changed, a fact confirmed by the Communist take-over on the mainland. Hong Kong soon reverted to what it had become by 1939, an Imperial outpost on a hostile shore. As early as September 1948 the newly renamed Far East Station had moved its headquarters to Singapore. In late 1957 it was announced that the Hong Kong Naval dockyard would close, as it did on 28 November 1959. The only ships based in the colony would be a small constabulary flotilla. This was certainly no longer the 'China Station' as it had been understood since the 1840s. An important era in British naval history had come to an end.

Notes and references

1   For good accounts of the China war see B. Greenhill and A. Giffard, *Steam Politics and Patronage,* (London, 1994) and G. S. Graham , *War and Diplomacy,* (Oxford, 1978).
2   Graham, *War and Diplomacy.*
3   Official 'Lists of Her Majesty's Ships in Commission' held at Naval Historical Branch, London.
4   W. L. Clowes, *The Royal Navy, A History,* (London, 1903), vol. 7, 125.
5   W. L. Clowes, *The Royal Navy,* vol. 7, 196-207.
6   A. Lambert, *Battleships in Transition,* (London, 1984), 84.
7   Station Orders for HM Ships and Naval Establishments on the China Station. Naval Library.
8   G. Fox, *British Admirals and Chinese Pirates,* (London, 1940), 65.
9   Oscar Parkes, *British Battleships,* (London, 1990), 155–6.
10 'Naval Force for the China Station', M Branch copy, held in the naval Library.
11 'Naval Force for the China Station'
12 Table 1 in J. F. Beeler, *British Naval Policy in the Gladstone-Disraeli Era*, (Stanford, 1997), 29.
13 A. Marder, *The Anatomy of British Sea Power,* (London, 1954), 240.
14 A. Marder, *Anatomy,* 240.
15 Parkes, *British Battleships,* 398-9.
16 N. Lambert, 'Economy or Empire; The fleet unit

concept and the quest for collective security in the Pacific, 1909-14' in G. Kennedy and K.Neilson, *Far Flung Lines*, (London, 1997), 57. The next section relies on this fine and seminal chapter.

17 Quoted in Lambert, 'Economy and Empire', 59.

18 Parkes, *British Battleships*, 449.

19 *Conway's All the Worlds Fighting Ships 1860-1905*, (London, 1979), 256.

20 P. Halpern, *A Naval History of World War One*, (Annapolis, 1994), 70.

21 P. Halpern, *A Naval History*.

22 Pink List for 16/11/18, Naval Historical Branch.

23 See J. Neidpath, *The Singapore Base and the Defence of Britain's Eastern Empire 1919-41*, (Oxford, 1981).

24 For carrier deployments see R. Sturtivant and D. Cronin, *Fleet Air Arm Aircraft, Units and Ships 1920 to 1939*, Tunbridge Wells, 1998: see also Jonathan Parkinson's paper in this volume.

25 Pink Lists, the sources also of subsequent deployment details.

26 *Conway's All The World's Fighting Ships 1922-1946*, (London, 1980),78.

27 Quoted in Neidpath, *The Singapore Base*, 114.

28 Staff History, *The War with Japan* (reprinted HMSO, 1995) vol 2, 39.

29 See picture in Admiral of the Fleet Sir Edward Ashmore's autobiography *The Battle and The Breeze*, (Thrupp, 1997). Ashmore gives a good account of life on the Station in its closing years and the uneasy relationship with the Japanese He was a Midshipman in HMS *Birmingham*.

30 M. J. Whitley, *Cruisers of World War Two*, (London, 1995).

31 Staff History, pp. 39-43.

32 See the author's *Vanguard to Trident*, (London, 1987), 127-137.

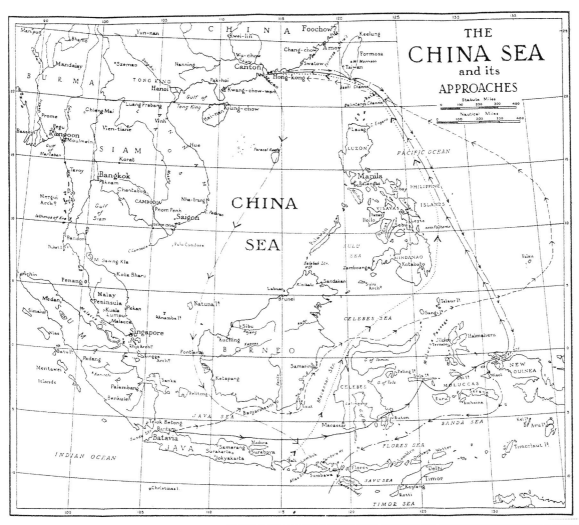

The China Sea and its approaches.

16

Lords of the East: the ships of the East India Company

Jean Sutton

The ships which sailed from this country to the China Seas from 1600 to 1834 were overwhelmingly English built and owned and were chartered exclusively, according to a unique system, by successive East India Companies. They were ships in the true nautical sense of the word at that time: three-masted, square-rigged on all masts, with an additional lateen course on the mizzen. Although the tonnage varied over the Company's life from only 150 tons to over 1400 tons, all were larger than other English merchant ships operating at any one time throughout the period.

These ships' activities in the China Seas fell naturally into two distinct periods: the first coincided exactly with the seventeenth century; the second covered the remainder of the period up to 1834. In the first, the Company endeavoured to gain access to the produce of China, particularly the fabled wrought (or woven) silks, by trading at a port on the Chinese mainland; failing that, indirectly at a port visited by Chinese junks. A direct trade was achieved in 1699 when a ship was allowed to trade at Canton. Throughout the second period the Company tried in vain to improve the conditions of trade imposed by the Chinese at Canton while continuing the search for indirect access to Chinese goods

The charter granted to a group of London merchants by the Crown in 1600 and renewed at intervals throughout two and a half centuries gave them a monopoly of trade between England and the lands 'beyond the Cape of Bona Esperanza to the Straits of Magellan for fifteen years…',[1] but the Company's commercial freedom was not entirely unrestricted: successive charters required that ten per cent of the exports comprise the growth or manufacture of England, which in the economy of the time

meant woollen cloth and some metals of which only lead ever found a ready market in the east. Throughout the Company's trading life these conditions hung like a millstone round the Company's neck. What the Council at Chusan wrote to the Court of Directors in 1702 in the typically robust language of the day could have been repeated at any time until the end of the Company's trading life:

> *We cannot tell what to advise your Honours to send to these Parts, the Natives being fond of nothing but Silver and Lead; and probably if the rest of your Goods were thrown over board at Sea, your Cargoes home would not be much the less.*[2]

In recognition of this the Company was permitted to take out of the country up to £30,000 of silver annually, a concession generally viewed with alarm, voiced among others by Robert Keale who labelled the Company 'enemies of Christendom as they carried away the treasure of Europe to enrich the heathen'.[3]

Once arrived in the eastern seas the merchants, or supercargoes, charged with conducting the fleets' trade had to lock into the vast, extensive, timeless trading system of the eastern seas and try to secure some advantage for the subscribers in England while dealing with problems on every front. The ships were victualled for two years until reliable sources of food were discovered along the routes. The failure of the beer to last that long and finding supplies of wholesome water were constant problems. The rhythm of the monsoon winds regulated trade in the eastern seas, ships failing to arrive in time suffering long additional delays. Navigational instruments were very basic, charts unreliable, and the body of experience contained in sailing directions, mainly Portuguese and Dutch, was jealously guarded. Disease weakened crews and replacements were very difficult to find. Where the ships were allowed to trade they suffered harassment and long delays, necessitating constant vigilance and ready arms, while the ships had to be on their guard in the early decades against Portuguese and, after only a brief honeymoon, Dutch hostility. Long voyages presented problems of maintenance, necessitating finding suitable places for careening.

Bantam was chosen as the base for the President of all the Company's fleets in the east, his job being to seek out the best trade. His attention soon focused on obtaining the fabled products of Cathay, part of an amorphous area often referred to as the Indies. He accepted from Dutch experience that mainland China was completely closed. He therefore concentrated on gaining indirect access to Chinese products. Japan was attractive as a source of silver to purchase Chinese goods, a policy adopted by the Dutch. An English seaman, who had been shipwrecked on the coast of Japan and subsequently benefited from the protection of a powerful overlord, informed him:

> Now my good friend can our English merchants get the handling or trade with the Chinese, then shall our country make great profit here, and your worshipful Company of London shall not have the need to send money out of England, for in Japan is gold and silver in abundance, for with the traffic here they shall have money to serve their need, I mean in the Indies, etc.[4]

From a factory, or trading base, established at Hirado (Firando) a trade was opened with Siam at Patani and Ayuthia where deerskins and redwood, both in great demand in Japan, were obtained, but the results were disappointing. Dutch seditious rumours alienated the Japanese against the English and a new Emperor expelled them on his accession.

Macao, the Portuguese-administered territory at the mouth of the Pearl River, offered the best means of gaining access to the China trade. A truce and free trade agreement between England and Portugal in 1635 seemed to offer mutual advantages: the English neutral flag for moving Portuguese goods in hostile Dutch infested seas, and an entry into the China trade for the English. An attempt in 1635 failed through the jealousy of the Portuguese Governor of Macao and harassment by Chinese officials while an aggressive visit by English interloping ships licensed by Charles I damned the English in Chinese eyes for generations.

After a long period of inactivity a reinvigorated, well capitalised company renewed its attempts to obtain China goods on three fronts in 1673: Tongking, Taiwan (Formosa) and a fresh attempt at Japan. In contrast to the fleet of very large ships built during the first two decades at the Company's own shipyards at Deptford and Blackwall, three small ships built in private yards on the Thames were now chartered to reconnoitre and

The East India Company shipyard at Deptford.
National Maritime Museum, Greenwich

establish trading bases where they were well received and profits might be made. According to an officer on board the 250 ton *Experiment*,

> ...*we were bound to a place where no English ship had been in 40 years before, which was to the island of Fearmosa upon the coast of China, and also to Japan to settle a factory at both places if we could...*[5]

The little 180 ton *Zant* succeeded in opening a factory at Tongking which obtained the greatly desired Chinese woven silks, but at great cost, trade being conducted only at the whim of the ruler and on his terms. The *Experiment* and *Return* failed in their attempts to trade at Taiwan, and they were too late in the season to go on to Japan. To minimize the waste of tonnage, the *Experiment* was sent back to Bantam, but was unfortunately taken by the Dutch in the Strait of Banka as news of the outbreak of war between England and the Netherlands had not reached her. The 350 ton *Return* was disappointed at Nagasaki: the Dutch had successfully spread the news of Charles II's marriage to a Portuguese princess, alarming the Emperor who had had trouble with Jesuits converting his people to Catholicism. She went on to Macao as the only secure place where she could careen and managed to sell her stock among the islands, just breaking even. By now three years out of England, her crew were mutinous.

The first factory established on mainland China was at Amoy, a tributary to Taiwan, which was one of the last areas to resist the Manchu expansion. But Manchus controlled all the surrounding country, preventing access to China goods. Amoy soon fell to the enemy and subsequent attempts to trade there met with little success.

The New East India Company, created in 1698 in opposition to the old, which was a creature of the Stuarts, opened a factory at Chusan. The Directors were keen to establish a trade at or near Nanking, source of the best silks, while they hoped to find in these cooler, more northerly climes 'a considerable vent for our Woolen Manufactures'.[6] Chinese suspicion

and harassment forced them to withdraw and they eventually obtained Company approval for a fortified base on the island of Pula Condore with a view to making it a great port which would attract China junks and ships carrying spices and other products of the east, but the garrison was massacred. In all these ventures it had been impossible to find a trade free from extortion, arbitrary and capricious rules, and physical danger.

The Manchu dynasty was firmly in place in China by 1683 and the policy of permitting foreigners to trade established. In the final year of the century the New Company's 250 ton *Macclesfield Galley* was allowed to trade at Canton. She returned with a cargo of wrought silks to find that Parliament had responded to the native silk weaving industry's fears of oriental competition by prohibiting the wearing of all woven silks from India, which by extension included China. Tea, on the other hand, which had enjoyed only a sluggish demand since first tried in 1666, was rapidly increasing in popularity and quickly became the major import from China, with raw silk replacing wrought silks in second place.

The actual physical achievement of navigating this strange and dangerous sea is incredible. Navigational instruments were basic, little changed since mediaeval times; latitude could be calculated within a few minutes but the navigators had to work out their east-west position by keeping a record of their course, the winds, the currents and their speed from the last sight of land whose longitude was known. Latitude sailing and constant use of the lead were the order of the day. However, we must not underestimate knowledge of strange seas communicated by word of mouth or encounter, overriding narrow national interests. European navigators in the eastern seas at that time comprised a very small elite whose *esprit de corps* probably surpassed their paymasters' rivalries. Surviving accounts by seamen of the times reveal much greater cooperation than might be supposed. Edward Barlow tells us that in 1673 the *Experiment* was piloted by a Chinese junk –

the best sailing ship he had ever seen – owned by the Company; the route was that followed subsequently and recommended in nineteenth century sailing directions for the China Sea. On a later voyage, when Barlow, as first mate, was paid extra to take the ship from Java to Canton as the captain had never sailed in the China Seas, he knew that it was too late in the season to follow the coast and sailed over between the Paracels and the Macclesfield Bank, exactly what was advocated a century later. These men considered their own lives and their livelihood more important than national rivalries.

The opening of the eighteenth century marked the beginning of a new era in the Company's trade. The Old and New companies merged to form the United Company of Merchants of England trading to the East Indies. Securing its legitimacy by a £3.2m loan to the state it became, with the Bank of England and the Royal Exchange, one of the pillars of the emergent world financial centre - the City of London. The Company had secured its long held ambition: a foothold on mainland China. But Canton had many limitations. It was far removed from Nanking where the best silk was produced, and from Fukien, the main source of teas, while there was little demand there for English woollen cloth. From the first the Company sent ships at frequent intervals to the more northerly ports of Amoy and Ningpo (Limpo) to seek out a trade but obstacles were put in the way. The Chinese authorities were determined to restrict

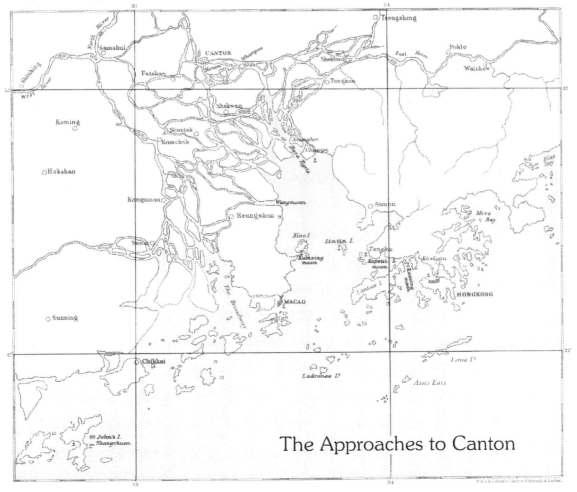

The Approaches to Canton

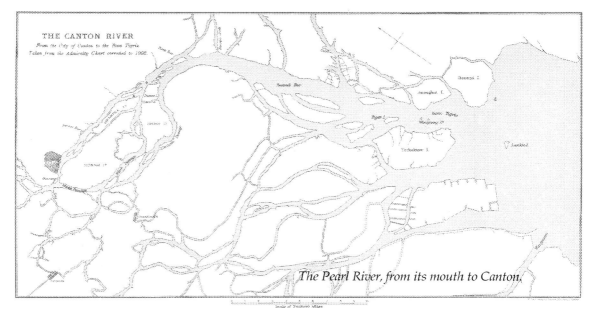

THE CANTON RIVER
From the City of Canton to the Boca Tigris
Taken from the Admiralty Chart corrected to 1906.

The Pearl River, from its mouth to Canton.

the European trade and the European barbarians – 'The Seamen and Officers, some or the Major part, are Brutes'[7] – to a part of the coast as far away from Peking as possible.

The Company despatched small fleets of ships over the winter months scheduled to arrive in the China Sea at the time of the south-west monsoon, between June and September, to take them up to Canton. The ships' absolute dependence on the south-west monsoon to reach Canton was broken in 1759 when Captain Wilson of the *Pitt* successfully sailed via the eastern islands, a passage which enabled commanders who had lost their passage to avoid wintering until the next monsoon. Early in the century the ships were small, of about 300 tons, and only about two a year were sent to China, returning via India to fill up with Indian goods. As the demand in England for tea increased throughout the century, despite the extremely high English customs duties, the ships increased in number and size, reaching about 750 tons by the 1770s. These ships were built in the private merchant yards along the Thames. They carried crews of 100 men and were armed with 26 nine pounder guns. Their cargo differed little from that carried by the ships in the previous

century: silver specie with some woollen cloth and metals. Most sailed via Madras where they picked up more silver, largely supplied from Bengal, to add to the tea investment.

Whether the ships entered the China Sea by the Strait of Malacca or Sunda, they headed for Pula Condore and Pula Sapata, then the Macclesfield Bank, hoping to avoid a typhoon which could overtake them without warning, and exercising particular caution at the change of the monsoon.

They looked out for the Lema Islands, the first indication that they were approaching the mouth of the Pearl (or Canton) River. They then looked out for the landmark, the Asses Ears, and sailed between that and the island immediately to the west. They passed the Grand Ladrone, the larger of the two Ladrones Islands, and anchored in the Taipa or Macao Road. From there a pilot took the ship up to the Boca Tigris, or the Bogue, where a river pilot took charge of the ship up the Pearl River to the European anchorage at Whampoa, about ten miles from Canton. A Chinese compradore was allocated to each ship to undertake victualling and supply of boats for unloading and loading. The English ships shared the anchorage at Whampoa with several much larger ships. Some belonged to the East India companies of France, Holland and Denmark; the rest were largely owned and commanded by English and Scots employed by the Austrian or Swedish companies to protect them against action by the English Company for infringing its monopoly. All were there to buy tea, mainly for the English market. By the 1760s it was estimated that the foreigners supplied smugglers with about half of the tea consumed in England.

The arrival in port of hundreds of men who had been at sea for five to six months and had easy access to alcohol always presented problems at Whampoa. The Company's instructions to their commanders urged them to see that their men observed 'sobriety and civil deportment' in China and prevent 'all quarrels and frayes' with the French and other Europeans.[8] Separation of the English and French, with the latter confined to French Island, the English to Danes Island, the other nationalities free to frequent either, was adopted early as a preventive measure. Each of the Company's ships erected a banksall on Danes Island in which all the masts and yards were stored while the ship was unloaded and completely overhauled in readiness for the return voyage. It was two or three months before the ships were partly loaded with a flooring of chinaware packed with sago on which the cheaper black teas, then the more expensive green teas and raw silk were laden. They then dropped down to the Second Bar where loading was completed, the ships surveyed and the Grand Chop issued by the Chinese authorities permitting them to leave. The ships usually sailed for England in two fleets: the first in November or December, the second by the end of January or early February. The commanders gave the Council one month's notice of the date of departure given in their respective charter parties the Company paying *demorage* to the owners if the ships were detained beyond that date, exposing them to a winter passage round the Cape.[9] Should a ship subsequently suffer damage as a result of such detention, the commander had the right to protest to the Company.

The commander's instructions ordered him to proceed to Canton to place himself and his ship under the orders of the named supercargoes who had travelled out on the ship in order to sell the cargo and buy a return cargo through the agency of one of a small group merchants, or Hongs, each of whom had paid an enormous sum of money for a licence to conduct the trade with the Europeans. Each of these merchants was appointed 'security' to one or more ships, and was responsible for everything connected with that ship. The supercargoes worked from factories, or hongs, rented from the Security Merchants along the river outside the city of Canton. The

The European anchorage at Whampoa.
National Maritime Museum, Greenwich

commanders rented their own hongs to carry on their private trade while enjoying the hospitality of the supercargoes in the factory at the Company's expense, flouting the Directors' instructions. Over the decades the supercargoes of the various ships combined to form small councils in order to be in a stronger negotiating position when dealing with the Security Merchants. From 1755 a single Council with a President and nine assistants conducted the business for all the ships of the season. The merchants' response, to the great alarm of the Council, was to form themselves into a combination, the Conghong, or Cohong, but it was dissolved after a few years. However, as the number of Hongs rarely exceeded ten, and often fell below that number, a free market in the sale of the Company's imports and purchase of the teas, raw silk and, until 1823, nankeens, was limited. After the completion of the business for the season, the ships departed and the Council of Supercargoes left Canton, as required by Chinese regulations, and removed to Macao until the arrival of the following season's ships. According to charter party requirements the supercargoes paid each ship £200 per month on behalf of the Company during their stay in China.

A major event on the ship's arrival at Whampoa was the ritual of the measurage. The Quanpoo, Imperial Commissioner of the Canton customs, always called the Hoppo by

the English, arrived resplendent in his official robes, surrounded by his creatures who flailed the air round his advancing person to prevent any form of human lower life fouling his path, to measure the ship from main mast to foremast, on which a charge was calculated. This was in addition to the 'presents', a fixed sum for distribution to various officials, were the dues each ship had to pay. As a Manchu, the Hoppo was an administrator not in any way involved in trade, which he considered beneath contempt. The Celestial Empire needed nothing from the European barbarians, but the Emperor in his generosity was willing to make available the abundant wealth and superior culture of the empire on a tribute system. The Hoppo, together with the Viceroy, or Tsungtu, the highest civil official in Canton province, together controlled the European trade. The Europeans could communicate with these mandarins only through the Security Merchants and linguists, while the mandarins themselves were the sole channel of communication with Peking. When the Company sent one of its own men with a knowledge of Chinese to the Emperor direct, he was imprisoned for his effrontery and his assistant Chinese linguist was executed.[10]

It was a system tailor-made for corruption, and the officers and commanders of the Company's ships supplied the medium in their private trade. Separated from the centre of power in Peking, the Hoppo's only means of gaining influence and possible promotion was through acquiring *curiosities* on behalf of the Emperor: clocks, watches, musical boxes and mechanical toys, known generally among Company personnel in the China trade by the terms sing songs and toys. Canton was not a very lucrative market for East India commanders' and officers' private trade ventures. There was no wealthy expatriate community, such as that in Bengal, able and willing to buy the luxuries of European life. Their ventures comprised mainly flints taken out as ballast for use in the Chinese porcelain industry, and some metals, such as lead. They were allowed to take out £3,000 in silver to

exchange for gold, which was less valuable in China, and £2,000 in coral or amber. They grasped the opportunity offered by the Emperor's love of toys. On 30 June, 1766, Francis Steward, surgeon of the Neptune East Indiaman, wrote to his sister-in-law, Captain Steward's wife, from Madras Road on the eve of sailing to China. He assured her that if her husband's homebound investment was as profitable as his outward bound was 'you will never more experience the pangs of so long a separation'.[11] He told her how he and the Purser had had an hour's conversation the previous evening with the Nawab of the Carnatic, when they had shown him the captain's clocks. He had bought the best pair, which had cost 1,000 guineas in London. As an indication of the value, Captain Steward's ship probably cost 5,500 guineas when launched. He obviously had other clocks for disposal in Canton. That he sold them to his satisfaction is indicated by his retirement from the service on his return after only two voyages as captain, both to China, and his spending the rest of his life as a man of property.

A typical mechanical clock or 'sing-song'.
By kind permission of Christie's

The Hoppo was always anxious to see any of these *sing songs*, while the Council exhorted the captains to forbear showing any such things to the Hoppo's people – a futile request since it was only the captains who could afford to invest in such expensive goods and their future prospects depended on selling them. They had paid upwards of £5,000, rising to £10,000 in the following decades, for their commands for the purpose of making a fortune and retiring from the service as quickly as possible. It was in the Hoppo's interest to purchase the most splendid items obtainable, often costing far more than the amount provided by the Emperor to buy and transport them. The sufferers were the Security Merchants. Any infringement of regulations by any of the European officers or seamen on board an Indiaman placed the merchant who was the security for that ship in a vulnerable position. The Hoppo's power to stop the trade until a suitable bribe – in the form of *sing songs* – had been paid was unlimited. Bribing their way out of trouble became increasingly costly. The Council wrote to the Court of Directors:

> We beg leave to observe to your Honors (sic) that the Merchants here are under very great apprehensions that the Toys brought out on board the Hon'ble Company's Ships to such a large amount as have been lately, will be the ruin of some of them; since the dissolution of the Conghong the Merchants are no longer responsible for each other: therefore there is great Reason to apprehend that the Company may be involved in their Misfortunes, at present the Merchants are too few in number, as well as deficient in Capitals, for our Trade here, Ruin happening to any of them will yet (further) reduce the Number.[12]

The vulnerability of the trade and the geographic unsuitability of Canton stimulated the continuing search for an alternative port visited by Chinese junks and other traders. In the early 1760s two possibilities opened up simultaneously: Alexander Dalrymple, on the staff of the Madras Council, seduced by accounts of the early voyages, was convinced of the possibility of creating an *entrepot* in the eastern seas attracting Chinese junks and vessels carrying the valuable spices which the Dutch had successfully monopolised. He sailed to the Sulu Sea and acquired the concession of the island of Balambangan from the ruler. His over-ambition and excessive demands precluded his being put in charge by the Company and the project failed through the venality of the appointee from Benkulen. The brief venture alerted the Dutch to possible intrusions on what they considered their sphere of influence and put them on their guard against English ships sailing via the eastern passage. The other development which promised deliverance from the tensions of the Canton system was the capture of Manila from the Spanish during the Seven Years war. Indiamen carried soldiers there from Madras to form a garrison, but Manila was returned to Spain at the peace and the Indiamen returning from China in 1763 carried back the garrison to Madras.

A sea change occurred in the European trade with China towards the end of the eighteenth century. By the India Act of 1784 Government divested the Company of all political and diplomatic powers, leaving only the conduct of the trade to the Court of Directors. At the same time the Commutation Act reduced the custom duty on tea to 12.5%. In return the Company undertook to supply the British public with 13m pounds of tea annually at a reasonable price, otherwise the trade would be opened up. This legislation had far-reaching effects on the Company's shipping, on the trade, and on the administration and situation in Canton.

The successful employment of a few very large ships convinced the Company that larger ships were more economic. For the first time the Court of Directors laid down specifications for the shipping it employed: a special class of 36 ships of 1200 tons burthen was created specifically for the China trade, most stationed for China direct.[13] Many of these ships actually greatly exceeded the chartered tonnage and brought back large surpluses of teas, especially in the last decades of the Company's life. Protecting the sheathing with copper plates was adopted from about this time, an improvement on the practice of covering it with large-headed nails which, when oxidised, formed a carapace offering some deterrent to the *teredo* worm. Coppering, and rules requiring a minimum of eighteen months between laying the keel and a ship's launch, ensuring thorough seasoning, enabled ships safely to perform six, eight, and eventually ten voyages, with periodic major repairs. The large merchant yards specialising in building East Indiamen and naval ships up to 74s were careful to preserve the quality of their materials and workmanship to meet the exacting standards of the surveyors of the Company and the Navy Board.

Maintaining the health of a crew on the long voyage to China without a landfall required commanders to manage their ships well. Cleanliness in their bodies, clothing and bedding helped to keep scurvy and most diseases at bay. The Company's general exhortations hardened into demands for evidence of good practice: the ships' logs record weekly scrubbing of the ships' beams, carlings and bends with disinfectant, usually vinegar but sometimes oil of tar, and regular washing of the seamen's persons, clothing and hammocks. Frequent lighting of fires and washing the inside of ships with quicklime helped to keep the ships dry and reduce chest complaints. Attempts were made to prevent the spread of infectious diseases by lowering funnels below decks to extract the foul air and burning gunpowder to fumigate them.

Scurvy was the great scourge of the China direct route until the nineteenth century. Most ships' crews arrived at Whampoa weak from the disease though the knowledge existed both to prevent and cure it. It is noticeable that not every ship's crew suffered. Keeping the people active was a known prophylactic: the Company's instructions to a commander as early as 1762 ordered him to 'keep them stirring and in motion', though they would not have known the reason which is that active muscles produce vitamin C.[14] For the same reason the seamen knew that fresh meat was a cure for scurvy, and fresh beef particularly – as well as fresh greens – were always the first items demanded of the *compradores* for debilitated crews arriving at Canton.[15] Boiled wheat and plum pudding appear to have been a favoured treatment of scurvy on Indiamen, although the antiscorbutic properties of lemon juice had been recognised by the Company since 1600 (and proved by James Lind in 1747) and all Indiamen carried ample quantities throughout the Company's trading life.[16] Captain Wilson of the *Pitt* put into Madagascar on his way to Madras in 1758 to pick up limes to cure his men of scurvy, a practice encouraged by the Company.

Imports of tea doubled immediately following the passing of the Commutation Act: almost twice the usual number of Company ships were sent to China in 1785, eliminating the competition of the other European ships. The lower prices boosted the demand for tea which soon surpassed the 13m lb target. The earlier smaller ships had carried 710,000 lbs; the large China ships loaded 1.5m lbs of tea each, with an additional 5% or 6% in the commanders' and officers' private trade.

Finding the money for the tea investment concentrated the minds of the Company and of the Government. There was no question of England supplying more silver. The investment would have to be supplied partly by increasing the export of the produce and growth of England: the amount of woollen cloth was increased, and copper and Cornish tin boosted the supply of metals. Though these products still sold at a loss in Canton, the simple barter system of woollen cloth for teas which had developed quite early on was refined into a formal division of shares to which the supply of tea was linked, reducing the amount of specie required for the purchase of the return cargo.

The commanders' and officers' interests benefited from the need to increase exports to China: they were encouraged, as a result of a more enlightened policy embracing British and not just Company interests, to fill up any room left in the ships' holds after the cargo had been loaded with their private trade goods freight free.[17] Furs and skins appeared, no doubt from the Hudson's Bay Company, while some Indiamen called at the north-west coast of America en route to Canton to buy from the trappers.

The remaining investment had to come from the growth and produce of India and the eastern seas. Cotton became a major part of this trade as famine in China forced the government to transfer land to rice growing, so diminishing that available for growing cotton. The Company actually built ships in its Bombay dockyard to carry this cotton to Canton on behalf of the Bombay government, but the latter never had sufficient funds to finance more than one ship a year: the bulk of the cotton trade to Canton was left to the country ships belonging to British or native firms in Bombay, Madras and Bengal. About four East Indiamen each season were stationed for Bombay and China – plum voyages for those commanders favoured by the Chairman and Vice-chairman of the Company in whose gift the voyages lay. By 1804 the commanders and officers were allowed $2/_5$ of the tonnage freight free and had first refusal on any remaining tonnage not required by the Company at reduced freight. After the English acquired Malacca some Company ships called there to pick up pepper, sandalwood betelnut, tin from Banka, together with a variety of minor products in the commanders' and officers' private trade; some commanders trans-shipped these products from country ships in the Strait of Malacca.[18] The silver acquired from the sale of all these goods and products was paid into the Company's treasury in Canton to contribute to the tea investment in return for bills – always called certificates in the case of the commanders – drawn on London, providing the Anglo-Indians with a much-needed channel to remit their fortunes to England.

Over half the silver needed for the tea investment came from one Indian product: Bengal opium. Though a Company monopoly, its import into China was left entirely to the country trade, the trade within the eastern seas. Commanders traded in opium on their own account but, apart from one or two unfortunate occasions, forwarded it to Canton on country ships. A major disruption to trade might result from the discovery of opium on board Company ships and commanders were repeatedly exhorted to refrain from carrying any opium. Sailing orders to the commanders of Company ships from Bombay to Canton directed that:

> You must take the most particular care that no Opium is laden on board your Ship by yourself , Officers or any other person, as the importation of that article at China is positively forbid & very serious consequences may attend your neglect of this Injunction.[19]

With the Company's emergence as the major purchaser of teas the British Government believed it was now in a position of strength to negotiate better conditions for the Company's trade at Canton and decided upon a direct approach to the Emperor of China from the British monarch. Embassy had been mooted even before the Canton system crystallised but it did not materialise until 1792.[20] In the face of Company disapproval, and at enormous cost which the Company had to pay, Lord Macartney, representing King George III, sailed to Tientsin on board one of HM ships with a proposed charter of rights for the English trade, one clause of which requested a piece of territory on the mainland or an island which the Company could use as a base to defend its stores, preferably near a northern port where the Company's woollens would be more marketable.[21] The ambassador was cordially received by the Emperor at Peking, but he achieved absolutely nothing. The commencement of war with France forced him to abandon the second part of his embassy: to travel to Japan and attempt to re-open the trade there.

The Canton system therefore continued under the Hoppo's arbitrary direction. Stoppages to the trade occurred regularly, increasing over the decades. The first lasted up to several weeks, any time between early October to 27 December, the date on which the Hoppo finalised his accounts. This was designed to keep down the returns for the year and so avoid creating a precedent which the Emperor would expect to be maintained. Wartime delays extended the season well into the following year, entailing a further stoppage of trade during the Chinese New Year. Paying each ship £200 per month became so expensive that the Select Committee stopped payment. Keeping up to 3,000 men well-behaved over such long periods became increasingly difficult, especially with strong liquor available despite all the efforts of the European and Chinese authorities. The Select Committee gave the commodore, the senior commander of the Company's fleet of the season, special powers: each commander was required to provide a boat manned and under an officer to patrol the river whenever the commodore decided. All liberty on that ship was prohibited that day. The officer was empowered to arrest any seaman committing a breach of the peace and carry him on board the commodore's ship to be tried by a Court of Enquiry composed of the captains.

The situation at Whampoa was so explosive that when mutiny occurred on the *Belvedere* East Indiaman in 1787 the Court of Enquiry decided on the most severe punishment for those found guilty. The enquiry revealed that there were no serious reasons for the mutiny – that the men had acted in that way mainly because, the *Belvedere* being a merchant ship, they felt there would be no recrimination. In view of the tense and dangerous situation at Canton the Court of commanders felt they must make it quite clear to all the seamen at Whampoa that such behaviour would not be tolerated: the two ringleaders were sentenced to receive 100 lashes and 70 lashes respectively at different ships round the fleet.[22] The commanders asked for the Court of Directors'

protection against damages awarded to them should they be sued (a growing practice) on their return to England. During the following decades, as radical movements in Britain elicited severe responses from the home government: emergency measures included the suspension of habeas corpus and the passage of laws against sedition; punishing seamen for 'mutinous and seditious behaviour' figures frequently in the ships' logs.

The wounding or, worse, the death of a Chinese at the hands of a European presented the greatest threat to the stability of the trade. The Select Committee and the commanders were reluctant to hand over an accused man to the Chinese authorities as the judicial process did not place sufficient emphasis on the rights of the individual: the Chinese, with their different culture, wanted a life – any life – for a life. The sentence was likely to be public strangulation. Unless the Select Committee and the Security Merchants managed to compensate the family without the incident reaching the ears of the mandarins, the latter seized the opportunity it offered for extortion. Security Merchants were imprisoned and sometimes tortured while the mandarins employed the various weapons in their armoury: pilots were refused in 1809 following the stabbing of a Chinese, and the Grand Chop withheld so that the ships could not clear, involving the Company in enormous costs of *demorage*.[23] On this occasion two security merchants were imprisoned until a man – any man – was given up. In this case, probably due to the helpful mediation of a naval captain and the India commanders between the Ladrones pirates and the Chinese government, the latter agreed to an enquiry by the commanders and allowed the culprit if discovered to be judged by the laws of England.

Such crises brought the Security Merchants and the Select Committee closer together as they faced the common enemy: extortionate mandarins. It was not in the Committee's interests that the number of Hongs should be reduced still further by bankruptcies, especially as really rich Chinese merchants were increasingly unwilling to take up the licences to trade with Europeans. The merchants complained that the expense of 'the Clocks Watches and other pieces of Mechanism' they were forced to buy to sell to the Hoppo for transmission to Peking were largely the cause of their financial embarrassment and hinted that they would like the Committee to prohibit their import.[24] The Committee expressed its opinion to the Court of Directors that the refusal of the Grand Chop that year was not to do with the homicide but was a move in the game of clocks and sing-songs 'which it seems are now become the established vehicle of Corruption between the Officer and his Superiors at the Capital'.[25] In 1813 the Security Merchants again complained to the Committee of the cost to them of these clocks and watches: 'Every year all the Hongs collectively spend for Clocks and Watches a hundred thousand Dollars'[26] – £25,000, up to £2m in today's terms – and asked the Committee to stop their import. Of the ten Hong merchants only three were entirely solvent, seven in debt, a situation which they believed would become progressively worse. The Committee shared the cost, subsidising the junior Hongs, as it was not in the Company's interests that the number of merchants should be reduced.

For almost half the period between the India Act and the end of the Company's trade in 1834, Britain was at war, putting an added strain on an already tense situation. Because of the great value of their cargo, which the Company did not insure, the China ships always had naval protection out and home. They sailed from England with one of the large convoys of merchant ships organised according to a regular timetable by the Admiralty and continued their passage with a single consort. Those stationed for Bombay and China sailed in the first convoy, in December, but this was cancelled after the resumption of war in 1803, the February convoy becoming the first of the year when most of the China ships sailed together. Prolonged delays at Portsmouth or Plymouth,

even extending to ports en route such as Rio de Janeiro, disrupted the regular schedule dictated by the monsoon winds and the China ships, especially single ships which had on occasions to sail without convoy, were forced increasingly to take the eastern passage, a generic term applied to all variations on the route pioneered by the *Pitt*. They were not the only Company ships to arrive at Canton via the Bashi Channel between Formosa and Luzon: those calling at the north-west coast of America, and those Indiamen regularly chartered by the British government from 1790 to carry convicts to New South Wales, proceeding to Canton to bring home teas for the Company.

French warships regularly waited off Pula Auro for the returning China fleet. The captain of the convoy assigned by the admiral in charge of the East Indies station decided the route to be followed. The Select Committee could only advise: they addressed letters to the naval commanders anxiously but deferentially pointing out the hazards of following a particular route and respectfully suggesting alternatives, no doubt after consultation with the India commanders whose knowledge of the conditions in the eastern seas greatly exceeded that of the naval officers.[27] But the final decision rested with the naval commander. When for some reason convoy was not available, as at the renewal of war after the Peace of Amiens, the Select Committee decided which route should be followed, but only after the most thorough consultation with the senior commanders.[28] Admiral Rainier, commanding the East Indies station, applauded the Select Committee's decision on this occasion, following the returning China fleet's successful repulse of a very powerful French naval force off Pula Auro. The Committee gave detailed orders on which route to take to commanders sailing alone, but the latter occasionally refused on good grounds, such as the heavy wear and tear on ground tackle suffered in the eastern passage.

Depleted crews were always a problem:

The battle of Pula Auro in February 1804.
British Library,
Oriental & India Office Collections

malaria and dysentery ravaged the men in the great heats of summer at Whampoa. Not until the final decades of the Company's trade were measures taken to counter this. The Court advised the Committee in 1822 to keep the ships below the second bar until the summer was over. In 1829 a better way of tackling the problem was accidentally revealed: the Select Committee decided on a trade embargo and the ships were kept to the east of Lintin in Urmston Road, Capsingmoon, Hong Kong Road and at Kowloon and the crews were much healthier as a result. The Select Committee suggested to the Court of Directors that it might be a good idea to keep the ships outside the river 'until the summer's back was broken', to which the Court agreed. The problem of weakened crews was exacerbated in wartime through pressing, either at Indian ports en route, or on arrival in Chinese waters. The crews were made up by Chinese who were returned the following season as passengers. As emigration of Chinese was against the law this operation carried its own perils. In the early years the Chinese boarded at Lintin or the Bogue, but as the mandarins appeared to be increasingly unconcerned by the practice the commanders grew negligent and the crimps and *compradores* were delivering men at the second bar. The authorities suddenly became more vigilant in 1805, the Security

Merchant Puiqua suffering financially as a result, and the Committee gave the commanders strict orders to return to the earlier practice.

The problem of shortage of men did not diminish with the coming of peace. Large numbers of men serving on Indiamen volunteered for service on naval ships on their arrival in the eastern seas: the East Indies station was very unhealthy and always undermanned; the only limiting factor on the number of volunteers that a no doubt hard-pressed naval lieutenant could accept from a ship was that the ship 'should not be distressed'. The secretary to the naval Commander-in-Chief, Prince of Wales Island, addressing the Select Committee at Canton on another matter in 1821, said that his superior recognised:

> …the great inconvenience to which the ships of the Honourable Company in this country have been subjected by the extent to which their crews have gone in volunteering for the Kings Service…

and had suggested to the Admiralty that limits be prescribed so that individual opinion was not the only criterion in deciding on the number of volunteers accepted.[29]

The great value of the fleets, both out and home, necessitated the greatest attention to the defence of the ships. Although they resembled

74 gun ships, and were regularly mistaken for them by the enemy, they were never equivalent to ships of war as they could not carry sufficient men to man the necessary number of guns while also handling the sails. Commanders were always encouraged to defend, not attack, but the Company were at pains to maximise the ships' fighting capacity: the commanders were ordered to carry more than the specified thirty-six guns and 130 men for the large China ships, the Company contributing to the cost; all guns on each deck were to be standardised and rest on Gover's carriages, which enabled the guns to be fired by smaller gun crews. But the Company placed greatest emphasis on the provision of two stern chasers (large, heavy guns designed to discourage a pursuing enemy) and on deterring boarders. A sergeant at arms was to exercise the men in the use of small arms and the great guns; boarding netting was to be provided and a 'sufficient number of men posted in the tops with swivels or musquetoons and pole axes' to fire down on boarders trying to climb up the nets. The ships' own boarders, armed with tomahawks, cutlasses and pistols, would join the rest armed with pikes to board the enemy should an opportunity arise. There is every indication that the Indiamen now closely followed naval practice at the time and the station and quarter bills resembled those of naval ships.[30]

The physical dangers faced by these valuable fleets remained but the nineteenth century commanders were immeasurably better equipped to deal with them than their seventeenth century predecessors. Professionalism triumphed over bigotry and prejudice: the younger officers who embraced a scientific approach to navigation in the more enlightened climate of the late eighteenth century were given the chance to practise it when the abolition of the sale of commands heralded an age in which only skill and experience counted. Though dead reckoning continued as the basis of finding east-west position at sea, improved nautical instruments, used in conjunction with lunar tables introduced in the 1760s, enabled navigators to calculate longitude to a much greater degree of accuracy. From the 1780s chronometers were carried in greater numbers on Indiamen and by the end of the Company's trading life had become the sole means of estimating longitude.

Although commanders had been instructed for some time carefully to note in their logs new discoveries and remarkable incidents for the improvement of knowledge and navigation, little use appears to have been made of this information until Dalrymple was employed as Company hydrographer.[31] He patiently assembled the body of experience of the commanders and officers of Company and country ships and disseminated it, involving them all in applying it for the common good. He set down on the charts which he published for the Company the longitude of many places and hazards to a far greater degree of accuracy and provided the commanders with far more reliable sailing directions. It was his successor, James Horsburgh, an ex-country captain, who produced charts and sailing directions which greatly improved the safety of navigation in the China Seas. The development of a sophisticated signalling system by the end of the eighteenth century greatly facilitated communication between Indiamen, who were always instructed to sail in company, and between a convoy and its naval escort.

The failure to obtain any improvement in the conditions of the trade at Canton and to gain access to other Chinese ports stimulated the search for an *entrepot* attracting Chinese junks and *prahus* bearing the products of the eastern archipelago. Enthusiastic country captains prowled amongst the islands of the eastern seas looking for potential ports. Balambangan was briefly revived. Great hopes were pinned on Penang, ceded to the Company and renamed Prince of Wales Island, but it was on the wrong side of the Malay Peninsula. Dalrymple's dream of a free port to which all the trade of China and the east would resort was at last answered in 1819 with Raffles' acquisition of Singapore. Following removal of restrictions at the renewal of the Company's charter in 1813 all the shipping free to sail from England to the east was now free to trade at Singapore, though the Company retained the monopoly of buying tea until 1833. Opium could now be transported as far as Singapore in Company ships and carried from there in the country trade. Singapore became a regular port of call for the China ships. The principal points in Lord Macartney's abortive Charter of Rights for the English trade – permission for the Company to trade at northern ports and to occupy a small unfortified island in the neighbourhood of Canton to store their unsold goods and house their people – were not achieved until almost a decade after the Company withdrew from the China trade.

Notes and references

1   F.W. Madden and D.K. Fieldhouse, (ed.s), *Select Documents on the History of the British Empire and Commonwealth*, (London, 1985), vol. 1, 235-6.

2   Quoted by H.B. Morse, *Chronicles of the East India Company trading in China*, 5 vols, (Oxford, 1926), vol.1, 114.

3   Morse, *Chronicles*, vol.1, 47n. The silver exported to China was the coin then known as the *real of eight*, later occasionally the *piece of eight* and throughout the eighteenth and nineteenth centuries the Spanish dollar constituting the medium of international exchange in China until 1857; R. Keale, *Trades Increase*, (London, 1615), 32.

4   British Library (BL), OIOC, First Letter Book, Will. Adams in Firando to August in Spalding, 12 Jan. 1613.

5   B. Lubbock, (ed.), *Barlow's Journal*, 2 vols, (London, 1934), vol. 1, 204.

6   Morse, *Chronicles*, vol.1, 109.

7   Morse, *Chronicles*, vol. 5, 40, Translation of the First Edict concerning the European Trade at Canton, 1755.

8   Orders and Instructions by the Court of Directors to Gabriel Steward, commander of the ship *Neptune*, 1763. Original in the family's hands.

9   The charter party was the contract between the owners of the ship and the Company. Demurrage was an extra charge paid as compensation to the owners of a ship for delay caused by the charterer's failure to load before the time of scheduled departure: always spelt 'demorage' in Company documents.

10   Morse, *Chronicles*, vol. 5, 298.

11   Letter in family hands.

12   Morse, *Chronicles*, vol. 5, 154.

13   BL, OIOC, L/MAR/C/531, f610, 12 Oct 1793, Court of Directors' opinion.

14   Instructions to Gabriel Steward, original in family hands: actually referring to the soldiers being transported as they always suffered most from disease through neglect.

15   Morse, *Chronicles*, vol. 2, 128.

16   J. Sutton, *Lords of the East: the East India Company and its Ships (1600-1874)*, (London, 2000), App. 7, 143, Victualling bill and stores of the ship *Durrington*, 1746. In 1803 the Court of Directors recommended that ships carry 1 gallon of lemon juice for every 4 men out and home. The amount would therefore vary considerably according to the number of troops being transported.

17   C.H. Philips, (ed.), *Correspondence of David Scott, 1787-1805*, 2 vols, (London, 1951), vol 1, no26, 30 March 1795, p23.

18   C.N.Parkinson, *Trade in the Eastern Seas, 1793-1813*,(Cambridge, 1937), 206.

19   Morse, *Chronicles*, vol. 2, 282, Council of Bombay to commanders of ships Bombay to Canton, 28 Nov 1783.

20   Lt-Col. Charles Cathcart was appointed ambassador to the Emperor of China but died en route in 1788: BL, OIOC H434, Letters from George Smith to Henry Dundas, President of the Board of Control, f11 and ff15-30 of 16 Feb 1783.

21   Morse, *Chronicles*, vol. 2 , 232-242, App. G: Instructions to Lord Macartney, 8 Sept 1792. Also BL OIOC G/12/264 Canton 1792-4 for the proceedings of the Secret and Superintending Committee created for the purpose of overseeing the Embassy and dealing with any agreement that may ensue. It was superior to the Select Committee, comprising the President and the two senior supercargoes, which had replaced the Council of Supercargoes in 1779, but it was concerned with policy, leaving the management of the trade to the Select Committee as before. The President headed both committees.

22   BL, OIOC G/12/88: composition of Court of Enquiry, its proceedings and decision, 15 Dec to 21 Dec 1787.

23   It was necessary to obtain the Grand (or Red) Chop or Clearance to quit the port, otherwise if the ship was blown back on to the China coast she would be liable to pay all the charges again.

24   Morse, *Chronicles*, vol. 3, 155.

25 Morse, *Chronicles,* vol. 3, 147.

26 Morse, *Chronicles,* vol. 3, 194

27 For example, see BL, OIOC G/12/269 of 28 Feb 1810: Select Committee to Captin Austen, RN.

28 BL, OIOC G/12/268 of 12/01/1804: Proceedings of the Select Committee considering the route to be taken by the returning fleet without convoy after the renewal of war with France in 1803.

29 BL, OIOC G/34/80, f272, Prince of Wales Island Consultations: Letter from the Secretary to the Naval Commander-in-Chief on board HMS *Topaz*, 21 Aug 1821.

30 See NMM HMN 33, Captain Hamilton's Station and Quarter Book.

31 Company's instructions to Gabriel Steward's Orders and Instructions.

The Country ships from India

Anne Bulley

In the later eighteenth century a cormorant's eye view of the Pearl River a few miles from Canton in October would show, among the junks (some over 1000 tons) and crowds of local vessels, a forest of masts belonging to English ships. But not all of them belonged to East Indiamen which had arrived from half the world away. An equal number or more sprang from the decks of the so-called country ships. These hailed from India. The wealth of the merchants of India was held in the cargoes within their teak walls.

When John Pope, a boatswain in the East India Company ships, planned a career for his only son (whom he had christened rather grandly John Adolphus), he chose the country trade as having the best prospects of a lucrative career, especially for someone lacking powerful patronage. Years ago on a passage to India he had made a useful contact with a Bengal merchant who was travelling as the First Mate's servant. When in years to come he and his partners had come to own several country ships, John Pope, aged thirteen was dispatched to India to become third officer in one of these ships. He had, like many others, received his initial training in seamanship in the Indiaman that brought him out. Once arrived in Bengal trouble was obviously taken that his captain was a suitable choice to 'have the care of youth' while his father provided the financial assistance for his first voyage. In a way John Pope's career mirrored the fortunes of the country trade with China in the late eighteenth and early nineteenth centuries.

The so-called country ships of India were British merchant ships that were privately owned but operated in the East under licence from the East India Company. With British officers, licensed as free mariners, and with lascar crews, they operated from port to port following traditional trade routes in the same way as had, over the centuries, thousands of other vessels built on the coasts around the Indian Ocean, the China or Arabian seas – great junks from China, Muslim ships from the Gulf, Gujerati trading vessels from the north or any small harbour or river estuary where ships could be constructed and launched. By the terms of their licence they were forbidden to trade to the west of the Cape of Good Hope, although exceptions increased when in certain years country ships joined the Company fleet to England as 'Extra ships'. These voyages provide almost the only logs for the country ships.

By the end of the eighteenth century this country trade was dominated by the British and their Indian associates. They had managed to out distance their European rivals, the Portuguese, the Dutch and the French. The outbreak of war in the 1770s played a major part, as the British continued to operate throughout under foreign neutral colours. For instance, in 1783 only three English country ships are recorded in China, but there is a suspicious increase in Imperial, Swedish, Danish, Spanish and Prussian vessels no doubt owned and manned by the British. Due to the war, it was impossible to obtain Spanish silver in London to pay for the China exports. The Canton supercargoes instead relied on specie from India but this source too dried up. So they were increasingly dependent on funds generated by the country trade. Thus by the end of the war in 1784 the owners of the country ships had money to invest in the ships to trade with China.

The country trade complemented that of the East India Company whose ships by the 1780s were scheduled only to sail between England, India or China and, after early attempts, almost never engaged in the coastal trade. Except for the traditional woollens and lead, little could be provided in London in the way of cargoes which were valuable to the Chinese. On the other hand the country ships could bring produce and smuggle opium, funds from which could be paid into the Company's Canton Treasury. In exchange, the country owners received bills on London payable a year later and were enabled to transfer their wealth to England while the Company had the means to finance its large annual tea purchases. The Canton agents had links with Bombay and London. As one example, in the early nineteenth century, William Baring could issue bonds on their London house.

Apart from some isolated attempts in the seventeenth century to trade with other ports in China, Canton from the end of the eighteenth century became the sole mart open to Europeans. In early days the Company records take no particular note of country ships in China so there are but infrequent references to them. This does not mean that they were not there in some numbers. Captain Alexander Hamilton arrived at Whampoa, the port for Canton, in 1703 in command of a large country ship from Bombay. This shows that although he was employed from time to time by the East India Company he had also made several country voyages.

In the eighteenth century most British country ships hailed from either Bengal or Bombay. There was, of course, no harbour in Madras. The ships from Bengal were the smaller. They were built for the estuaries and small harbours where they looked for their trade in the Malay archipelago. In 1785, when the young John Pope joined the 350 ton *Princess Royal* on what turned out to be a three year voyage, his letters describe how her trade along the way enabled her captain to pay, during two visits, funds into the Company's Canton Treasury. He writes of days of calm, with the lascars always on deck as they kept no watches, fishing and singing their songs with which the First Mate joined in without knowing the words; the Captain, a stern disciplinarian, with his 'seraglio', the occasional passenger to break the monotony or

days of storm when they were constantly soaked in the so-called 'Sumatras'. The British were no strangers in these remote estuaries. The country captains followed in each other,s wake and revisited from time to time. Embassies arrived – the object to find 'places of refreshment' for the Indiamen on the route to China since Malacca (Melaka) and Rheo were in the hands of the Dutch. The country ships were now welcomed by their former enemy and Malacca was used as an entrepot. Many a captain left his girl here to wait for his return from China, but not Pope's captain. He smuggled his into Macao. At exactly the time of this voyage Penang was founded and then in 1819 superseded in importance by Singapore and finally Hong Kong.

Opium played a major part in the country trade to China. Normally grown as a Company monopoly in Bengal, it was bought by the ship owners at the Calcutta auctions. The East India Company's involvement was normally then at an end but exceptions prove the rule. In this case the MacIntyres, owners of the *Princess Royal* and some other owners that year, were assigned chests of opium at a special rate if they guaranteed to pay a certain sum into the Canton Treasury. Arms were provided by the Board of Ordnance to be sold before the voyage was completed. After 1794 naval convoys became obligatory and arms were provided as a matter of course for the China ships to protect them not only from the French but also from 'pirates'.

Trade was often a hit and miss affair. On this voyage, efforts to barter some of this opium in Junk Ceylon (now the popular Thai resort of Phuket) was a complete failure. The King of Pegu's fleet was busy besieging the island which was subject to his enemy, Siam. They were more successful in Kedah. Chests of opium and piece goods were exchanged for block tin. There was a ready market for tin in China since it was used in religious ceremonies. But, sailing southwards, trade was disappointing. No tin was to be bought in Pera or on Pulo Penang (the following year to be settled as Prince of Wales Island) where they were unable to open trade 'with the shy natives'. So from there they crossed to the north east coast of Sumatra. Here it was a matter of trial and error. The sultan of Pedir was ferociously hostile. 'No white face goes on shore here' said Pope nervously. And error it was that, some years before, the *Flyer*, a vessel from Bengal, had been 'cut off' and all her crew massacred – even so his captain's trading methods shocked Pope as he and the fourth officer 'with musket and blunderbuss' intercepted boats laden with betel nut and forced them to do business with their ship. But other harbours under an independent rajah were more co-operative – up to a point. At one small place, they did make a pepper contract but when there were delays and excuses, the captain, suspecting foul play, simply kidnapped the official's son 'as surety for a debt of 8000 dollars' and took him off in the ship for the round trip to China.

The vessel made its way into the China Sea from island to island. On the return voyage they were lost among the islands to the 'south east of the Strait of Sincapor' and had to 'blunder our way through as well we could'. (Incidentally Alexander Hamilton on his fourth voyage to China in command of a 700 ton ship with 40 guns and a crew of 150 had been generously offered the island of Singapore by the sultan but refused, remarking presciently that it was of 'no use to a private person tho' a proper place for a company'.) The country captains were the pioneers in these waters, none more so than James Horsburgh, who was to become the East India Company's hydrographer. In the future he and Pope were to be friends, both commanding country ships to China for Bombay partnerships. Preparing his charts and sailing instructions back in England, Horsburgh was to rely on a correspondence with his former colleagues to tap their expertise on rocks and shallows or which routes they favoured on entering the China Sea, such as that which some took to the west of the island of Sapata.

Off the Great Ladrones, a pilot was taken on board at the fee of 20 dollars and having reached Macao, the captain made contact with one of the ship's owners, John MacIntyre, a permanent resident and – a rare accomplishment – a Chinese speaker. Through him, 40 chests of opium were smuggled into China. (The East India Company Canton supercargoes had also appreciated his talents and used him for some years as their unofficial opium agent.)

The letters suggest that the methods for disposing the opium were as efficiently organized as any legal business. The trade had been initiated by the Portuguese and Armenians, but from 1780 the English had muscled in and established depot vessels to the south of Macao. In 1788, the first American 'Consul' to Canton, Major Samuel Shaw, having gone on board one of the MacIntyre's ships bound for Bengal, watched as opium was delivered to vessels 'among the islands'.

The *Princess Royal* having taken on a pilot, (armed with a bamboo cane to plumb the shallows), she proceeded the hundred miles and more up the Pearl River to Whampoa, the anchorage for Canton, where masts and rigging were off loaded into a *'bankshall'*.* Then began the measurement of the ship by the Hoppo, magnificently dressed and accompanied by a dozen 'squalid henchmen', to decide the custom dues. He drew alongside, Pope records:

> …*in an immense boat half as big as our ship. An accommodation ladder being fixed on the ship's side for him – a table and chair covered with scarlet cloth is placed for him on the Quarter deck… He asked a number of questions about the ship and drank a glass of wine. The Ceremony of Measurement then began. A line being previously stretched from the Foremast to the Mizen mast, that space is measured for the Length, and the measure abreast of the Main mast for the Breadth…*

The Hoppo traditionally gave a present to the ship, in this case two bullocks and ten jars

---

* A warehouse or other building belonging to a port authority

of a rice liquor called *samshu*. A Comprador was assigned to the ship to oversee her provisioning. (Hamilton said his main outgoings in China had been the Comprador's account, cloth for the lascars, canvas for sails, and arrack, another locally-distilled spirit. A century later, Horsburgh recorded the same list to the owner of his ship, Pestonjee Bomanjee brother of the Bombay Master Shipbuilder.) A Security merchant, organized the trade, one of the celebrated Co-Hong, in this case Munqua. That he entertained the ship's officers at his splendid house in such regal style shows that, as far as trade was concerned, from the Chinese point of view, a country ship was of equal importance to one of the Company's, with its predictable trade. The country ships usually arrived earlier in the season than the Indiamen but the method of trading was the same. The factories or warehouses used by the country captains lay on neighbouring creeks to Respondentia walk.

Once more at Malacca, Pope discovered that the voyage would be extended by a further year. They were to proceed to Bombay to pick up a cargo of cotton. It so happened that 1786 was the beginning of a boom in the trade. China was suffering a dire famine and cotton fields were now put down to grain. There was a perfect scramble by the Bengal owners to enter a trade previously monopolized by the Bombay merchants. In 1784, before the boom began, only four Bombay ships brought bales of cotton to China. In 1786 eight or so Bengal ships extended their normal voyages to pick up cotton from Bombay. But it could not have been a success for the next year, when the *Princess Royal* arrived, only two Bengal ships came. They were probably too small, and unprepared for such a bulky but light cargo or the threat posed by the lee shore of the Malabar coast. For whatever reason the Bengal merchants were discouraged or, like the owners of the *Princess Royal* from a variety of causes, which included the wreck of some of their ships, went bankrupt.

From now on the most important import to China, besides opium, was to be cotton. The 24 country ships in China for that season included a fleet of 17 Bombay ships loaded with it. Twice as much cotton was imported by the country ships as by the Company. The next year the number of English country ships had increased to 33 and space chartered by the country merchants on the Company's ships increased cotton exports dramatically. In this period there was no mention of opium in the official Canton records at all.

Not surprisingly, by 1790 the cotton market in China was glutted. When a prime Chinese merchant defaulted, the fact that 11 Indian agents in Canton petitioned the supercargoes because they could not get full payment for their cotton. This, they wrote, 'will…distress the English merchants in Bombay and wholly ruin some individuals without weight or consequence', showing a large native Indian involvement in the trade. (The debt stood at 600,000 dollars, $^2/_3$ of which was owed by Eequa)

The *Princess Royal*'s long voyage, which had encompassed two visits to China, ended with her taking on a cargo of beetel nut in Sumatra, bartered in Rangoon, for a load of timber for Calcutta. This final stage was organized by another of the ship's owners who lived in Burma. Such a network of owners indicates an efficient, if rudimentary, sort of early shipping company.

In this period, Bombay, with her great harbour and, since the mid eighteenth century, the only dry docks in the east, had considerable maritime advantages over Calcutta. The great forests of Malabar and Gir provided a superlative supply of teak but most important of all were the talents and experience of the Parsi Wadia shipwrights. The Bombay ships which carried the cotton to China were large, often larger than the Company ships and specially adapted for the cargo with, for instance, no orlop deck to create extra space for the bales compressed in the great screws in the dockyard. Many of the ships came season after season. The 660 ton *Milford* launched in 1786 visited China for 21 years. The *Lowjee Family* also built in the dockyard, launched in 1791, only ultimately met her end by fire in Bombay harbour in 1849. Amazingly, except in time of war, as far as building new ships was concerned, the Company's dockyard was rented principally by the private merchants to build their own ships. The way these vessels were organized on board mirrored the Indiamen, as increasingly they did service as 'Extra ships' in the Company's fleet to England. So sometimes, too, they were tendered as troop ships for military expeditions and, as a result, as in 1802, on account of the Red Sea expedition, there were almost no Bombay country ships in China. The officers appointed to command these ships were normally experienced and reliable men. Horsburgh became famous for his chart making and sailing instructions but he was not perhaps the best of country ship commanders. Upbraiding one of his young officers for his 'supine, indolent un-officer like custom of sitting down and sleeping or lolling on his watch or even taking a glass too much', he recalled smugly his own experiences as Chief Mate between 1786 to 1798:

> *… all the time in large ships, never having less than three officers, and in some of them five or six but I never knew an expression made use of by any of these officers to one another, or to myself… which was the least unbecoming of a gentleman.*

On the *Anna* it was a different story – so many quarrels among the officers that he had to discharge some of them in 'the hopes of unanimity'. In 1798 she had gone as an 'Extra ship' to England which may have had something to do with it. It was Horsburgh's first command. She was certainly not a happy ship and this can usually be laid at the door of the commander. He also reported serious health problems with his lascars. Was he too pre-occupied with his chart-making and nautical observations?

The country ships could be owned or more likely part-owned by the captain or by one of the private partnerships or agency houses such as in Calcutta Fairlie Fergusson or in Bombay, Scott, Tate and Adamson, Forbes and Co, or

Bruce Fawcett. Parsis, if not owners in their own right, were frequently in partnership if not by name with the Europeans as were Company servants, until forbidden, to oil the wheels. In fact the Parsi merchants had relatives or close contacts operating not only in China but in most of the harbours around the Indian Ocean, Arabian Sea and the Persian and Arabian Gulfs and had been engaged in the country trade for decades if not for centuries. The Parsi family of Cowasjee, for instance, were to be prominent ship owners in both Bombay and Calcutta In the 1820s Jamsetjee Jeejeebhoy, (the 'first Parsi baronet'), made his fortune as a ship owner in the Bombay China trade.

In 1801 it was judged that the Bombay fleet brought to China around 80,000 bales of cotton, each half a maund (or 53 lbs) in weight. With astute foresight, having served several years in the Bengal ships, John Pope before the end of the century had moved over to Bombay where he was to command ships for the next sixteen years for well-heeled and respectable agency houses – Alexander Adamson and after Adamson's death, his Parsi partner Ardesir Dady and finally Framjee Cowasjee. After commanding the large 1000 ton *Minerva* for ten years, in 1813 as the Company's monopoly of Indian trade came to an end, he retired to run a rope walk and marine agency in Bombay. His fortune had been made, as his father had hoped, in the country trade. But now the commercial scene in China appeared less promising.

As far as ship building was concerned, from the end of the eighteenth century Bengal had begun slowly to initiate dockyards on the Hoogli and for two decades produced a great many vessels with teak imported from Rangoon or Chittagong. With a few exceptions they were small and they also appeared extraordinarily vulnerable to capture by the French in the Bay of Bengal and to hazards of wind and tide. But they carried the opium to China and increasingly cotton grown in Bengal. In 1828 appeared the first of the famous Calcutta 'built for speed' opium clippers. Over in Bombay, from the beginning of the century, fewer ships were now built. The docks were required for repairing men of war and with the enlarging of the docks, the Navy woke up to the advantages of actually building them here. In 1808 the Company, belatedly hoping to compete in the China cotton trade, began building the first of six large ships, such as the *Charles Grant* and the *Buckinghamshire.* Because of a depression in trade none of these were to fulfil their original purpose. Until then the country merchants had dominated the scene. The Governor of Bombay had written to Canton in 1803: 'On account of the superabundance of country shipping this season we have been unsuccessful in our endeavours to let the Honourable Company's proportion of chartered tonnage'.

From about 1802, Bengal began to compete with Bombay, producing a finer cotton more economically than on the west coast where it was apt to suffer from being grown in areas outside the control of the Company. The Bengal ships carrying the cotton now made direct trips to China, a safer voyage after the capture of the French Naval Headquarters in Mauritius in 1810.

Return cargoes from China were a problem, and they were forbidden to leave without them. As an example, a large country ship in 1802 carried 3000 piculs of sugar and sugar candy (a picul, by the way, was roughly the weight a man could carry on his shoulder) and for the rest small quantities of black and green tea, raw silk, cassia, tutanague, alum, chinaware, camphine, vermilion, glass beads, galling gall, china root, musk, parasols and gold thread. In 1800 Horsburgh left Canton $^2/_3$ full – the cargo mostly light except for 5000 piculs of tutanague. Unrecorded were the Chinese who were smuggled out to settle around the Indian Ocean – for instance in 1786 on Pulo Penang.

John Pope had chosen to retire as a slump hit the Bombay China cotton trade. It was caused by multiple factors – a famine in the cotton growing areas in Gujerat, the end of the Company's monopoly of trade with India in

1813, the end of the Napoleonic wars, an increase in cotton goods from England and the Chinese finally increasing their own cotton production. By 1820 the Bombay merchants were forced to look elsewhere for their profits. John Pope died in 1821 as the merchants' interest shifted from cotton to the export of Malwa opium grown in the west of India outside the Company's sphere of influence. It had already been exported in small quantities, for instance in 1804 in Forbes & Co's *Lowjee Family* and the following year in James Horsburgh's former command, the *Bombay Anna.* (At that time Mr. Beale, of the future Jardine Matheson partnership, superintended the sales of opium in Macao.) Since opium grown in Bengal was a Company monopoly, it naturally did all in its power to restrict, or to benefit by some form of tax on, the export of Malwa. By 1825 the country ships from Bengal exported 2,576 chests of Patna and Benares but from Bombay came almost twice as much.

The seeds of future wars were sown in these years. Leaving aside the moral issues, over which the merchants did not lose much sleep in this period, how could a satisfactory trade be built on a galloping increase in the importation of a prohibited smuggled article? Yet the Company's Supercargoes could not finance their business without the proceeds or the collateral thus provided by opium sales. All pretence was given up when in 1825 the Company's opium accounts appeared in black and white in the East India Company's Canton Diary for the first time. Opium was openly acknowledged as being the principal source of income for raising a supply of silver. The influence of Jardine Matheson and other British Canton firms in keeping alive the opium trade which was by now managed by Indian merchants and ship owners cannot be over-estimated.

The cheapness of Malwa compared with the Company-grown Bengal opium encouraged the small ship owners and speculators. It also signalled a shift from European and Indian owned Bombay country ships to the majority being owned solely by

Indians. Also gradually evolving in England was a more modern distaste for the drug. The country service was no longer a favoured career as it had been for the boatswain John Pope's son – a lucrative and respectable alternative to the East India Company. Only four ships of between 500 and 900 tons were built for private merchants in the Bombay dockyard between 1828 and 1833 and with one exception, these were for native Indian owners such as Jamsetjee Jeejeebhoy. They were the last, although one clipper ship, the *Ardeseer*, was built in 1836. Indian ship building could not compete with an increasingly industrialized Victorian Britain with its access to raw materials and world-wide banking facilities.

In the early 1820s, the ships which brought the cotton also brought the opium and attempted to unload everything at Whampoa but this soon became too dangerous. Early on two vessels were adopted specifically. The *Jamesina* (382 tons commanded and owned by Alexander Grant) was registered at Calcutta but in 1826 would be registered at Bombay and in 1829 was owned by Jardine Matheson & Co. It is probable that the latter always had an interest in her. The other was *Samarang* (405 tons) that had previously belonged to the Bombay agency house, Bruce Fawcett. Vessels like these were much smaller than the old ships of the cotton fleet. Their registration often alternated between Calcutta and Bombay. In Calcutta the first of the famous opium clippers, the *Red Rover* was launched in 1829, part owned in 1833 and finally completely by Jardine Matheson. She and others like the *Water Witch*, *Sylph* or *Cowasjee Family* were speedier on the round trip between Bengal and China than any others until the arrival of steam. The ships which anchored at Lintin and elsewhere, delivered opium, took in prohibited sycee and imported or exported without paying customs, did so through the efficiency of the British firms and it being to the Hoppo's interest, with notable exceptions, to turn a blind eye to the illegal trade.

From 1833, when the East India Company lost the monopoly of the China trade, private ships could now export teas. This caused a rush from England. They and the country ships found themselves in competition with the rest of the world. Merchant ships from England with captains and crews eager to cash in on the novel situation made for Canton, often ill-prepared. Jamsetjee Jeejeebhoy's son complained in 1840 of 'the utter inability of our Indian shipping to compete with Free traders and Yankees' but by then his father, with a fortune made in the China trade, had transferred his attentions to England.

Original Sources
J. A. Pope, *Common Place Book*, in possession of the author.
Parish records, Plymouth.
Hamilton, Alexander, *A New Account of the East Indies* (Edinburgh, 1727)
Forrest, Thomas, *A Voyage from Calcutta in the Mergui Archipelago etc.* (London,1792)

British Library: East India Company Records
　　Factory Records/China
　　Marine Records
　　Bengal Public Proceedings
　　Bombay Public Proceedings
　　Bombay Commercial Proceedings
　　Eur MSS (F 105) Letterbook of James Horsburgh

Cambridge University Library: Jardine Matheson Archive: Newspapers etc:
　　Calcutta Gazette
　　Bombay Gazette
　　Bombay Courier
　　East India Register
　　Asiatic Annual Register
　　Asiatic Journal

Parliamentary Papers

At British Library OIOC reading room: Anne Bulley:
　　Register of Bombay Country Ships with Commanders and Owners 1790-1833 (unpublished)

Secondary sources
Bulley, Anne, *Free Mariner. John Adolphus Pope in the East Indies 1786-1821*, (London, 1992). An account of his career, together with his letters, which describe a three-year country trading

voyage 1786-1789 from Calcutta with two visits to China. (His copies of the original letters, bound, are in the possession of the author.)

Bulley, Anne, *The Bombay Country Ships 1790 –1833*, contains a bibliography for the subject.

Bibliography

Furber, Holden, *John Company at Work* (Harvard, 1948)

Greenberg, Michael, *British Trade and the Opening of China 1800-42*, (Cambridge, 1951).

Horsburgh, James, *Directions for Sailing to and from the East Indies*, (London, 1798).

Milburn, William, *Oriental Commerce*, 2 vols, (London, 1813).

Morse, H.B. *Chronicles of the East India Company Trading to China*, 5 vols, (Oxford, 1926).

J. A. Phipps, *A collection of Papers relative to Shipbuilding in India*, (1840).

Shavakshah, Hormasji Jhabvala, *Framji Cowasje Banji* (1920).

Shaw, Major Samuel, (ed J.Quincy) *Journals*, (Boston, 1847).

Siddiqi, Asiya 'Business world of Jamsetjee Jeejeebhoy', *Indian Economic and Social History*, XIX,3,4, (1996).

The Competitive Advantage of British Shipping in China Seas

Howard Dick

*Introduction**

Between the First Opium War (1840-42) and the country's re-opening to the West in the mid-1970s, China's sovereignty was either compromised or, after 1949, not widely recognised. Its economy was exposed very unevenly to globalisation. These unusual circumstances gave opportunities for foreign firms to provide intermediary services, including shipping. From the 1870s to the 1960s, it was British-flag shipping that predominated. The early period of Anglo-American steamship rivalry up to the 1870s has been well documented, as have been the main companies and their fleets.[1] Yet the sustained competitive advantage of local British-flag shipping has for the most part been taken for granted. This paper argues that the explanation is more complex than Britain's global maritime dominance and that contractual forms evolved in response to shifts in state power and the status of local capital in China.

At the outset it is helpful to identify the range of operational and contractual forms. Home-based liner operators such as P&O and Holts' Ocean Steamship Co. linked main Chinese ports into international liner trades. British firms based in China, most notably the China Navigation Co. (John Swire & Sons) and the Indo-China Steam Navigation Co. (Jardine, Matheson & Co.), provided river, coastal and shortsea services, while delegating procurement of cargo, stevedoring and crewing to Chinese compradores. Local tramp operators such as Moller & Co., Williamson & Co. and John Manners & Co. registered ships under the British flag in Shanghai and Hong Kong and chartered them to Chinese firms. Finally, these and other firms registered under the Hong Kong Companies Act served as

beneficial owners for Chinese principals. Hence, there were degrees of British-ness from full ownership and control to virtual flag-of-convenience.

Competitive advantage began with the security of property under the British flag through the protection of British consuls and the Royal Navy. Technological advantage dated from the 1870s, when British shipyards overtook American yards in the design of specialised steamships for the China coast and rivers; in China this expertise was backed up by company marine departments, ships' engineers and local British dockyards. British firms enjoyed network advantages of access to capital, insurance, deepsea cargoes, and transhipment. Finally, there were early-mover advantages: after overcoming American competition in the 1870s local British firms protected their position through commercial agreements.

This paper begins with an overview of British-flag shipping in Chinese waters in the mid-1930s and compares the size of fleets with those elsewhere in Asia. It then analyses the main forms of competitive advantage for British liner shipping and how they were gradually eroded over time. The final section considers British shipping in Chinese waters, especially since 1949, from the viewpoint of flag of convenience.

Companies and Fleets

Table 1 ranks the British and other main China Coast liner fleets by size in 1935, just before outbreak of the Sino-Japanese War. The largest fleet was Dairen Kisen, based in Japanese-controlled Manchuria, which included coastal, shortsea and deepsea ships. Next came the two leading British fleets, China Navigation Co. (CNC) and Indo-China Steam Navigation Co. (ICSNC), which were the dominant firms in the British sphere of Central

---

* I am grateful to Stephen Kentwell and Bill Laxon for comments on previous drafts.

and South China. Next largest British firm was Moller & Co., a Shanghai family business which in the depression years of the early 1930s had assembled a motley secondhand tramp and charter fleet operating on a shoestring budget. Williamson & Co. was a smaller Hong Kong-based tramp fleet. Stuart Williamson, a New Zealand marine engineer, had been superintendent of the Douglas Steamship Co. (DSSC) before in 1932 buying a controlling interest. Incorporated in 1883, DSSC represented the shipping interests of Douglas Lapraik, who since the 1850s had run ships from Hong Kong to South China Coast ports, including Taiwan – Lapraik had also been a leading light in formation of the Hong Kong, Canton & Macao Steamboat Co. (HCMSC) and the Hongkong & Whampoa Dock Company. A merger of ferry interests since 1865, HCMSC, controlled by Jardines, operated jointly with China Navigation in the Pearl River delta.[2]

Table 2 relates the China Coast fleets to some of the main shipping groups in East Asia. The aggregate 722,000 tons of the main China Coast fleets exceeded the huge fleet of British India S.N.Co. (BI, 600,000 tons), which monopolised the coastal and shortsea shipping of India and East Africa. However, it may be more informative to compare the main shipping groups to which some of the China Coast firms were feeder lines. As detailed below, China Navigation was part of a combination of Holts', Swire's and Straits S.S. Co. with around 800,000 in tonnage, rising to 900,000 tons by takeover in 1935 of the rival Glen Line. This was still smaller than the huge BI-P&O combine (1.1 million tons even without other subsidiaries serving Australia and New Zealand) but matched the combined tally of the Dutch lines (Koninklijke Paketvaart Maatschappij or KPM and Java-China-Japan Lijnen or JCJL) and their parent home lines (Stoomvaart Maatschappij 'Nederland' or SMN and Rotterdam Lloyd or RL) serving colonial Indonesia. Just as BI-P&O and Holts-Swires-Glen were rival groups under the British flag, so also were Nippon Yusen Kaisha

(NYK, 785,000 tons) and Osaka Kisen Kaisha (OSK, 513,000 tons) under the Japanese flag. Both Japanese lines operated extensive services to China in addition to those of the jointly affiliated Nisshin Kisen.

Unlike the situation in some colonies, where local shipping became concentrated in virtual monopolies, shipping in China was therefore always contested by powerful interests. This situation flowed from the partitioning of China into western spheres of influence without any strong central government. In the mid-nineteenth century the main competition was between British and American shipping. Sale of Russell & Company's Shanghai S.N.Co. to the newly formed China Merchants S.N.Co. (CMSNC) in 1877 ushered in a brief period of Sino-British competition that was soon regulated by commercial agreements.[3] French and German interests tried to establish a presence but the former was never commercially significant and the latter, though well subsidised, ceased with the outbreak of war in 1914.

In the long-run only Japanese interests presented a serious foreign threat to British dominance. Britain and Japan make an interesting contrast. British shipping interests in China were at the utmost possible distance on the other side of the world with only the colony of Hong Kong as a reliable base. This involved difficulties of management, communication and logistics. By contrast, Japan's colonies of Taiwan (1895), Kwantung/ Dairen (1905), Karafuto (Southern Sakhalien) (1905) Korea (1910) and Manchukuo (1931) were as adjacent as northern Europe to Britain. Japan's leading steamship lines NYK and OSK therefore began with coastal and shortsea services, only gradually opening long deepsea lines to the other continents. Eventually some of these shortsea interests were hived off into separate companies such as Nisshin Kisen (1907), to serve the China coast and Yangtze, and Kitanippon Kisen (1914), serving Karafuto. Other specialist companies emerged such as Dairen Kisen (1913), a subsidiary of the South Manchurian Railway, and Chosen Yusen (1913) serving Korea. In 1939 Nisshin was merged with the China interests of NYK, OSK and several other firms into a much larger Toa Kaiun (dissolved in 1946).[4]

The other long-run threat to British shipping was from Chinese shipowners. The early challenge from the state-sponsored China Merchants was soon accommodated by pool agreements, after which 'the inertia of mandarin management', underinvestment and state opportunism hobbled the company.[5] During World War I, however, private interests accumulated capital and saw opportunity to expand into shipping. Firms such as San Peh S.N.Co. (with the associated Hoong On S.N.Co. and Ningshin S.S.Co.) in Central China and Ching Kee S.N.Co. in North China became significant forces in the interwar years. In addition to these three main Chinese fleets represented in Table 1, there were also many Chinese-flag fleets of less than 10,000 gross tons, accounting in 1933 for at least another 155,000 tons of shipping.[6] By an overall accounting, the total Chinese shipping fleet of around 300,000 tons was therefore not much less than the local British-flag fleet but ownership was much more fragmented.

The Sources of Competitive Advantage

Security of property

British-flag shipping in Chinese waters enjoyed no greater benefit than the application of British laws that were administered extraterritorially by British consuls in the treaty ports and enforced when necessary by the might of the Royal Navy. Other countries also had consuls and a naval presence, most notably the United States, France and later Japan, but no other consular network was so extensive, the ships so numerous or the prestige so great. British power rested not so much on the ships themselves, which for the most part were small and outmoded gunboats, but on the capacity and determination to deploy superior force. This had been forcibly demonstrated in the two Opium Wars of 1840-42 and 1856-58 and the Boxer rebellion (1900-01). In Hong Kong, the prize of the First Opium War, Britain had the infrastructure of a naval station able to despatch or reinforce the token naval presence at any treaty port.

Protection applied to the ship, cargo, passengers and manning. In the first instance protection was needed against piracy, which was endemic along the South China Coast. In the nineteenth century piracy was brought under control by naval patrols and the greater speed and manouevrability of steamships but with the breakdown of central political authority it flourished again between the two world wars. The modus operandi was now for pirates to board with the deck passengers, seize control of the ship and sail it to a pirate base. China coasters were designed with grilles to close off the access ways to the bridge deck and engine room, manned by armed Sikh or Russian guards and on the bridge they carried weapons for use by the ship's officers. Such measures discouraged casual attack but did not protect even British ships against organised depradation. The piracy of the *Haiching* in 1929 was particularly gruesome. Retaliation was, nevertheless, assured.

Protection was also required against arbitrary detention by Chinese authorities. Traditionally bureaucrats would expect to be paid regular 'squeeze' money, but might act against any ship or cargo owner who was tardy or reluctant in payment, or had become a political foe. Shipping by a British-flag steamer meant that the consequences of hold-up would be much more serious. Some of the early steamers in China under the British flag were in fact owned by Chinese principals.[7]

There was sometimes the need for protection against foreign powers. During the Sino-French War (1884-85), the Sino-Japanese War (1894-95) and the Boxer Rebellion (1900-01), China Merchants ships at risk were temporarily transferred to foreign registry, mainly British and, in 1894-95, German. After the outbreak of the Sino-Japanese War in 1937, the threat of seizure obliged China Merchants and by then numerous private Chinese shipowners to resort to flags of convenience, including British,

Norwegian, Italian, Greek and American. The nominal owners were typically expatriate Shanghai or Hong Kong businessmen and the transfers were made at the local consulate. It became common practice for the foreign flag to be painted prominently on the hull, a practice carried over into the 1950s when British-flag ships were running the Nationalist blockade of the People's Republic of China (PRC).

Finally, the British flag gained entrée to all ports of the world. After 1949 the PRC flag was not recognised in ports of the United States and various allies, while conversely other countries discriminated against that of Taiwan. Registration in Hong Kong avoided all these problems (see also below).

Technological advantage
In the decades of the mid-nineteenth century, most steamships in Chinese waters were American built. American traders brought out wooden-hulled coastal and river steamers with 'walking beam' engines from New England via Cape Horn. Steamers were also sailed out from Britain around the Cape of Good Hope but were either secondhand or of fairly standard coastal design. There was no cost advantage to building any but the smallest steamships in China. Although skilled labour was abundant and cheap, most components except for wooden hulls and decking had to be imported. Local yards were therefore little more than assembly or repair shops.

In the late 1860s the greater durability of iron-hulled steamers caused the American Shanghai S.N. Co. to switch to more advanced British shipbuilders. Leading Scottish builders William Denny & Bros., Robert Napier & Sons and Thomas Wingate had already built iron steamers for Jardine's and Lapraik but designs seem as yet to have differed little from vessels built for Indian, South East Asian or Australasian waters.[8] In 1867 the Shanghai S.N. Co. took delivery of the *Chihli* from Napier's, followed by the *Hupeh* (1870), *Shantung* (1870), *Chihli* (1871) and *Shingking* (1873) from A. & J. Inglis.[9] In 1872 John Swire also turned to Inglis for four iron paddle steamers of improved

American design to run on the Yangtze River for the new China Navigation Company.

Subsequently Swires relied almost entirely upon another Clyde shipbuilder, Scott & Co. of Greenock, which to all intents became an affiliated firm (Table 2). The principal, John Scott, was in 1872 a founding shareholder in China Navigation. His third son, James Scott, joined the China agency of Butterfield & Swire in 1866, rising to manager and partner.[10] In 1874 John Swire persuaded John Scott to place two new but idle freighters built for the UK/Spain trade in a new joint venture, the Coast Boats Ownery, to work China's coastal trade.[11] From 1876 Scott's delivered the first of a long series of specially designed cargo ships that became known as 'beancakers' after the staple beancake trade between North and South China. They also built 'tweendeck China coasters and river steamers. Between 1875 and 1909 Scott's built 68 of China Navigation's 74 new ships.

The pattern for Jardine's was somewhat different (Table 3). Although they relied just as heavily on British shipyards, they distributed their custom and bought more secondhand ships. Between 1881 and 1909 the Indo-China S.N. Co. took delivery of 40 new ships from Britain: 15 from the London & Glasgow Iron Shipbuilding & Engineering Co. of Glasgow, 8 from Wigham Richardson (later Swan, Hunter & Wigham Richardson) of Newcastle, 7 from Hall, Russell & Co. of Aberdeen and the balance from other yards.

The twentieth century saw a marked shift towards shipbuilding by colonial British yards in China (Tables 2-4). By the 1900s both Jardine's and Swire's had acquired large fleets. Well-equipped local drydocks and machine shops were therefore essential. Capabilities to replate hulls and replace boilers were needed to keep ships in commission and modernise as necessary. From there it was not a large step to shipbuilding. Marine departments could supervise the work and modify designs and fitting out as appropriate. In 1863 Jardine's and Douglas Lapraik, along with P&O, had been founding shareholders and directors of the

Hongkong & Whampoa Dock Co. (HWD), which merged various dockyard interests in Hong Kong. In Shanghai the firms Boyd & Co. and S.C. Farnham & Co. both emerged in the 1860s.[12] Early work was mainly docking and repair but these yards followed other local Chinese builders in construction of small and mainly wooden-hulled craft, including river steamers. However, between 1879 and 1901 the two Shanghai firms delivered to Jardine's six iron-hulled river steamers of increasing size and one to China Navigation. With technical assistance from Scots engineers, in 1903 HWD delivered the large steel-hulled river steamer *Kinshan* to the Kong Kong, Canton & Macao Steamboat Co. (HCMSC), which was controlled by the same Jardine and Lapraik interests. The underpriced contract delivered a massive loss to the yard but established a capability.[13] Between 1906 and 1941 all but one of Jardine's new river steamers and most of its China coasters were built by HWD (11) or Shanghai yards (5) compared with only 5 new ships in Britain. Postwar, however, Indo-China operated with a much reduced fleet and relied more on secondhand purchases: six new ships were built in Britain, none by HWD and none in Shanghai (whose yards of course passed out of British control).

In 1900 Swire's decided that they would also benefit from a local shipbuilding, drydock and repair yard and settled on a site adjacent to their Taikoo sugar refinery in Hong Kong. Technical assistance was provided by Scotts. The Taikoo Dockyard & Enginering Co. of Hong Kong Ltd (Taikoo) docked its first ship in 1908 and launched its first ship two years later.[14] Thereafter it built most of the company's new ships, first coasters and river steamers and later cargo liners. Between 1910 and 1970, Taikoo built 45, Scott's 19 and other yards 9 of the 73 new ships delivered to China Navigation (Table 2).

Table 4 calculates the proportion of locally built ships for the main China coast liner companies up to 1970. Swire's and Jardine's built as high a percentage of ships in Hong Kong and Shanghai as China Merchants and

twice the percentage of the Japanese-controlled Nisshin. It may be concluded that the ability of British lines to control or form close relationships with local shipbuilders was a significant source of competitive advantage by reducing both capital and maintenance costs. Local yards could match British yards in cost and delivery time for all classes of ship on the China coast and Yangtze. Between Taikoo and Scott's, Swire's supplied most of their own needs; Jardine's relied less heavily on the affiliated HWD.

Network advantages
Chinese principals did not necessarily lack funds to invest in steamers but faced difficulty in raising loans from foreign banks or placing orders with foreign shipyards because their reputation did not extend beyond China, or even beyond Shanghai. The same problem arose with insuring ships and cargo. These difficulties, the converse of those faced by foreign shipowners in seeking Chinese cargoes, could be mitigated by use of foreign agents or partners. The Hongkong & Shanghai Bank was also an intermediary with extensive local networks.

Over time, as Jardine's and Swire's extended their liner networks and made transhipment agreements with the homeward lines, access to international cargo became more tightly controlled and market entry more difficult. Table 6 summarises the networks of the main lines. Jardine's, which looks to have the most extensive network, had begun with the old 'Country' trade between Bengal, the Straits, and China, later extended by steamship to Japan. Coastal and Yangtze lines were grafted onto this during the 1870s and the whole network was amalgamated in 1881 into the Indo-China S.N. Company. Over time the network was extended to Manila, North Borneo and Bangkok. In addition, from 1869 Jardine's held the China agencies for the Glen Line's fast cargo liners trading between Britain and China via Suez.

Swire's network was more restricted by the lack of reach to India or Japan but this is somewhat misleading. Butterfield & Swire had been established in 1867 to serve as local agents for Holts' Ocean Steamship Co. (Ocean), which quickly became the main freight carrier between Britain and China. The Holt brothers were founding shareholders in China Navigation, which provided a local feeder network. Though nominally a subordinate party, John Swire acted to all intents as a principal of Ocean and mapped a good deal of its commercial strategy.[15] By the 1900s, Ocean had extended its network from China and Japan via the Philippines across the North Pacific. The main gap was in Southeast Asia, where in 1899 Holts' had shortsightedly sold out its ill-managed East India Ocean Steamship Co. to the German Norddeutscher Lloyd (NDL). This was remedied in 1914 when Holts' took up a one-third shareholding in the Anglo-Chinese firm of Straits Steamship Co. Limited (Straits).[16] In 1932 Swire's and Straits together took over the formerly Chinese-owned Ho Hong Steamship Co. which carried deck passengers and cargo between South China, the Straits and Rangoon. Through G.S. Yuill in Sydney, a former employee of Butterfield & Swire and in-law of the Scott family, Swire's maintained their interest in the China/East Australia trade, while Ocean ran a line between Western Australia and Singapore.

Of the other lines, Nisshin itself provided only Yangtze River and limited coastal and shortsea services to Japan but acted as a feeder to the global networks of the parents, NYK and OSK, whose overall networks were even more extensive than Swires-Ocean-Straits-Yuills. China Merchants developed shortsea lines as far as Singapore and Hawaii in the late nineteenth century but in the twentieth century retreated to the China Coast and Yangtze. San Peh built up a large fleet for tramping and charter but its liner services were restricted to the Yangtze and coastal lines from Shanghai to Ningpo and Foochow. China Merchants, San Peh, Ching Kee and smaller Chinese operators were therefore completely outflanked internationally by British and Japanese lines, although between the world wars China

Merchants in particular enjoyed some patronage from the lines of rival nations such as Germany.

Chinese lines still remained competitive for local cargo, which required access to local business networks. British and other foreign lines initially gained access by appointment of prominent merchants as compradores.[17] Although some early compradores like Tong King-sing were extremely powerful, giving firms the character of joint ventures, over time the power and status of their successors tended to diminish as information became more widely disseminated and functions became more routine. The booking of cargo, stevedoring and recruitment of staff nevertheless remained largely in Chinese hands. Swire's and Jardine's British lines enjoyed a good reputation as generous and wise employers, looked very well after established shippers and sought to maintain a very high standard of service. China Merchants' organisation, by contrast, was often lax and revenues leached out. Local networks therefore did not become a competitive strength, except when nationalism came into play as during the anti-British boycott of the mid-1920s or the anti-Japanese boycotts of the 1930s.

Early-mover advantages: commercial agreements
Curiously, the China Coast and Yangtze River were among the first steamer trades to be organised into modern cartels, not just rate agreements but sophisticated traffic- and revenue-sharing pools. This outcome reflected the close involvement of John Swire, who had little faith in conventional rate agreements and went on to organise his principals and competitors in the Britain/East Asia trade into the first liner shipping conference.[18] He thereby earned the sobriquet of 'the father of shipping conferences'. These arrangements clearly worked to the benefit of the British firms.

The China Coast and Yangtze had been contested until 1877, when Russell & Co. sold their Shanghai S.N.Co. fleet to the new China Merchants' S.N.Company. Tong King-sing immediately reached a rate and traffic sharing agreement with Jardines, for whom he had formerly served as compradore.[19] After some bitter rate warfare and the arrival in China of John Swire himelf, these agreements were, in 1878, extended to Swire's. Thereafter Swire's, Jardine's and China Merchants signed pool agreements that divided up the trade between them. Although periodically challenged and renegotiated, these agreements set a structure for the working of all the main China Coast trades. Over time the blows of the Sino-French (1884-85) and Sino-Japanese (1894-95) wars, eroded the position of the China Merchants to the benefit of both Swire's and Jardine's.

These agreements extended to other British firms on the China Coast. Lapraik's Douglas S.S.Co. (1883) reached agreement with Swire's and Jardine's not to intrude upon its regular trades from Hong Kong to Swatow, Amoy, Foochow and Taiwan, but in return had to agree not to extend beyond those trades to challenge the larger firms. HCMSC, in which Lapraik's and Jardine's held the controlling interest, in turn reached agreement with Swire's to share the local river trades against competition from local Chinese firms.

Agreements between Swire's, Jardine's and the China Merchants to share the traffic of the Yangtze and China Coast raised barriers to new entrants. The contrasting experience of French, German and Japanese challenges is instructive. In 1905 the Shanghai firm of Racine, Ackermann & Cie, agents for the French line Cie des Chargeurs Réunis, sought to break into the Yangtze River trade with three French-built river steamers trading as Cie Asiatique de Navigation. After fierce competition and indifferent results, they sold out in 1911 and went into liquidation. The ships were taken over one each by the pool partners Swire's, Jardine's and China Merchants.

German merchants had been prominent in China since the mid-nineteenth century. A steamship line best known as the Kingsin Linie opened from Hamburg in 1871.[20] The German Norddeutscher Lloyd (NDL) of Bremen opened a subsidised line of mail steamers to China and Japan in 1886. German interest intensified after the occupation of Shantung in 1897 and the development of the port of Qingdao (Tsingtao). Both the Rickmers Linie (1896) and the powerful Hamburg-America Line (1898) opened East Asian lines. The local firm of Jebsen & Co. opened a subsidised coastal line while both Rickmers (3) and NDL through its local agents Melchers & Co. (4) placed Shanghai-built river steamers on the lower and middle Yangtze.[21] In 1901 the Hamburg-America Line (Hapag) took over the Rickmers river steamers, which thereafter ran jointly with those of NDL as the 'German Yangtsze Service'.[22] Hapag also took over the Jebsen coastal line, while over the next five years NDL bought out Rickmers eight coastal feeders. NDL had already built up an impregnable position in South East Asia. In China the two subsidised German Lines with their excellent local agents presented a tough challenge to British supremacy. When World War I broke out in 1914, however, Japan seized German Shantung and the ships were all interned. Neither line sought to revive their own feeder services between the wars.

The Japanese challenge was better coordinated, more heavily subsidised and enjoyed an element of good fortune. The Treaty of Shimonoseki (1896) that ended the Sino-Japanese War extended to Japan extraterritorial privileges, including the right to operate commercial steamers on the Yangtze. Over the next three years and under subsidy Osaka Shosen Kaisha (OSK) opened lines from Japan to Taiwan, from Taiwan to South China and on the Yangtze.[23] Unable to withstand the subsidised Japanese competition, in 1904 the small Douglas S.S.Co. withdrew from the South China/Taiwan trades.[24] In 1904 Hunan Kisen, an affiliate of Nippon Yusen Kaisha (NYK), also commenced operations on the Yangtze. Despite subsidies, both OSK and Hunan operated at a loss on the Yangtze, leading in 1907 to a compulsory merger of all Japanese interests on the river into a single company, Nisshin Kisen (Nisshin), which was established with a fleet of 14 ships and an even larger subsidy to withstand British, Chinese and German competition.[25] By 1913 Nisshin was the leading operator on the river and was able to broker a pool agreement from a position of strength. Nisshin succeeded in breaking into the trade because it was a national policy objective generously underwritten by the Japanese government. Suspension of German competition in 1914 and the increased Japanese presence in North China favoured Nisshin to a greater degree than its rivals.

Another successful entrant on a more modest scale was the San Peh S.N.Co. (San Peh) of Yu Ya-ching (Xiaqing), a Ningpo merchant and banker who in 1909 had ventured into shipping by becoming shareholder in and general manager of the Ningpo-Shaohsing S.N.Co. (Ningshao).[26] In 1914 Ningshao challenged the foreign companies and China Merchants by running a large steamer between Shanghai and Hankow. Forced to step down as general manager, Yu instead became chairman of the Hoong On S.S.Co., an Anglo-Chinese firm which since 1904 had run two small ships on the Yangtze. Having accumulated funds during World War I, in 1918 he bought control of the company and the following year transferred the two ships to the Chinese flag. In 1922 he also acquired a small shipyard in Shanghai. Yu hedged his political risks by astute networking. Besides being a leader of the Shanghai business community, he cultivated ties with both the Anhui clique in Beijing, which appointed him as assistant governor of the port district, and with underworld leader Tu Yueh-sheng. In December 1926 he pledged business support to General Chiang Kai-shek and financed his bloody seizure of the city with support of Tu Yueh-sheng. From 1929 Yu was the Chinese representative on the Shanghai Municipal Council. By 1933 Yu's San Peh and Hoong On together ran 8 large steamers between Shanghai and Hankow and six smaller steamers on the upper river. Capital costs were modest because most of the ships were secondhand. Yu could draw on Chinese patriotism to draw traffic from both British lines: he organised the 1925 anti-British boycott in Shanghai and, after the Manchurian invasion of 1931, from Nisshin.

The Japanese invasion from 1937 onwards cancelled out most early-mover advantages. Nisshin had lost business during the 1930s but after 1937 could exercise strong political leverage. In December 1941 all British shipping was seized. Under the Treaty of Chungking in 1943, Britain and the United States renounced extraterritoriality, including the right to sail ships between Chinese ports and on the Yangtze. After the end of the war, surviving river steamers were sold to Chinese owners or for scrap. Coastal steamers, however, continued to operate out of Hong Kong, where Swire's, Jardine's and smaller British firms retained a strong base.

The Gradual Decline

The decline of British-flag liner shipping in Chinese waters was more gradual than the rapid ascendancy and reflected the erosion of competitive advantages. Technological advantage was lost fairly quickly as Japanese and Chinese rivals closed the gap. By the twentieth century British firms were building mainly in local yards in Hong Kong and Shanghai. Network advantages also diminished as Japanese firms built up first regional and then global liner networks. The property-rights advantage of the British flag also diminished. On the one hand, Japanese occupation of Taiwan and Manchuria and the spread of Japanese influence elsewhere in North China reduced British leverage while Japanese subsidies and patronage undermined commercial viability. On the other hand, consolidation of Nationalist control of Central China after 1927 improved property rights security and official patronage for well-connected Chinese firms. Had the Japanese not invaded in 1937, British lines would have faced intensifying competition from emerging Chinese companies that were more aggressive than the bureaucratic and corruptly managed China Merchants. Under pressure on two fronts, British lines had therefore to rely more heavily on established reputation, good organisation and efficiency. Cartel agreements helped to maintain some stability but were not in the long run sufficient to defend market share against adverse trends.

The Japanese invasion of July 1937 marked the end of the old rules of the game. Much of the Chinese fleet was scuttled in barrages across the Yangtze. The surviving ships were either withdrawn up river or re-registered under foreign flags. The Japanese imposed blockades of ports still under Nationalist control. Normal trade was impossible and many ships had to be laid up in Shanghai and Hong Kong. After the attack on Pearl Harbour in December 1941, the Japanese seized most foreign ships remaining on the China Coast. Little survived the Allied onslaught in 1944/45. Meanwhile, under the wartime Treaty of Chungking (1943), Allied governments had agreed to revoke extra-territoriality. After the Surrender in August 1945, the Chinese government was therefore able to impose cabotage between Chinese ports, which was a great encouragement for former and aspiring shipowners quickly to buy up old secondhand tonnage.

British lines thereby lost much of their local cargo base but continued to engage in foreign trade with Chinese ports, including transhipment trade through the British colony of Hong Kong. Both Swire's and Jardine's diversified more into deepsea liner trades, most notably between the booming economies of Hong Kong and Japan on the one hand and Australia and Southeast Asia on the other. In the longer term, however, Swire's were more entrepreneurial in development of their regional liner shipping interests, entering new regional trades between South East Asia, Australia, the Pacific Islands and East Asia. Jardines' traditional Calcutta-Straits-China-Japan line suffered from the stagnation of the Indian economy and intensifying Indian and Japanese competition. Its North Borneo-Hong Kong timber trade was abandoned in 1968. Most of the Australian interests were merged into the joint venture Dominion Far East Line,

which in 1968 formed a new firm to build a roll-on, roll-off ship for a consortium in the Australia/East Asia trade. Meanwhile both Swire's and Jardine's invested heavily in bulk shipping and, in the case of Swire's, tugs and supply vessels for the offshore oil industry.

Containerisation was another watershed. During the 1970s most traffic in main liner trades switched to cellular containerships. Together with P&O, Ocean was a prime mover and shareholder in Overseas Containers Limited (OCL), which in 1972/73 with other British, German and Japanese lines introduced containerships to the Europe/East Asia trade.[27] This was associated with closer integration between Ocean and Swire's for containerisation of other East Asian and Australasian trades. In 1986, however, Ocean sold its 33% stake in OCL to P&O (which twelve years later merged with the Dutch Neddloyd group to form P&O-Nedlloyd Lines). The China Navigation Co. thereby regained its autonomy and continues to be an active participant in regional and feeder shipping in the western Asia-Pacific. Jardine's, however, which was now a small and fairly isolated liner operator, sold off both its residual liner shipping interests and also its bulk fleet in the mid-1980s.[28]

Flag of Convenience
The security premium of foreign flags and the British flag in particular has varied according to political stability within China and threats from hostile foreign powers. A Chinese shipowner could transfer a ship's registration very simply by signing an agency agreement with a resident foreign principal or firm acting as the registered owner, lodging registration papers with a fee at the local consulate and appointing a British master. Such arrangements were made most readily in the International Settlement in Shanghai or, in the case of the British flag, also in Hong Kong. Temporary transfers to protect against seizure were made during the Sino-French War (1884-85), the Sino-Japanese War (1894-95) and the Boxer Rebellion (1900-01).

A more permanent arrangement was to form a new shipowning company under the relevant national companies act and register it with the local consul. As far back as the 1860s and 1870s Chinese merchants were setting up British shipping companies in conjunction with local British residents. In some cases such as the North China Steamer Co. (1866) and Union S.N.Co. (1867), the Chinese were minority shareholders; others such as Jardines' China Coast S.N.Co. (1873) and Yangtze Steamer Co. (1879), the precursors of the Indo-China S.N.Co. (1881), were genuinely Anglo-Chinese joint ventures.[29] Although the capital of Indo-China S.N.Co. was anglicised – and that of the China Navigation Co. was British from the outset, this pattern persisted among smaller local firms. Sometimes the British party seems to have been little more than a nominee. At other times, the Briton may have been a genuine principal but capital was mainly Chinese. Some of the early Moller shipowning interests seem to have been of this kind.

Some foreign shipbrokers had a sideline in fostering would-be shipowners. Typically the broker, such as Eric (N.E.A.) Moller or Haakon Wallem, would have a ship for sale but the potential Chinese buyer would have neither the capital to buy the ship outright nor the foreign credit-rating to take out a mortgage. The broker would stand as registered owner and guarantee the loan in return for a commission on the ship's earnings until such time as the loan was discharged and the ship could be transferred to the Chinese flag. In the event of default, the ship would be repossessed and put up for sale. In the 1910s Eric Moller appears to have acted in this way for Yu Ya-ching, principal of the San Peh S.N. Co. and associated firms. In the 1920s, when Eric Moller was for several years an undischarged bankrupt, his Chinese business partner/compradore Chun Y(o)ung Zan registered ships in his name, an unusual reversal of normal practice.[30]

The Japanese invasion of Manchuria in 1931 and subsequent anti-Japanese boycotts altered the relative convenience of foreign flags. British ships could still trade freely, which created opportunities for firms such as Moller & Co. of Shanghai and Williamson & Co. of Hong Kong to build up secondhand tramp fleets for charter to Chinese and Japanese principals. Chinese firms such as San Peh and Ching Kee also chartered ships to Japanese firms for trade with Japan, while Japanese firms placed ships under Chinese nominees for trade with China. Two such nominees were shipowner and shipbroker Yih Zeu-fong and his associate Song Vung-kwe (Wen-Kwei), business partner of Shanghai-British entrepreneur George Marden.

Japan's declaration of full-scale war in July 1937 made the Nationalist Chinese flag untenable. However, in view of the threat of war, the British flag was no longer so convenient, especially after the outbreak of war against Germany in 1939. Instead the pro-Axis Italian flag, the neutral Norwegian flag and the new Panamanian flag gained instant popularity. The well-established Norwegian shipbroking firm of Wallem & Co. with branches in Shanghai and Hong Kong played a leading role in this flagging out.[31] China Merchants ships that were neither scuttled in the Yangtze nor withdrawn into the upper river – and excluding four new China coasters sold outright to Jardine's – were transferred to American and Portuguese registration (the old American firm of William Hunt & Co.).[32] The San Peh fleet went mostly to the Italian flag (Chinese-Italian Navigation) with two new acquisitions to the Panamanian flag.[33] Yih Zeu-fong, since 1932 the principal of the Wah Shang S.S.Co., transferred his ships to the Norwegian and Panamanian flags.[34] The young C.Y. Tung registered the Island Navigation Corporation in 1940 in the tax haven of Delawere and through Wallem & Co. acquired two ocean-going ships under the Panamanian flag; with British associates he also set up in Hong Kong the Chinese Maritime Trust (1941) Ltd.[35]

Marden and Song operated British and Chinese flags-of-convenience operations for Japanese principals. In 1933 they had set up a shipbreaking venture in Shanghai and established a good relationship with Osaka shipbreaker Miyachi & Co.[36] The steel industry of Osaka-Kobe was based on scrap feed, mainly from breaking up old ships. In 1937 when the United States began to dispose of its laid-up fleet of warbuilt standard ships, the Japanese became concerned that their declaration of war against China would lead to discrimination. Marden agreed to borrow funds from the Hong Kong & Shanghai Bank on Miyachi's behalf and travelled to the United States to bid for lots in the name of both Song and Yih but for resale of charter back to Miyachi. The next step came in February 1938 when the shipowning firm Miyachi Kisen became a subsidiary of the Kawasaki steel, shipbuilding and shipping zaibatsu; Kawasaki Kisen (52%) and Miyachi Kisen (48%) in turn invested in a new joint venture, Kokoku Kisen.[37] Some of the ex-American ships were transferred to Miyachi or Kokoku but others registered to Marden under the British flag with British masters and a few British officers for charter to Miyachi/Kawasaki. Though reportedly seized by the Japanese on 8 December 1941, it appears that most of this flag-of-convenience fleet had in fact been sold to Miyachi a short time previously, a favour in return.[38]

The British flag again became a flag of convenience in 1949 on establishment of the People's Republic of China. Because Britain recognised the new government, British ships were free to trade with China, which had lost most of its shipping fleet by withdrawal to Taiwan and whose ports were now blockaded by Nationalist forces. Swires and Jardines continued to trade from Hong Kong to Chinese ports until two ships hit mines in mid-1950 and the war risks became too great.[39] More enterprising firms including Moller's, Manner's, Wheelock's and Williamson's were prepared to charter older and smaller ships to Chinese principals, including nominees of the Chinese Government, at very high rates, relying on the Royal Navy to intervene in the frequent event of seizure by Nationalist forces.[40] Some of these ships also plied under permit between Chinese ports. Chinese shipowners who had removed their ships from Shanghai also reregistered in Hong Kong, often under nominees.

Especially after 1952, when the United States applied pressure on Panama to deny its flag to ships on the China Coast, there was an explosion in the number of ships on the Hong Kong register. Three different types of ownership can be distinguished. First, as mentioned above, there were British principals, of whom Robert de Lasala of John Manners & Co. quickly became the most prominent.[41] Their trampships with British and Commonwealth officers and Chinese crews traded on charter throughout Asia and Australasia. During the Vietnam War, such Hong Kong registered British ships were prominent in running the American blockade of Haiphong.

Secondly, there were the fleets of refugee Chinese principals, mostly from Shanghai or Canton. At first when the political situation was highly uncertain their ships were registered to nominees such as Wallem's or Wheelock's but over time more and more shipowning companies were registered in Hong Kong and their ships typically flew either the British or Panamanian flag. C.Y. Tung's Chinese Maritime Trust and other subsidiaries were (re)registered in Hong Kong. In the mid-1950s Y.K. Pao laid the foundations for his World-Wide shipping group and was followed in the late-1950s by T.Y. Chao (Wah Kwong). In the 1960s they began rapidly to expand fleets in their own name by building new ships with finance from the Hong Kong & Shanghai Bank against the security of long-term charter to Japanese lines.[42] Many of these ships, however, were placed under Liberian or Panamanian flags of convenience.

Thirdly, there was the People's Republic of China (PRC). Since the PRC flag had little recognition internationally and was at high risk of seizure, in 1949 the PRC had used the shipbroker Wallem & Co. and later also Wheelock Marden & Co. to buy and operate deepsea ships under the Panamanian flag. When this option was closed off, the PRC turned to joint ventures with Eastern bloc countries, in particular Poland and Czechoslovakia. Also Sinofracht took Hongkong-registered ships on long-term time charter. From 1958 the PRC used a third tactic of registering its shipowning companies in Hong Kong to operate ships under the British flag. Ocean Tramping Co. and the associated Hemisphere Shipping Co. and Peninsular Shipping Co. bought up a number of old China coasters while Yick Fung Shipping & Enterprises and later Chiao Mao Enterprises acquired mainly larger standard 10,000-ton freighters. After a hiatus during the Cultural Revolution, the rate of purchase rapidly accelerated from the late-1960s into the 1970s, by which time Yick Fung in particular was operating a very large deepsea fleet. Despite China's liberalisation of trade and shipping after 1976 and increasing recognition of the People's Republic, this flag-of-convenience fleet was retained until Hong Kong reverted to China in 1997.

Conclusion

British shipping in China was always an anomaly. The opportunity flowed from Britain's ability to seize a beachhead in Hong Kong and impose a neo-colonial extra-territoriality along the China Coast and Yangtze River. Entrepreneurs quickly emerged to seize the opportunity and in a few notable cases to establish shipping and shipbuilding firms to consolidate and sustain core competencies. Their ability to defend market position in the long run may be summarised as the outcome of five interacting elements. First was the strength of the British presence in China: extra-territoriality effectively ceased in 1941 but Hong Kong remained a British colony until 1997. Second was the growing power of Japan in China after the Sino-Japanese War of 1894-95 and the Treaty of Shimonoseki (1896). Third was the weakness of the Chinese state and, after 1949, its political and commercial isolation, which was a tremendous handicap to the development of Chinese firms. Fourth was the gradual shift in economic competitiveness between Britain and East Asia, especially

Japan: British firms in China could combine the advantage of nationality with a Chinese cost structure but they still had to compete with Japanese and Chinese firms. Finally, there was the element of entrepreneurship and business organisation: British, Japanese and Chinese firms could do better or worse than environmental factors might predict according to the quality of management.

The interaction of these five factors over the long-term can be summarised in the following periodisation:

<1872: *American monopoly*
  Shanghai S.N.Co. (Russell & Co.) dominant
1872-1882: *Rivalry*
  Entry of Swire's, Jardine's, China Merchants
1882-1896: *The British heyday*
  Swire's, Jardine's dominant
1896-1914: *Foreign challengers*
  Entry of (French), German, Japanese firms
1914-1937: *Stable oligopoly*
  Swire's, Jardine's, Nisshin, China Merchants
1937-1945: *Sino-Japanese war*
  Closure of Yangtse; Japanese supremacy
1945-1949: *The Nationalist era*
  Cabotage applied to Chinese ports
1949-1976: *The closed economy*
  Restrictions on PRC shipping
>1976: *Liberalisation*
  Chinese-flag shipping gains ascendancy

The eventual outcome is what might have been expected: modern Chinese shipping, which had begun to prosper in the 1870s and again in the interwar years but both times had been thwarted, has finally achieved the dominance which natural advantage, entrepreneurship, capital and expertise would predict. That dominance would almost certainly have been achieved by the 1950s, with or without extraterritoriality, but for the *force majeure* of Japanese intervention, which in the 1940s both destroyed the Chinese merchant fleet and paved the way for the Communist takeover and the suppression of private business.

This analysis has two important insights for the long-term history of British shipping in Chinese waters. First, there were only ever two large British liner firms on the China Coast, Swire's and Jardine's, and, although they long behaved like duopolists, the parallelism is deceiving. Swire's were always the market leader from the entry of the China Navigation Co. in 1873. John Swire was a remarkably modern businessman: a fine strategic mind, a shrewd financial brain and a very good organiser. Jardine's, by contrast, never escaped the mentality and organisational limitations of the traditional agency house. It is therefore not altogether surprising that Jardine's, who had been reluctant investors in coastal shipping in the first place, withdrew from shipping in the 1980s in consequence of heavy losses in the Hong Kong property market, whereas Swire's have defied history by outliving the parent Ocean Steamship Co. and, apart from P&O-Nedlloyd, most of the once proud British liner shipping fleet. Although the principals continue to reside in London, the Hong Kong-based Swire Pacific group and Cathay Pacific Airways have grown into substantial corporations in their own right that rely not on the privileges of nationality but on well-developed core competencies. This is a fascinating business history of continuity in strategic vision combined with flexibility to adapt to tremendous changes in market environment.

Secondly, the rest of the long coda of British shipping in Chinese waters, certainly the seventy years between 1937 and 1997, is really a 'flag-of-convenience' story about *Chinese* shipping under the British flag. Until the 1990s the Chinese flag was a flag of inconvenience. What held China back as a shipowning nation was not lack of entrepreneurship, capital or expertise but the weakness of property rights in shipping under the Chinese flag. To gain adequate legal protection from seizure or extortion, Chinese capitalists therefore had to work with or through foreign interests. Market distortions thus created scope for intermediaries, often opportunists, who were numerous in Shanghai and Hong Hong. The phenomenon was most apparent at times of disturbance when ships were transferred to foreign registered owners but it was always to

some extent a feature of the commercial environment. The watershed was 1949. Chinese maritime capital had shifted to the British and other flags in 1937 but there was a vigorous revival of the Chinese flag between 1945 and 1949. In 1949, however, the Shanghai capitalists had to choose between fleeing to Taiwan, to Hong Kong or, in a few cases, remaining behind. Hong Kong now came into its own as the nearest and most convenient international port of registry. With the protection of the British flag, ships could venture back onto the China Coast and trade internationally without risk of exclusion or seizure. By the 1980s 'local' shipowners such as Y.K. Pao (World-Wide group) and T.Y. Chao (Wah Kwong) were strong enough to take over (Wheelock Marden/Wharf) or marginalise (Jardines) the old British 'hongs' that had once been their joint venture partners. For its part the PRC used the British flag to build up a large merchant fleet to trade with countries that had not yet granted recognition. All this is part of the story about Chinese shipping. Britain, in effect, just charged commission on the business.

Table 1. Main China Coast Fleets, 1935 (gross tons)		
Dairen Kisen	Jp	166,345
Nisshin Kisen	Jp	45,473
China Nav. Co.	Br	145,942
Indo-China S.N.Co.	Br	89,814
Moller Line	Br	80,925
Williamson & Co.	Br	23,714
HCMSC	Br	12,473
Douglas S.S. Co.	Br	10,129
China Merchants	Cs	66,609
San Peh S.N. Co.[1]	Cs	47,373
Ching Kee S.N.Co.	Cs	33,496
Summary		
British flag	363,000	
Japanese flag	211,800	
Chinese flag	147,500	
Total	722,300	

[1] Includes Hoong On S.N.Co., Ningshin S.S.Co..

Source: Calculated from *Lloyds Register*, 1935/36.

Table 2. Some Main Shipping Groups, 1935 (gross tons)	
British India	672,075
P&O	419,853
Total	*1,091,928*
Ocean	585,245
NSMO (Dutch flag)	37,534
China Nav.	145,942
Straits	38,065
Ho Hong	10,832
Total	*817,618*
+ Glen Line	93,383
Total	*911,011*
Japanese flag	
NYK	785,203
OSK	513,098
Dutch flag	
KPM	275,274
JCJL	94,886
SMN	289,796
RL	251,627
Total	*911,583*

Source: Calculated from *Lloyds Register*, 1935/36.

Table 3. China Navigation Co.: Newbuildings by Yard, 1873-1970

Period	Scotts	Other UK	Taikoo	Other China	Total
1873-09	68	6	-	4	78
1910-70	19	9	45	9	73
Total	*87*	*15*	*45*	*13*	*151*

Source: Calculated from Dick & Kentwell (1988)

Table 4. Jardine Matheson & Co.: Newbuildings by Yard, 1855-1970

Period	UK	HWD	Other China	Total
1855-80	15	-	2	17
1881-09	40	1	4	45
1910-41	5	11	4	20
1946-70	7	-	-	7
Total	*67*	*12*	*10*	*89*

Source: Calculated from Dick & Kentwell (1988)

Table 5. Main Fleets: Newbuildings by Yard (iron and steel hulls), 1862-1970

Firm (period)	UK	Japan	Local	Total	Total
Swires, 1873-70	102	-	49	151	32
Jardines, 1862-70	67	-	22	89	25
Douglas, 1862-41	19	-	-	19	0
HCMSC, 1865-41	4	-	4	8	50
Nisshin, 1907-41	-	26	4	30	13
CMSNC, 1873-41	22	-	8	30	27

Source: Calculated from Dick & Kentwell (1988, 1991)

Table 6. Main Coastal and Shortsea Liner networks, mid-1930s

Line	ICSNC	CNC	Nisshin	CMSNC	San Peh	Ching Kee
Yangtze	X	X	X	X	X	
N. China	X	X	X	X		X
S. China	X	X	X	X	X	X
Haiphong	X		A			
Saigon		X	A			
Bangkok	X	X	A			
Straits	X	X	A			
Bengal	X		A			
Borneo	X		A			
Manila	X	X	A			
Japan	A	A	A			

X = served directly; A = served by affiliated liner firm

Source: Various

Notes and references

1 K.C. Liu, *Anglo-American Steamship Rivalry in China, 1862-1874* (Harvard, Cambridge Mass, 1962); E.K. Haviland, *American Steam Navigation in China, 1845-1878*, Reprint (Salem, Mass, 1956-58); E.K. Haviland, 'Early Steam Navigation in China: Hong Kong and the Canton River', *American Neptune*, 22 (1962), 3-45; E.K. Haviland, 'Early Steam Navigation in China: Hong Kong and the Canton River, 1858-1867', *American Neptune*, 34 (1974), 17-58; E.K. Haviland, 'Early Steam Navigation in China: The Yangtsze River, 1861-1867', *American Neptune*, 43 (1983), nos 2-4. S. Marriner & F.E. Hyde, *The Senior, John Samuel Swire, 1825-98: Management in Far Eastern Shipping Trades* (Liverpool, 1967); M. Keswick, *The Thistle and the Jade: A Celebration of 150 Years of Jardine, Matheson & Co.* (London, 1982); H.W.

Dick & S.A. Kentwell, *Beancaker to Boxboat: Steamship Companies in Chinese Waters* (Canberra, 1988); H.W. Dick & S.A. Kentwell, *Sold East: Traders, Tramps and Tugs of Chinese Waters* (Melbourne, 1991)

2 Dick and Kentwell, *Beancaker to Boxboat; Sold East* contain brief histories of these British-flag companies.

3 Liu, *Anglo-American Steamship Rivalry.*

4 S. Kizu, *A 100 Years' History of the Ships of Nippon Yusen Kaisha* (Tokyo, 1984), 213-14.

5 K.C. Liu, 'British-Chinese Steamship Rivalry in China, 1873-85' in C.D. Cowan (ed), *The Economic Development of China and Japan* (Allen & Unwin, London 1964); Chi-kong Lai, 'The Qing State and Merchant Enterprise: The China Merchants' Company, 1872-1902' in J.K. Leonard & J.R. Watt (eds), *To Achieve Security and Wealth: The Qing Imperial State and the Economy, 1644-1911* (Ithaca 1992).

6 *China Yearbook* (1933).

7 Y.P. Hao, *The Commercial Revolution in Nineteenth-Century China: The Rise of Sino-Western Mercantile Capitalism* (Berkeley, 1986).

8 D.J. Lyon, *The Denny List*, Part I (1844-86) (Greenwich, 1975).

9 Haviland, *American Steam Navigation,* Appendix III.

10 Mariner & Hyde, *The Senior*, 22-3. A descendant, Edward Scott, was Chairman of John Swire & Sons until his death on 29 January 2002.

11 ibid. 60-61, 79-82.

12 A. Wright & H.A. Cartwright, *Twentieth Century Impressions of Hongkong, Shanghai and other Treaty Ports of China* (London, 1908), 456-60.

13 A. Coates, *Whampoa: Ships on the Shore* (South China Morning Post, Hong Kong, 1980), 151-55.

14 Taikoo Dockyard & Engineering Co, *Fifty Years of Shipbuilding and Repairing in the Far East* (Hong Kong, 1954).

15 Mariner & Hyde, *The Senior*, 114-21.

16 K.G. Tregonning, *Home Port Singapore: A History of Straits Steamship Company Limited, 1890-1960* (Singapore, 1967), 44-8.

17 Hao, *The Commercial Revolution.*

18 Mariner & Hyde, *The Senior*, Chapter 8.

19 K.C. Liu, 'A Chinese Compradore: Tong King-Sing' in Keswick, *The Thistle and the Jade*, 103-27.

20 O. Seiler, *Ostasien Fahrt im Linienschiffahrt der Hapag-Lloyd AG im Wandel der Zeiten* (Herford 1988).

21 Wright & Cartwright, *Twentieth Century Impressions*, 618-20; A. Kludas, *150 Years of Rickmers, 1834/1984* (Herford, 1984), 36-9.

22 E. Drechsel, *Norddeutscher Lloyd Bremen, 1857-1970: History, Fleet, Ship Mails*, Vol. 1 (Vancouver, 1994), 253-8.

23 M.F. Kline, *Official Guide for Shippers and Travellers to the Principal Ports of the World* (Osaka, 1935), 17.

24 Dick & Kentwell, *Beancaker to Boxboat*, 127-8.

25 Dick & Kentwell, *Beancaker to Boxboat*, Chapter 5.

26 Dick & Kentwell, *Sold East*, Chapter 7.

27 M. Falkus, *The Blue Funnel Legend: A History of the Ocean Steam Ship Company 1865-1970,* (London, 1990), Chapter 14.

28 Dick & Kentwell, *Beancaker to Boxboat*, Chapter 1.

29 Y.P. Hao, *The Commercial Revolution.*

30 Dick & Kentwell, *Sold East*, 36-7.

31 Dick & Kentwell, *Sold East*, Chapter 3.

32 Dick & Kentwell, *Beancaker to Boxboat, Chapter 6.*

33 Dick & Kentwell, *Sold East*, Chapter 7.

34 Dick & Kentwell, *Sold East*, Chapter 3.

35 M. Conners & A. King, *C.Y. Tung: His Vision and Legacy,* (Hong Kong, 1984), 9-10.

36 R. Hutcheon, *Shanghai Customs: A 20th Century Taipan in Troubled Times* (Sydney, 2000); Dick & Kentwell, *Sold East,* 167-68.

37 *Kawasaki Kisen: A 50-year History* (Kobe 1969).

38 R. Hutcheon, *Shanghai Customs*, p. 148.

39 Dick and Kentwell, *Beancaker to Boxboat.*

40 Dick and Kentwell, *Sold East.*

41 Dick & Kentwell, *Sold East,* Chapter 5.

42 R. Hutcheon, *First Sea Lord: The Life and Work of Sir Y.K. Pao* (Hong Kong, 1990).

British Ships and Mariners on the Upper Yangtze

Fraser Stuart

Many of the cargoes which moved from and to British ships in the ports of China did so via the great rivers of that country. One of the main channels for this commerce was the 3000-mile long Yangtze with its tributaries and land transport links. The flow of cargoes on the Yangtze was impeded above and below by several hundred miles of gorges and rapids. Navigation in this section was expensive, slow and very dangerous with much loss of life, vessels and cargoes. It could be conducted only by combinations of specially designed junks, portages and hauling from the shore. The commerce was in the hands of Chinese merchants, highly skilled junkmen and local pilots, and had been so for many centuries.

Into this scene on the Yangtze there appeared at the turn of the twentieth century a British businessman and a mariner who were to transform the trade and shipping for all time, with many consequent technological, economic, social and even military impacts. They were Archibald Little and Cornell Plant. This paper provides an outline of their achievements and also their partnership with the highly skilled Chinese Yangtze River pilots, who moved from navigating the junks to the subsequent steamer trade run by British shipping companies and ship's officers. It traces the period of active trade by these companies to their decline under a period of turbulence and war in China.

Captain Plant, who pioneered steam navigation on the Yangtze, was so highly regarded in China that a massive monument was erected to him in 1922 above the Hsintan, where it still stood when this paper was read, but it disappeared in 2003, with the Gorges and Rapids under the waters of the new Three Gorges Dam. It is fitting at this time to recall this small but vital piece of maritime history of China and the part played in it by British mariners. We start by recalling the Yangtze as it was before the intervention of Little and Plant.

The River

The Yangtze Kiang, as the river is known to foreigners, is known to the Chinese as Ch'ang-Chiang (the Long River), the Ta'kiang (the Great River), or simply the Kiang. It is over 3000 miles long. The river from the sea to Hangkow is called the Lower River; between Hangkow and Ichang, the Middle River; from Ichang to Chungking, the Upper River and Chungking to Suifu, the Top River. This paper specifically deals with navigation on the Upper River. The Upper River, over a distance of 350 miles, is tortuous and passes through several narrow gorges where vertical cliffs rise on each side to heights of several hundreds of feet above the level of the river. In late July or early August the melting snow and monsoon rains cause an abnormal rise in the river level which may amount to 53 feet at Ichang and 108 feet at Chungking. In the Gorges an abnormal level may reach 150 feet.

The strength of the stream varies with the season. In some areas a rate of $1^1/_2$ to 3 knots at low river in the winter, to 4 to 8 knots or more at high river in summer and in other areas and in certain conditions attains a rate of 13 knots, which constitutes a rapid. There are 72 or so rapids between Ichang and Chungking and all of them within 150 miles of Ichang. The Gorge district extends from Ichang to Kueichoufu a distance of 110 miles, though the combined length to the Gorges is actually 49 miles.[1]

Junks and junk trade

Trading through these stretches of the river was conducted for centuries by junks. In 1880 the British Consul at Ichang estimated that 8000 down river junks arrived at Ichang that year and some 7000 up river.[2] G.R.G. Worcester in *Sail and Sweep in China* said the upriver passage could take from 28 to 30 days during the winter low level water season and 50 to 60 days during the summer level, and the down river passage from Chungking to Ichang could be made in 6 to 10 days.[3]

The largest type of junk was approximately 120 feet in length and carried about 60 tons up river and about 80 to 90 tons down river. A junk was an expensive vessel to build and passage from Ichang to Chungking would amount to £70 to £80 per junk load, a high price for that time.[4] Down river cargo consisted of Tung oil, lumber, hides, tea, pig gut, bristles, tobacco, silk and opium. Up river cargoes were salt, cotton piece goods, kerosene, medicines, wheat flour and sugar and light consumer goods.[5] Small junks were preferred for the most valuable cargoes, as they were considered less liable to accidents on the rapids.

There was also the Upper Yangtze Passenger junk which came in two sizes, the K'ua-tze, 70 feet or more in length and the Shin Potze, about 40 feet in length. These were frequently used by government and commercial people.

Crews

The junks employed hundreds of men, namely, the crew, pilots and trackers. In his *Glimpses of the Yangtze Gorges*, Cornell Plant describes the junk folk as 'a fine body of men, physically and temperamentally; they were hardy, merry and bright not withstanding the arduous nature of their calling'.[6] Archibald Little described the junkmen thus:

> …a more cruelly worked or more poorly paid and withall a better tempered set of fellows are not to be met with the whole world over. Dirty and ill paid, usually covered from head to foot with sores, and treated like dogs, they work with a will and are always ready for a job.[7]

Pilots

Local pilots were always taken on above and below each rapid. No junk would venture to negotiate the rapid either way without them.[8] The pilots were also magnificent sailors, trained by their fathers in this hazardous hereditary work, they were deservedly looked upon as the aristocrats of the Upper River.

When a junk is underway, the pilot stands on a plank, on the after part of the junk, which gives a clear view over the mast house. From this vantage point he watches with a practised eye the surface of the water. This is called 'reading the water'. With bent elbow his hand is raised, the index finger aloft, and, without the slightest change in facial expression, he bends or flicks this finger in a beckoning manner, now to the right, now upright, now to the left. Meanwhile the laodah standing beside him, struggles obediently with the tiller, 15 feet long, to alter course in the direction indicated by the mute signal. In the same way the men on the huge bow sweep receive their orders. Close to the pilot stands a man who, under the orders of the pilot, controls the actions of the trackers far ahead on the shore. This is done by the rhythmic beat of a drum, the note being varied; the signal 'stop' is given by a short sharp beat; 'slow' is indicated by an even rhythm, and 'full speed' denoted by a rapid and frenzied constant drumming.

Not a word is spoken; indeed it would have been useless, for the roar of the angry river drowns all sound. This thunderous roar of the water and the beat of the drum are a large factor in the memory of anyone who has experienced a fiercely running rapid.[9]

Trackers

The trackers were engaged in hauling the junk from the shore. On the upper Yangtze, tracking was done by professionals, and junks on passage between Ichang and Chungking always carried a small gang of long distance trackers to haul the junks along in the comparatively calm reaches between rapids when they cannot operate on sail alone. On arrival at the bad rapids the junks would bank in and wait their turn to be hauled over the rapids; this would involve employing up to 200 local men in what was a dangerous and arduous task.[10]

Before attempting a difficult rapid some of the heavy cargo would be discharged and portaged to a point above the head of the rapid. Warps would be laid out and all hands would go ashore leaving 10 to 16 to man the bow sweep. Three or four special swimmers called *Tai-wan-ti* or water trackers would stand by to jump into the water and free the towline should it become fouled on a rock. Because of the constant fraying on the rocks a towline was renewed after every voyage.

A large junk of 150 tons carried a crew of 100 men; 70 or 80 trackers on shore and about 20 men on board to man the bow sweep and the iron topped poles used to fend the junk off boulders and rocky points. The trackers were guided and directed by the beat of a drum, the drummer being under the direction of the helmsman.[11]

Little and Plant – Pioneers of steam

The trade and traditions of the River which have been outlined were centuries old when steam technology was spreading in China. Two British men above all others pioneered the use of steam on the treacherous Upper Yangtze. They were Archibald John Little who had the dream and the drive, and Samuel Cornell Plant, a mariner who proved steam could overcome the navigational problems. It may be useful to detail their backgrounds and contributions before considering more fully the developments on the river.

Archibald John Little

Archibald John Little came from a prominent expatriate Shanghai family, one of his brothers being a doctor in Shanghai and another the editor of the *North China Daily News*. He was born on 18 April 1838 in London and educated at St Paul's School and Berlin. He went to China in 1859 and commenced his career at Kiukiang as a tea taster with a German firm. After a few years he started the firm of Lattimer, Little & Company in Shanghai. In 1883 he made a journey from Hangkow to Chungking and back by junk, and returned a keen enthusiast for steam navigation on the Upper Yangtze. In 1884 he started an all-year-round service outside the rapids, between Hangkow and Ichang with a small twin screw steamer of 139 tons called the *Y-Ling*.

The experience he gained with the *Y-Ling* convinced him that steamer navigation on the Middle and Upper Yangtze was perfectly feasible. Therefore in 1887 he formed the Upper Yangtze Steamship Company and built a larger steamer of 459 tons at Bow and MacLachlan, Paisley, which was sent out in sections and assembled in Shanghai. This was the *Kuling* a paddle steamer, 175 feet long, flat-bottomed, which drew only 2 feet 6 inches when light. Little said he was doubtful of her ability to navigate the Upper River.[12] Already in 1861 the British surveyor Blakiston had expressed the opinion that steamers of any kind would have to be towed over the rapids and that only short, flat-bottomed, full-powered steamers with separate engines could navigate the river above Ichang.[13] L.S.Duncan, the Senior Surveyor, who took part in a special mission of inquiry into the trade of the River Yangtze in 1869, said in his report to his commanding officer that steam navigation could not be carried out because of the force of the current, want of anchoring ground, intricacy of navigation and the changeable condition of the river's bed.[14]

Despite these adverse opinions, Little brought the *Kuling* to Ichang in February 1888. As the Chinese authorities refused to allow the vessel to sail above Ichang, Little was forced to sell the *Kuling* to the China Merchants Steam Navigation Company, which was partly owned and subsidised by the Chinese Government. Little was undeterred and determined to be the first to take a steamer to cross the rapids up to Chungking and in 1898 he had built at Shanghai a small 58 ton teak launch, 55 feet in length, with twin screw reciprocating engines of 20 hp capable of 9 knots. With Little himself in command and accompanied by Mrs Alicia Little, an engine room staff of a middle-aged engineer from Ningpo and two stokers, the *Leechuan* set off for Chungking on 15 February 1898.

At some of the bad rapids 300 trackers had to be employed and after considerable strain and anxiety the *Leechuan* arrived safely 10 miles below Chungking. The accomplishment was more symbolic than practical. The *Leechuan* could carry neither cargo nor passengers. However, Little was sufficiently encouraged by the success of this venture that he formed a company to build a larger steamer of commercial size on the Clyde, the *Pioneer*.[15]

In 1900 the *Pioneer* was built for Little's Yangtze Trading Company; the hull at Blackwood and Gordon's shipyard at Port Glasgow to Denny's design, and the engines and boilers at Denny's own works at Dumbarton. She was a paddle steamer, 182 feet in length, 60 feet in beam over the paddle boxes and 9 feet 6 inches deep with a fully-loaded draft of 6 feet. She could carry 50 tons of cargo and could accommodate several European passengers and also tow a flat alongside with another 100 tons of cargo and Chinese deck passengers. The hull and machinery were sent out in sections and assembled at Shanghai, a method that Denny's had developed for many steamers they had built for the Irrawady Flotilla Company.

In 1899 Archibald Little was dining at the Oriental Club in London and expounding to companions his frustrated attempts to steam up the rapids on the upper Yangtze. Dining nearby was a shipmaster who had just returned from three years in Arabistan on the Tigris and Euphrates rivers, but more importantly had spent 16 months as captain of a sternwheel steamer on the rapids of the Upper Karun River, Southern Persia. This was Captain Samuel Cornell Plant. In 1900 Little persuaded him to come to China and command the *Pioneer*. On 12 June 1900 the *Pioneer* with Captain Plant in command left Ichang with 150 tons of cargo on board and many passengers.

When she arrived at the Hsintan rapid she hung for a time on the lip but managed to get over. The greatest difficulty came at the Yehtan where she was delayed for 3 days before she could be hauled over with the aid of hawsers to the shore. She arrived at Chungking having taken 8 days from Ichang and anchoring at night, and only taking 58 hours actual steaming time.

The voyage was a great success very largely as a result of the skills of Captain Plant. Unfortunately, Little was again prevented from exploiting this enterprise. The Boxer troubles were then approaching their climax at this time and the Royal Navy chartered the *Pioneer* to evacuate British and foreign nationals from Chungking and West China. After another trip to Chungking, again under Royal Navy charter, the *Pioneer* remained as a guard ship until 1921 when she was sold to Chinese owners.[16]

Captain Samuel Cornell Plant

Samuel Cornell Plant was born in Framlingham, Suffolk on 8 August 1866, son of Samuel Plant, Captain in the Merchant Service.[17] He followed his father to sea and was trained in sail and steam. Plant spent three years in Arabistan (Southern Persia) employed by the Euphrates & Tigris Steam Navigation Company.

Captain Plant's experiences navigating the rapids of the upper Kárún river over a period of approximately 16 months are contained in a manuscript he wrote in 1891 which is now held in the Middle East Centre, St Anthony's College, Oxford. It was on the Upper Kárún that Captain Plant learned the skills which were to stand him in good stead on the Upper Yangtze. After meeting with Archibald Little at the Oriental Club he accepted his offer to go to China in command of the *Pioneer* which was being built at Port Glasgow. The *Pioneer* made 2 trips to Chungking with Captain Plant in command, during which time he trained Chinese junk pilots to handle a steamer and when the Admiralty acquired the *Pioneer* they considered they could save money by employing Chinese pilots trained by Captain Plant, whom they dismissed.

In October 1901 Captain Plant was engaged by Lt De Vaisseau Hourst of the French Navy to pilot their gun boat *Olry* from Ichang to Suifu. Lt Hourst had a very high opinion of Captain Plant. He quoted Plant's honesty, serenity and natural ability:

I owe him a lot and I was very happy when I once had to say to Captain Henniker-Hughan in command of the English fleet in China who was talking about him (Plant) that I considered him the most splendid sailor I have seen on the seas.[18]

After the *Olry*'s voyage Captain Plant was retained by the French Navy to advise it on Upper Yangtze navigational problems. In 1902 he had built a large junk-houseboat, the *Junie*, and while trading profitably between Ichang and Chungking also made a thorough study of the Upper River under all conditions and became fully convinced the feasibility of steam navigation. In 1908, when his contract with the French Navy was terminated, Captain Plant persuaded a group of Szechwan Government officials and business men to combine to form a steamship company to trade on the Upper Yangtze. The company ordered a steamer from Britain and Captain Plant went to Southampton to supervise the building of the company's first ship, the *Shutung*.

This was a twin screw tug boat, designed to tow a passenger and cargo flat alongside. She was 115 feet in length and drew 3 feet of water, and could carry 12 first class passengers and 66 deck passengers. The flat could carry 60 tons deadweight, or 120 tons measurement of cargo. The *Shutung* was sent out in sections and assembled at Shanghai. She arrived at Ichang in July 1909, but because of violent opposition from junk owners and junk men, she only made 8 round trips between Ichang and Chungking towards the end of the season. There was no night-time sailing and nights were spent either at Wanhsien, 140 miles above Ichang, or at an anchorage chosen by Captain Plant. By 1912 the *Shutung* had made many trips without mishap and a second steamer, larger and more powerful than the *Shutung*, which would dispense with the flat, was ordered from Yarrow's on the Clyde.

In 1915 it was recognised that there was a need for a River Inspector for the Upper River and the Maritime Customs appointed Captain Plant. It was generally acknowledged that the success of the *Shutung* was due to

Captain Plant, as much by his ability to win the confidence and co-operation of his Chinese associates as his technical ability. In 1916 the Maritime Customs published what became the basis for the Upper River Sections of the Admiralty Pilot book, Captain Plant's *Handbook for the Guidance of Shipmasters on the Ichang-Chungking Section of the Yangtze River*. As a shipmaster, I would suggest that Captain Plant's *Handbook* is a work of science in which he has recorded every, rock, rapid and whirlpool and his charts are works of art. In the preface to the first issue, Captain Plant writes 'The object of this book is to provide a first-aid to shipmasters about to navigate the Upper Yangtze between Ichang and Chungking.[19]

During 1919 Captain Plant was intending to retire, but was persuaded to take a year's leave and then return to the Upper River for a further three years. When he retired, and out of gratitude for his services, the Chinese Government and Maritime Customs built a bungalow for him and his wife above the Hsint'an. In June 1920, Cornell Plant entrusted the publication of his book entitled *Glimpses of the Yangtze Gorges* to Ivan P Donnelly, who added numerous of his own illustrations and drawings. The book is a gem, intended for the general public: full of interest and teeming with legend and Chinese folklore, with descriptions of the great gorges and the wonderful journey from Ichang to Chungking, as well as the interesting old towns and hamlets, pagodas and temples – everything that went to make a journey through China one of the most fascinating trips in the world. There is a chapter on the various types of junks, their masters and crews and methods of handling them in the rapids. The third chapter deals with modern steamers and describes their cargo carrying capacities and other characteristics.

Cornell Plant's style in this book is self-effacing and nowhere does he mention his own major contribution to the introduction of steamers on the Upper Yangtze.

Charting the river and its dangers

Although the pilots knew the river and its dangers well there were no reliable charts until the nineteenth century. Parts were mapped by French Jesuits in the sixteenth and seventeenth centuries. More work was done by the Royal Navy in the nineteenth century and by Thomas Blakiston and his party in 1861. Blakiston's book *Five Months on the Yang-Tsze* and his chart published by John Arrowsmith in 1862 provided the first detailed description of the Upper Yangtze but it was on too small a scale for navigational purposes. In 1903 the Hydrographic Department of the French Navy carried out detailed surveys of the Upper River from Ichang to Suifu which were supplemented by further surveys in 1910, 1913 and 1921. In later years the British Officers of the Upper River Inspectorate of the Maritime Customs made good use of these surveys and produced charts covering the Upper River and Top River.[20]

Yangtze lifeboats

Despite the skills of the pilots and junkmen and progress in charting there was considerable loss of life. Nonetheless, worse tragedy was avoided by the excellent Chinese lifeboat service.

In 1854 a prosperous merchant Li Yun-Kuei, who lived near the dreaded Hsin-tan, conceived the idea of collecting subscriptions from those junks which had to face this danger. With this money he built three life-saving craft. To distinguish them they were painted red from which their general name of red boats, Hung-Ch'uan, originated, though these particular ones were known as Kan-ssu-tang – the 'dare to die' service.

In 1899 alone they saved 1,473 lives from 49 junks and in 1900 some 1,235 from 37 junks. By 1901 there were 44 of these boats in commission. The crew consisted of a helmsman and four boatmen and the yearly upkeep was $200 for each boat. The service was very well organised. Plots of land were bought for the burial of the bodies found in the river and matsheds were erected on the banks for the crews and the rescued. When a wreck occurred a gun was fired to summon all boats to help. After the rescue the circumstances of the disaster, the name of the junk master and number of the crew were reported and the red boats' crew received 1,200 *cash* for each life saved and 400 *cash* for each body recovered. The salvaging of a cargo was expressly forbidden. This duty was undertaken by especially registered fishing boats from the nearest village and returned to the owners who rewarded the fishermen.[21]

Entry of the British companies

Plant had effectively established a level of technology for navigating the rapids which was reliable. He also provided the necessary directions for navigation and he trained the very knowledgeable Chinese pilots in steamship manoeuvring. The way was now open for the entry of major commercial companies.

In 1917 the Asiatic Petroleum Company, the Far Eastern arm of the Shell Oil Company, built the *An Lan* at the Kiangnan Dock and Engineering Company in Shanghai. A twin screw steamer equipped to carry petroleum products in bulk and with accommodation for 12 First Class passengers, she could navigate the rapids without the assistance of trackers. The *An Lan* was the first British flag merchant ship on the Upper Yangtze. For the first few trips the *An Lan* returned to Ichang empty, but from late 1919, Butterfield and Swire chartered her for the down river trip and this can be considered as the China Navigation Company's real entry into the Upper Yangtze trade.

In 1921 Mackenzie & Company of Shanghai, an established trading company, made their first venture into shipping by building the *Loongmow*, which was much larger and more powerful than any previous Upper Yangtze steamer. She was 1127 GT, 195 feet in length with twin screw steam reciprocating engines of 2000 ihp, speed 14.7 knots. She had luxurious accommodation for European passengers and was promptly christened *The Queen of the Gorges*.

It was in 1922 that the China Navigation and Indo-China Steam Navigation Companies finally made a full-scale commitment to the Upper Yangtze. Each had a ship built in sections by Yarrow and Company, Glasgow. B & S had the *Wanhsien* assembled at Hong Kong and Jardine's had the *Fuhwo* assembled at Shanghai. The former was the largest ship on the Upper Yangtze. The *Wanhsien* was 1060 GT, 214 feet long and had twin screw oil fired steam reciprocating engines of 3600 hp. Both had a fully-loaded draught of about 8 feet.[22]

During 1923 Mackenzie and Company sold the *Loongmow* and *Shutung* to China Navigation Company, who renamed the former, *Wanliu* and a year later Jardine's built the *Kiawo* for the Upper River and China Navigation Company increased their Upper River fleet by 6 ships. They achieved this by buying the Dollar Company's *Alice Dollar* and building 5 ships at Yarrow's. They were the turbine oil fired steamers *Kiating*, *Kiangting* and *Kingtang*, and the smaller motor ships *Suisha* and *Suiting*. The former were the most modern ships on the whole river, 150 feel long, twin screwed, 483 GT and a loaded draft 5 feet 4 inches, suitable for operation between Ichang and Chungking during the low water season. One of the main cargoes was wood oil for which they were fitted with special tanks. Unfortunately they had one great disadvantage; a slow change from ahead to astern power and so no more turbine steamers were built for the Upper Yangtze.

The motor ships were 121 feet long, 296 GT with twin screw Gardner diesels and intended for operation between Chungking and Suifu. Unfortunately, because of the unsettled political situation, it proved too hazardous to operate ships on the Top River and after a few months they were withdrawn to the Upper River.[23]

By the time of the second issue of the Plant *Handbook*, published in 1932, the development of steamer traffic on the Ichang-Chungking Section of the Upper Yangtze had produced several types of vessels suitable for operating at different levels. As a general rule these vessels were of light draught, twin screw, built of mild steel and fitted with three rudders with both steam and hand steering gear.

Unfortunately Captain Plant did not live to see the burgeoning of steam ship commerce on the river which he had so ably pioneered. In February 1921, Captain and Mrs Plant decided to go home to England and sailed from Shanghai on a Blue Funnel steamer but Captain Plant died from pneumonia before the ship reached Hong Kong. The shock was overwhelming for his wife and she, too, died as the ship was entering port. They were buried together in Happy Valley, Hong Kong. A memorial, an obelisk thirty feet high made of blocks of pink granite on a brown sandstone base was erected above the Hsin T'an by public subscription among the foreign community. His old friends thanked him for all his hard work and called him *The Father of the Gorges*; father that is, of steamship navigation on the Upper River. His professional influences on many subsequent events remained.

British mariners on the new river vessels

The new generation of river vessels working the Yangtze were commanded by British captains and officers from Britain and crews recruited in China. The traditional companies trading coastwise in China were by the 1930s dominant on the River, although great reliance was placed on the detailed knowledge of the Chinese pilots.

The two principal British shipping companies trading within China and on the China coast were Butterfield and Swire's China Navigation Company and Jardine Matheson's Indo-China Steam Navigation Company. Officers signed 3-year contracts and volunteers for service on the Upper Yangtze were recruited from Middle and Lower River ships, and usually received a bonus and local leave after a season of 6 months. The volunteer system was stopped in 1932.[24]

At this time officers on British tramp ships, which comprised 70 per cent of the merchant fleet, were living on hard tack, carrying donkey breakfast mattresses around with them, very poorly paid and fortunate to get a job when foc'sles were full of men with certificates. By contrast, officers on China Coast and Yangtze River ships were living like gentlemen. Each had his own personal steward who did his laundry, cleaned his cabin and provided a standard of service which was absent on most British ships.

These officers on the Upper River Ships considered themselves the aristocrats of the China Coast Shipping fraternity. They fitted into the social scene and were accepted as members of the clubs at Ichang and Chungking when river conditions imposed delays of several days at each end. Here more than anywhere else on the coast, reliable navigation, ship handling and machinery performance was essential to avoid serious mishaps. To quote Cornell Plant:

> The general idea was that it required a man of exceptional nerve to navigate the Upper Yangtze. This idea was misleading. The quality required above all was caution, and next to it calmness and stability of temperament. The man who 'took chances' on the Upper Yangtze when he had neither sufficient knowledge nor experience ran very grave risks.[25]

These Upper River ships usually had six British Officers, Master, Chief and Second Mates, Chief, Second and Third Engineers. With the establishment of the shipyards in Shanghai and Hongkong, Chinese time-served engineers were recruited by China Navigation & Indo-China Steam and replaced the European junior engineers. By the 1930s the Chief Engineer was the only European in the engine room.[26]

The Chinese crews

In a system inherited from the Indian Coast, the Chinese deck, engine and catering departments were recruited by the bosun, No.1 Fireman and Chief Steward respectively. Each of them selected and employed his own men and in many cases it included a large proportion of sons, brothers, nephews and other relations which meant that the head of

the department exercised close control over their behaviour.

The usual practice was to select each department from different provinces. The deck department usually from North China, Tientsin in particular, the engine room department from Canton and Shanghai (engineers and fitters were trained in Shanghai and Hong Kong shipyards) and the catering department from Wenchow. Coming from different provinces, speaking what were really different languages, this was a form of 'divide and rule'.

Wages in the early 1920s and 1930s were pitifully low, but in the conditions of the time in China a job on a Jardine or Swire ship was highly prized. It was secure, they were fed, clothed (in company uniform) and in addition to regular wages there was always the chance of an extra dollar through 'pidgin' or 'squeeze' when deck passengers were carried.

Whether as sailors, firemen or stewards Chinese crews were reliable hardworking, trustworthy and sober, and relations between British Officers and crew were almost invariably excellent and survived periods of anti-British boycotts on-shore and Anglo-Chinese hostility.[27] Each department had its own galley and cook, and the head of the department was paid a victualling allowance for each man, per day and an allowance of rice was also paid by the owner. This was essential since, coming from different parts of China, their food tastes were quite different.

The Chinese pilots

Captain Plant attributes to a skilled Chinese pilot the same peculiar instinct which enables the American Indian to follow a trail; to him the river provides its own aids; its surface is its compass and on their efficiency the safe navigation of steamers depended to a very great extent. These Chinese pilots were excellent and capable men as a rule, but at the same time it was necessary for the Master of a steam vessel to be at all times on the alert.

To appreciate the skill of the Chinese pilot one can do no better than recount the first hand experience of Captain Graham Torrible when in command of the China Navigation Company's *Wanliu* on the Upper River in 1938.

> *Towards the end of a hard day's run from Ichang against a powerful and increasing freshet the* Wanliu *was driving hard to get clear of the 25 miles long Wushan Gorge before nightfall. The gorge itself, due to the rapid rise in the level was an unforgettable picture, foaming water swirling from cliff to cliff. Having entered the gorge there was no stopping until we reached the top and darkness comes earlier in a gorge.*

> *The senior pilot was a proud old man, who, once asked by a jaunty passenger in Chinese about his ability, replied quite simply that he was the best pilot in the world. He excelled himself that day with the ship hugging the cliff sides in order to avoid the main current, he would suddenly hurl the ship (there was no other word to describe it) at the cliff face, a matter of feet away. The ship would rise up on a bulge of trapped water which he knew he was going to meet, and be flung clear, thus retaining her position close inshore, instead of finding herself in mid-stream. Just inside the head of the gorge there was a huge stationary whirlpool. It spanned the full width of the river and in the gathering dusk and overshadowing cliffs, looked like a mediaeval picture of hell.*

> *This whirlpool was something I had never experienced and never want to see again. It was as though the power of the freshet trapped by the sudden restriction of the gorge, which would be less than 150 yards across at that point, and the rugged outline of the shore, were lifting the whirlpool above the level of the river itself.*

> *We crossed it safely, keeping well clear of the vortex; the dip towards it was very noticeable and it was necessary to slow down the starboard propeller to stop it racing. The whirlpool and the freshet should have had the river to themselves.*[28]

Political and social relationship

The introduction of steam was in a sense inevitable and it was accomplished remarkably smoothly, with Plant's guidance. However, there were tensions right from the start. Between 1919 and 1923 some 20 steamers were plying between Ichang and Chungking and Chungking and Suifu, but the political situation was increasingly chaotic.[29] In 1922 the Szechwan opium crop was reputed to be the largest for 10 years and General Liu Ch'ing-hsun, commandeered many Chinese-owned vessels to carry troops and opium down river. To avoid their ships being commandeered by the military, Chinese owners registered them under French, Italian, Swedish flags but the fall in freight rates forced some small Chinese companies out of business.[30]

British ships were rarely interfered with for the first few years but anti-foreign boycotts became the feature of the scene as nationalism and the anti-foreign movement gathered strength. As the number of steamers increased it proved disastrous for junks, junk crews and traders. Not only did it reduce their opportunities to secure cargo but also insurance rates on steamers were far lower than junk-borne cargo. The resentment of the junk men and trackers at the loss of their livelihood and the increased perils of the river with the wash from steamships caused them to vent their wrath on foreign-owned steamers. In 1925 there was a boycott of British goods and shipping but the most disturbed years from a British point of view were 1926 and 1927 with the spread of nationalist influence throughout the Lower and Middle Yangtze. The British ships were subject to repeated interruptions and for a time there were no services above Hangkow.

British ships were forbidden by the British Embassy to carry troops but at times found it politic to carry 'volunteers', that is soldiers in plain clothes and without arms.[31] On 27 August 1926 the China Navigation Company's SS *Wanhsien* arrived at her name port to discharge cargo and passengers and anchored near HMS *Cockchafer*. During the night the *Wanhsien* was boarded by 100 Chinese soldiers, commanded by General Kuogu Tung, a subordinate of the warlord General Yang Sen. General Kuo announced he was commandeering the *Wanhsien* for the carriage of his troops. The captain of the *Wanhsien* sent a call for help to HMS *Cockchafer* and the captain of the gunboat soon came on board and became involved in a heated discussion with General Kuo. Eventually the General agreed to remove his soldiers, but immediately complained to his superior, General Yang, who was determined to force the *Wanhsien* into his service.

On 29 August another of China Navigation Company's ships the *Wanliu* arrived at Yan Yang some 30 miles below Wanhsien. As was the practice when making brief calls the *Wanliu* remained underway whilst passengers disembarked, and while this was taking place several troop-laden sampans came alongside and some troops managed to get on board and storm the bridge which had been isolated by the Captain and his Officers. As an anti-piracy measure, China Coast and Yangtze River ships were fitted with steel shutters which, when closed, isolated the navigating bridge. In this state of siege the *Wanliu* proceeded to Wanliu and eventually anchored near HMS *Cockchafer*. An armed party from the gunboat boarded the *Wanliu*, disarmed the Chinese soldiers, sent them ashore and the *Wanliu* left for Chungking.

In the meantime, General Yang Sen had put 400 troops on board the *Wanshien* and announced he intended to hold every British ship until he was compensated for the loss of a pay chest containing $85,000 which he said was in a sampan that had been deliberately rammed and sunk by the *Wanliu* at Yan Yang.

Later that evening another of China Navigation Company's ships, the *Wantung* arrived at Wanhsien and after she anchored she was boarded and siezed by 300 armed Chinese troops. General Yang refused to negotiate with the captain of *Cockchafer* and threatened to fire on his ship unless the Royal Navy boarding parties were withdrawn from *Wantung* and *Wanhsien*. The Captain was

forced to comply. He reported to the Rear Admiral at Hangkow and awaited reinforcements. Meantime, General Yang Sen consolidated his troops and artillery on the river bank opposite the anchorage.

At Ichang the Royal Navy chartered the Jardine Matheson ship *Kiawo*, placed her under the White Ensign and fitted protective plating and barricades of coal bags around her bridge. Various armaments were transferred from the gunboats to the *Kiawo* and on 4 September the *Kiawo* and the gunboats *Scarab* and *Mantis* left Ichang and anchored for the night in the Wushan Gorge, where the *Kiawo*'s funnel and hull colours were painted out.

At 1815 hours on 5 September the *Kiawo* and the gunboats arrived at Ichang and as *Kiawo* approached the detained ships she was heavily fired on from the river bank. The British gunboats and the river gunboats returned the fire. In the stiff fight that followed 3 naval officers and 4 ratings were killed and the Chief Engineer of the *Wanhsien* was shot and drowned while attempting to swim to the *Kiawo*. All Europeans were evacuated from the China Navigation Company ships and the *Kiawo* and the two gunboats withdrew to Ichang where a large naval force was assembled ready to proceed to Wanhsien had the *Kiawo* expedition been unsuccessful. General Yang Seng however now decided to negotiate and eventually the *Wantung* and *Wanhsien* were released in an indescribable condition and returned to the China Navigation Company. [32] [33] [34]

Repercussions of the *Wanhsien* incident lasted for a long time. China protested to the League of Nations about Britain's 'brutal' bombardment of the peaceful town of Wanhsien, which had caused the death of many innocent people and many thousands of pounds of damage. Foreign property (especially British) was looted in Chungking by 10,000 ruffians armed and organised by General Yan, who called themselves The Wanhsien Revenge Society. There was a boycott of British trade, which lasted for nearly a year on the Upper Yangtze, four years at

Wanhsien itself and for shorter periods at some Lower Yangtze ports.[35] Consular opinion was that if further action had been taken by the Royal Navy at Wanhsien all the Szechwan Generals would have joined forces against the British, a circumstance which might even have led to a full scale war.[36]

In 1929 and 1930 trade improved on the Upper Yangtze. The Nationalists were in control of most of the Lower and Middle River, but independent War Lords still controlled much of Szechwan and Yunnan. There were some 2 million soldiers in the former, some of them so-called regular troops of War Lords and others militia men or bandits.[37]

In 1932 and 1933, following seizure of Manchuria by the Japanese, and their encroachment into North China there was a boycott of Japanese goods and shipping which benefited British and Chinese shipping. The Sino-Japanese war erupted in earnest on 7 July 1937 with the fighting at the Marco Polo Bridge outside Peking and five weeks later the war reached Shanghai which was shelled by Japanese war ships on 18 August. Nanking fell to the Japanese four months later and Hangkow fell on 26 October 1938.[38]

Withdrawal of the British companies
Conditions under which foreign ships operated on the Yangtze steadily deteriorated, as it became obvious that the Japanese intended to establish a commercial monopoly on the River. On 10 March they announced that all ports on the Lower River would be blockaded until the war was over. All merchant ships would require permits and would only be allowed to trade at specified ports. British ships were the specific targets for the Japanese tactics.

As the Japanese advanced up the Lower and Middle Yangtze the situation on the Upper Yangtze became more chaotic. With the fall of Hangkow, Ichang became the end of the line and more and more crowded with men, materials and shipping trying to escape to the West and conditions there became indescribable. There were no adequate repair facilities at either Ichang or Chungking. Ships ran non-stop, grossly overloaded with little or no attention paid to river conditions or safety precautions of any kind. Fuel supplies became an increasingly serious problem; the military commandeering the best coal early in the war and supply of fuel oil and diesel from the Lower River dried to a trickle. Various mixtures of rapeseed, cabbage seed and peanut oil were all tried, all with little or no success.[39]

Junk traffic in the gorges was revived, but not successfully. Many had been out of commission for a long time following the increase in the number of steamers on the river. Many were ill-found and tended to get over-loaded, and almost certainly their tracking ropes were old and had been in use longer than was prudent. Red Boats had disappeared by this time so loss of life must have been heavy.[40]

The final operations of British ships on the Upper Yangtze were drastically reduced services between Wanhsien and Chungking. Two Jardine gorge ships, the *Kiawo* and the *Hsin Chang Wu* and the Taikoo *Wanhsien*, all oil burners without fuel, were laid up alongside the APC installation at Ichang, together with a fleet of Taikoo lighters. A single Japanese bomber dropped incendiary bombs on the *Kiawo* and the *Hsin Chang Wu*, which were soon gutted. So ended Indo-China Steam Navigation Company's Upper Yangtze adventures.[41]

In May 1940 Ichang fell to the Japanese. The last British ships remaining on the Upper Yangtze, the China Navigation Company's *Kangting*, *Wanhsien* and *Wanliu*, were handed over to the Chinese Government and the British Officers returned to Hong Kong by road from Chungking to Kunming, then by rail to Haiphong, and finally by sea.[42] This ended British shipping on the Upper Yangtze.

In 1995 the writer Simon Winchester made a journey up the Yangtze from estuary to source and visited the Plant Memorial above the Hsintan. He was told that in 1963 the Red Guards had tried to blow it up. They could not destroy it so they had a group of boys with iron tools break out every letter. It is now submerged under the waters retained by the Three Gorges Dam.[43]

Notes and references

1. *Yangtze Kiang Pilot,* 2nd Edition, (London, 1928), 181,188-9.
2. A. D. Blue, *British Ships in West China 1875-1941* Unpublished thesis, Open University, (1978), 87-88.
3. G. R. G. Worcester, *Sail and Sweep in China,* (London, 1966), 108.
4. S. C. Plant, *Glimpses of the Yangtze Gorges,* (Shanghai, 1921), 39.
5. L. P. Van Slyke, *The Yangtze – Nature, History and the River,* (New York, 1988), 110.
6. S. C. Plant, *Glimpses,* 43.
7. A. J. Little, *Through the Yang-tse Gorges,* (London, 1888), 331.
8. A. J. Little, *Yang-tse Gorges,* 124-5.
9. G. R. G. Worcester, *Sail and Sweep,* 110.
10. G. R. G. Worcester, *Junk and Sanpans of the Yangtze,* (Annapolis, 1971), 51.
11. A. J. Little, *Yang-tse Gorges,* 111-2.
12. A. D. Blue, *British Ships in West China,* 92-3.
13. T. W. Blackiston, *Five Months on the Yangtsze ,* (London , 1862), 129.
14. A. D. Blue, *British Ships in West China,* 74.
15. G. R. G. Worcester, *Junk and Sanpans,* 149.
16. A. D. Blue, *British Ships in West China,*132-134.
17. Birth Certificate of Capt. S C Plant.
18. Hourst, Lt de Vaisseau E. A. L., *Dans les Rapides du Fleuve Blue,* (Paris, 1904), 12-15.
19. A. D. Blue, *British Ships in West China*, 136-7, 139, 142-4.
20. A. D. Blue, *British Ships in West China*, 139.
21. G. R. G. Worcester, *Junk and Sanpans,* 528-529.
22. A. D. Blue, *British Ships in West China*, 179, 182-3.
23. A. D. Blue, *British Ships in West China*, 186-7.
24. G. Torrible, *Yangtze Reminiscences ,* 2nd Edition, (Hong Kong, 1990), 43.
25. S. C. Plant, *Handbook for the Guidance of Shipmasters on the Ichang-Chungking* Section of the Yangtze River, *Second Issue, (Shanghai, 1932),* 2.
26. A. D. Blue, *British Ships in West China*, 213-8.
27. A. D. Blue, *British Ships in West China*, 218-9.
28. G. Torrible, *Yangtze Reminiscences,* 78, 81-2.
29. A. D. Blue, British Ships in West China, 181.
30. A. D. Blue, *British Ships in West China*, 185-6.
31. A. D. Blue, *British Ships in West China*, 188-90.
32. A. C. Hampshire, *Armed With Stings,* (London, 1958), 66-80.
33. A. R. Williamson, *Eastern Trader,* (Privately published, 1975), 209-10.
34. H. G. W. Woodhead, *The Yangtze and Its Problems,* (Shanghai, 1931), 35-6.
35. A. D. Blue, *British Ships in West China,* 193.
36. A. C. Hampshire, *Armed With Stings,* 80.
37. A. D. Blue, *British Ships in West China,* 197.
38. A. D. Blue, *British Ships in West China,* 221-3.
39. A. D. Blue, *British Ships in West China,* 227-228.
40. G. Torrible, *Yangtze Reminiscences,* 77.
41. G. Torrible, *Yangtze Reminiscences,* 85.
42. G. Torrible, *Yangtze Reminiscences,* 86.
43. S. Winchester, *The River at the Centre of the World,* (London, 1996), 274-6.

Chinese Seafarers in the Global Labour Market: A Focus on Seafarers as Labour Export[1]

Bin Wu

Despite some significant periods of international maritime activity, exemplified by the fleet led by Admiral Zhang He in the fifteenth century, China's history has generally been dominated by its shore-based economy, characterised by high levels of self-sufficiency in its various sectors. Among the consequences of the Opium War in 1840 were not only the 'inflow' of outside capital and commodities, but also an 'outflow' of its surplus labour abroad. Today there are Chinese communities to be found in most parts of the world. Seafaring must be considered a part of this outflow. British merchant shipping was significant in the transportation of Chinese labour to other parts of the World and in employing Chinese as seafaring ratings (on deck, in the engine room and in catering).[2] In the first half of the twentieth century, China was, perhaps, one of the largest suppliers of seafarers in the world. By 1933, according to official statistics, Chinese seafarers numbered 126,000, of whom three quarters were employed in foreign deep-sea shipping, and a quarter in the Chinese coastal trade and the Yangze River transportation, which were dominated by China's national fleet.[3] The process of Chinese emigration was interrupted for three decades from the late 1940s until it was restored owing to economic reform and a more open policy on emigration from the late 1970s.

Owing to the growth of the Chinese population and economic change, migration pressures have increased in recent decades.[4] Linked with the demand from the global labour market, various channels and models have developed for tapping China's labour resources. It is well-known that a great number of Chinese skilled workers have emigrated to the USA, Canada, Australia, United Kingdom and other West European countries.[5] Nevertheless, maritime disasters have also drawn international attention to the increasing trend in Chinese illegal migration and international criminal gangs.[6] Between the two ends of the spectrum, however, there is a wide range of temporary migrants who are either sent by the Chinese government or by Chinese business companies on contracted projects abroad, or they are imported by host countries owing to shortages of labour (*e.g.* cooks, nurses, Chinese medical doctors and teachers). The term 'labour export' refers to all those Chinese who work abroad temporarily and legally. Differing from other types of migration, labour export contains some common elements such as: a valid visa, a defined period (short-term migration), involvement with intermediate companies or state owned enterprises, and authorisation or approval by the Chinese government.

A good example of labour export is Chinese seafarers working in foreign fleets, not only because they are one of the major fields of China's labour export since the economic reforms of the 1970s, but also because the international shipping industry is the first globalised industry which has established a global labour market to seek and recruit cheap and qualified seafarers in that same post-reform period.[7] As a result, China has become a major seafarer supplier alongside the Philippines, India, and East European countries.[8]

The global labour market, however, is full of competition and uncertainty. While the Philippines have been dominant for more than a decade, their leading position is questioned in recent debates because of the supposed increasing costs of employing Filipino seafarers.[9] Owing to China's advantages in human capital stock, maritime education facilities and cheaper labour in particular, it is hardly surprising that the demand for Chinese seafarers is expected to increase.[10] In contrast to the increasing demands, however, the supply of Chinese seafarers seems to lag far behind. According to the China Co-ordination Council for Overseas Seaman Employment (COSE), the average growth rate of Chinese overseas seafarer numbers has been four per cent per year during the past decade, and had reached 32,448 by the year 2000.[11]

Three main interpretations are generally recognised with respect to the gap between demand and supply. The most popular assumption is that the language competence of Chinese seafarers suffers in comparison with other seafarer supply countries such as the Philippines or India.[12] Such an assumption does not recognise that China might work to overcome the disadvantage by reallocating its English teaching resources so as to enhance the capacity of its labour export, which has been listed as an important objective of national economic development.[13] The second interpretation is that the improvement of wages and welfare in shore-based industries has led to a decline in the number of seafarers wishing to work for foreign fleets.[14] Such an explanation seems to conflict with the fact that China has been suffering from a rapid increase in urban unemployment in recent years, resulting in an enlargement of the labour supply for foreign fleets, if the government offers training and recruitment opportunities.[15] The third approach considers the deficiencies of regulation and harmony systems which constrain labour export.[16] Compared with the first two approaches, this interpretation draws attention to the role of government intervention in labour export affairs, but leaves a question untouched: what is the fundamental base upon which the regulation system can be properly established and implemented effectively?

This paper does not attempt to answer the above questions, but rather to provide an empirical base upon which the assumptions above can be tested and adjusted. Therefore it is necessary to know what progress Chinese seafarers have made in entering the global labour market. What are the similarities and differences between 'exported seafarers' who work on 'foreign' ships and their counterparts who work for the national fleet in terms of skill, rank, age and working conditions? What position do Chinese seafarers hold in the global labour market compared with other seafarer supply countries, such as Filipinos and Indians?

The above issues are addressed through an on-going global seafaring labour market survey conducted by the Seafarers International Research Centre (SIRC) at Cardiff University. Comprised of a global seafarers database and a regional seafaring labour market survey, the SIRC project attempts to map out the composition and distribution of global seafarer labour forces on the one hand, and identify the main factors and dynamics driving change in the global labour market on the other. Based upon sampling and collecting crew lists from ports world-wide, a global seafarers database has been established, and the first SIRC global labour market survey report has been published.[17]

Through a combination of a descriptive analysis of the SIRC seafarers database and other relevant information, this paper attempts to provide a profile for Chinese seafarers involved in international cargo transportation in general, and to reveal their competitive capacity and comparative advantages in the global labour market in particular. This chapter outlines the evolutionary processes of China's ocean fleet and the impact of economic reform on seafarer export. This is followed by a profile of Chinese seafarers, and a comparison between exported and non-exported seafarers. Chinese seafarers in foreign fleets are further compared with Filipinos and Indian seafarers. In summarising the results of this analysis and comparison, the conclusion highlights policy implications.

The Chinese Fleet and Chinese Seafarers in the Globalisation Era

The role of Chinese seafarers in the global labour market cannot be separated from the development and reform of China's shipping industry. Constrained by the post World War II political environment and its alliance with the Soviet-Union, China's shipping industry was small and limited to river and coastal transportation. During the 1950s, for instance, the water transportation share of the national total cargo turnover was only a quarter.[18] China's contemporary ocean fleet did not exist until 1961. Under the environment of the planned economy, deep-sea transportation was monopolised by the China Ocean Shipping Company (COSCO), and seafarers were one of the top occupations amongst urban Chinese who were permanently employed by the state-owned company. By 1980, China's water transportation accounted for 44 per cent of the national total in cargo turnover whilst its ocean fleet had 955 vessels, and total gross tonnage had reached 6.87 million tonnes.[19] Benefiting from economic reform and open-door policies, China's shipping industry in general and ocean shipping in particular entered a period of rapid expansion from the 1980s. By the end of 2000, China's ocean fleet had reached 2,525 vessels with 37 million deadweight tonnage (DWT), contributing 5.3 per cent of the world total, ranking fifth amongst the world fleets. Among the Chinese ocean fleet, furthermore, 1986 vessels used the national flag, contributing only 46.3 per cent of its total ocean fleet in DWT, whilst the remaining 539 ships were registered to flags of convenience (FOC), accounting for 53.7 per cent of its total DWT.[20] This is an indicator that China's ocean shipping industry has become part of the globalised industry.

Beside the growth of the national ocean fleet, one of the major changes resulting from China's economic reform is related to increasing competition in the international freight market. By 2000, there were a total of 290 shipping companies registered for international shipping in China, of which the three largest state-owned companies, COSCO, China Shipping Group Company (CSG) and China National Foreign Trade Transportation Corporation, accounted for over 65 per cent of the national ocean carrying capacity.[21] Alongside the reconstruction of China's ocean enterprises, more and more

foreign companies have entered China's shipping market since 1986. By the end of 2000, a total of 562 representative offices from 30 countries had been established in 35 cities in China, including many interior cities. Foreign shipping companies altogether established 21 foreign-funded shipping companies with 62 branches in cities such as Beijing, Shanghai, Dalian.[22] As a result of the opening of the freight market, for instance, the Chinese fleet share is less than 40 per cent in the dry cargo and tanker freight markets, and less than 30 per cent in container transportation.[23]

Associated with the expansion of its shipping industry, China has established a comprehensive maritime education and training system, including five universities (offering bachelors' and higher degree courses), six colleges (offering three year diploma courses), over twenty shipping schools and 34 training centres.[24] It is said that these establishments can provide 5,000 officers and 20,000 ratings annually.[25] In keeping with institutional change and the requirements of the International Convention on the Standards of Training and Certification of Watchkeepers (STCW 95), the global seafaring labour market has been added into the objectives of the training structures, resulting in an adjustment of curriculum design and resources. Of no less importance, many foreign agencies have been allowed to enter China's maritime education and training systems, which offers a new dynamic for Chinese seafarers to gain access to the global labour market.[26]

Globalisation has not only reshaped China's shipping structure and freight market, but also led to the adjustment and reallocation of seafarer resources. With the opening of international freight markets, many coastal and even river shipping enterprises have become involved in international shipping, resulting in an enlargement of the seafaring labour force.[27] Owing to increasing overstaffing in almost all state-owned enterprises, the permanent employment system has been abandoned and a 'contract employment system' has been introduced instead, which has resulted in increasing unemployment in urban areas.[28] In response to the demand of the global labour market, more and more crewing agencies have been established. To promote and manage seafarers' labour export, in 1989 the government established a new institution, the China Co-ordination Council for Overseas Seamen Employment (COSE). By 2001, a total of 56 crewing companies had been registered as members of COSE.[29]

To conclude, an evolutionary image emerges regarding the demand and supply of Chinese seafarers. Before the 1980s, China's ocean fleet and coast/river ships were separated, whilst all seafarers in the ocean fleet were permanently employed by the state-owned company. Since economic reform and the adoption of open-door policies, Chinese seafarers have being reallocated owing to many factors such as: plurality of ocean transportation, enterprise system reform, participation of foreign capital, and the development of maritime education. This has resulted in a new system being created for seafarer recruitment, training, employment and management. Involving complex economic and political factors however, the process is far from complete.

Many conclusions may be drawn from the review of the processes that enabled Chinese seafarers to return to the global labour market. Their return was a gradual process, involving many factors including economic reform and the open door policy, maritime education infrastructure, adjustment of national regulation system and recruitment policy, demand from the global labour market, and so on. The contribution of Chinese seafarers to the global labour market is not in a simple linear relationship of demand and supply dealing with foreign fleet managers, but involves the complex reallocation and reconstruction of Chinese labour forces among three sectors: coastal/river transport, national ocean fleet and foreign fleet. Different from its planned economic system, therefore, an increasing flow or exchange of seafarers can be found crossing borders.[30] Alongside the state-owned shipping companies,

maritime education and training systems have become a major channel to provide young and qualified seafarers to foreign fleets, resulting in an improvement of seafarers' profile compared with those working in the national fleet.[31] The above assumptions are subject to confirmation by empirical data, the task of the following sections.

The Distribution of the Chinese Seafaring Labour Force

Chinese seafaring labour forces can be distinguished in three categories: seafarers who work in coastal shipping; those in the national ocean fleet (or national controlled fleet, including both Chinese flag and fleet managers registered as Chinese), and exported seafarers who are contracted to work aboard foreign fleets (all fleets beyond the central government control, including Hong Kong and Taiwan). To reveal the extent and potential of Chinese seafarers' participation in the global labour market, this section begins by clarifying the size of the labour force working in China's shipping industry, and then distinguishes those aboard the national fleet from those in foreign fleets.

Table 1. Crewing level comparison between the Chinese and world fleets

Type	Size	PRC Crew L	N	SIRC total Crew L	N	PRC/SIRC
Tanker	5- 20,000	24.1	7	20.0	383	1.21
	50-70,000	31.8	4	27.3	115	1.16
Bulk carrier	20-50,000	27.8	72	23.4	1477	1.19
	50-70,000	29.7	23	24.4	371	1.22
	>=70,000	26.4	16	22.9	532	1.15
Gen. Cargo	5- 20,000	25.7	20	20.9	1211	1.23
	20-50,000	26.5	8	23.9	412	1.11
Container	5- 20,000	23.5	22	20.4	637	1.15
	20-50,000	28.2	32	22.8	556	1.24
	50-70,000	24.0	7	20.3	142	1.18
Total	—	—	211	—	5836	1.18

According to official statistics, the total personnel employed in the water transport sector numbered 443,000 nation-wide in 1999.[32] Taking out river transport and shore based personnel, it is estimated that the total supply of Chinese seafarers was 338,000 seafarers by that year.[33] The total number of ocean seafarers, according to the BIMCO/ISF 2000 report, was about 87,000. It is not clear, however, whether the above figure includes those seafarers who work on foreign ships. To reveal the scale and distribution of Chinese seafarers, the SIRC Seafarers' Database will be employed to facilitate the analysis which follows. There are three assumptions behind the following computation. Firstly, that there is no difference between China's flag and China's registered fleet managers in terms of crewing policy (e.g. crew level, payment, management styles). Secondly, all China's fleet, no matter what flag it uses, employs Chinese seafarers only. In other words, it assumes that the Chinese fleet is operated by 100 per cent of Chinese from mainland China (some ships may have a few Filipinos or Polish seafarers). Finally, it assumes that there is a fixed relationship between Chinese crewing levels and the world average, which can be identified by the SIRC Seafarers' Database. Based upon the assumption above, Table 1 indicates the crewing levels of the Chinese fleet in selected ship types and size. Compared with the mean of SIRC samples, Table 1 shows that crewing levels in China's fleet are about 20 per cent higher than the world average.

Taking the data in Table 1 as a benchmark, the total number of Chinese seafarers working on China's fleet can be estimated through the following procedure.

1. All fleets registered as under Chinese fleet management are classified to match the ship type and size in the SIRC Seafarers' Database.
2. Applying the SIRC crewing level as the benchmark of the world average, the differences in the sample of ships described in Table 1 is extended to all the Chinese fleet, resulting in an estimation of the number of active seafarers in its ocean fleet.
3. By adopting the BIMCO/ISF assumption of back-up ratios, the total number of Chinese seafarers employed by Chinese ocean fleet can be estimated. [34]

Formula: Total Employment of Chinese Seafarers in National Fleet

Total Chinese Seafarers = {$\sum\sum$(Chinese fleet$_i$ x SIRC crewing level$_j$)$_j$} x a x b

i - ship size: 1, 2, 3…9; j - ship type: 1, 2 ,3:7;
a - ratio of crewing level between Chinese fleet and world average;
b - back-up ratios

Applying the above Formula, the total number of active seafarers working in the Chinese ocean fleet at any time is estimated as 48,000 or 81,600 (back-up ratio = 1.7) by 2000. The above figures, however, do not cover the vessels of less than 300 tonnes deadweight. Allowing around 4.3 per cent less than from Chinese official data, the total demand for Chinese seafarers in national ocean fleet is estimated at 85,000 by 2000. With respect to the distribution of the demand for Chinese seafarers in the national fleet, Figure 2 provides a comparison between deadweight and seafarers. By adopting a similar procedure, the total number of Chinese seafarers working in foreign fleets is estimated as around 33,500 by 2000. [35] This result is very close to official data. [36] Combining the two groups together, roughly there are in total 120,000 Chinese seafarers at work in ocean shipping industry, of which about three quarters are employed by the Chinese fleet, whilst about one quarter provides services for foreign fleets.

Profiles of Chinese Seafarers by National and Foreign Fleets
Bearing in mind the two groups of Chinese seafarers related to the global labour market, it is reasonable to ask: what differences are there between them in terms of skills, age and rank? And what changes can be found related to economic transition in recent years? Using the SIRC Seafarers' Database, the following paragraphs make a comparison of their profile first, and then examine the changes from 1997 to 2000.

Regarding the distribution of Chinese seafarers by ship types, Figure 1 shows a comparison between the national and foreign fleets. Compared with a relatively balanced distribution in the national fleet, two thirds of the exported seafarers are concentrated on bulk carriers. Turning to the distribution of Chinese seafarers by rank, the SIRC survey shows that senior officers, junior officers and ratings share 15.7, 27.6 and 56.7 per cent of the total number of seafarers respectively, and there is no obvious difference between the national and foreign fleets.

Figure 1: Comparison of Chinese Seafarers by Ship Type and Fleet Managers (%)

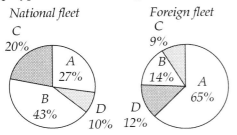

National fleet   *Foreign fleet*

Sources: Bin Wu, 'Modelling Inter-Regional Flow of Global Seafarers…': national fleet data weighted (2000); foreign fleet data (1998) is from the SIRC Seafarers' Database, and is unweighted.

The mean age of Chinese seafarers was 36.8 years, according to the SIRC survey, 1.4 years younger than the world average. With respect to the differences between the national and foreign fleet, not surprisingly, the mean age in the national fleet was 38.5 years, 2.2 years older than for the foreign fleet. Focusing on 1998, Figure 2 provides a detailed comparison of age profile by rank and fleet managers, whilst the curve line illustrates the distribution of senior officers by age. The complexity of the age profile can be illustrated from a time series analysis of Chinese seafarers' ages. Figure 3 shows a continuous growth in both foreign and national fleets. From 1997 to 2000, the mean age of Chinese seafarers has grown four years on average and reached 39 years, of which three years was the increase in the national fleet ages (from 36.1 to 39.2 years old), whilst four years was the increase in foreign fleet ages (from 34.7 to 38.9 years old). Linked with increasing unemployment in urban China in recent years, two conclusions can be drawn from Figure 3.[37] Owing to the heavy pressure of urban unemployment, older seafarers tend to maintain their seafaring careers as long as possible, resulting in a significant increase in seafarers' mean ages. Secondly, Chinese seafarer labour export cannot be separated from, and is closely related to, the reform of state-owned shipping enterprises. While the national fleet faces pressures from overstaffing, more seafarers would like to stay onboard or remain in the foreign fleet, resulting in an increase in seafarers' ages until they are in balance with those of the national fleet. The conclusions above can be further verified by breaking down the seafarers' ages by rank and fleet manager. Comparing the foreign and national fleets, Figure 4 seems to suggest that the major dynamics of seafarers age growth in the late 1990s, are mainly caused by the growth in ratings' ages. It seems to suggest that the Chinese shipping industry is

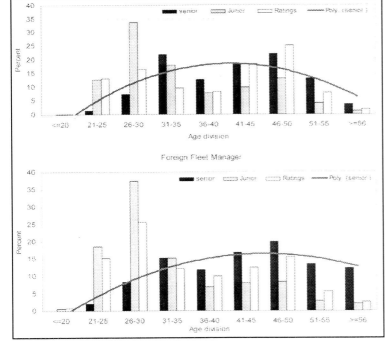

Figure 2 : Comparison of Chinese Seafarers Age Profiles by Fleet Management (1998)

facing the pressure or challenge of overstaffing, which impedes the inflow of ratings into the ocean fleet and the promotion from junior to senior officers. In addition, the stability of junior officers' ages in the foreign fleet can be explained by the continuous supply from the maritime education systems and the attraction of the foreign fleet to them.

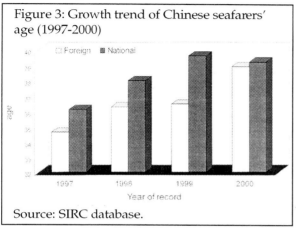

Figure 3: Growth trend of Chinese seafarers' age (1997-2000)

Source: SIRC database.

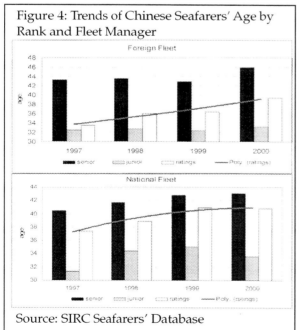

Figure 4: Trends of Chinese Seafarers' Age by Rank and Fleet Manager

Source: SIRC Seafarers' Database

A Comparison Between Chinese, Indian and Filipino Seafarers
The role of Chinese seafarers in the global labour market can be further illustrated by a comparison between Filipino and Indian seafarers. Among the top ten seafarer supply countries by year 2000, according to the SIRC report, the Philippines leads the way, accounting for 28.5 per cent of world seafaring labour forces, whilst China was 5.4 per cent, followed by India with 5 per cent.[38] These three countries together share about 40 per cent of the world total. The absolute population of Chinese seafarers, however, does not represent its competitive capacity in the global labour market. Compared with only one quarter of Chinese seafarers working on foreign ships, the SIRC database shows that nearly 90 per cent of Filipinos and 95 per cent of Indian seafarers are employed in foreign operated shipping. This suggests that China has not yet become a seafarer labour export-oriented country.

The distribution of seafarers among foreign employers is shown in Table 2 which indicates the geographic difference of employment patterns among the selected nationalities.

Table 2 Comparison of Selected Nationalities by Top 10 Fleet Manager (1998, %)

Filipino %		Indian %		Chinese %	
Japan	20.9	Hong Kong	11.2	Hong Kong	38.6
Greece	16.5	Philippines	9.0	Taiwan	18.2
Germany	7.5	Japan	8.5	Japan	11.0
Norway	7.3	Norway	7.6	Philippines	8.9
Panama	4.5	U.K.	5.9	Singapore	6.3
U. K.	3.2	U.S.A.	5.5	U.S.A.	3.5
Hong Kong	3.1	Switzerland	4.2	Panama	3.5
Singapore	2.7	Monaco	4.2	Greece	1.5
U.S.A.	2.7	Singapore	3.9	Liberia	1.2
Liberia	2.4	Greece	3.3	S. Korea	0.7
sub-total	*70.9*	*sub-total*	*63.3*	*sub-total*	*93.4*
Total cases	41789	Total cases	6989	Total cases	8273

Source: *SIRC Seafarers Database (2002).*

Two conclusions can be drawn from Table 2. Firstly, Chinese seafarer labour export is more concentrated in the hands of a few fleet managers' nationalities than that of the Philippines and India, which can be seen as 90 per cent of Chinese seafarers working in the top 10 fleet manager registered countries or regions. This is 27 and 30 per cent higher than the Filipino and Indian figures respectively. Secondly, over 80 per cent of Chinese exported seafarers are actually employed by the East

Asian (Northeast and Southeast) fleet compared with less than one third for the Philippines and India. This suggests that Chinese seafarers have not yet become a real rival of either the Filipinos or Indians at a global level.

Figure 5: Comparison of Seafarers Distribution by Ship type

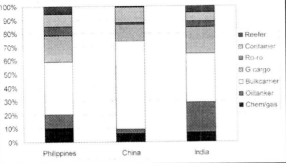

Figure 6: Comparison of Rank Comparison by Nationality

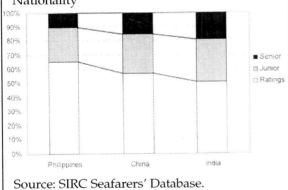

Source: SIRC Seafarers' Database.

Figure 7: Mean Age of Seafarers by Nationality and Rank (1998)

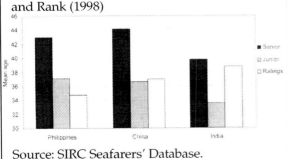

Source: SIRC Seafarers' Database.

Figure 8 Age Change of Junior Officers by Selected Nationalities

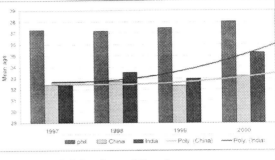

Source: SIRC Seafarers' Database.

Turning to the speciality of seafarers fitted to the labour market, Figure 5 takes into account seafarer distributions by ship types. It indicates that compared with the distribution of Filipino and Indian seafarers, the Chinese are heavily concentrated in bulk carriers. The distribution of seafarer ranks for selected nationalities is shown in Figure 6. About two thirds of Filipinos are ratings whereas half the Indians are officers. Although the Chinese share a similar proportion with India in terms of junior officers, the percentage of its senior officers is less than the latter's. The trend of seafarer supply, Figure 8, compares the change of junior officers' ages between the three countries. It shows an increasing difference between Indian and Chinese junior officers. This suggests that as the development and enhancement of its maritime education system continues, China's comparable advantage in the supply of junior officers will be increasingly recognised.

Many conclusions can be drawn from the comparison between exported Chinese seafarers and their Filipino and Indian counterparts. Firstly, China is a big country in terms of the total seafarer population but still a small one in the supply to the global seafaring labour market. Secondly, the main employers for Chinese seafarers are limited at a regional level, and concentrated in the bulk carrier sector. Thirdly, the comparative advantage of Chinese seafarers in the global labour market is in its junior officers, because of its strength in maritime education. Finally, taking account of the on-going economic transition and the short experience of labour export (only two decades), China has great potential in enlarging its share of the global labour market in general, and that of its young and well-trained junior officers in particular.

Conclusions and Implications

Using the SIRC Seafarers' Database and other information as a basis, this paper has attempted to address such questions as: to what extent have Chinese seafarers participated in the global labour market? What is the profile of those seafarers exported to foreign fleets and how does this compare with their counterparts in the national fleet? And what competitive capacity and development potential do Chinese seafarers have, compared with other major seafarer supply countries in the world? Taking China's on-going economic transition and two decades of experience of labour export into account, a number of conclusions can be drawn. Firstly, despite the increasing demand from the global labour market, the supply of Chinese seafarers is a complex and gradual process, which involves many factors including maritime education and training, national regulation and managerial institutions related to shipping enterprises and labour export. The evidence displayed in this paper indicates that these factors are not separated but interwoven. This seems to suggest: firstly, competence in English is an important but not determinative factor. Secondly, instead of a single factor or linear analysis, a multidimensional approach is necessary to understand the nature and process of Chinese seafarer labour export. If China's accession to the world trade organisations offers good opportunities for China to accelerate its economic transition and opening processes, many questions arise. How will it influence the participation in the global labour market? What interaction and interface between national and global labour market for seafarers exports will occur? What barriers set up by state-owned enterprises restrict the establishment of a national seafaring labour market? This paper offers an estimation of the total number of Chinese seafarers and distribution by sector and fleet manager registered nationality. Bearing in mind the increasing pressure of urban unemployment and its strength in maritime education and training facilities, China's seafarer labour export performance is not reaching its potential. It remains at the preliminary stage characterised by a small proportion (one quarter) of the total seafaring population, and is limited within the regional level (mainly East Asian fleet managers). It seems to suggest that great potential exists in Chinese seafarer supply on the one hand, and yet it has a long way to go to raise itself from the regional labour market to global level on the other. With the objective of enhancing their competitive capacity for service with western ship owners and companies, individual seafarer export should be considered and encouraged alongside the group pattern of seafarer exports. Finally, in the short term, the comparative advantage of Chinese seafarers in the global labour market is with junior officers. To release the potential mentioned above, great attention should be paid to improve and enhance China's maritime education and training system to interface with international regulations and a multi-cultural environment. It would be helpful for China to enhance its capacity for seafarer labour export by encouraging foreign companies or agencies to invest in Chinese maritime education and training systems.

Notes and references

1   I am indebted to Professor Gregor Benton for his constructive comments on an early draft of this paper.
2   Ronald Hope, *A New History of British Shipping* (London, 1990), 341, 383; see also Gregor Benton & Frank N. Pieke, *The Chinese in Europe* (London, 1998).
3   Chinese Navigation Association, *The History of Chinese Navigation* (Beijing, 1989) [in Chinese].
4   Judith Bannister & Jeffrey R. Taylor, 'China: Surplus Labour and Migration', *Asia-Pacific*

Population Journal, Vol. IV, No. IV (1989), 3-19; see also F. N. Pieke & M. Malee (eds.), *Internal and International Migration: Chinese Perspectives* (1999).

5   See Pieke & Malee, *Internal and International Migration: Chinese Perspectives.*

6   F. N. Pieke, 'Recent Trends in Chinese Migration to Europe: Fijianese Migration in Perspective', International Organisation for Migration, *Migration Research Series No. 6* (Geneva, 2002).

7   T. Alderton & N. Winchester, 'Globalisation and De-regulation in the Maritime Industries', *Marine Policy*, Vol. 26, No. 1 (January, 2002), 35-43.

8   See Tony Lane, *et al.*, *Crewing the International Merchant Fleet* (Redhill, 2002).

9   Alec Almazan, 'Looking for Cheaper Seafarers', *Lloyd's Ship Manager* (January/February 2002); 'China a Burgeoning Supplier of crew Despite Lingering Doubts', *Lloyd's List* (9 November 2000).

10 Li K. X. & Wonham, J., 'Who Mans the Fleet? A Follow-up to the BIMCO/ISF Manpower Survey', *Maritime Policy & Management*, Vol. 26, No. 3 (1999), 295-303; David Osler, 'Crew Firms Tap Chinese Market', *Lloyd's List* (14 November, 2000); Almazan, 'Looking for Cheaper Seafarers'; 'China a Burgeoning Supplier of Crew'; 'Chinese Crews Set to Increase', *Lloyd's List* (23 October 2000); 'Philippines Challenged on Manning Supremacy the Future Source of Labour for the Shipping Industry is a Continuous Concern for those in Manning and Crewing', *Lloyd's List*, 27 November 2001). Li, Shanmin, 'Good Prospects for China's Export of Seafarers', *China Ocean Monthly*, No. 79 (No. 7, 2001): according to this report, the mean wage of Chinese seafarers is 32 per cent lower than that of Filipinos.

11 Yanping Gong, 'Discussion About the Situation with Chinese Seamen Export', *China Ocean Monthly*, No 78 (No. 6, 2001) [in Chinese].

12 Yanping Gong, 'The Key Points for Chinese Seafarers Joining the International Labour Force', *China Ocean Monthly*, No. 71 (No. 11, 2000) [in Chinese].

13 Lingfu Chen, 'Issues and Policy Suggestions for Improving the Management of China's Labour Export', China Internet Network (16 March 2002), http://www.China.come.org.cn

14 Yanping Gong, 'Seamen Export: China Expects Becoming the Second Largest Supplier in Asia', *China Ocean Monthly*, No. 88 (No. 4, 2002) [in Chinese].

15 Meng Xin, 'Recent Developments in China's Labour Market', a paper presented at the China Update Conference, Canberra, 1998; US Department of Commerce (USDC), 'China: Foreign Labour Trends', National Trade Data Bank (6 May 1999), http://tradeport.org/ts/countries/china/flt/htm; Social & Economic Policy Institute (SEPI), 'Overview of Current Labour Market Conditions in China', Global Policy Network (GPN) (14 January 2002), http://GlobalPolicyNetwork.org.

16 Shanmin Li, 'Good Prospects for China's Export of Seafarers'; Chen, 'Issues and Policy Suggestions…'.

17 Lane, *Crewing the International Labour Fleet.*

18 Ministry of Communications of China (MOC), *China's Shipping: A Development Report for the Year 1999* (Beijing, 2000), http://www.moc.gov.cn/shuiluys/shuiluys.htm.

19 MOC, *China's Shipping: a Development Report for 1999*; *Lloyd's Register of Shipping* (London, 1980).

20 MOC, *China's Shipping: a Development Report for the Year 2000* (Beijing 2001), http://www.moc.gov.cn/shuiluys/shuiluys.htm.

21 MOC, *China's Shipping: a Development Report for the Year 2000.*

22 MOC, *China's Shipping: a Development Report for the Year 2000.*

23 MOC, *China's Shipping: a Development Report for the Year 1999.*

24 MOC, *China's Shipping: a Development Report for the Year 2000.*

25 Minghua Zhao, 'Chinese Seafarers at the end of the Twentieth Century', *Seaways* (February, 2000); Li, "Good Prospects for China's Export of Seafarers.

26 Osler, 'Crew Firms Tap Chinese Market'; Gong, 'Discussion About the Situation with Chinese Seamen Export'.

27 Minghua Zhao, & G. Shen, 'Seafarers' Labour Market in China: an Overall View', a paper presented at the Global Labour Market Working Meeting, Cardiff (30 June 2001).

28 Xin, 'Recent Developments in China's Labour Market'; USDC, 'China: Foreign Labour trends'.

29 China Co-ordination Council for Overseas Seamen Employment (COSE), 2002.

30 Zhao & Shen, 'Seafarers' Labour Market in China: an Overall View'.

31 Keith Wallis, 'HK Owners Step Up China Crew Training Ties', *Lloyd's List* (12 June 2001).

32 MOC, *China's Shipping: a Development Report for the Year 2000.*

33 Zhao & Shen, 'Seafarers' Labour Market in China: an Overall View'.

34 Baltic and International Maritime Council & International Shipping Federation (BIMCO/ISF), BIMCO/ISF 2000 Manpower Update: the World-Wide demand for and Supply of Seafarers: Main Report (Coventry, 2000). The back-up ratio is the ratio of the number of active seafarers to the total number of seafarers. Besides active seafarers, the latter also includes those who are on leave, ill, or engaged in shore-based training. In the *BIMCO/ISF 2000 report*, the back-up ratios of Chinese seafarers vary from 1.7 to 1.9, depending upon ship type, size, and seafarers' rank. This paper adopts a value of 1.7 regardless of the above variation.

35 Bin Wu, 'Modelling Inter-regional Flow of Global Seafarers: an Assessment of the Demand for and Supply of Chinese Seafarers', in preparation 2003.

36 Gong, 'Discussion About the Situation with Chinese Seamen Export'.

37 Xin, 'Recent developments in China's Labour Market; USDC, 'China: Foreign Labour Trends'; International Labour Organisation, 'China: Labour Market and Income Inequality' (Geneva, 2001), http://www.ilo.org/public/english/protection/ses/info/database/china.htm; SEPI, 'Overview of Current Labour Market Conditions in China'.

38 Lane, *Crewing the International Merchant Fleet*.

Law and Disorder on the China Coast: The sailors of the *Neptune* and an Affray at Canton, 1807.[1]

Patrick Tuck

A trial of fifty-two sailors of the East Indiaman *Neptune* occurred at Canton in April 1807. It was the outcome of a violent commotion in which a Chinese was killed on the quayside of the Western factory settlement. No culprit could be identified, but all assumed a British sailor to have been responsible. Failing production of the actual culprit, the Chinese authorities insisted on the nomination of a substitute culprit, and the British refused to name one. At stake was the continuance of China's maritime commerce with Britain, a trade of immense value to both sides. The case brought two legal traditions, the Chinese and the British, into confrontation, achieving a deadlock that proved soluble only through a corrupt bargain.

The *Neptune* trial case is usually treated by historians as having only procedural interest. Hosea Morse, for instance, emphasises the fact that this was the first time British trade officials had participated directly in a Chinese trial process.[2] It was also the first time that the Chinese had allowed a trial to take place in a foreign 'factory' on the Canton waterfront outside the city walls. However, the trial seems of far greater significance when the issues it raised are considered as part of the learning process by which the British were coming, after nearly a century of direct trading, to understand how Chinese law functioned. It also illuminates one of the major points of difference between Chinese and British legal tradition.

Prior to this case, Chinese law appeared to the British commercial community at Canton to be capricious in its operation, unjust in its procedures for determining the guilt of the individual, and both cruel and excessive in its

Illustrations for this article, by kind permission of the Royal Asiatic Society, can be found inside the rear cover.

punishments. But the *Neptune* trial, its verdict, and the final report issued on it by the Board of Punishments, reduced local British fears of Chinese juridical process, and led to clarification of the ways in which it was intended to apply to foreigners. All the same, on the main point at issue in the trial, the need for a symbolic culprit, the British would still fail to achieve an understanding of the underlying rationale of Chinese law. They viewed Chinese law neither in relation to the Chinese system of moral and cosmographical belief, nor as a reflection of China's social traditions of collective responsibility, nor as an integral part of the government's administrative machinery for maintaining social control. Hence British resistance to Chinese demands for a substitute in place of the real culprit epitomises a fundamental point of incompatibility not only between two traditions of law, but also between different belief systems and systems of governance, and the way this case was handled on both sides offers scope for reflection on some of these differences.

British Sailors, 'liberty' and affrays on the China Coast

We know from anecdotal accounts, and from ships' logs, that incidents of assault, theft, affray and homicide involving British sailors with Chinese were very common on the China coast in the later eighteenth and early nineteenth centuries.[3] Most incidents involved crews of East India Company vessels and privately owned 'country' shipping rather than Royal Navy ships, which rarely stopped off at Whampoa and Canton in this period. It was extremely difficult to control the behaviour of crews ashore.[4] On occasion the East India Company tried to limit the privilege of 'liberty', or shore leave. But Canton and

Whampoa lay at the end of one of the longest of all long-haul voyages. Ships took five months to make the outward journey, and spent three months at anchorage off Whampoa before taking five months on the return. So liberty on arrival, and the chance to drink, were considered vital for morale.[5]

Most cases involving violence were aggravated by alcohol. The Dutch supplied strong spirits at Whampoa, but it was the brews purveyed in Chinese liquor shops that had a particular propensity to drive sailors wild. On Dane's Island at Whampoa, a potent drink called 'samshu' was illicitly distilled; and the liquor shops in Hog Lane on the Canton waterfront sold a firewater consisting of raw alcohol, tobacco juice and sugar, reportedly with a light dash of arsenic to give it bite. This concoction was described by the Reverend Edwin Stevens as causing 'a degree of inebriety more ferocious than that occasioned by any other spirit', leading sailors into 'riotous scenes of the greatest enormity'.[6] Affrays, assaults and thefts occasioned or suffered by drunken sailors on liberty occurred least often at Canton itself. The more usual locations were Danes Island, a place of recreation set aside for British sailors to prevent them fighting with other European mariners, or at anchorages below the Bocca Tigris, particularly Chuenpi. The problem of assaults and affrays caused by drunkenness was perennial, yet few Chinese trials resulted from such incidents. Cases were usually settled informally without reaching the ears of Chinese mandarins. According to Hosea Morse, the chronicler of the East India Company trade with China, only twelve incidents of homicide led to international difficulties during the whole period of European commerce there before the Opium War of 1839.[7]

But the danger of major diplomatic incidents was ever-present, and some cases had fairly spectacular repercussions, since proceedings tended to run into deadlock over incompatibilities between Chinese and British law. An impasse could lead, for example, to Chinese threats to arrest and indict the president and members of the Select Committee of supercargoes responsible for managing the East India Company's trade at Canton. One such deadlocked case, in 1839, contributed significantly to starting the Opium War.[8] More usually, such judicial deadlocks prompted threats to suspend trading operations, a threat sometimes used in desperation by the British, but more usually by the Chinese. Threats of trade stoppage made such judicial cases highly significant for both sides. The China trade had become extremely valuable not only to the East India Company but also to the British government and to the Chinese imperial court.

At the beginning of the nineteenth century, the value of British export manufactures to China reached a million sterling, and the annual value of goods carried from Canton by the China fleet averaged six or seven million sterling, and on occasion up to sixteen million.[9] In tax alone, receipts to the British government on Chinese imports exceeded three, and sometimes four, million a year.[10] At a tenth of British government income this was an especially vital resource at a time of intermittent war with Napoleonic France and her satellites. Not only was British commerce through Canton the only fully profitable part of the East India Company's entire commercial operation, but as a major outlet for the Company's Indian cotton and opium, the trade provided in effect the main channel of remittance through which the surplus revenues of its Indian possessions could be transferred home to Britain.[11] The importance of the trade for the Chinese, too, was considerable. China's agricultural economy was obviously vastly larger than her maritime trade, so that the Chinese could speak of commerce with westerners as unnecessary, and as a privilege conferred merely to 'sooth and civilize' undeserving barbarians. Nevertheless, they valued the Canton interchange highly. The terms of trade with Britain were still broadly in China's favour in this period, and customs duties derived from it usefully supplemented a declining government income. Moreover, since the emperor personally received into the *Nei wu-fu* (Imperial Household Treasury) a direct and substantial proportion of Canton customs revenue, as much as 855,000 taels annually, he showed a particular concern for its continuation.[12]

British fear of Chinese law.

Despite emphatic and reiterated orders from the directors to the supercargoes of the East India Company to show strict obedience to Chinese laws, the chance of a stoppage of trade caused by a judicial deadlock in a case of affray was always high. British scruples and prevarications tended to irritate Chinese officials, and some early cases went to extremes simply due to British ignorance of the Chinese legal system. The British were also inclined to challenge Chinese judicial procedure from fear of the extreme brutality of the Ch'ing system of prescribed punishments, some of which had been visited on foreigners already in the 1770s. In 1801 when, after repeated requests, the governor-general of the two Kwangs finally supplied the President of the Select Committee at Canton with fifty copies of extracts from the Ch'ing penal code relating to foreigners,[13] the British found that it contained a tariff of horrific penalties attached to what appeared in many cases to be relatively trivial infractions. Their impression of the exceptional cruelty of the Chinese system of penalties was reinforced by the arrival at the factory in 1805 of an elegantly illustrated publication entitled *The Punishments of China*, by George Henry Mason, showing in vivid colour the various ways in which judicial punishments were administered. Although Mason's lurid book omitted any reference to the penalty of 'death by slicing'– *ling ch'ih*, or the famous 'death of a thousand cuts' – it offered examples such as blinding with lime, strangulation, beheading by the sword, hamstringing and ankle-breaking.

Even more important than the British community's fear of Chinese punishments, was its impression of the apparent arbitrariness of the legal process. Prior to the *Neptune* case of 1807, British ignorance of the way that the system of justice operated meant that they were constantly apprehensive as to how Chinese officials might choose to apply Chinese laws. They had little to go on but experience of how cases had actually been handled by Chinese officials in the past.[14] In this regard, their impressions of how capriciously Chinese law operated were very largely based upon the spectacularly brusque way that the Chinese had resolved one particular manslaughter case in 1784, involving the gunner of a private British country ship, the *Lady Hughes*. Since the shadow of this precedent lay heavily across the *Neptune* case of 1807, it needs to be looked at briefly first.

The Lady Hughes *affair, 1784*

The *Lady Hughes* case was a significant stage in the learning process for the Select Committee at Canton. When in November 1784 an elderly gunner from a privately owned British 'country' ship, the *Lady Hughes*, fired a ceremonial salute accidentally killing two Chinese in a passing Chop boat, Chinese officials demanded the gunner's surrender on threat of halting the season's trade. The gunner went into hiding, so the cargo manager of the *Lady Hughes* was arrested in his stead and was threatened with being charged with homicide in place of the gunner. The Select Committee, on being notified that in China manslaughter was usually treated as a capital offence, initially resisted Chinese demands to yield up the gunner. It went against the grain to surrender a man for what the supercargoes thought an excessive punishment for accidental manslaughter. They reported: '[In China] life only can atone for what in Europe is thought rather a man's misfortune, than his crime'. The committee's resistance provoked an armed invasion of the Hongs [Company waterfront factories] by Chinese troops.

The president of the Select Committee was then told by a number of officials that if the gunner were not produced, he would himself be held responsible for the crime. Reporting sardonically to the directors in London that the Chinese had pronounced themselves lenient in not requiring *two* culprits to be nominated to atone for the two Chinese who had been killed by the gunner's salute, the president complained of the committee's subjection to the 'absolute and tyrannical power' of the Chinese government. Merchants from the other European factories rallied behind the British Select Committee, and there was an exchange of fire with Chinese troops on the river. But the seizure of the cargo manager, and the threat to arrest the president weakened the resolve of the Select Committee and made it ready to negotiate. Relying on a vague assurance from a senior mandarin that the gunner would probably be treated leniently, the committee complied with the official demand for his surrender, and was then invited to discuss matters with the *An-ch'a shih*, or judicial commissioner for the province. However, the committee later discovered that at the approximate time that the president and supercargoes were being given the judge's explicit assurance that the culprit would remain unharmed until the emperor's will was known, the gunner himself was being strangled outside the city wall.[15]

From this uncomfortable experience the British developed new impressions as to the way the Chinese administered their laws, and this influenced their future conduct. Most obviously they learned to mistrust official assurances of leniency. More important, since in China accidental homicide could be treated as a capital crime, and since it was normal practice to match the number of culprits to the number of victims, they began to realise that for the Chinese the intentions of the culprit was less important than the fact of the crime itself, so that for every life that had been taken, a life was deemed forfeit.[16] Most alarming of all, it appeared that the threat to indict the president of the Select Committee had not merely been a pressure tactic to obtain compliance in yielding up the *Lady Hughes* gunner. The British found that the practice of redistributing responsibility for a crime was integral to the Chinese system of justice. They learned that if the culprit could not be apprehended, the Chinese would not

simply drop the case: they assumed complicity by others, and could reallocate full liability for the crime to them.

The underlying rationale of the system naturally remained invisible to the British. To the Chinese, lawbreaking was not merely a threat to social harmony and to governing authority: it was a violation of the cosmic moral order. For every crime reported, the Chinese considered that a criminal should be produced, whose public denunciation and punishment was a requirement for repairing damage to the moral continuum binding society and the cosmos together.[17] If the criminal evaded capture, a substitute must be produced who could be deemed accountable; and that substitute could be any figure carrying responsibility within the criminal's social group, family or clan.[18] This principle was most prominently expressed through the famous *pao-chia* system of collective communal responsibility, by which individuals in social, family or clan groups stood guarantors for each others' good behaviour, and could be made to suffer if a guilty co-guarantor could not be apprehended. *Pao-chia* – collective responsibility – was a practical mechanism for maintaining ethical order in the cosmos, as well as the prime instrument of social control upon which orderly government in China relied.[19]

The *Lady Hughes* affair showed in greater detail than any previous case how these principles might be applied to foreign commercial enclaves. Forcing the custom of collective responsibility upon the foreign trading community increased the Select Committee's sense of insecurity, but it conferred some collateral benefit too. Foreigners found that in legal matters between themselves that did not involve homicide, they were sometimes allowed to discipline their own nationals without official interference. They were not formally apprised of having any rights in the matter, and remained uncertain of how far self-regulation was allowed. Only in cases of homicide, or when Chinese were harmed by Europeans, were judicial officials invariably bound to confront foreigners, either to discover the culprit, or in his absence to apply the principle of reallocating blame. On the whole, few such cases reached the point of trial. Affirmations by British traders and supercargoes suggest that normally complaints of injury or homicide perpetrated upon Chinese by foreigners would be hushed up by means of surreptitious compensation to the victims or their families. But if a crime was notified and became officially visible, Chinese officials themselves came under pressure from the Board of Punishments at Peking if they failed to find culprits to match reported crimes. If culprits were not readily found, the integrity of officials became suspect, and they themselves could be considered complicit and threatened with liability. So, faced with a lack of culprits in cases involving foreigners with Chinese, officials tended, for their own protection, to show alacrity and persistence in extending the radius of blame.

When problems were caused by the drunken violence of crews of incoming British ships there was never any lack of substitute culprits. Ultimate responsibility for the good behaviour of the British was theoretically borne by the Chinese security (or 'Hong') merchant in charge of the lading or unlading of each foreign vessel. In the absence of a culprit, and according to the circumstances of each case, accountability could extend from the Hong merchant to the supercargo of the trading vessel, or to its captain, and finally to the president and supercargoes of the Select Committee in their role as trade officials ultimately responsible for all British commercial activity. The hierarchisation of responsibility and transfer of blame for public order disturbances had never been exercised on foreigners in so clear and thorough a fashion before the *Lady Hughes* case, and their application came to the British as something of a shock.

Finally, the *Lady Hughes* case taught the British something of the mechanics of Chinese legal procedure, which left the accused with little scope for self-defence. The *Lady Hughes* gunner had not been provided with any advocate to argue his case. Not only was there was no profession of legal defenders in China, there was not even an independent judiciary as such. Magistracy was a function of government, exercised by mandarins as one of many rotating administrative roles. The intention of the trial process was not to hear argument. Guilt was established by prior administrative investigation and enquiry. The purpose of formal trial was simply to proclaim sentence and calculate punishment.[20] There was no presumption of innocence. In fact, accusation carried the presumption of guilt. Since confession of guilt was always required before sentencing, torture was legally and routinely used to extract confessions from the accused, in order to confirm guilt.

The British were encountering a system of law in which the chief priority was to publicize repairs to the moral and social order, rather than to show scrupulous equity in identifying the culpability of the individual. Whatever its rationale, the shocking dénouement of the *Lady Hughes* case of 1784 convinced the foreign community that the Chinese legal system was capricious, cruel and perverse.

The case of the **Neptune** sailors' affray at Canton in 1807

However, the deadlock produced by the *Neptune* case of 1807 would reveal a very different aspect of Chinese law to the British. They already knew that officials could behave unpredictably. In 1807 they were to find how the very flexibility with which law could be applied might work to British advantage. After an exceptionally hotly contested, deadlocked, proceeding, the anticlimactic outcome of the *Neptune* case would reveal the Chinese legal process as a less intimidating, and more humane system. Even though this case reaffirmed the fact that British and Chinese laws occupied different moral worlds, it offered hope that the mitigations built into the Chinese system could enable deadlock to be unravelled by negotiation, rather than forcibly sundered by trade stoppage or threats to the lives of British trade officials.

In the case of the accidental death of a Chinese in an affray at the hands of some sailors from the East Indiaman, the *Neptune*, on 24 February 1807, the Select Committee at once displayed its anxiety to co-operate with the Chinese authorities. But deadlock was soon reached on a far more intractable issue than in the previous case. In the *Lady Hughes* affair, the gunner had undoubtedly been guilty of accidental homicide. The Select Committee had resisted demands for his surrender from a reluctance to see him suffer an unjust punishment. In the *Neptune* case, the Select Committee readily accepted that a manslaughter verdict would result in execution, and were prepared to swallow their repugnance, and co-operate in the culprit's discovery. The impasse arose over the impossibility of identifying any particular culprit. The Chinese were insistent that a culprit – any culprit – be produced. But sending an arbitrarily chosen sailor to his death without clear proof of guilt contravened British notions of natural justice. As the Select Committee observed to the Chinese governor-general:

> *Does Your Excellency call upon us to deliver up to you an innocent person? We trust that Your Excellency does not. Neither the laws of China not of any country can require so absurd and unjust a sacrifice… No consideration whatever can induce us to commit an act which is not only revolting in human nature but for which we would be expected to forfeit our lives on return to our own country.*

The Chinese demand was too much for the Select Committee to accept, so that it felt forced to dig its heels in once more.[21]

The facts of the case are simple. On 23 February 1807, a number of drunken sailors from the East Indiaman *Marquis of Ely* were robbed, stripped and thrown into the river by Chinese boatmen, leaving the liberty men from all the other East Indiamen in an angry mood. The following day at Canton a prolonged series of affrays occurred between a large Chinese mob and fifty-two liberty men of the starboard watch of the *Neptune*, another East Indiaman. A full three days after these affrays, on 27 February, a Chinese, Leau A-ting, died of an injury said to have been received in the fighting. When the dead man's family carried their complaint to the local magistrate, the president of the Select Committee was ordered by the Chinese authorities to investigate the matter and deliver up the culprit for punishment.

In ordinary circumstances this case need never have arisen. The Hong security merchant for the *Neptune*, Mowqua, would have smothered the family's complaint with an offer of compensation before it could reach the hearing of officials. But the family had been prompt to approach the magistrate before Mowqua could be informed of the death, and he had lost his chance to intervene. The victim was a dependent of the family of an extremely influential official, the *Chong-quan*, or general of the Manchu troops,[22] so the case was highly visible, and the authorities were more than usually incapable of ignoring it. The Chinese were happy to let the British conduct their own enquiry so long as they could produce a culprit for sentencing. The Select Committee, commanded by the directors to show obedience to Chinese laws, was perfectly willing to surrender the culprit, if guilt could be credibly attached to a particular individual or group.

So a shipboard enquiry was held on the *Neptune*, presided over by the captains of three East Indiamen, on 1 March.[23] But the chances of discovering the guilty party were remote. There had been many injuries inflicted during the fighting, and since Leau A-ting had died three days after the affray, none of the sailors involved were conscious of having delivered a mortal blow. Nor, given the likely consequence, was any of them willing to implicate a shipmate.

The first enquiry was considered unsatisfactory, even by the British. It reported that many of the fifty-two sailors had been less than frank. Then Chinese officials belatedly produced a witness, a child of eight who, though unable to identify any of the sailors, was able to explain some of the circumstances. So it was decided to hold a second shipboard enquiry on 6-8 March, partly to investigate the implications of the child's evidence.[24] This reflected more thorough probing. The board reported, mainly on the testimony of the *Neptune*'s captain, Thomas Buchanan, that eleven of the crew, being drunk, had behaved with violence. From the minutes of the proceedings a sailor named Philip Murray seems to have attracted greatest suspicion. A witness was prevailed on to testify that Murray had been seen beating a Chinese with a black knotted staff the size of a broomstick. Suspicion of Murray deepened when, during the enquiry, he transhipped without permission to the *Antelope* and had to be secured and returned to the *Neptune* under the express orders of the senior Royal Navy officer at Canton, Captain Robert Rolles, convoy commander of the China fleet. But suspicion against Murray was not capable of proof.

When the Select Committee informed the Chinese that no single culprit could be confidently identified, Chinese officials applied stronger pressure. On 11 March they threatened the Captain of the *Neptune* with arrest and accused him of trying to buy off the child witness with $5, an accusation indignantly denied.[25] Then the officials threatened to arrest and ruin Mowqua, the *Neptune*'s Hong guarantor, whom the committee defended as 'that innocent and highly respectable merchant'.[26] In mid and late March the mandarins referred in sharp terms more than once to 'the personal responsibility of the Chief of the factory for the murder, in the event of the real offender not being surrendered to their tribunals of justice'.[27] This was a chilling reminder of the threat issued to the president of the Select Committee during the *Lady Hughes* affair. The mandarins also warned that if the emperor got to hear of these proceedings he would withdraw the privilege of trade permanently from the East India Company.[28] Sir George Staunton, the secretary

of the Select Committee, who merely served as translator of these exchanges, was himself threatened with arrest, and a Chinese attendant of the *Neptune* was beaten.[29] Mowqua was then ordered to produce the culprit within ten days on pain of paying a huge fine. If he failed, the Select Committee reported, 'it would be concluded that Mowqua knew the culprit and purposely concealed him, a crime in the eye of the Chinese laws equal in guilt with the crime itself'.[30] Anticipating such a threat, Mowqua had already offered a reward of $20,000 to the *Neptune*'s crew as an inducement to the sailors to break ranks and identify one of their number as the culprit. But the offer had been 'universally rejected by the seamen with indignation'.[31]

The problem of determining a culprit was only resolved after prolonged and dogged negotiation by the committee, and particularly by Captain Rolles R.N. Rolles' pronouncements were said to have been rendered particularly effective by the blunt translations of Sir George Staunton, secretary and interpreter to the committee, as yet the only member of the East India Company ever to have achieved fluency in Chinese.

On 14 March, the Chinese magistrates had asked for all the suspects to be handed over for trial to the magistrates of Canton 'and that they should have the liberty to employ engines of torture to draw from the sailors the required confession',[32] a proposal which aroused particular indignation and was rejected out of hand.[33] The magistrates then offered assurances that the offender, once determined, would be leniently treated 'so that his life would not be endangered', but the *Lady Hughes* precedent still operated powerfully on the minds of the mistrustful Select, and they demurred.[34] Finally, a totally unprecedented procedural compromise was reached on 31 March. It was agreed, on certain conditions, that since the British could not find the real culprit, the Chinese would seek a nominal culprit for themselves from among the sailors of the *Neptune*. The magistrates gave a solemn undertaking that they would treat with leniency any culprit they selected, and would levy only a fine. They would question the whole of the starboard watch at a formal magistrates' hearing that would take place, not within the city walls but, on British insistence, at the English Company Hong on the Canton waterfront. Crucially, to prevent any last minute chicanery by the authorities, as had occurred in 1784, the British demanded and received an assurance that they could retain custody of the culprit's person, even after his sentence had been pronounced.

So the trial proceedings were to be an agreed charade. Despite all the bluster, neither side wanted to prolong the stoppage of trade. The Chinese only wanted a symbolic culprit. The British had been assured in advance of his lenient treatment, and would keep custody of his person. For the one side, the arrangement reflected the Select Committee's wariness of Chinese justice; and for the other side, it fulfilled the absolute duty incumbent on Chinese officials to produce a culprit to match the crime. The *Quang-cheou-fu*, governor or prefect of Canton, was to preside over the trial, with three other officers as his assessors. These latter were the district magistrates of East and of West Canton, and the Anchassee, [*An-ch'a shih*] or judicial commissioner of the province, who was responsible for conducting the trial. A representative of the Imperial Customs Commissioner was also to be present as an observer. The composition of the court suggests that the Chinese authorities had abandoned their normal routines and were conflating all three stages of primary judicial process -preliminary investigation, report to the prefect, and pronouncement of verdict - into one continuous trial proceeding.

On 8 April the Chinese officials all appeared in great state in palanquins and sedan chairs, and there exist several contemporary copies of two magnificent and very unusual scenes in oils by a Chinese artist, thought to be Lamqua, which show both the officials' arrival at the waterfront Hongs, and the scene of the trial inside the British factory.[35] The Select Committee and Captain Rolles had demanded to be present at the trial, and to be given positions of prominence in the court. Captain Rolles also suggested installing a full contingent of marines in the improvised courtroom, ostensibly to magnify the dignity of the proceedings, but more probably to prevent a repeat of the *Lady Hughes* incident when the European Hongs were invaded by Chinese troops. The Chinese objected, but agreed to the ceremonial presence of two marines with fixed bayonets, to keep off the crowd and, in Rolles' phrase, ' preserve due decorum.'[36]

The ostensible resolution of the case

The trial took place over three days. On the first day, the seamen were not brought up in cages, as would have been the usual treatment for Chinese criminals about to be arraigned and sentenced. Instead, they were walked up in groups of five, signifying that the first part of the proceedings represented the preliminary interrogation. The Chinese merely put a few simple questions to each seaman[37] and, in the words of Staunton, '…obtained no answer…tending in the least degree to criminate any of the parties'.[38] The Chinese only needed one culprit, 'selected', in the words of Sir George, 'so as to render their enquiries apparently successful'.[39] They made some attempt to turn witnesses against each other by misrepresenting evidence. This effort drew indignant protests from the Select Committee president, John Roberts, and from Captain Rolles, and was without result.[40] On 11 April, Mowqua and another security merchant Pouqua, possibly on the advice of the magistrates, proposed a solution intended to emphasise the accidental aspect of death. They suggested that the dead Chinese should be said to have hit *himself* on a sailor's stick. But the Select Committee stated its objection to such a 'glaringly false' account.[41]

On the third day of the proceedings a deal was arrived at before the hearing by which the Chinese magistrates would accept an expression of belief on the part of the *Neptune*'s captain, that eleven sailors of the starboard watch had all struck various Chinese during the course of the affray.[42] The magistrates would interrogate all eleven, and then choose one, but the charge would be 'shaped in such a way as should effectively acquit [the chosen culprit] of all ill-intentions',[43] a plan to which the Select Committee assented without being prepared to endorse any specific details of the verdict. The court finally chose to fix the blame 'almost at random' on Edward Sheen, despite the fact he had only carried a tobacco pipe, on the grounds that he had been one of those listed as being drunk and violent.[44] Sheen was then charged at the final hearing with 'accidental homicide', and delivered over to British custody at the factory. A number of his companions tried to smuggle him back to the ship before the *Neptune* set sail, but they failed. On 17 April, as the British factory community prepared to depart to Macao for the summer, with Sheen among them, some mandarins entered the factory and tried to abduct him. They were chanced upon by Staunton and thwarted. Sheen was subsequently sentenced to pay a nominal fine, the equivalent of four pounds three shillings,[45] and rejoined his ship a year later without loss of pay.[46]

How the case was actually resolved
No previous historical analysis of this trial has yet explained how this case was technically resolved as a legal issue.[47] 'Accidental homicide during an affray' was a capital crime under the Ch'ing penal code, for which strangulation was mandatory and non-commutable. Since an affray had plainly taken place, the mere fining of an arbitrarily chosen culprit could not in itself get the Chinese officials off the hook. How, therefore, did these officials manage to convert a case of accidental homicide during an affray, invariably carrying the death penalty, into a case of purely accidental manslaughter, for which the death sentence was commutable to a fine?

Neither Morse nor Peter Auber raise this issue at all in either of their lengthy treatments of the *Neptune* affair.[48] However, in 1808 Sir George Staunton obtained a copy of the complete series of reports that were sent to,

and endorsed by the Board of Punishments at Peking, and he published his translation of these in a footnote in his edition of the Ch'ing Penal Code, the *Ta Tsing Leu Lee*, in 1810. The official reports make clear that the magistrates solved their problem simply by concealing all mention of an affray, and composed a fictional narrative to fit the pre-concerted sentence. When notifying the case to the Board of Punishments, the governor-general of the two Kwangs plainly covered up for the magistrates.

The account devised by the magistrates of the death of Leua A-ting is an elaborate invention. The affray had been of spectacular scale and duration and had attracted notoriety. It had involved a large number of drunken sailors and a much larger Chinese mob, had taken place on the quayside not far from the Chow Chow factory, had gone through several sallies and sorties, had caused several injuries, had occupied much of an afternoon, and had resulted in a belated death by beating. The governor-general stated in his own report that he had 'personally and strictly' examined the affair himself. He represented Sheen not as a drunken sailor on liberty, but as a peaceable assistant to Captain Buchanan, helping to land goods at the British factory at Canton, the Fung-tay Hong, after which he had

> ... accompanied Captain Buchanan and others to the upper story of the said warehouse or factory, in order to dwell therein until, the returning cargo having been received, the period of departure should arrive. This upper story was contiguous to, and overlooked the street and pathway towards which a window was opened with moveable shutters. On the morning of the 18th day of the first moon of the 12th year of Kia King, Edward Sheen employed a wooden stick in an oblique direction to keep open the shutter of the above-mentioned window; but in doing this the wooden stick slipped and fell downwards... Leao–a tong... passing at the same moment under the said upper story, was struck and wounded by the end of the

stick falling, as aforesaid, upon his left temple… and the wounded man died on the evening of the following day, the 19th of the moon… Now the aforesaid Edward Sheen, having been repeatedly examined, has acknowledged the truth of all the facts here stated without any reservation. Consequently in this case there is no appeal against the conviction of this offender Edward Sheen; who having been proved guilty of accidental homicide may be sentenced to pay the usual fine to redeem himself from the punishment of death by strangulation.[49]

There had been no such accident, and Sheen had never confessed his guilt. But this account enabled the homicide to be dealt with under clause 192 of the Ch'ing Penal Code, which gave a narrow definition of 'deaths by *pure* accident'[50] as '[accidents] in which no previous warning could have been given'.[51] The penalty was still strangulation, but unlike the non-commutable capital offence of 'accidental homicide in an affray', the punishment was reducible to a small fine of twelve *liang*, four *fen* and two *lee*.

The main victim of this whole affair was not Sheen, but Mowqua. As security merchant for the *Neptune* he was formally obliged by his office to take responsibility for the behaviour of its British crew, who were effectively escaping punishment. He, rather than Sheen, was treated by the officials as the real culprit. Forced to resort to bribes to evade the punishment of strangulation for manslaughter in an affray, he suffered an enormous financial penalty. Purchasing the magistrate's verdict and the governor-general's endorsement brought Mowqua almost to the point of ruin. H. B. Morse, in a very detailed account written in the 1920s, was unable to establish the sums he had laid out, and merely deduced from the course of Mowqua's subsequent career that he had been 'bled white'. On this point there is no need for conjecture, however. Morse did not make use of the notes on the affair given in appendix XI of Sir George Staunton's *Ta Tsing*

Leu Lee, the first translation of the Chinese penal code to be published in any European language, in 1810. Staunton states that the factory received information at the time that Mowqua had been forced to pay 'a sum little short of £50,000…'. [52]

Clearly, the Chinese officials had not only resolved the diplomatic incident but had also satisfied their obligation to find a more appropriate culprit for the crime. By violating the letter of the law in a way that carried some risk, they felt entitled to profit. After a fashion the moral order had been repaired as the system demanded, but only by corrupt means. Of the fabricated outcome Staunton commented that the Chinese officials 'contrived to do that which was just in itself, though they certainly resorted to means which were far from defensible'. [53]

Consequences

The *Neptune* affair was made much use of by Staunton, in his translation of the Ch'ing Penal Code, to make a substantial adjustment to contemporary British views of the horrors of the Chinese legal system. Staunton cited the *Neptune* case, along with other examples, to emphasise the gulf between the draconian penalties of the code, and the notable flexibility of their application. Arguing their 'severity in denunciation and lenity in execution',[54] he pointed out that the prescription of cruel punishments for often trivial crimes was rhetorical in intent, designed to inspire awe;[55] and that the code was so amply provided with exemptions and mitigations, and officials so flexible in their application of it, that it operated in many ways more humanely than contemporary British law.[56] Finally, the report of the Board of Punishments on the trial verdict contained explicit reassurance on a point that had long been uncertain in the minds of British traders, namely how far they would be made subject to Chinese law in non-capital cases where no Chinese were involved. This report announced that, in all cases other than for deaths in an affray, whenever the law 'declared palliating circumstances, and which are therefore not capitally punishable, the offender shall be sent away to be punished by his countrymen in his own country'. Staunton noted: This paragraph is particularly important as it announces an exception in favour of foreigners, which however essential to their well being and security in China, was never before so distinctly declared and understood.[57]

The British at Canton were reassured and better informed as a result of the *Neptune* trial. They had been brought to a clearer understanding of the relationship between criminal proceedings and the code of punishments. And they better understood the role that corruption could play in influencing the outcome of a difficult case. They had been shown how flexibly and leniently the penal code could operate in practice, and had acquired a clearer view of the potential for offering resistance to unacceptable Chinese legal demands.[58] The trial had also led the Board of Punishments to issue the clearest and most reassuring statement yet formulated by the Chinese on the way that the law should be applied to foreigners, confirming that all non-capital cases occurring solely between Europeans could be referred to European courts. Finally, although the British derived no insight into the underlying rationale of Chinese law, and would never be reconciled to judicial torture or to some forms of punishment, the system now looked to them less capricious, and more flexible and negotiable than it had previously appeared.

Conclusions

British and Chinese law inhabited different moral worlds that had been brought into confrontation and deadlock by the *Neptune* case, resulting in an exceptionally awkward attempt to bend the facts to fit an outcome desired by all. For both sides the resolution of this case was a product of diplomatic and economic necessity. Chinese insistence on finding at least a symbolic culprit – the main issue characterising the *Neptune* trial, but also prominent in the *Lady Hughes* case – was an issue that illuminated particularly strongly the

gulf between the two juridical systems. Chinese resort to substitute culprits was a practice rooted in a wholly different structure of governance and social control, defined partly by the notion of collective responsibility, and partly by the need of officials to ritualise and proclaim the effectiveness of their repairs to the moral order. However mendacious or corrupt the behaviour of officials in each case, even their abuse of the legal process reaffirmed the values for which the law stood as an arm of government. Meantime, the *Neptune* trial was an important stage in a learning process for the British. Their understanding of the workings of Chinese law was clarified, though not deepened, by the ordeal. While the trial and its aftermath conferred no profounder insight into the political, administrative and cultural rationale of Chinese juridical practice, it brought greater accuracy to British understanding of the structure, procedures and penalties of Chinese law, dispelling at least some of their fearful conceptions of it.

Seen in conjunction with the *Lady Hughes* affair, the *Neptune* case is an historical issue that for us, too, sharply defines significant differences between two governing cultures, as well as between two systems of law. And it had taken a gunner's clumsiness and the misbehaviour of a few drunken sailors to bring these differences into clearer light.

Notes and references

1 I would like to thank my colleague, Dr Dmitri van den Bersselaar for casting a critical eye over an earlier version of this paper.

2 Hosea Ballou Morse, *The Chronicles of the East India Company Trading to China*, (Oxford, 1926-9), 5 vols, Vol. III, 'The *Neptune* Affair', 51.

3 For instance, Alexander Shank, a young Scottish merchant working for the agency house of Reid and Beale at Canton, wrote home in 1807: [At Canton] quarrels and affrays [are] very common… when the ignorance and rascality of [the Chinese] can be equalled by their laughable cowardice, for one or two English sailors will at any time clear the Quay and put a hundred Chinese to flight…' National Archives of Scotland, Melville Muniments, GD51/535/1-2, p. 175R. Alexander Shank to Thomas Reid, 22

March 1807. More soberly, a former president of the Select Committee, Sir George Staunton, wrote in retirement: 'The riots and irregularities which frequently took place when sailors from the Company's ships were allowed to visit Canton on liberty are well known'. Sir George Thomas Staunton, 'A Note Relative to the Suspension of Trade of the East India Company at Canton on 1807', *Miscellaneous Notices relating to China and our Commercial Intercourse with that Country, including a Few Translations from the Chinese Language*. 2 vols. Second edition enlarged. (London 1822). p. 261. Finally, the secretary to the E.I.C. directors, Peter Auber, in his chronicle of the Company's trade with China, cites an effort made in 1788 to reduce these disorders: 'The conduct of the British seamen in China having long been most turbulent and disorderly, occasioning frequent complaints from the representatives of other European nations, and causing affrays which tended to involve the supercargoes in frequent embarrassment , regulations under the sanction of the Court [of Directors] were framed to check this evil.' Peter Auber, *China. An Outline of its Government, Law and Policy: and of the British and Foreign Embassies, and Intercourse with that Empire*, (London, 1834), 191.

4 The Select Committee at Canton had no court or jurisdiction to try British nationals. But it had long possessed powers of arrest and seizure of British property, ships and persons, which were confirmed in 1786 under 26 George III Cap. lvii, section 35. All cases involving the exercise of these powers were referred home to British courts for judicial proceedings. In 1788 the Company's Court enacted further regulations to check the occurrence of drunkenness and affrays by seamen on the China coast. See Auber, *China. An Outline*, 189.

5 While serving as secretary to the Select Committee at Canton, Staunton referred to the custom of liberty as 'an indulgence to which [seamen] have a strong claim after the fatigues of a long sea voyage and are in some degree intitled by immemorial usage'. British Library, India and Oriental Collections, India Office Records, Canton Consultations, G12/ 154, p. 13, Sir George Staunton, secretary to the Select Committee, to the Viceroy,[governor-general of Kwangtung and Kwangsi], 7 March 1807.

6 Edwin Stevens, 'Seamen in the Port of Canton.' *Chinese Repository* 2, (Canton and Macao, 1834),

423-4.

7 Hosea Ballou Morse, *The International Relations of the Chinese Empire*. 3 vols. (London 1910), III, 100.

8 Ping Chia kuo, *A Critical Study of the First Anglo-Chinese War with Documents*, (Shanghai, 1935), 119-122

9 In 1804, when Captain Nathanial Dance defended the China fleet against attack by Admiral Linois, the cargo at stake was valued at £16 million. Peter Auber, *China: an Outline of its Government*, 211.

10 Sir George Thomas Staunton, *Ta Tsing Leu Lee, Being the Fundamental Laws and a Selection from the Supplementary Statutes of the Penal Code of China*, (London, 1810), 515. 'A trade which employs upon average annually upwards of 20,000 tons of English and 10,000 tons of Indian shipping, which carries off each year more than a million sterling in value of our manufactures and productions....'

11 Michael Greenberg, *British Trade and the Opening of China, 1800-42*, (Cambridge, 1951), chapter 1.

12 Te-ch'ang Chang, 'The Economic Role of the Imperial Household (*Nei wu-fu*) in the Ch'ing dynasty', *Journal of Asian Studies*, 31, 2 (February 1972), 258.

13 Auber, *China: an Outline of its Government*, p. 207. Auber was secretary to the Court of Directors of the East India Company, with full access to all the Company's China correspondence.

14 It was not until Sir George Staunton published his analysis and translation of the Ch'ing dynasty law code in 1810 that it was realised that the code also contained so many exemptions and mitigations that it was markedly lenient in its application. Staunton particularly singled out Mason's work for ridicule. See the introduction to Staunton, *Ta Tsing Leu Lee*. Bodde and Morris consider that Staunton's translation remained the standard work on Chinese law, until superseded in some respects by Philastre's translation of the Annamite law code, which incorporated the Ch'ing penal code of 1740 almost in its entirety. See D. Bodde and C. Morris, *Law in Imperial China exemplified by 190 Ch'ing Ddynasty Cases (translated from the Hsing-an hui-lan) with Historical, Social and Juridical Commentaries*, (Harvard, 1967), 73-4.

15 Morse, *International Relations*, III, pp.102-3; Morse, *Chronicles,*, II, 104-6.

16 Clause 185.1 of the Ch'ing Penal Code stated: 'For any destruction of a human life there has to

be a proper requital (*ti*). '*Ti*' or *ti-ming*' was understood to mean 'a life is forfeit in requital for another'. See Bodde and Morris, *Law in Imperial China*, 183, 330.

17 'In the final analysis, a disturbance of the social order really meant, in Chinese thinking, a violation of the total cosmic order because, according to the Chinese world-view, the spheres of man and nature were inextricably interwoven to form an unbroken continuum.' Bodde and Morris, *Law in Imperial China*, 4.

18 T'ung-tsu Ch'ü, *Law and Society in Traditional China*, (Paris, 1961) 74-6.

19 Philip A. Kuhn, *Rebellion and its Enemies in Late Imperial China. Militarization and Social Structure, 1796-1864.* (Cambridge, Mass. 1970), 24-7, 94-5. Simpler explanations are offered in Morse, *International Relations*, III, 114-6; and Staunton, 'Considerations upon the China Trade' in *Miscellaneous Notices*, 127-9.

20 Bodde and Morris, *Law in Imperial China*, 97-8; Morse, *International Relations*, III, 113-4.

21 Sir George Staunton, on behalf of the Select Committee, to the Viceroy, [governor-general] of Kwangtung and Kwangsi], 7 March 1807. B.L.I.O.C., I.O.R., Canton Consultations, G12/156, p.13

22 'Leau- A-ting, though an individual of the lowest class, was in some degree a dependent of the family, and therefore under the peculiar protection of the *Chong-quan*, or general of the Tartar troops, a mandarin of the highest rank and influence…' Staunton, *Miscellaneous Notices*, 263.

23 'Proceedings of the Court of Enquiry held on board the Honble Company's ship Neptune at Second Bar, first of March 1807.' Captain James Tweedale of the *Albion* presided, with Captains Benjamin Richardson of the *Perseverence*, and Thomas Buchanan of the *Neptune* as members. B.L.I.O.C., I.O.R., Canton Consultations, G/12/154.

24 'Proceedings of the Second Court of Enquiry held on board the Honble Company's ship *Neptune* at Second Bar, sixth day of March 1807.' Captain James Tweedale of the *Albion* presided, with Captains Benjamin Richardson of the *Perseverence*, and Robert Patterson of the *Royal Charlotte* as members. B.L.I.O.C., I.O.R., Canton Consultations, G/12/156.

25 Morse, *Chronicles*, III, 43.

26 Staunton, *Miscellaneous Notices*, 269.

27 Edict of the Anchassee [*An-ch'a shih*], or Grand Judge of the Province of Kwangtung, addressed to Mowqua, Hong Merchant, pointing out that the French, Portuguese and other foreigners always handed over culprits when a Chinese was mortally wounded by their nationals, and adding: 'Whoever designs or connives at the offence of a criminal is held by the laws to be equally guilty'. B.L.I.O.C., I.O.R., Canton Consultations, G12/156, 20 March 1807; Staunton, *Miscellaneous Notices*, 270.

28 The Consultation of 22 March records that: 'The mandarins said that we might be assured that if the emperor were acquainted with these circumstances His Majesty would insist upon the strict execution of the Law against the offender, or upon being informed that he was not given up, would direct the punishment of the Chief who concealed and withdrew him from justice, and would moreover deprive our nation of the benefit of trading to this country…' B.L.I.O.C., I.O.R., Canton Consultations, G12/156, 22 March 1807

29 Staunton, *Miscellaneous Notices*, 269-70.

30 Edict of the Anchassee [*An-ch'a shih*], or Grand Judge of the Province of Kwangtung, addressed to Mowqua, Hong Merchant. B.L.I.O.C., I.O.R., Canton Consultations, G12/156, 20 March 1807

31 Staunton, *Miscellaneous Notices*, p. 272; B.L.I.O.C, I.O.R., G12/156, China Consultations, 16 March 1807.

32 Staunton, *Miscellaneous Notices*, 275.

33 'The President (of the Select Committee, John Roberts) replied that the mandarins might be assured that he would never be the means of exposing any number of unconvicted British subjects to so dreadful a trial or to any form of Chinese trial whatsoever, except such as the mandarins might think proper to carry into execution within the factories, and therefore if the former was their intention, they must have recourse to absolute force, for the consequences of which he was not responsible'. B.L.I.O.C., I.O.C., China Consultations, G12/156, p. 77, Consultation of 14 March 1807.

34 On 31 March, for instance, when the Hoppo, or Customs Commissioner, was consulted and gave his opinion that the death penalty would probably not be demanded, the Select Committee minuted suspiciously: '…there is every reason to suppose that they [the Hoppo and other mandarins] would rather sacrifice any number of Europeans rather than expose themselves to the chance of disgrace, a danger

they must inevitably incur unless the perpetrator of the murder is discovered.' B.L.I.O.C., I.O.R., China Consultations, G12/156 Consultation of 31 March 1807.

35 I have traced four pairs of contemporary versions of these paintings of the exterior and interior scenes. One pair, said to have belonged to Staunton, is in the National Maritime Museum, London, and another pair is in the Hong Kong Museum of Art. The other two pairs have been split up and are variously located. One, a version of the court scene, is in the Royal Asiatic Society, London , and is of unimpeachable provenance, having been gifted by Staunton himself, as co-founder of the society. The Peabody Museum, Salem, Massachusetts, and the Henry Francis Dupont Winterthur Museum, Delaware hold two further versions; and there is also a copy of one scene in private hands. The exterior and interior scenes are reproduced, with a useful commentary, in Carl Crossman, *The Decorative Arts of the China Trade,* (Woodbridge, 1991), 108-9. H.B. Morse gives a helpful explanation of the positioning of figures in the court scene in his *Chronicles of the East India Company Trading to China*, III, 51-3. But his article of 1927 attributing these paintings to an anonymous British artist seems wide of the mark, and Crossman's attribution is more authoritative: see H.B. Morse, 'The Factories at Canton in 1807', *Journal of the Royal Asiatic Society*, (1927), 313-5. I would like to thank the Royal Asiatic Society, London, for its kind permission to illustrate this paper with close-ups from the society's version of the trial scene. I thank particularly its librarian, Michael Pollock, for his assistance in enabling this painting to be photographed in a clear light on the Society's doorstep.

36 B.L.I.O.C., I.O.R., China Consultations, 31 March 1807.

37 B.L.I.O.C., I.O.R., China Consultations, 8 April 1807, Transcript of the first day of the trial.

38 Staunton, *Miscellaneous Notices*, 277.

39 Staunton, *Miscellaneous Notices*, 278.

40 Upon his re-examination on 9 April, the magistrates tried to extract an admission from Sheen by misrepresenting the testimony of another seaman, Julius Caesar, who had supposedly accused Sheen of striking a Chinese. Sheen's indignant denial was supported by outraged protests to the magistrate from both Captain Rolles and the president of the Select Committee, John Roberts. B.L.I.O.C., I.O.R.

China Consultations, G12/156, Trial evidence, 9 April 1807..

41 B.L.I.O.C., I.O.R., China Consultations, Consultation of 11 April 1807.

42 *ibid.*

43 *ibid.*

44 The précis of Sheen's actual testimony states: 'Was a little drunk. Had a pipe in his hand, was struck on the head with a stone, but did not attempt to strike again as the Chinese were a great way off.'. B.L.I.O.C., I.O.R. China Consultations, G12/156, Trial evidence, 9 April 1807. See also Morse, *Chronicles*, III, 44-5.

45 In Chinese currency 12 liang 4 fen and 2 lee. Staunton, *Ta Tsing Leu Lee*, 521.

46 B.L.I.O.C., I.O.R., L/MAR/B, 98 GG/1, Wages book for the *Neptune*, 1806-8; L/MAR/B, 98 0, Ship's Log, *Neptune*, 1806-8.

47 Morse, *Chronicles*, III, 'The Neptune Affair', pp. 27-53; and Auber, *China. An Outline of its Government, Law and Policy*, 225-9. See also Morse, *International Relations*, III, 103-4.

48 See n. 45 above.

49 Staunton, *Ta Tsing Leu Lee*, appendix XI, 521.

50 My italics.

51 'By a case of pure accident is understood a case of which no sufficient previous warning could have been given, either directly by the perceptions of sight and hearing, or indirectly, by the inferences drawn by judgement and reflection….' Staunton, *Ta Tsing Leu Lee*, 314.

52 Staunton, *Ta Tsing Leu Lee*, 516.

53 *ibid*, 517. Staunton's fuller judgment was as follows: '…although the falsehood in which so many persons concurred, was no doubt base and criminal in itself, it neither produced, not was intended to produce, the slightest deviation from substantial justice in respect of the person accused; he was well known to be innocent, or at least unconvicted of the murder; but the strictness of the laws unfortunately rendered it impossible for the magistrates to ground a verdict of acquittal upon a true statement of the case, without at the same time in some degree implicating and condemning themselves; they therefore, under these difficult circumstances, contrived to do that which was just in itself, though they certainly resorted to means which were far from defensible.'

54 Staunton, *Ta Tsing Leu Lee*, xxvii . Staunton's view of the Ch'ing Penal Code as an essentially flexible, if intransigently expressed, body of laws is shared by Geoffrey MacCormack, *The*

Spirit of Traditional Chinese Law, (Athens, 1996), 113-4.

55 '...although every page of the following translation may seem at first sight to bear testimony to the universality of corporal punishments in China, a more careful inspection will lead to the discovery of so many grounds of mitigation, so many exceptions in favour of particular classes, and in consideration of particular circumstances, that the penal system is found, in fact almost entirely to abandon that part of its outward and apparent character.' Staunton, *Ta Tsing Leu Lee*, xxvi.

56 A major feature of the code's application was the need to offset grounds for mitigation against a tariff of finely graded degrees of culpability, such that '...the sections of the Chinese code may...perhaps not unjustly be compared to a collection of consecutive mathematical problems.' Staunton, *Ta Tsing Leu Lee*, xxvi.

57 Staunton, *Ta Tsing Leu Lee*, 521.

58 Three years later the Select Committee behaved with aplomb when a deadlocked case similar to that of the *Neptune*, the Ah-shing affair, occurred leading again to threats of arrest addressed personally to the Select Committee by Chinese officials. The Select Committee took the opportunity to ask the Court of Directors in London for guidance as to how to handle every type of legal impasse that might arise with the Chinese. The examples given were: 1. cases where a Chinese was killed accidentally, as from a stray gunshot; 2. cases where a European, acting in self-defence, killed a Chinese committing a crime such as robbery or burglary; 3. cases where a European, while acting as a sentinel or watchman, kills a Chinese; 4. cases of homicide in an affray where a European offender could not be determined; and 5. cases where proof of guilt would be insufficient to convict a man under English law. The Directors declined to give the Select Committee advice appropriate to any specific type of case, proclaiming that the supercargoes should respond to demands to surrender culprits whose guilt was provable, but withhold compliance in cases when it was not. So, in effect, resistance to Chinese legal demands that were deemed unacceptable in terms of British legal procedure was now sanctioned as official policy, despite the risks to British trade. This suggests that the Directors too, were coming to feel that incompatibilities between Chinese and British legal procedure were becoming negotiable. For the handling of the Ah-shing case, see Morse, *Chronicles*, III, 153-6, 172-3, 188.

Go East, young woman (but not often): inter-war British India line stewardesses[1]

Jo Stanley

In the interwar years, 'British women' and 'Far East' were categories that seldom coincided, particularly in the field of recreational tourism. The main reasons for this were firstly, that women had less access than men to spatial mobility (with all its social connotations). Secondly, the 'Far East' was indeed socially and spatially far, and radically distinct from near, in the days before commercial flying. In Britain it was socially constructed as different from 'home' and west.

Ships' stewardesses were women who had unusual access to travel. In 1931 there were just over a thousand: 0.005 per cent of the female population of England and Wales. That is, any woman who went to sea was in an exceptional position and those who went far were even more exceptional. This study focuses on the 44 British India line stewardesses who exceptionally travelled far beyond India in the 1920s and 1930s as part of their working life. They were 25 per cent of the 171 seagoing female employees of the British India shipping company. Stewardesses working for other shipping firms such as P&O, Blue Funnel, Glen, and Bibby Lines[2] also sailed East, but the focus in this study is BI, because there is substantial data on the seagoing workers in its catering department.

This paper explores what can be known about this group of British women who accessed 'abroad' by virtue of their job and their employers' policies and practices, particular in relation to troop ships. It discusses whether these 44 stewardesses had any personal characteristics that enabled this exceptional travel and how such voyages fitted with their overall patterns of travel in their career. Using perspectives from cultural geography, tourism sociology and gendered imperial history, this chapter explores some meanings of their travelling and visiting roles during a very particular period of imperial history. Its foundational and unanswerable question is 'What difference did going far, in this way, make to women? How did it divide them from those who went near – and even from those who stayed at home?'

So who were the British women who – as workers – sailed to Far Eastern destinations such as Singapore, Hong Kong, China and Japan? And what do we make of them? Stewardesses were seafaring service workers on the hospitality side of ships' operations, usually called the stewards, victualling or catering department. Before World War Two they were not required to be concerned with a ship's operation as conveyance.[3] But they were deeply implicated in providing the kinds of service that the shipping company required in order to get return custom. They were the majority of, if not the only, women workers on ship. (Sometimes there were nurses). Their job was to look after those women and children not being looked after by the Asiatic stewarding crew. A stewardess's role was a mix of chambermaid, hostess, ladies maid, mother's help and nurse and their usual self-description was 'I looked after the lady passengers'.[4] Some worked as matrons on some trips; in that role they looked after the women and children travelling in steerage, usually unaccompanied by men. Depending on their shipping line's policy on employing Asian stewarding workers, stewardesses aboard might form as much as 50 per cent of the white stewarding crew, even though they could be only one or two in number. Stewardesses were largely solo women, over 30, often widows, often women with a wider experience of travel than their sisters at home.[5] They were employed for their competence and practicality, not their glamour.

How were stewardesses different from the

passengers and those rare senior male officers who might write their memoirs? The key distinctions about their position are that, unlike passengers, they were paid to serve, not travel: thus their sense of agency was reduced. And they were involved in the business of re-location but by only by proxy. Their working life was set in an alternating sequence of floating British-style interiors and foreign landscapes including seascapes. Departure and arrival were routine, not special, occurrences. They endlessly witnessed others' travel and migration but themselves seldom actually settled anywhere east of Southend. Unlike the captains and chief engineers who later penned memoirs, these women were non-newsworthy workers who were assigned a lowly status because they were doing feminised work in a workplace that valorised the masculine.[6]

Why study them? One of the main reasons is that, as with the study of any subaltern or potentially counter-hegemonic group, in looking at the hidden history of the marginalised we better understand the history of that which is constructed as more mainstream. Examination of these women working for British India line helps provide a more discerning account of imperial and maritime history that shows the part played by gender, race and class. This chapter offers both quantitative and contextual information by which to understand the qualitative experiences of a group of subjects who are no longer available to speak for themselves.

Primary evidence about the stewardesses comes from British India line records of seagoing staff (which are revealed mainly in the detail of each voyage).[7] This data is supplemented by secondary readings of BI[8] history and extensive primary and secondary sources on stewardesses working for other lines. No other shipping company in the UK has extant archives that show us which stewarding crew went to which destinations in the inter-war years. Therefore these collated statistics allow a unique quantitative insight into female crew movement.

Women going east with BI
According to imperial historian Stephen Constantine, the British Empire's:

> *... integration of, eventually, about one quarter of the world's land surface into what purported to be a single polity seemed to British observers to open up dizzying possibilities of enhanced global mobility for the ethnically diverse people of the empire… There also seemed a prospect of free movement into and between other imperial territories.*[9]

But this mobility was restricted by gender. As feminist geographers and historians of women have shown,[10] it was unusual for unmarried working-class women to travel widely in the inter-war years before mass tourism, commercial flying, au pairing and backpacking. Going to sea as a ship's stewardess was almost the only way it could be achieved. The exceptions were nannies and nurses who accompanied travelling lady employers; the occasional adventurous nurse or stenographer who ventured solo; and missionaries. And ship's stewardesses were a tiny proportion of the female population: 0.005 per cent in 1931: just 1128 women.[11] Few stewardesses went to far-distant destinations. This is because their numbers aboard reflected the number of women passengers on ship; such opportunities generally occurred on popular passenger routes such as the transAtlantic. In the early twentieth century before round-the-world cruises became common, the main long-haul trips with women aboard were the emigration-fuelled route to the Antipodes (on which White Star and P&O were the principal operators); BI voyages to India; and P&O and BI trips to the Far East.

BI was one of the major companies sailing east; its main rivals were Blue Funnel, Glen, P&O (with whom it amalgamated in 1914) and Bibby Line. By the opening of World War Two BI had 105 ships of 675,000 gross tons and at any one time employed about 2 per cent of the UK stewardessing workforce: 30-plus women.

In the interwar period, an average of 16 BIS ships carrying non-Asiatic stewarding personnel was sailing each year, and 93 per cent of BI voyages carried women stewarding crew to India, East Africa and other ports.[12]

Charles Allen, who collected oral testimony from British administrators who had sailed out to the Far East, briefly explains the relative cultural meanings of these lines.[13] BI was larger but seen as less snobbish than P&O.[14] It had about 30 stewardesses at any one time in the inter-war years, and most of these made about four trips per year. BI's women crew usually sailed in a very different social situation from women on other lines such as Cunard and Canadian Pacific. The three main differences appear to be women's rarity on ship;[15] the large number of matrons, as opposed to stewardesses, employed;[16] and the higher status of these white women that resulted from their working on black-crewed ships.[17]

BI was associated with trooping history from the mid-nineteenth century. Post-World War One its role was '…maintaining the Commonwealth's garrisons and consolidating the long tradition of co-operation between the Company, the Services and the Board of Trade, (the Government Department responsible for the chartering of tonnage for trooping)',[18] according to the published summary of its trooping history.[19] That connection to the empire's armed might inscribed BI almost as an arm of the government. How could crew experience themselves as other than imperial subjects? This position implicitly positioned the countries to which troops were taken as in need of protection and governance, and lesser than Britain, and therefore the ports crew women visited as 'backward'.

When troops travelled with wives and children, it was the custom to employ white stewardesses, not Asian stewards, on troop ships to care for such passengers. It is because of this custom and three State practices that BI stewardesses sailed to the Far East: deploying British troops in particular overseas locations (to which they had to sail, not fly in that period); sending accompanying families in

some cases; and using BI as the carriers.

Only 44 (25 per cent) of BI's 171 inter-war stewardesses and matrons went to the Far East in their career. Nor did those who went make the trip often. Table 1 shows that only 123 (7 per cent) of the 2074 voyages made by stewardesses in the 25-year inter-war period were to the Far East.

Table 1. Far East voyages by BI stewardesses 1918-42

Destination	No. of stewardess voyages	As % of total voyages by BI stewardess
China	33	2
Kure	0	0
Hong Kong	36	2
Shanghai	42	2.
Singapore	12	1
Sub-Total	123	7
East Africa	381	19
India	1288	60
Other	282	14
Grand Total	2074	100%

Source: National Maritime Museum, BIS 30/34,35,36: compiled from details of individual voyages in 'Stewarding Staff Afloat'.

The reason why there were so few women voyaging to the Far East was not that they were excluded from ships on those routes. They were not. Stewardesses and matrons sailed on 93 per cent of all 123 voyages to the Far East from 1918-1942.[20] The rarity of such a trip for a woman was simply that relatively few BI voyages were to the Far East. Duncan Haws' fleet history of BI shows that China and Japan were destinations to which the company only sailed 'as inducement offered'.[21] The inducement that took these women to the Far East was the UK government trooping contracts that BI had secured.

Stewardesses and matrons sailing to the Far East usually sailed on one of four BI ships which formed about 25 per cent of its passenger fleet at any one time: *Dilwara* and *Dunera*, *Neuralia* and *Nevasa*. *Neuralia* and

Nevasa were built as passenger ships but given over entirely to peacetime trooping after 1925, except in the off-season. *Dilwara* (1936) and *Dunera* (1937) were the first two ships ever designed as troop ships. Large numbers of women passengers were evidently expected aboard the *Dilwara* because there was an entire seven-bed women's ward off the side of its main hospital.[22] Spatial arrangements reflect and reproduce social order and thus it is no surprise to find that stewardesses – who are generally quartered near the passengers they serve and far from single men – were indeed housed together in a tiny cabin on the upper deck, near the ironing room and families gallery.

Women on east-bound ships

What was it like aboard, for these women crew? Troop ships were socially segregated and largely male situations, where the wives and children of 'other ranks' were kept apart from their men. Officers' families travelled together. The latter were attended by saloon stewardesses and the former by troop matrons who were specifically employed to look after the western women and children travelling to and from the east, in that cocoon of British class-based social division. No oral testimony from BI women crew is available, so the subjective experiences of these relatively lowly stewardesses and matrons during their encounters with the east and those voyaging to it are a mystery. But P&O stewardess Edith Sowerbutts on the TSS *Canberra* in July 1919, records that 'my most vivid recollection of the voyage on the *Canberra* was of laughter. We had never had so much fun. Life was magic'.[23] This jollity may be part of the immediate post-war festivity; the atmosphere on ships taking out troops to situations of conflict would surely have been more sober. Other seafarers in similar situations, such as bride ships, describe a chaos of frantic mothers with cooped-up children, rather like the first days of the January Sales or post-blitz 'making shift'. Often seasick, their jobs included trying to find space to dry children's nappies in every possible bit

of the ship. Some tried to wangle ways to transcend the imposed separation and meet their husbands (feigning sea-sickness was a ruse in which many helpful stewarding crew were complicit.)[24]

The women passengers these BI stewardesses and matrons served to and from the Far East were mainly missionaries, wives of colonial administrators and traders, and a very few exceptional wealthy lady travellers such as Isabella Bird. By looking at the nature of the female passengers we may discern both the ways that woman was treated on those gendered ships and the working situation for the stewardesses. Some of the grander female passengers can be understood through making our own nuanced inferences from stereotypical white male accounts such as Somerset Maugham stories: a world where fickle privileged women inclined to dalliance romanced across the Andaman Sea and down the Malacca Straits to the tunes of Cole Porter and Ivor Novello, drinking gin-slings with men brought up on Kipling.

Passengers are also the subject of occasional anecdotes by the imperial administrators interviewed by Charles Allen. Although such vignettes mainly refer to P&O vessels, which was seen as more pukka than BI, they offer a sense of young white women as focus of masculine attention and older women as uncompromisingly interested in their own separate sphere. Cecil Lee, who went out on the *Patroclus*, recorded that:

> All the lovely girls coming out East were the attraction of all the officers – and ourselves – there were daughters going out to join their parents, fiancées coming out as brides-to-be and wives following their husbands after an extended leave'.[25]

There were other women, who were not romantically available and 'who seemed very hard cases, played bridge from morning till night' aboard their ships.[26] Such fragments suggest that the ship was a sexualised space and that women's stage in their lifecourse determined their shipboard practices.

Quantitative data

What kind of women were these stewardesses and matrons who went to the Far East? They varied enormously in age and experience at sea. Apparently an elderly widowed greenhorn could as easily be rostered for the 14-week 20,960-mile round trip to Shanghai as could a 40-year old spinster who had been diligently voyaging to Bombay and Calcutta every trip for ten years. The available statistical information about three facets of this workforce available to us from BI archives enables us to trace the faint common patterns in their age when they went there; their marital status; their experience of travelling with BI before and after going to the Far East.

Firstly, were they young women? The census summaries show that stewardesses generally, working for all the different companies, were a relatively elderly workforce, mainly in their late thirties, forties and fifties. The 1931 census shows the greatest clustering in the 35-45 year age band[27] and this is confirmed by P & O's data for 1920 which shows that 47 per cent of all their stewardesses were 30-39 and 17 per cent 40-49.[28] However, table 2 shows that the majority of the 44 BI women going on their first trip to the South China Seas were far older than the norm: 27 per cent were in their 50s. Eight per cent of those who went were over 60 and no-one in their twenties went. That is, BI emphatically did not say 'Go East, young woman'. If anything it said 'Go East, mature woman'.

Table 2. Ages of stewardesses on their first trip to the Far East, as percentages of all inter-war stewardesses to that destination.

Age	Number	% at this age of all steward-esses going to Far East
20-29	0	0
30-39	12	27
40-49	9	20
50-59	13	30
60-69	3	7
Other	7	16
Total		*100*

Source: See Table 1

So were these – mainly older – women long-married or widows who might be conceived of as stable, stoic, with grown-up children; women who would not be flighty with the troops and with Far Eastern locals. Or were they single women who may (but not necessarily) have had fewer pressing family ties to prevent them from taking four-month trips? Sixty two per cent of Far East-bound women had been married at some point, as table 3 shows.

Table 3. Marital status of BI stewardesses going to the Far East

Status	married	widowed	single	n/a	total
Number	13	15	16	1	44
Percentage	29	33	36	2	100

Source: See Table 1

This is a very high percentage, although the statistical sample is only small (44) and so not too much significance must be given to it. While 62 per cent of those Far East-bound were once-married, only 55 per cent of women going to other destinations were married or widowed. The census for England and Wales shows that in the UK stewardessing workforce in general, once-married accounted for 55 per cent in 1921 and 46 per cent in 1931. This also indicates that the number of once-married going to the Far East was exceptionally large.

Were these women novices or experienced travellers who might take in the sights of Chinese ports with eyes used to seeing many far-flung ports? They went at very differing times in their career with BI and there appears to be no consistent pattern. As table four shows, twenty five per cent went on their very first voyage with the company (this may have been because newcomers were often given the role of matron and troopships to China had need of matrons). And 38 per cent went on one of their first five trips with the company. By contrast, two women aged more than 60 went after doing 50 voyages with the company. The point in stewardesses' careers when they went varied from their very first trip to their fifty-third; the mean was to go on voyage seven and the most constantly recurring figure was voyage one.

Table 4: Stewardesses' and matrons' voyages to Far East as place in their career, 1918—42

Times women went to Far East in their career	On Voyage						Overlap in more than one category	Total
	1-5	6-10	11-15	16-25	26-35	36+		
Once	10	4	-	2	2	-	-	18
Twice	5	-	-	1	1	-	2	9
Thrice	-	-	-	-	-	-	3	3
4-5 times	2	-	-	1	-	1	3	7
6-10 times	-	-	-	-	-	-	2	2
Over 11 times	-	-	-	-	-	-	5	5
Total	17	4	0	4	3	1	15	44

Source: See Table 1

For ten (22 per cent) it was their last trip, and 18 per cent their next-to-last trip. Possible reasons for this include that such a long and difficult voyage made them disinclined to work for BI or as seafarers again. But it could also have been that they had seen what they wanted to see: it was a pinnacle of their career. They had 'gone East'. For some women it was their first and last journey. In the inter-war years, of the 29 women doing just one trip to any destination, 13 per cent (4 out of 29) were to the Far East. There is no information about why people left, so we do not know if this disproportionately high number of Far Eastern trippers left of their own volition or at the company's behest.

Even when women went to the Far East, only 40 per cent went more than once, as table 5 shows. It was usually a one-off experience. However, once a woman became someone who BI sent to the South China Seas, she tended to do several trips there. 18 per cent of stewardesses did two consecutive trips and a further 38 per cent went on four or more consecutive voyages. That is, some became old hands at the Far East: a core of about six, by comparison to the score who just went on trip after trip to India. There was a tendency for BI to have two tiers of semi-permanent female seagoing employees: those who went on plying regularly to and from Bombay and Calcutta with all the routine of any office worker, and those who changed ships and destinations almost every trip: the ones used more flexibly.

Table 5 Recurrence of voyages to Far East, 1918—42 during stewardesses' and matrons' careers

Times women went to Far East in their career	Total voyages	As % of all stewardesses going the Far East
Once	18	41
Twice	9	20
Thrice	3	07
4-5 times	6	14
6-10 times	3	07
Over 11 times	4	11
Total	44	100%

That is, eighteen stewardess and matrons – 41 per cent of the women going to the Far East – did so only once. At the other end of the scale only four women (11 per cent of Far Eastern-bound stewardesses) went more than 11 times.

Did matters change over this 25-year period, when Britain was building up her Singapore base and tensions in China were mounting? Table six shows the fluctuations year by year; for example there were 12 stewardess voyages to China in 1930. Post war, voyages to the Far East became even more common with a very different pattern of kinds of stewardess: younger, and more likely to be single, but to a proportionately greater extent than might be expected given that the workforce became younger post-1945.

Table 6. Number of BI voyages with stewardesses aboard, by year and destination.

	Shanghai	China	Hong Kong	Singapore	India	East Africa	Other	Total stewardess voyages to anywhere that year	Total voyages of ships with stewardesses*
1918	-	1	-	-	-	-	-	1	1/21
1919	-	2	-	-	45	-	7	54	23/36
1920	-	-	-	-	43	11	5	59	22/28
1921	-	1	-	-	48	4	7	60	23/30
1922	-	-	-	-	68	13	-	81	35/43
1923	-	-	-	-	72	9	2	83	37/45
1924	-	-	-	-	85	12	-	97	41/45
1925	-	-	-	-	85	29	-	104	52/56
1926	-	-	4	-	74	24	10	112	47/49
1927	-	-	1	-	84	30	-	115	53/53
1928	4	-	-	-	81	26	10	121	53/53
1929	5	1	-	-	73	21	13	113	51/51
1930	-	12	-	-	65	22	7	106	48/48
1931	4	3	-	-	57	26	3	93	46/46
1932	4	3	-	-	50	23	9	89	41/41
1933	6	2	-	-	41	26	13	88	38/38
1934	4	-	-	-	50	23	10	87	37/37
1935	-	3	-	-	48	23	14	88	38/38
1936	-	5	3	-	49	22	27	106	43/43
1937	8	-	6	5	54	10	36	119	45/45
1938	-	-	11	4	61	2	47	125	48/48
1939	7	-	11	3	46	4	46	117	38/38
1940	-	-	-	-	9	14	-	23	13/33
1941	-	-	-	-	-	3	16	19	11/17
1942	-	-	-	-	-	-	-	0	0/18
Total	42	33	36	12	1288	381	282	2074	885/947

As % of all BI stewardess voyages

	Shanghai	China	Hong Kong	Singapore	India	East Africa	Other		
1918-42	2	1.6	1.7	0.6	62	18.3	13.5	100	

* In the final (right-hand) column, the figure **before** the oblique refers to number of stewardess voyages that year. The figure **after** the oblique indicates the number of voyages made by BI passenger vessels that year. Hence in 1919, there were 36 voyages made by BI passenger ships, and on 23 of those there were stewardesses. As there were 54 voyages made by stewardesses that year, we can infer that on most of those 23 voyages there were two stewardesses.
Source: See Table 1

And finally, were they women who chose to 'Go East'? It is unlikely. In the inter-war years workers were not encouraged to have a sense of agency about their career. Oral testimony from inter-war stewardesses in other companies suggests that self-selection was unlikely. They said 'You went where you were put, or woe betide you'.[29] Staff were simply grateful for any job. From the personnel ledgers it appears that BI women's postings to ships making particular voyages were based simply on availability and their surname's place in the alphabet. The headquarters staff responsible for staffing rosters used an alphabet-based placement pattern.

There were also three disincentives to such travel: political trouble and no financial recompense for that, distressing weather and (probably) an intense pace of work. The Far East for Britons was a politically tense situation with increased military presence. 1925 was an uneasy time with the fear of revolution in China and aggression from Japan.[30] And in 1937 world crisis mounted as Japan began eight years of undeclared war against China.[31] Most of the women in this study went within a military and tense situation. But wages on troop ships that might be caught up in such conflicts were no higher than on any other ship (for example £13 15s per month in 1920); there was no bonus for war risks then. From at least 1925 staff had argued – unsuccessfully – that they deserved extra pay. A letter of complaint from stewarding crew on a BI trooper in February 1936 protested that:

> …we have now become civilians on board a fighting vessel, of which we do not approve. Sir, In a time of hostilities one is prepared to make the best of a bad position, but at the moment we are suffering many things we didn't sign for.[32]

Secondly, the weather was often bad, which meant employment was seasonal and, if the ships sailed despite monsoons, uncomfortable. Even stewardesses travelling on the India trips found that the route to Bombay was affected by monsoons in the Arabian Sea from June to August; Calcutta-bound ships were faced with tropical storms in April, May, October and December.[33] And thirdly, it is likely that women's work as matrons on troop ships (the main vessels going to China) was done on such a scale and at such a pace that there was insufficient job satisfaction or rest.

Visiting the East

When they went east, what did they encounter? BI was a company that also serviced other parts of the Empire – India and East Africa. So almost all its seagoing female staff witnessed the Far East in the context of the whole British empire, parts of which they saw on other trips the rest of the year. This necessarily meant that their perspective was very coloured by colonial, military[34] and orientalist discourse,[35] and any gendered and classed variants of that created by the women passengers and crew with whom they worked. That is, they saw the Far East through particular, nuanced eyes. But without personal testimony we cannot know what oppositional discourse the women may have created. Further, they saw only particular Far Eastern places, the more European, indeed anglicised ports. That is, they saw only a selected and littoral Far East, that which could be erroneously used as a metonym. As seafarers, and people associated with military use of space they did not see representative spaces and not the less developed hinterland. Their knowledge of the area was spatially constrained and thus socially limited. It was only after World War Two that BI stewardesses sailed to Japan; before that a woman anxious to see Japan would have been better off working for P&O instead.[36]

The women seafarers who accompanied such lady passengers and their lowlier co-voyagers on the lower decks have three inter-related social positions, which affected the terms of their encounter with the East at the apex of each trip. Firstly they were seafarers. As such they were in port briefly, which circumscribed their activities. They met those socially designated as suitable (*e.g.* shop assistants, expatriates) and were involved in activities which were also deemed appropriate *e.g.* shopping for souvenirs, visiting sanctioned sites of interest. As off-duty seafarers they were semi-tourists. And a goal of tourism is to encounter that which is different from our usual lives. They were therefore expected to consume the place as the site of particular kinds of extraordinariness and difference. This was enabled by the cultural products of the period such as novels and the rare autobiographies of women travellers such as Alma Karlin's.[37]

Secondly, these stewardesses and matrons were female, not male. And they were women without permanent men attached. That is, they were socially positioned as the second sex, who were permitted even less agency than their male colleagues and the single ones were part of a social problem because of their 'superfluity'. The Dominions Royal Commission in 1911 had calculated that 'in England and Wales there were at least 346,000 women of ages suitable for migration with no 'statistical prospect of marriage'. A transfer would enable such women to fulfil their biological destinies.[38] Seafaring women intimately witnessed the increased female migration that arose because of such social attitudes. They served such women: they saw the hopes. And they also saw some migrants who returned bearing stories of what migration meant – including entrepreneurial prosperity and failed marriages. They could not help but be aware of the repertoire of possible female fates if they left the ship for good in a foreign place.

Also women were seen as a fit target for male sexual desire and therefore in need of protection from it. This very desirability was both a problem on long voyages where sexual desires can get out of hand and in foreign ports during that White-Slavery-obsessed period with its anxieties about women's danger from rapacious foreign men in ports.[39] Such patriarchal concern affected women's touristic practices ashore. For example, in 1920s Shanghai traveller Alma Karlin confined her local seaborne travels because 'people who take sampans out to distant steamers are often never heard of again'.[40]

This restricted gendered access ties in with the third point: that these stewardesses were white British people who could not but help, as part of the ship's British population, but have hegemonised hostile views towards the foreign Other as lesser, and as 'naturally different'. As Stephen Constantine points out, 'For most of this century, discrimination by the white settler societies against all "Asiatic" was not even relaxed for those of empire origin'.[41] In the interwar years colonial administrator John Harrison found when travelling on the Malay express that:

> …without any orders or regulations, the First Class was only used by European, the Second Class was mainly occupied by Chinese and the Third Class compartments were occupied by the Tamils. The races seemed to segregate in that manner, of their own accord. They didn't mix and they didn't mind not mixing.[42]

Visiting women such as stewardesses not only encountered this lower Other but had additional duties because of their sex and the problems of managing sexual order out there.[43] They were expected to behave as exemplary white-gloved ladylike representatives of imperialism. The long arm of British law would have forcibly imposed it if women had not anyway been prepared to behave as British 'ladies should'. Cecil Lee found in Singapore's raffish van Wijk hotel that it was:

> …the 'place of assignation' for European women of easy virtue – where you could get a French, German, Dutch or Russian girl but not an English girl. If an English girl came out on the mail boat the CID sent her back on the next one. They wouldn't have it.[44]

These three positions – seafaring, female and British – affected the ways seafaring women from BI ships could encounter the far-off places that were utilised as economic resource for Britain and one of the some-time jewels in the imperial crown.

Distinctively far away
Why does the far nature of the destination matter? How might going there affect women's identity? By going to the Far East these women went to places which – because of their distance and relative unvisited-ness – could have brought them cachet and new knowledge. 'Going East' in the interwar years had at least two connotations: far away and different. As modern cultural geographers argue, spatial relations can function as

metaphors for social relations. Shields points out that:

> …space was understood by Kant to be one dimension of all perceptions, the other being time. For Durkheim and Mauss the division of geographical space into near and far, quadrants and places was one of the first forms of "primitive classification" underpinning all social divisions.[45]

Thus those British people leaving western homes and travelling east for thousands of miles on the China seas went 'very far' spatially and encountered cultures that were 'very distant' socially. In western cartographic terms, China and Japan were often pictured so far to the right of stylised maps that they were almost out of the frame. There was thus a radical difference from hops across the Atlantic.

'Going far' had increasing status between the world wars when the new breed of mass tourist was starting to go to near destinations such as the Mediterranean. It was a mark of cultural distinction, in Bourdieu's terms, for the more privileged classes to visit the unfamiliar and far, and thereby acquire the cachet society bestows. It is worth considering the possibility that such a cachet may have also been acquired by seafarers who paid for their passage in labour, as well as by those passengers whose money bought the licence to roam. That is, the fact of visiting, despite the economic basis of how the visit is achieved, could have produced in stewardesses a sense of pride and status. And it probably had a price.

On British India ships such as the *Dilwara*, *Dunera*, *Neuralia* and *Nevasa*, passengers and crew sailed to the furthest reaches of that continuum and binary: home/away. They went to that which was cast as the 'opposite' to the West, that place that was used as synonym for Civilisation, Home and The Mother Country. Contemporary popular discourse configured the East as 'mysterious' and its denizens 'inscrutable' even though, as oral historian of colonial administrators in the area,

Charles Allen, points out 'the South China Sea may be compared to the Mediterranean in the sense that is the cradle of ancient and affluent civilisations'.[46] And indeed in demographic terms China was nearly as great as the British empire, with a population in 1913 of 358 million, by comparison with 396 million in Britain and its empire.[47] Borne far to the east in cocoons of Britishness, ships' passengers and crew made a marked spatial move that was configured as correspondingly socially marked. Thus they were psychically destabilised by a sense of themselves in the unknown and unknowable, a state which people deal with by valorising their existing prior knowledge, for example belief in British superiority over the 'yellow' Other.

Visitors' encounters with the radically 'othered' are affected by the cultural capital and by their particular spectating positions, Urry argues.[48] Western visitors, both passengers and crew, not only viewed the extraordinary new places from that high and impressive viewing platform: the great ex-metropolitan ships that positioned their inhabitants as ordinarily superior, and bearers of gifts and order. They also disembarked with particular cultural baggage: the idea that they were visiting a place that, as Said contends, had been constructed into 'a quintessential Orient', a cumulative vision shaped by 'the prestigious authority of the pioneering scholars, travellers and poets'.[49] Such an Orient, according to BI and P&O pictorial advertising material, was a place of rickshaws and pagodas, deferential women with 'slanting' eyes and men with pigtails under conical hats. In fact even by the interwar years it was a place of cultural mixture. Photographs and travellers reminiscences such as Alma Karlin's show us, the 'front-stage' spaces such as those in 1922 Hong Kong 'round the quays with their modern offices and open squares' had been constructed to look 'civilised' to Europeans but 'most of the streets are narrow and very Chinese'.[50] It was experienced as dangerous because tour operators had not yet obliterated these places' differences from the west in the interests of making occidental visitors feel safe, as they have done in the shop-lined Orchard Road, Singapore, for example, today.

Lack of oral testimony means we cannot ask these 44 BI stewardesses and matrons what it meant to them to go so far east. No evidence is available to clarify whether they experienced a radical change to their knowledge and cachet through having encountered the far, with all its metaphorical meanings. We might imagine that going far made a distance to self-perception and social understanding. Aware of the differing impacts of travel on travellers we may presume that in some subtle subjective ways the experience of the worlds scale and of different cultures divided some stewardesses from their sisters who went to nearer destinations as workers and passengers, and from those who stayed at home. But the question remains unanswered: what was it like to be a working woman who had that kind of spatial mobility in those days?

Summary

This paper has demonstrated that few shipping lines offered solo women of limited means an exceptional opportunity to see the Far East at a time when solo women's access to distant parts of the world was limited. BI was one of these, but even so, 75 per cent of the inter-war female workforce did not get posted to such voyages, but mainly sailed to India and Africa. That is, going to ports such as Shanghai was exceptional, even within this most promising of shipping companies. These inter-war stewardesses were able to visit the Far East because of Britain's military arrangements in that area, and not because they were accompanying commercial or leisure voyages there. They would not have been there had it not been for three linked factors: Britain's supplying of troops to such parts; the practice of sending out families with such troops; the assumption then that female passengers had to be cared for, at least in part, by people of their own sex and race and BI's preparedness to adhere to this convention. That is, these women's exceptional voyages were enabled by routine macro-social arrangements that were in no way a response to the women's own individual desires. They were cogs in a militarised commercial operation rather than adventurers travelling under their own mental aegis.

The imperial exhortation borrowed for the title of this chapter,' Go east, young woman', as opposed to 'Go west, young man' benefits from examination in this summary if we are to have a sense of the meanings of these women's travels. Firstly, the saying implies a command to not just voyage but to settle. The seafaring service workers who accompanied the mass migrations and imperial business travel in the days of Empire were in a unique position: they saw adventurers setting out and (sometimes) coming back and heard their stories. So they had special knowledge of what 'going east' meant, for many people; they almost migrated by proxy. They were bystanders and witnesses, but not settlers. The actual brief encounter with Far Eastern ports was a disruption, not the point; a side-encounter and not the main agenda. So the 'going', the travelling element, was the important one for shipboard workers - unlike their passengers' focus on arrival. They went, and came back.

Secondly, the women studied here were not young. We do not know if they were adventurers or simply people doing their usual job on what happened, this trip, to be an unusual stretch of water for them: the South China seas. But they were people who had experienced several decades of life and hence had a history of expectations; they did not go with empty hands but with assumptions that can obscure direct experience.

Thirdly, the exhortation normally implies a masculinist project; the muscular, often military, adventurous wrestling with 'primitive' foreign elements discussed by Green and Dawson, for example.[51] In fact, these stewardesses and matrons went to the Far East and travelled briefly there within a discourse of traditional white and virtuous femininity. They were placed there to nurture, to help create domestic harmony and comfort on ship.[52] That implicitly means that to seek an exciting experience of the extraordinary and far would require them to transcend the gendered, raced and classed norms within which they were positioned.

The foundational question of this chapter has been 'What difference did going far, in this way, make to women? How did it divide them from those who went near – and even from those who stayed at home?' The absence of personal testimony means there is no certain answer. But we consider that although these women went far geographically, not all may have been in a position to travelled far psychically, given that they were surrounded by a British cocoon. Going East with BI may not have seemed very different from going to the other destinations, if they did not take firm individual steps to make the experience a distinct one for themselves. But maybe the very exceptionality in most of these 44 women's careers of such a trip made the Far East seem special. They had seen what few at home in Plaistow had seen, and only once. That, in a period before television transformed the far into the seemingly familiar, had to mark these stewardesses as somehow distinct; they had gained knowledges of the radically Other, the exceptionally far, that could function as a kind of power to assist them in their negotiations of the near, at 'home'.

Notes and references

1 I thank many colleagues for help in this voyage of exploration and interpretation including Hilda Kean, Sarah Palmer, John Urry and John Walton. A grant from the Society for Nautical Research enabled me spend time at the National Maritime Museum (hereafter NMM) extracting statistical data from four ledger accounts of BIS stewarding staff afloat 1914-1952. For that funding, and for access to the archive, I am grateful.

2 Charles Allen (ed.) *Tales from the South China Seas: images of the British in South East Asia in the twentieth century*, (London, 1983).

3 Indeed so exceptionalised were women among the crew that pre-WW2 they were exempted from having to take the lifeboat skills exam that became compulsory for all men, although some stalwart women took it voluntarily - and proudly.

4 This is the main description of the work from over 20 stewardesses from other lines (such as Canadian Pacific and Cunard) whom I have interviewed.

5 This is because some had been daughters of armed forces men working abroad, some had been lady's companions or army nurses, according to P&O archives for the early 1920s.

6 Pat Ayres, 'The making of Men: Masculinities in Inter-war Liverpool', in Margaret Walsh, (ed), *Working Out Gender*, (Aldershot, 1999); Valerie Burton ' "Whoring, Drinking Sailors": Reflections on Masculinity from the Labour History of Nineteenth-century British Shipping,' in Walsh, op cit.

7 These records are held at the NMM's outstation.

8 I use the term British India and the abbreviation BI for simplicity. The company was officially known by the name British India Steam Navigation Co.

9 Stephen Constantine, 'Migrants and Settlers' in R.W. Louis and J.M. Burns (eds), *The Oxford History of the British Empire,* 5 Vols, vol. 4, (Oxford, 1999), 163.

10 Feminist geographers include Mona Domosh and Joni Seager, *Putting Women in Place: feminist geographers making sense of the world*, (New York and London, 2001); Alison Blunt and Gillian Rose (eds.), *Writing women and space: colonial and post-colonial geographies*, (New York, 1996). Feminist historians of women's role in imperialism and migration have primarily focused on the late nineteenth century. Foundational works include Claire Midgely (ed.), *Gender and Imperialism*, (Manchester, 1998); Vron Ware, *Beyond the Pale: White Women, Racism and History,* (London, 1992).

11 *Census of England and Wales, Summary tables.* There were 933 or 0.004 in 1921, 1128 in 1931. Note this refers only to enumerated stewardesses. There were more than this in the workforce but they were at sea on census night.

12 This figures is based on my own calculations from BI company records of stewarding staff afloat, NMM BIS 30/31-34.

13 Charles Allen, op cit. briefly discusses their relative cultural meanings. Blue Funnel was only one class and was full of planters (p.31) whereas P&O were snobbish and took out

officers and high civil servants to Penang and Singapore (p.17) To Hong Kong they carried men who worked for the big banks 'the Honkers and Shankers' and the Chartered, as well as the trading institutions such as Bousteads and the Asiatic Petroleum Company (p.23). Malaya Police probationers were 'advised that it was compulsory for them to travel out on the P&O' (p.29).

14 P&O was a company so distinct that it was often popularly described as the third navy.

15 Firstly, there were fewer women passengers to these countries than to northern America, so there were just 1-5 stewardesses on board BI vessels, as opposed to 15-25 on the transatlantic ferries and cruises operated by other lines. However, because they were on troop trips, with a large number of wives aboard, there were more women on board than on, say, Elder Dempster vessels going out to West Africa on non-trooping voyages. I make this general point from a wide range of crew agreements with different companies, many of which are kept at Memorial University, Newfoundland.

16 Because these were troop ships, that is, carrying large numbers of low status women and children in conditions akin to steerage, so there were more matrons aboard than on most ships. There were up to three matrons on a troop ship to the Far East whereas a normal Canadian Pacific migrant vessel had only one.The majority of women were stewardesses but some took the role of matron for a voyage or two. Most of the troop ships such as the *Neuralia* and the *Nevasa* carried one matron, sometimes two. The formal arrangement of the listing suggests that the troop dept was seen as lesser than the saloon. An effect of working in low-status situations is that workers then internalise that stigmatised identity, so matrons may have experienced a sense of denigration. Often the ships with a relatively large number of stewardess eg three on *Dilwara* in 1939 also had the largest number of matrons, suggesting that many officers' families as well as other ranks' families travelled.

17 BI women were affected by the company employing many Asian workers. Stewardesses were a large proportion of a very tiny group of white stewarding crew, because most of the stewarding staff were Lascar men. Sometimes there were only 3-10 white people in the stewarding department, and over 50 per cent of them could be female. This was very different to ships that used European stewarding crew, such as Cunard and Canadian Pacific, where stewardesses had a much lower status.

18 Troops were taken out for the Boer war and the Boxer Rebellion. Fifty BI ships were converted to troopships and hospital ships in WW1, and many more transported essential stores. After that war 'routine peacetime trooping [resumed, particularly the *Nevasa* and the *Neuralia* to] 'India, Hong Kong, West Indies, Egypt and other Dominions and Colonies.' No author, *British India: 100 years of trooping* 1856-1956, (BISN Co, UD, c1956), 4, NMM BIS/36/19.

19 *100 years of trooping*.

20 They were usually on 100 per cent of voyages, except in war time when women were first informally and then formally restricted from seagoing service.

21 Duncan Haws, *British India Steam Navigation Co*, (Hereford, 1991), 28-29. Other destinations BI only visited when inducement offered were Port Swettenham, Malacca, Ceylon, Quilon, Mallipuram, Tirumalalvasaal, New Zealand, Portonovo, Ibo, Mocimboa, Kilwa, Rivu Bay and Middlesborough.

22 NMM BIS 37/1, cuttings box.

23 Imperial War Museum Archive, Edith Sowerbutts, c1974, *Days Of Empire* Part II, 101

24 See, for instance, Ken Attiwill, *Steward*, (London, 1936); Graham McInnes, *The Road to Gundagai*, (London, 1965), 22-34.

25 Lee cited in Allen, *Tales*, 35.

26 *ibid*.

27 *Census of England and Wales, summary tables*, 1921 and 1931.

28 P&O age summaries extracted by me from individual records in Chief Steward's Conduct Report, (1919-1929) NMM P&O 77/23.

29 Oral evidence to me from inter-war Cunard, Shaw Savill and Canadian Pacific stewardesses.

30 David Howarth and Stephen Howarth, *The Story of P&O*, (London, 1994), p126.

31 Howarth, *The Story,* 135.

32 Policy file, NMM BIS 33/13.

33 In 1943 two of the four main ships on which stewardesses went East – the *Dunera* and *Dilwara* – were 'laid up during the SW monsoon, May to September, and trooped only during the favourable weather of the NE monsoon ... After the war they worked throughout the year.' Captain Brian Mc Manus Ellwood (letter) *Sea Breezes*, vol. 73, no 644, (1999), 313.

34 This is suggested by BIS' h*undred years of trooping,* It had been involved in trooping since the mid nineteenth century, and saw itself as 'maintaining the Commonwealth's Garrisons and consolidating the long tradition of co-operation between the Company, the Services and the Board of Trade' In WW1 about 50 BI ships were converted to trooping and hospital ships 'a great number of them were manned (sic) by Officers and men (sic) to whom the Government Charter Parties and regulations were familiar, and who understood the particular requirements of the carriage of troops'.; *100 years of trooping*, 3.

35 The main work on orientalism is Edward Said's *Orientalism*, Penguin, London, 1995. For a summary of feminist arguments on orientalism see chapter one of Reina Lewis, *Gendering Orientalism: Race, Femininity and Representation*, Routledge, London, 1991. On orientalism in popular discourses see also foundational writers such as John Mackenzie, *Propaganda and Empire: The Manipulation of British Public Opinion 1880-1960*, (Manchester, 1984); Anne McClintock, *Imperial Leather: Race, Gender and Sexuality in the Colonial Conquest*, (London, 1995).

36 Stewardesses sailing on to Japan 1919-29 were on the *Caledonia, China, Dongola, Karmala, Kashgar, Khashmir, Khiva, Macedonia, Malwa, Mantua, Morea, Narkunda, Nellore.* Source: Chief Steward's Conduct Report, (P&O, 1919-1929) NMM P&O 77/23,

37 Alma Karlin, *The Odyssey of a Lonely Woman*, transl. Emile Burns, (London, 1933).

38 Constantine, *Migrants,* citing *Final Report, PP,* (1917-18), X, Cmd 8462, 96, 166 .

39 For discussion on white slavery fears see Donna J. Guy, *Sex and Danger in Buenos Aires,* (Lincoln and London, 1991); Ronald Hyam, *Empire and Sexuality: The British Experience,* (Manchester, 1990). However, the latter does not refer much to

destinations more easterly than Singapore. It has been critiqued for its lack of feminist insights into imperial sexuality. See, for example M.Berger, 'Imperialism and Sexual Exploitation: a Response to Ronald Hyam's "Empire and Sexual Opportunity"', *Journal of Imperial and Commonwealth History*, 17: 1, (1988), 83-89.

40 Karlin, *The Odyssey,* 391.

41 Constantine, *Migrants,* 183.

42 Allen, *Tales,* 63.

43 Hyam, *Empire,* shows that the British management of paid sexual relations out there included making brothels illegal throughout the Straits Settlements in 1929 (p.151) In the British navy, VD was its highest on the China station: 304 in every thousand RN men there in 1921-26, by comparison to 22 per thousand among RN men at home (p89).

44 Allen, *Tales,* 65

45 Rob Shields, *Alternative Geographies of Modernity,* (London and New York, 1991), 29.

46 Allen, *Tales,* 44.

47 Constantine, *Migrants,* 183.

48 John Urry, *The Tourist Gaze,* (London, Thousand Oaks and New Delhi, 2002).

49 Said, *Orientalism,* 221.

50 Karlin, *The Odyesey,* 390.

51 Graham Dawson, *Soldier Heroes: British Adventure, Empire and the Imagining of Masculinities,* (London, 1994); Martin Green, *Dreams of Adventure, Deeds of Empire,* (London, 1980).

52 Indeed, Mrs Bella Lee, a BI stewardess, had been sacked by her former employees P&O for being 'too familiar with men passengers - unsuitable for service'. There were very particular ways that British women should be seen to be behaving, though obviously BI appear to have been less strict than P&O in Mrs Lee's case. Chief Steward's Conduct Report, (P&O, 1919-1929) NMM P&O 77/23, 464.

The China Coast Blockade in the 1950s

Peter Armstrong

Few people have heard of the China Coast Blockade in the 50s, apart from seeing an occasional picture in the national press of an old freighter with a huge Union Jack motif painted on its side. The Yangtze incident involving HMS *Amethyst* raised some British interest in that far-off part of the world, but it was soon forgotten and the blockade was by international standards just a little local difficulty. However, in the China Sea, nothing is *little*.

Being a marine engineer, my involvement was of a practical nature up at the sharp end, and my thoughts and conclusions are personal – they could be said to be the view of the man on the Kowloon Omnibus. I kept no diary at the time of these events and rely solely on memory. This human faculty is not constant and I find that good times are more readily remembered than bad times and this may be for the better, but the account of the men, crews and ship conditions is factual.

This may be a good time to explain the existing situation that caused this incident, Mau Tse Tung led the Communist Army on the *Long March* and had defeated the Nationalist Army led by Chang Kai-shek, forcing them out of mainland China, except for a few small islands off Foochow, on to the island of Formosa, now Taiwan. From these small islands the Nationalists threatened to re-invade China and strangle the coastal shipping: this was unacceptable to Red China, which was desperate to get coastal shipping re-started. The internal river traffic was not affected, nor was international trade in and out of Hong Kong.

This was not easy. The young Red Guards had caused havoc throughout the business community of the country, including those in the maritime industries, such as the owners and managers of shipbuilders, ship repairers and docks. Ships' captains, engineers and crew were sent to rehabilitation prisons or even worse. The major shipping companies, long-time providers of transport on this coast, were reluctant to serve lest their ships be confiscated on a trumped-up charge, and in any case the communist authorities did not want foreigners in their country for fear of spying, sabotage or other subversive groups. The Chinese government sought a solution, bearing in mind that foreign currency was scarce and there was a shortage of almost everything, including all types of oil. Dock facilities were poor and the Chinese professional classes had been decimated. On the other hand, there were abundant supplies of coal and cheap manpower. The obvious solution was to employ cheap old coal-fired ships with foreign officers and Chinese crew. Hand-fired coal burners had long been obsolete with most owners and in most trades, but one of the exceptions was Australia. Here they still plodded around the coast, with bulk cargos, the owners making no money and therefore not willing or able to buy new ships. The export of meat, wool and cereals was carried out by overseas ships. The owners could not believe their luck when buyers arrived for their veterans. There was an added bonus for the buyers – these ships were under the British Flag and the British officers were under the protection of the Royal Navy wherever they sailed. The officer situation was resolved by money: mercenary it may be, but the rates of pay were far more than the Australian rates, which were themselves far more than British rates. Officers signed on rapidly, knowing little of the conditions that faced them in the future. The only catch was that they had to sail the ships from Australia to China, some 5000 miles non-stop in old tubs that had not travelled more than 500 miles in one go for years.

Bunker space was insufficient, so extra coal was loaded into holds, and holes cut in the bulkhead so it could be passed through to the stokehold when required. Two ships left together, one towing the other which had the extra coal. The latter was pulled alongside to transfer coal when required. The final obstacle was the crew, or *crowd* as they were known in British ships. To understand this, think Football Crowd to gather the full meaning - liable to riot at any time. An agreement with the union required that a ship leaving the coast for good had to be sailed out to the nearest foreign port by an Australian crew on coastal wage rate, which would be astronomical. They were working by the ship up until sailing but as usual had all gone home or to the pub by 5pm.

At this point I now refer to a particular ship, namely the SS *Aeon*, built in Scotland in 1910 and by then 40 years old. It was basically sound, but with a few cement boxes filling in holes in the hull to make it watertight. The name was now changed to the *Neapean Breeze* and regulations required that the name be gouged into steel at the stern, but here the cement had been liberally used and the Australian boilermaker called in to do the job was heard muttering that a stonemason should have been called for this task. It was around midnight that about 80 Chinese crewmen arrived by coach direct from the airport, joined the ship and immediately started raising steam. In three hours we were ready, slipped moorings and steamed out of Sydney Harbour without tugs or pilot, towards New Zealand; the journey had begun.

This really set the scene for what was to come in the future off the China Coast; the law of commercialism without any official controls. The first call was Nelson and reaching this port was fraught with problems. The crew had mainly never been to sea before, and of those who had, only a few had experience of hand-fired coal burning vessels, which is probably the most difficult job you could possibly get on a ship.

On these vessels there were three boilers, approximately 16 feet in diameter each with three furnaces, some four feet wide and 12 feet long. Horizontally across the centre of each were fire bars or a grate ; coal on top and ash underneath. Once lit the fires could not be let out until port was reached, for steam was needed all the time for the engine, but the fires needed to be cleaned or poked at least every 12 hours, and this was achieved by a method called *winging* which was carried out as follows. Fresh coal was shovelled into the left hand half of the furnace on top of the existing burning coal. Coal from the right hand half, which when almost burnt out and made up of clinker, dross and cinders was raked out of the furnace onto the floor plates and quenched with water. The top coal on the left hand side, by then burning strongly, was levered over to the bare right hand side with a ten-foot iron rod called a *slice* and new coal shovelled onto the burning coal would start to burn immediately. The same procedure was carried out on the right hand side, after which the furnace was now clean and would burn for 12 hours with only the occasional *poke*, and the addition of further coal.

It must be remembered that all this took place in front of a furnace with temperature of about 600^0f , with sulphurous smoke, ash and dust, maybe with the ship rolling too; it could not be any worse in Hell. Simple arithmetic tells us that three furnaces were cleaned every four-hour watch. Woe betide the watch that left dirty fires for the oncoming men; fists and shovels would be raised when this occurred. In addition to this, of course, was the clearing away of cinders and ash which were loaded into bins, hoisted to deck level and dumped over the side of the ship into the sea. Getting the coal from the bunkers into the stokehold became harder the longer the voyage went on. A fireman was needed to go into the bunker on top of the pile some 20 feet high, and shovel or throw it to the hatch leading into the stokehold. Sometimes it was necessary to break up large lumps of coal with a hammer to make them manageable. Watching this it is understandable how Welsh steam coal got such a good name in marine industry. A high heat fuel, of regular nut size, low in ash and producing little waste, it was easily shovelled into the boiler and included no dust which would fall uselessly through the firebars without burning.

Steaming through the harbour heads, steam pressure was down to 60lbs, from 180lbs and the engine barely turned, but as the firemen became used to the work it steadily improved. Unfortunately, after two days steam was noticed escaping from the boiler furnace and pressure in the boiler was reduced to prevent an explosion. This meant a reduction in our speed and in these reduced circumstances we limped into port. While we loaded scrap steel, which sold at a good price in Japan, major repairs were carried out to all three boilers. Repaired, we sailed around the coast, loading as much as possible. Our last port was Auckland and it was here that I learned some of the traits of our Chinese crewmen. Food was part of the crew wages and, in conjunction with the Chief Steward and the No.1 (*i.e.* crew working boss), the less they spent on food the more money they received. I saw three ways in which money was saved. The gangway watchman always had fishing lines into the water - the catch going straight into the galley, Entering the forecastle, which was used to store paint, ropes, etc, I found it full of live pigeons, grinning sailors indicating to me that they had trapped them from the quay. They were kept alive for food on the voyage. Invited to eat with the crew for a birthday party, I asked what the tubular type meat, cut into one inch lengths rather like cannelloni tubes, was. It proved to be chicken intestines, of which there are 20 inches per bird, cut washed and cooked.

With the loading, repairs, and learning curve behind us, the long haul from New Zealand to Japan began – non-stop across the Pacific Ocean for our old ship. As the trip wore on, the slower she travelled, boilers shooting and scaling up, weeds yards long trailing from the fouled hull, steam pressure down as coal had to be taken from the cargo hold into the boiler room, but she made it into Kobe Harbour, unloaded into barges and thence into dry dock. New accommodation cabins were welded on deck, heating and wash basins installed in the officers' accommodation and a little more work on the boilers. It was here that I first learned the value of an empty forty-four gallon drum in post-war Japan. In currency it was worth a taxi to a bar, drinks, taxi to a bathhouse, food, more drinks, overnight accommodation, and taxi back in the morning; very good value and from that time forth I never travelled to Japan without oil drums.

All good things must come to an end, and we sailed to Hong Kong. It was on this journey that we learned what troubles were in store. One night as we steamed through the Straits of Formosa the steering gear failed, the ship began to circle and take a zig zag course. The engine was stopped and we drifted for many hours while engineers and mates made a jury rig aft, steering with a hand-held compass and manually moving the rudder. The captain panicked and radioed for tugs. This was probably the reason why he was sacked on arrival in Hong Kong. So we made our way through the darkness, and at first light, through the gloom, close on our starboard bow was the large black shape of an American destroyer, all guns trained on us – a very daunting sight. This warship escorted us until we were clear of the Straits. On his radar our strange course would have suggested mine laying in this channel, however temporary repairs had been made to the steering and we clumsily made our way into Hong Kong Harbour.

Hong Kong is a sailor's town. For years they have received foreigners arriving in ships and are very good at it. After the monotony and sometimes hostility of the sea, here was a friendly place to enjoy the lights, the bustle, the noise, the entertainment and Johnnie was very welcome. The Chinese were very tolerant, and accepted bad behaviour as a matter of course. The ship was welcomed into this environment. The Chinese – Portuguese owner came aboard, introduced himself, inspected the ship and left and so did the ship within a few days to begin her new career. I did not sail with her for personal reasons, but waited for another ex-Australian boat that was on her way. This time was spent living ashore in the China Coast Seamen's Club, a magnificent building made of marble and glass. The running expenses were mainly provided by the large shipping companies for such was the number of seamen passing through Hong Kong that a base was needed. Those who had missed their ship waited for a UK-bound ship. They were known as Disabled British Seamen or DBS as it was stamped on the seaman's book: not a good reference. Some replacements waited for their new ship, officers on the higher floors, crews below, for it is not good policy to mix ranks when ashore, as many old scores may be waiting to be settled. For five Chinese dollars one had a cool, fanned *en suite* room and the services of a Chinese man servant who acted in the best tradition of this position. At the flicker of a bleary eye in the morning, tea was instantly served, clothes that had been discarded in pitiful condition the previous night, were now washed, ironed, hung and ready for more action. Not a word spoken, just smiles and bows and a generous tip. Next, a trip to the resident barber, for a shave, hot towels and massage. This really set one up for a lunch session and Dim Sum, some shopping maybe, an afternoon nap, and ready for evening festivities. Enjoy it while you can young man, for it will not last, and when back on ship and the engine room telegraph rings out *Standby – Slow Ahead* you leave Heaven and start towards Hell. You have only memories to keep you going.

My next ship soon arrived and the refit started. She was a smaller vessel than the last and a few years younger and this time the repairs were done while floating in the harbour. Wooden bungs were hammered into the ship's side to keep the water out while the sea valves were overhauled, which was typical of the quality of the work. Lots of new crew accommodation was welded on top of existing deck houses which made the ship top heavy and we never seemed to go anywhere without

a port or starboard list. My new cabin was right aft next to the steering engine, which noisily raced about throughout the voyage. Fortunately, this was drowned out by the constant thrashing of the propeller. However, the main worry was water. For some reason she had only 14 inches of freeboard (that is height above the water), and the cabin was often awash when at sea, so much so that I had to stand on the chair to get dressed. Often we carried timber logs, which were stowed in the holds and across the decks to about 15 feet high. To get to the engine room, which was amidships, it was necessary to climb on top of the logs, crawl along and climb down, all this on a rolling, listing ship. Having made a Chinese port, things did not get much better. Shanghai was the best. Being tied to a wharf felt good, but there were drawbacks. As soon as first light showed, numerous loud speakers started playing martial music. *The East is Red* was a favourite. All the happy workers were encouraged to sing along or, when coaling, hundreds would be on ascending benches with small baskets containing a few pounds of coal lifting to the next person only a few inches to a steady rhythmic chant, night and day.

While in port the ship was heavily guarded by the Chinese Army. Soldiers were always on the gangway. They demanded to see the little red passes that were issued when the ship first arrived. At that time all the crew would be lined up under guard and paraded through a suitable deck cabin in which sat many army officers at a long table. Each member would be questioned and have his papers inspected and all were counted. European officers only took copies of their documents in case originals were confiscated for some reason or another. Our cabins were also searched and life made very uncomfortable. In one incident, in another ship, the crew of inebriated Scotsmen decided to have a little fun by constantly rejoining the queue at the back, when several hundred crew were counted the joke was discovered, the Chinese officials, not understanding this type of humour, were incensed. Impounding and arrests followed for this behaviour. In the best traditions of communism the workers were directed to enjoyments and to this end the most exclusive club in Shanghai, the Shanghai Club, had been commandeered. A magnificent building, situated on the waterside *Bund*, the premises were situated on the finest road in town, but government surveillance was necessary and foreign users were required to order taxis from ship to club, using huge old American cars, in fact the only ones I ever saw in this city. We were transported in style to the 'Workers' Palace'. Here the entertainment was without parallel in the seaports of the world: non-stop jugglers, unicyclists, flag wavers, conjurors, fire-eaters, acrobats. There was no Punch and Judy, but there was very cheap, good beer. Having endured as much excitement as a sailor can for one evening and in the best tradition of capitalism, it was usual to hail a trishaw. This being a pedal-power rickshaw, we put the driver in the passenger seat and pedalled ourselves, racing our mates back to the ship. Perverse it may be, but it was necessary therapy. For those unable to pedal, it was customary to stand up in the back of the chariot-type vehicle and shower the hoards of children, who always followed us, with money in the form of one *bar* notes, about the size of a tube ticket and whose value outside China was so low as to be worthless.

One day I made a foray into the previously French Quarter of Shanghai, looking for antiques. I visited a huge warehouse, which I assumed to be a former department store of Selfridge's type. Floor after floor, there were beautiful articles stored in this dim and dusty place. They had, of course, been confiscated from the bourgeois in the revolution and the atmosphere seemed to reflect this state of affairs. Tragically orphaned furniture gives off its own signs. I did make a purchase of a piece of Jade but the misfortune it brought me convinced me that this was a place of ill omen.

Foochow was completely different from Shanghai. We always anchored in the river and took on cargoes from barges. What wharves there were had been blown up and huge broken concrete slabs sloped into the river.

Asking questions and directions always brought strange looks and negative responses from crews. Asking officials was not an option as spying was a serious offence. I did manage to get into the local town, or rather collection of dwellings alongside an unmade track, which could be classified as a pig town, except the smell would suggest there were many more hidden somewhere, to add to the ducks and the armed soldiers that wandered about. It was like something from the middle ages. Somehow we found an eating house. There was a long, long wait as all food had to be freshly killed. No passing trade, no refrigeration here, no electricity, but we enjoyed the meal by the light of paraffin lanterns. The trip back to the ship was most memorable. The Chinese boatmen all rowed while standing up with one long steering oar at the back, propulsion and steering being achieved by a figure-eight motion in the water. I remember well the sight of the boatman towering over the passengers in a black triangular cloak and a huge conical straw hat forcing his craft through the strong current. I did not dine ashore here again.

Another outstanding memory was the heat. At mid-day all breeze seemed to stop, as did the work. The engine room was untenable, boilers were shut down and left, generators stopped, the ship was lifeless. To find somewhere out of the sun and heat was the intention; an impossible wish as there was no shade. Decks were hot, cabins like furnaces, no shade anywhere. It was agony and the only time I questioned myself as to what I was doing here. After some 3 hours one noticed the slightest flicker of a breeze and was thankful, but now we knew that the second ordeal was about to start.

The farmers along the river now stirred themselves, and I mean this literally. For human sewage was used extensively on the farms, each holding having its own private supply hole. The fertilizer was stirred to get good consistency pulled out in buckets and the crops generously fed. The prevailing stink was very strong, and now we knew we had just one more trial to come, for with that down-river breeze came sewage barges. Having cleaned the city up-river, there now came long strings of barges, travelling very slowly and very close. One tried to stop breathing, but then the smell only came in through the ears. One thanked God for Mr Crapper and flush toilets in other places. Now it was gone and the air cleared and one tried not to think of tomorrow. Cargo working restarted going long into the cool night, as the dockers worked logs into the dark hold with only the dim light of hurricane lamps to guide them – no Health and Safety laws in these places. Reloaded, we would pound our way out of the river, leaning to one side or the other and hoping the weather would be kind to us.

The listing of a ship has far more effects than just uncomfortable living conditions, for the engine is meant to work in an upright position, and leaning to one side puts stresses on the wrong parts, causing overheating; coal in the boilers slides to one side and cargo tends to slide to a lower level, possibly causing the list to increase, an ever-increasing and unwanted condition that could lead to disaster.

It was coming from Foochow that we had one of our biggest frights. As we came into the estuary it was the custom to keep close to the mainland shore, for controlling this route was a Nationalist occupied island which was known as *White Dogs*. Suddenly the shout went up from the Chinese Supernumerary that we were being chased and when water spouts appeared astern we knew they were serious and were firing. Without any orders being issued, volunteer stokers arrived down below and fired those boilers as never before, giving steam pressure on the maximum the ship had ever recorded. The Nationalist vessel chasing us was an ex-American tank landing craft

(TLC) of about 3000 tons, without tanks but with naval guns. We radioed that we were a British ship on legitimate voyage and that we were calling for assistance from the Royal Navy in Hong Kong. The chase went on for some time, but on the appearance of a ship on the horizon ahead the TLC turned back. Just as well, for this rescuer was in fact another blockage runner. We warned them and they slowed so as to make a night arrival in darkness.

There was no help from the Red Chinese Navy, although they had many of this type of vessel moving all the way up the rivers. To the annoyance of the mates, they insisted that we dipped our flag when passing their warships and complained to the authorities if this was not done. So time passed, and up and down the coast we sailed, but with what I do not have full knowledge. Loading in Hong Kong was a frenzy and we were encouraged to take shore leave during these few days; an offer not to be refused. From what I did see it was small luxury items, refrigerators, electrical goods, perks for the party faithful no doubt.

Eventually, monotony overcomes all and it was time to move on. More and better second-hand ships were arriving from Europe, not for the blockade, but for voyages to communist States, like Russia, Poland, and establishing the Hong Kong Chinese shipping giants whose fleets now influence World Trade. They had cheap crew costs, negligible official control, minimum maintenance: all these factors resulted in the decline of the once-dominant British Merchant Navy. Hong Kong is slowly losing its importance in this constantly changing world. Maybe its wealth will transfer to the poor mainland, but a change in regime will also be required to make this a desirable place.

The Iron Hong : P&O and the Far East since 1845

Stephen Rabson

The arrival of steam

On 28 June 1866 P&O's 1,491-ton iron passenger steamer *Benares*, Captain Edward Browne, left Singapore on the last leg of the 15 June sailing from Bombay to the Far East. At 1.50am on the morning of 4 July she anchored off Hong Kong, getting under way again at 5.21am, but immediately colliding with the steamer *Agamemnon*, doing considerable damage, though surviving P&O records do not specify to which ship the damage was done, nor if it was shared. *Benares* docked at 6.41am after what was presumably P&O's first encounter with a Holt's ship in the China Seas.

P&O was in the China Seas more than a decade before the *Agamemnon* incident, and still sails there today in the diluted forms of the P&O Nedlloyd container shipping joint venture and the now-independent P&O Princess Cruises. On shore its most go-ahead business, P&O Ports, has significant interests at Shekou in the south and Qingdao in the north, but this paper is limited to the Company's presence in the China Seas over the century and a quarter between the Liverpool-built *Lady Mary Wood* paddling into Hong Kong harbour in August 1845, and the final passenger liner sailing home from Hong Kong by *Chitral* on the very last day of 1969.

Over this period, most references to the Far East in P&O's published Reports relate to the provision and development of mail contract services, the extension of feeder routes in response to commercial pressure, the hazards of navigation in Chinese waters, and the not infrequent chartering of ships to the British Government, and sometimes the French, for use in campaigns in or missions to China. Unmentioned in almost all these Reports was the opium trade. To quote Freda Harcourt:

Extraordinarily high freight rates for transporting opium gave P&O a financial advantage unique in steam shipping. Earnings covered not only the working expenses of the line itself but also the costs of the very valuable through traffic– silk and tea – from China to Europe

And after the opium was gone, there came World Wars, political unrest, economic change and technological revolution.

The drawbacks of sail for business communications with England and the carriage of opium to China account for the great interest in steam navigation in India in the 1820s and 1830s. Steam committees sprang up in Bombay, Calcutta and Madras, but by the early 1840s P&O had absorbed most of them, and as the only commercial concern running suitable ships east of Suez, since opening its Calcutta/Suez service at the end of 1842, it is not unexpected that its being granted a mail contract to Hong Kong two years later was more a matter of negotiation than of competitive tender.

A Minute of the P&O Board Meeting of 7 January 1845 reads as follows:

The Managing Directors report that after 16 months continual negotiation carried on by them with various departments of Her Majesty's Government, they have now the pleasure to lay before the Board the Contract duly executed for the conveyance of Her Majesty's mails to India, China etc.

Initially, P&O tried to obtain Government backing to take over the carriage of mails between Suez and Bombay, but the sitting tenant on the blue riband route, the East India Company, was not prepared to budge. Nor did Government seem interested in taking over the Honourable Company's support for P&O's service to Calcutta, but the proposal of an additional Ceylon/Far East connection and the support of some heavyweight friends in

Parliament were enough to bring the negotiations to a satisfactory end.

A fortnight later the Board appointed a Mr John Ryan as its Agent in Hong Kong, at a salary of £500 per year plus an allowance of £500 'on the understanding that the furniture etc., purchased therewith should be the property of the company'. In June Mr Ryan wrote from Calcutta that unless his salary was increased to £800 he would resign; P&O told him that they would pay him at £500 per year until a suitable replacement could be appointed.

Services and trades

The monthly contract service between Galle and Hong Kong via Penang and Singapore was worth £45,000 a year. P&O had new ships building, but under Government pressure, sent out two vessels originally built for the Peninsular run, the three-year-old *Lady Mary Wood* and the much-refitted 9-year-old *Braganza*, almost a year earlier than expected. To quote a letter to their Agents in Cadiz, Zulueta & Co, in January 1845:

> We shall begin to book passengers for China and the intermediate ports, by our steamer from Southampton of 20th June next…We have engaged to keep up a communication once a month between Suez, Ceylon, Madras, and Calcutta, and it is with this line that the China branch is connected. A passenger leaving Southampton on 20th June would arrive at Alexandria about 6th July, and would leave Suez in our steamer about the 10th, would arrive at (Galle) about the 28th, and start in the steamer for Hong Kong say the 29th, and arrive there about 15th August; say in all about 55 days from Southampton to Hong Kong.

Lady Mary Wood in fact left Galle on 27 July 1845 and arrived in Hong Kong on 4 August. The Southampton mails of 20 June thus arrived in only 46 days. On her return voyage on 1 September she carried 4,757 items of mail: 165 to Penang, 74 to Ceylon, 281 for Madras, 242 for Bombay, 6 to Aden and 3,989 to Europe. There was a good deal of excitement in Hong Kong, and the prepaid letters were all left behind, being sent by the steamer *Fire Queen* to Calcutta some days later, to be forwarded when opportunity presented itself, almost certainly by the next P&O steamer to Suez, overland and beyond.

Reg Kirk, assiduous chronicler of the movement of mails by P&O, reports that the earliest extant postal cover carried by P&O's China Mail was sent by a French sailor from his ship in Manila, by gunboat to Macao, thence by hand to Hong Kong, and left aboard *Braganza* in March 1846. On arrival in Southampton it was forwarded to London and thence via Dover and Boulogne at an extra charge of 1/10d, and the French charged the matelot's Mum 15 centimes for delivery in Paris.

As was usual, passengers who could afford it used the mail steamers, but demand for tickets East of Suez was seasonal. In February 1849 P&O made a 20% reduction in fares to the Straits and China on steamers leaving England in May, June, and July of each year in the hope that this would balance things out, and thus passage for a Gentleman to Hong Kong was reduced to £146, and for a Lady to £154, with similar reductions for homeward sailings in October, November, and December.

In 1847, two years after the Galle/Hong Kong service opened, P&O began carrying opium from Bombay to China. Being the first and *ipso facto* the longest-established operator on the route helped the company to deter any serious opposition. On the direct trade from Calcutta, however, carrying the higher-grade Bengal opium, P&O only operated from 1851 to 1857 before itself withdrawing in the face of opposition from established shippers, most notably Jardine's and the Apcar Line.

At the other end of the route, the 400-ton *Canton* arrived at Hong Kong in 1849 and was employed ferrying Malwa opium to Canton. P&O also put *Lady Mary Wood* on a Hong Kong/Shanghai line in 1850, where the three big opium carriers – Jardine's, Dent's and the American Russell company – combined to force freight rates down. To save costs, *Lady*

Mary Wood's master took to shipping silk at Woosung, outside Shanghai port limits, thus evading export and harbour dues, which illegality the three competitors duly reported to the authorities, although the ensuing conviction and fine were quashed on appeal.

On 31 August 1859, after a visit to Japan byThomas Sutherland of its Hong Kong staff, P&O's steamer *Azof* left Shanghai for Nagasaki, where she arrived on 3 September. Further voyages followed at irregular intervals until 1863, when a fortnightly Shanghai/Japan service was inaugurated connecting with the China Mail Line, and Japan was included in mail sailings from 1867.

Sutherland is undoubtedly the most celebrated of all P&O's representatives in the Far East. Born in 1834, he joined P&O in London in 1852 but was sent out East – first to Bombay, almost immediately transferring to Hong Kong – when only 20, and spent 12 years in China. He later became Managing Director and then Chairman for over 40 years. A colleague, Franklin Kendall, wrote home thus in December 1863:

> Sutherland is without doubt, the right man in the right place. He takes a liberal and practical view of everything, yet withal managing to keep on good terms with all the mercantile and official world, and is as capital a manager of the Company's business as one will often meet with.

He also found time to be a member of the Legislative Council and to help found the Hong Kong and Shanghai Bank:

> The P&O Directors sent for me to come to London, and again I was to come rather under a cloud: the cloud of independence. I can't have been more than 32 at this time. A young man, a mere Agent starting banks was a person required to be dealt with and suppressed!

He wasn't, of course, which was probably just as well.

In 1866, P&O issued a Report on its first 25 years. Its Far East services were by now well-established, but complex. Thus *Singapore* left Yokohama on 14 August for Shanghai, where her consignment joined local mails aboard *Aden* for passage to Hong Kong. Other mails came from Foochow aboard *Formosa*. The Hong Kong/Bombay steamer *Northam* took the consolidated mails to Galle where they trans-shipped to *Bengal*, coming from Calcutta, for passage to Suez. After the overland crossing of Egypt by train the mails were split: *Delta* took the faster and lighter element to Marseilles to make the French railway and cross-Channel steamer journey to London, while the heavier portion of the mails went from Alexandria to Southampton in *Massilia*, arriving on 20 October.

This complex pattern involved seven ships steaming some 13,274 miles between them and overland transit of some 982 miles, although only the faster and lighter element of the mails made the longer of the two land journeys. It is not surprising that P&O felt keenly the contemporary criticism of the rates it was paid by the Government, when compared with Cunard to North America and Royal Mail to the West Indies: the patterns of services they operated were hardly comparable!

The same 1866 Report listed the following properties in China and Japan:

> At Hong Kong: houses for the Agent and principal employees, offices and coal sheds, all held on lease; freehold stores and workshops, fitted with the machinery necessary at a terminal station; also lighters for coaling and cargo purposes, and the hulk Fort William.

> At Shanghai: the Agent's house, the office and godown, all held on lease; freehold coal sheds, and cargo and coal boats.

> At Yokohama: the hulk Tiptree.

It's nice to know that P&O had a coal shed or two. I used to have a coal shed, but it didn't hold anything like the 6,000 tons P&O could store at Shanghai, not to mention the 10,000 tons at Hong Kong. At Yokohama, very much the end of the line, it stored only 2,200 tons, probably the most that the obscure hulk *Tiptree* could manage.

In October and November 1871 the 'extra' steamers *Mirzapore* and *Pekin* were despatched from Southampton via the Suez Canal to Hong Kong and Shanghai respectively, but the mails still went overland from Alexandria to Suez as required by the 1864 contract, those for Far Eastern ports being forwarded in the Calcutta steamer and transferred again at Galle. In 1874, after lengthy wrangling, P&O was for the first time permitted to carry mails through the Canal, albeit only the heavy element loaded in Southampton, at the expense of increased penalties for late delivery and an overall reduction in subsidy.

Reg Kirk's summary of revised working under the 1874 contract, with the fast mails still crossing Egypt by rail, seems not much better than arrangements eight years before:

> *Previously, both Brindisi and Southampton steamers had called at Alexandria, where their mails had been unloaded and sent by rail to Suez, where the Suez/Aden/Galle/ Madras/Calcutta steamer was waiting. Future Brindisi steamers continued like this.*

> *UK steamers left London with cargo as before. The mails were collected at Southampton… At Suez this steamer transferred the India mails from Southampton, Gibraltar and Malta, to the waiting Bombay steamer [and] collected the mails from Brindisi which had come overland from Alexandria. At Galle, the Australian mails were transferred to the steamer bound for King George's Sound, and the China mails to the China steamer which left Bombay about 4 days before.*

> *In the tea season, which began in late May or early June, the [homeward] China steamer would go through from Shanghai to Southampton and London, where the tea would be unloaded for the first time. This required special arrangements for the mails between Calcutta and Galle, and between Galle and Bombay.*

Have you all got that?

Misfortunes

From *Douro* on the Paracels in 1854 to *Sobraon* on Tung Ying island in 1901, P&O lost 6 ships in Chinese waters, 25% of its total losses for the period.

Douro was westbound from Hong Kong when her engines were disabled in a typhoon, and while continuing under sail she ran aground on the Paracels on 26 May 1854 and became a total loss. One Lascar seaman fell overboard and was drowned. The Second Officer, a P&O First Officer who was going home on sick leave, four seaman and two passengers, one Chinese, sailed 300 miles to Hong Kong in the ship's jolly boat to summon aid, though en route the Chinese passenger was robbed when he boarded a passing junk to seek assistance.

Sobraon was wrecked 80 miles north east of Foochow in dense fog, en route from Shanghai to London. There were no casualties, passengers were taken off in native craft, and the mails were forwarded to Europe aboard a Norddeutscher Lloyd vessel. The crew remained on board to stop looting while an unsuccessful attempt was made to tow her off.

The most disastrous loss was undoubtedly that of *Corea*. On 29 June 1865 she left Hong Kong for Swatow, Amoy and Foochow with 103 aboard just as a typhoon was breaking, and was never seen again.

83 of those aboard *Corea* were either Chinese crew or Chinese deck passengers, but almost as many Chinese were lost when in January 1887 P&O's *Nepaul* ran down the transport *Wan Nien Chin* anchored in fog below Shanghai with the loss of 73 lives. P&O was found responsible, though it was able to settle out of court for only half its liability.

Sometimes injury to the locals was deliberate. *Canton*, herself a loss in 1859, ten years earlier took part in the celebrated incident on 29 September 1849 when she towed the becalmed brig HMS *Columbine* into action against Chinese pirate junks, which were quickly sunk or surrendered, with *Canton* taking Naval casualties back to Hong Kong.

Not that the locals were always unpleasant.

When *Bokhara* was driven aground on the Pescadores in October 1892, with the loss of 125 out of the 148 on board, the survivors were entertained with champagne by the local mandarin. Maybe he was a cricket lover upset by the loss of almost the entire Hong Kong cricket team, returning from a match in Shanghai.

Competition

A near-monopoly has its drawbacks. Someone complained about almost everything P&O ever did, and its inherent conviction of its superiority did not help. Here is a comment from 1882, when passengers were switching to Messageries Maritimes ships which were newer, more comfortable, quicker and more conveniently scheduled:

> *I think we came home by French Mail, as by that time my mother had taken quite a natural dislike to the P&O because one had to change at Colombo, and because they would not do washing on board...We had to take sufficient clothing to last the whole six weeks, and this with children and babies was no fun. Sir Thomas Sutherland refused to have his ships 'looking like laundry companies'. After his death this was altered and all laundry was done below decks, but the change at Colombo still continued for some years, the through ships going to Australia.*

Henry Joseph, a P&O Manager on a tour of inspection, wrote from Shanghai in 1906 to the same Sir Thomas Sutherland:

> *I will not write more about the laundry question...but I must say that I feel convinced that, laundry or no laundry, there is an opening for a great development in our passenger traffic with China, Japan and the Straits if we can give a regular service, fortnightly, of the better class of intermediate steamers...Two or three direct mail steamers at the height of the season would also add much to the Company's prestige in this part of the world.*

The French were taking P&O cargoes too: in 1867 Sutherland, temporarily in charge at Shanghai while the local Superintendant took a rest cure, reported that Messageries had increased its silk carryings from Shanghai from 11.7% of the total in 1863 to 42.4% in 1866 because its ships went direct to Suez, and sailed 2 or 3 days before P&O's. Silk contributed £119,000 to P&O's income in 1869, but within two years its freight rates had dropped by 65%.

When Holt's steamers began making direct voyages to and from the UK round the Cape – *Agamemnon* brought tea home in 62 days in 1866 – P&O had no real grounds for complaint. It had carried tea overland to England faster than the tea clippers (56 days) but more expensively (over £20 a ton) as early as 1859. However, it had not really prepared for the success of the Canal, and suffered accordingly. Trans-shipment of mails, and cargo on mail steamers, in Ceylon continued.

When the mail contracts were renegotiated in 1879, P&O faced competition from four other operators, though only it and Holt's quoted for all the various interlocking services. P&O won the day on both cost and speed, but both it and the Liverpool firm saw fit to publish pamphlets outlining their respective cases, P&O's at least in rather bitter terms. (As it was similarly beset by Orient Line on the Australian service, perhaps it felt particularly beleaguered: credible competition was not something it was used to, or liked).

One reason for trans-shipment was because P&O maintained its Bombay/China route, terminating at Shanghai from 1874, and thereby its stranglehold on the Malwa opium traffic, while Jardine's and Apcar's kept their control of the Bengal trade. When BI and Messageries wanted to get involved, they effectively found themselves limited to the inferior Persian crop which BI brought from the Gulf and trans-shipped to the French line in Ceylon.

To quote Freda Harcourt again:

> *The Bombay/China line...stood on its own. Opium earnings amply covered all the working costs of the line and those of the silk*

freight as well, so (profits from the latter) and the proportion of the mail subsidy allotted to the Bombay-Hong Kong Line – £68,543 – were left completely available for the benefit of the Company's other lines.

This was just as well, with growing post-Canal competition. Opium earnings brought relative stability over the whole range of P&O's lines for about four decades, and were not negligible thereafter, but the 1905 agreement between the Indian and Chinese governments reduced the trade by 10% per year from 1907 so that it would cease in 1917. Sutherland pronounced its valedictory at the P&O Annual General Meeting in December 1908:

The Bombay opium trade, at one time a source of princely revenue, has now fallen to a fragment of what it once was…As philanthropists you must rejoice at the extinction of the Indian opium trade but as shipowners you have considerable reason to grieve, and I doubt whether our philanthropic action will be followed by the Chinese Government in prohibiting the growth of the native opium in China. I believe that a Chinaman is constituently so created and exists in such a climate that the use of opium to a moderate extent is a necessary to him as the use of beer in England.

Unlike in earlier years, from 1905 until 1970 the P&O archives include, with some early gaps, copies of the annual reports submitted from its overseas agents. The 1905 file shows what business P&O was doing in the China Seas half way through the period of my survey.

Into Shanghai it carried only $2\frac{1}{4}$% of the raw cotton trade, but 38% of Indian yarn; only 20% of Bengal opium but a massive 97% of Malwa opium. Outward it carried 29% of silk exports, the same as Norddeutscher Lloyd, while Messageries Maritimes carried 17%, and 54% of general cargo to the UK while Ocean carried 30%. On the passenger front P&O carried only 446 to Europe against Messageries' 3,023 and NDL's 1,116.

P&O carried all the Malwa opium imported into Hong Kong, though only just over 10% of the Bengal crop, most of which was trans-shipped at Colombo from the Calcutta lines. Ocean's carried more Canton and Macao tea to the UK from Hong Kong (54% against P&O's 42%), but P&O carried more of the Foochow product, 34% against 12%. In each tea trade, the next largest carrier, Ben Line, was well down at only 3 or 4%.

The inter-war years
The first Lord Inchcape, who came into P&O with the takeover of BI in 1914, was an astute businessman, who turned a Company into a Group while in the process ensuring that companies he controlled took over almost all the local agency work East of Suez for P&O and its newly-acquired flock of subsidiaries. In about 1918, the P&O agencies in Hong Kong and Shanghai, formerly Company offices in their own right, were taken over by the BI agents Mackinnon Mackenzie & Co, on a 5% commission basis. This saved P&O £3,885 annually – but it also netted Mackinnon's £13,442 a year, of which Inchcape, as the senior partner, took a sizeable cut.

Inchcape's comments at the AGM in 1926 make an interesting contrast with Sutherland's eighteen years earlier:

I have spent a good many years of my life in the East, and…my belief is that we have, in a great measure, brought about the present condition of antagonism to us in China by sending missionaries there to endeavour to convert the people to Christianity. I ask you how the Chinese would be regarded here if they established all over the country a number of mission stations with the object of converting our people to Buddhism. Christian missionary efforts among uncivilised peoples…may be…fully justified; but the attempt to break down China's ancient faiths, as sacred to the Chinese as Christianity is to ourselves, is, I think, to be deplored. Such efforts, in my judgement, do far more harm than good.

After the First World War P&O's London/ Yokohama intermediate service regained its mail status as suitable tonnage became available. At the Annual General Meeting in 1927, Lord Inchcape pointed out that a return passage from London to Hong Kong, 20,224 miles in 68 days, cost a maximum of £175, and that after deducting costs of a comparable hotel ashore at £2 per day, the travel element of the journey cost £39, i.e. under $1/_2$ d a mile – something not even the Great Western Railway could match.

He suggested that airships might eventually take over the mail services, but 'not in my time', and bewailed the political unrest in China which had prompted the British Government to send ships and troops to defend British interests…P&O's *Assaye* and *Karmala* were both involved, while its cargo liner Nagpore was fired on from the shore while making her way down the Yangtse from Hangkow to Shanghai.

The political and military situation in China was to figure prominently in P&O's comments on affairs in the Far East right up the outbreak of the Second World War – and after. In 1930 the Hong Kong agency reported that 'with civil disobedience in India, civil wars in China, and a universal trade depression, the outlook for China cannot be said to be bright. There was also the renewal of piracy in Chinese waters, referred to in 1929.

By January 1930 the occasional Far East mail voyage was made via Bombay, a diversion which lengthened passages by 420 miles. Faster ships were needed to maintain mail schedules with an adequate safety margin, and *Corfu* and *Carthage* of 1931 were the first new passenger liners built for P&O's China service for many decades. By the end of 1932 almost all sailings were via Bombay, though that year's P&O Handbook of Information still listed its Far East passenger services as follows:

London to Straits, China and Japan fortnightly on Friday via Southampton to Colombo, Penang (27 days), Singapore (28 days), Hong Kong (33 days), Shanghai (37 days) and Japan ports. From Marseilles fortnightly on Fridays, usually at midnight…to Penang (19 days), Singapore (20 days), Hong Kong (25 days) and Shanghai (30 days).

There is also the following ominous note: 'China supplementary and local services may be dislocated under present conditions.'

Ex-Government standard-design cargo liners had been introduced on the Far East run after the War, and purpose-built ships were ordered in 1930. In 1925 P&O had regularised its relations with other British shipping companies in the area with the signing of the Victoria Point Agreement by P&O, BI, Alfred Holt, Straits Steamship and China Navigation. This was basically an agreement not to trespass on each other's coasting rights in the India, Straits and China spheres, and some of its provisions apparently held good right up to the container era.

If one of these is to be believed, it was usual for competing lines to co-operate enthusiastically in regularising traffic, especially when times were hard. The Far East freight and passenger conferences were active and powerful. But in the end, national and commercial pressures were quite likely to override formal agreements. In 1936 Alexander Shaw complained of Japanese intrusion into 'British' trades between Hong Kong, Singapore, Penang and Colombo, while American insistence on excluding lines from their own waters, but reserving the right to trespass on the historic trades of others elsewhere in the world, finds echoes in US attitudes generally.

In 1940 P&O's agents in China reported that passenger carryings were down by 90% – which was scarcely surprising – and that the tea trade had been killed off by the export priority given to essential commodities such as refrigerated eggs and egg products, silk (for parachutes?), china grass, bristles and oil – but not tea!

Hong Kong itself was now producing a variety of goods, from canvas and rubber boots and shoes, to rattan furniture and preserved ginger, but as none were priority commodities there was no business for P&O, though lots for NYK. The agent in Hong Kong noted the stranglehold of the Japanese military occupation in China, and wondered whether Japan would ultimately side with Germany and Italy....

On 2 March 1945, the Japanese steamer *Nichutin Maru* was bombed and sunk by US aircraft in the East China Sea. In a previous existence she had been the P&O coaster *Mata Hari*, trading on the Malayan coast and captured at the fall of Singapore. She was not the only P&O asset that the Japanese found useful, as Sir William Currie, the P&O Chairman, pointed out at the Annual General Meeting in December 1945:

> *The Company's office property in Hong Kong is intact – in fact it is reported to us that the Japanese have effected considerable improvements...[but] launches, tugs and barges have, I am afraid, mostly disappeared.*

Post-war recovery and terminal decline
P&O ordered four new ships for its Far East cargo service in 1945, as none of its pre-War vessels had survived hostilities. These were delivered in 1948-9, and four more between 1951 and 1956, with ships of P&O's tramp subsidiary the Hain Steamship Company, which had also provided Far East liner tonnage in the 1930s, filling the gaps when necessary. Despite terminating at Hong Kong, the average Far East cargo voyage in the Forties took 189 days as against 140 days prewar, with 58% of the time spent in port against 41% in the Thirties.

In 1950 the Shanghai agent reported that conditions neither warranted nor indeed permitted P&O ships to call there. The Government had begun minesweeping and reinstated the old fairway, but there was no pilotage and agents were required to guarantee that they would be responsible for clearing wrecks in case of accident. The companies they represented were unenthusiastic. Some North Chinese cargoes went via Hong Kong, and P&O also lifted 35% of that year's North China Spring Pack of frozen egg from Taku Bar, 4,790 tons in all.

In Hong Kong in 1950, P&O loaded 5,000 tons of cotton goods, 36% of the total and half as much again as Holt's; 3,300 tons of rubber canvas shoes, 38% of the total and about the same as Holt's; 2,000 tons of mats and matting, 15% of the total but only two-thirds of Glen Line's liftings; and 1,600 tons of ginger, 37% of the total, as well as lesser quantities of tea, canes, wood oil in drums, teaseed oil, cassia, feathers, hides, sesame seed, silk waste, torches, enamelware, seagrass, wool tops, rubber goods, and bristles.

Cargo was, of course, also carried on the UK/Hong Kong passenger service, reopened by *Canton* in October 1947, with the larger but one-off *Chusan* delivered in 1950 to bring the number of ships on the route up to four. By 1954 a monthly passenger/cargo service to Hong Kong and cargo service to Japan were operated, while calls at Shanghai, Tsingtao and Tsientsin re-opened links with China, but two years later the agencies were complaining that P&O's cargo ships were slower than the opposition and were losing market share both outwards and home, while the passenger ships suffered from competition from Lloyd Triestino, Norddeutscher Lloyd and Hapag, who had newer, better and more spacious vessels. P&O's Hong Kong agent commented on the situation in 1956 as follows:

> *Outside competition is serious but ...we do not do so badly at present, even with hopelessly old-fashioned ships. I am convinced that with good modern ships we can take passengers away from the others, rather than lose them... I think the sea will still be more popular [than air] for a long time yet. I think it of the utmost importance that an 'announcement of intent' to build should be made as soon as possible. This will put a bar on the present adverse publicity of lack of interest in the China run.*

There was no such announcement, though the ex-Belgian sisters *Cathay* and *Chitral*, introduced in 1961, were certainly an improvement.

By 1960, cargo liner visits to mainland China had ceased again in favour of Taiwan, served by an extension of the Japan service. In 1964 passenger calls to Japan were cut to 3 per year, and *Chusan* moved to the Australian run soon afterwards, though this change was offset to a degree by the promotion of 'New Way Home' sailings to the UK via the Pacific and Panama.

The cargo routes saw a major change in 1967 with the introduction of the three 12,500-ton 'Super Strath' fast cargo liners giving a 90-day round voyage between Europe and Japan, via Panama on the homeward leg. There were still three sailings per month to Hong Kong: *Cathay* or *Chitral*, the 'Straths', and the normal cargo run. The last was replaced in 1968 by two 18-knot 'Pando' services utilising some of the faster P&O Group cargo liners from the Australian service rendered surplus by the imminent containerisation of that route and sailing out alternately via the Cape or Panama, home via the Cape.

On 31 December 1969 *Chitral* made the last P&O line passenger sailing from Hong Kong, arriving in London's King George V Dock on 12 February 1970. After the closure of the Suez Canal the voyage to and from Hong Kong took 35 days instead of 25, and demand for passenger sailings had fallen right away. *Chitral* later joined her sister *Cathay* on Eastern & Australia's service from Sydney to Hong Kong, but here too the Boeing and the box were hovering, although that is another story.

The Gold Rush Passenger Trade and the history of Hong Kong 1849-1867[a]

Elizabeth Sinn

In 1849, 300 Chinese sailed for San Francisco, followed by 450 in 1850 and 7,785 in 1851.[1] In 1852, the number grew to 30,000.[2] Thus began the flood of Chinese into the United States that formed one of the major strands of the great global migration in the mid-19th century.[3] While the migration aspect of the California-bound movement has been much studied by scholars, the shipping aspect of it, especially the financial and organizational dimensions of the passenger trade, despite its long-term consequences for Hong Kong's development, has been largely neglected.[4] Significantly, even in Baruch Boxer's monograph *Ocean Shipping and the Evolution of Hong Kong*, this passenger trade was mentioned in exactly one-quarter of a sentence! As a prime contributor to Hong Kong's development as an international port-city and major hub of the global Chinese diaspora, the passenger trade surely deserves serious study.

Another reason for highlighting this particular passenger trade is the fact that very often when mid-nineteenth-century Chinese emigration is brought up, it is the 'coolie trade', *i.e.* the traffic of indentured/contract labour to places such as Havana, Peru, the West Indies, and to some extent to Southeast Asia, that is invoked in people's minds. Because of the

enormity of the tragedies and hardship that characterized the indentured labour trade, historians tend to devote their energy to condemning its immorality, often for polemical purposes, and few detached accounts have been constructed. One unfortunate result of such academic bias is that the various nineteenth-century emigration strands have been lumped together, their distinctions blurred.

My submission is that the Chinese Gold Rushers, unlike the indentured labourers mentioned above, were primarily free emigrants, an important fact that defines the California passenger trade, as will be shown below. Contemporaries were alert to the difference. The American Consul, F.T. Bush, reporting on the large numbers of Chinese leaving Hong Kong for the United States in 1851, commented, 'The emigrants are of different classes - merchants, small tradesmen, agriculturists, and artisans, all of them respectable people'.[5]

The Governor of Hong Kong was keen to point out that not only were they 'respectable people', they were in fact 'a superior class'.[6] What was more, they were free. 'There is a large class of emigrants proceeding to Australia and California, voluntary and self-supporting, paying their own passages and making all the necessary provisions for their departure', wrote Sir John Bowring. 'These persons are not collected by crimps, or kidnapped', he went on, emphasizing the difference:

> ...*nor would their liberty of action appear to be interfered with by fraud or misrepresentation. They are usually hale men, in the prime of their life, adventurous and laborious. The mortality on board the Emigrant Ships to Australia and California*

a   This paper is written with the support of a Research Grants Committee (Hong Kong) grant for the study of Chinese Emigration from Hong Kong. I am grateful to the following institutions for permission to use their archives and libraries: The Huntington Library; the Baker Library of the Harvard University Business School: Jardine, Matheson & Co. and the Cambridge University Library; the Bancroft Library and Ethnic Studies Library of the University of California, Berkeley.
    I am grateful to the Reverend Carl T. Smith for sharing his data and insights with me, and to Paul Cohen for his comments.

presents a most favourable contrast to that of coolies sent to the Colonies under labour contracts, who are so frequently in a low state of wretchedness and exhaustion, either suffering from or subject to latent diseases undermining their constitutions and to some extent accounting for the lamentable statistics of death which have naturally excited the attention of Her Majesty's government.[7]

Some of the California and Australia-bound emigrants might have borrowed money to pay for their tickets, or used the so-called credit ticket system,b but they were only obliged to repay the debt, and were not 'indentured'. As far as their being passengers was concerned, the fact that they went abroad voluntarily was crucial. These differences, so fundamental, have not been sufficiently stressed even by the most serious scholars. Gunther Barth, for instance, in *Bitter Strength*, still repeats the old belief that California-bound Chinese emigrants obliged to repay borrowed passage money were 'no better than serfs'.[8]

No doubt the inter-connectedness between the various strands of the Chinese emigration-business was real. The same ships operated by the same captains and crews, owned by the same owners and handled by the same charterers and agents were being used to carry Chinese anywhere. Prospective emigrants were sometimes confused about their own destination; for example, they would be told that they were going to 'Gold Mountain' when they were actually being shipped to less desirable destinations such as the guano islands in Peru.[9] Worse still, in the hands of politicians, these separate strands were deliberately mixed up for polemical ends. For instance, in the 1850s and 60s, anti-Chinese agitators in California habitually labelled all Chinese entering the United States as 'coolies', equated their regimented work routine at the gold mines with slavery, and proceeded to oppose Chinese emigration on the grounds of its being 'slave trade'. Such rhetoric has added greatly to the general confusion then and thereafter.

However, it is vital, I think, to disentangle the various strands of migration — based on destinations, nature of financial arrangement, background of the passengers, method of recruitment etc — because each had its own historical trajectory that resulted in widely differing social and economic, political and cultural impacts. For me, the difference is all the greater since my research interest is in migration-related *businesses* and not in moral or ideological issues. Thus, however interconnected the various migration strands might have been, and might have appeared, it is essential that we single out – even rescue – the trade of free passengers to California and Australia for analysis in order to achieve a clearer understanding of the development of the passenger trade, and its contribution to Hong Kong's development as a whole.

California Gold and Hong Kong

By the late 1840s, firms and individuals in Hong Kong were beginning to despair at the lack of economic progress. The newly acquired colony, which Sir Henry Pottinger hoped would become 'the Great Emporium' of British trade, was not quite fulfilling that promise. Despite being declared a free port – free of duties and open to ships and merchants of all nationalities – trade did not prosper. Hong Kong's economy depended on one trade: opium. Competition from the Treaty Ports proved detrimental, and colony's fate appeared to be sealed.

Then gold was discovered in California.

This event on a distant continent, presenting unprecedented opportunities, proved the break that Hong Kong had been waiting for that would help her fulfil her destiny, at least as envisaged by Pottinger, as one of the world's great ports.

It is not clear when exactly news of the gold discovery reached Hong Kong. Personal letters bringing news from California was one possible source, especially since a number of Boston merchants operating there had close China ties; ships' captains, seamen and passengers arriving from California might also have spread the news within their own circles. Wide circulation of the news, however, began when the US ship *Preble* arrived in Hong Kong and Macao in September 1848. It brought several numbers of the Honolulu newspaper the *Polynesian* that reported on the gold discovery and the rush for California: 'thousands are resorting to it from all quarters, suddenly seized with fever as our contemporary expressed it'.[10] The arrival of the *Julia* in January 1849, bringing with her a considerable amount of gold dust, set on the gold fever in Hong Kong.[11]

Thenceforth, Hong Kong newspapers were full of the news of California: the ease of finding gold, the high prices of consumables such as sugar, coffee and butter at California, that goods were selling at three or four times of ordinary prices. There was much gold but shortage of everything else,[12] which meant that anyone with anything to sell there would strike gold too. This obsession with California gold in the Hong Kong media led the *Alta California* to comment later, disdainfully and perhaps unfairly, that Hong Kong newspapers contained nothing but news of California.[13]

The early stories of gold were enough to induce a number of British, Americans and Europeans to leave Hong Kong for San Francisco. But as far as the passenger trade was concerned, it was only when the Chinese started going in large numbers that any real impact was felt.

By April, 1850, the Hong Kong government was reporting on the effect of the California trade, partially with reference to the large number of Chinese coming from the Mainland into Hong Kong. Some simply came to produce for the California market, such as carpenters come to build house-frames that were in great demand in San Francisco. The government also observed that no less than 23 vessels were sailing for San Francisco direct from Hong Kong, thus affording employment to a very considerable number of carpenters and other artificers.[14]

Most of the Chinese who came to Hong Kong, of course, came in order to sail to California. Foreign shipping merchants in Hong Kong and Guangzhou, quick to take advantage of the Chinese disposition to emigrate, actively seduced them by circulating placards, maps and pamphlets, presenting highly-coloured accounts of the 'Gold Mountain', as California was soon to be known among the Chinese. Numerous ships sent out native agents to obtain passengers.[15] When three or four Chinese passengers returned to Hong Kong on the *Race Hound* in early 1851, each bringing with them $3,000 to $4,000, and giving glowing accounts of the golden regions and showing them the dust,[16] gold fever among the Chinese was out of control.

Later in 1853, when the first Chinese-language newspaper, the *Chinese Serial*, was published in Hong Kong, like its English counterparts, it too monitored closely the conditions of Chinese in California, Australia and elsewhere. Indeed, its very first issue carried a translation of California's 'Regulations for Chinese Gold Diggers' The translation had beed made in California and the Editor of the *Chinese Serial* even took the trouble to re-translate passages that he believed contained inaccuracies.[17] Through newspapers and other sources, Chinese at home were kept informed of conditions abroad. Though reports of mutinies, kidnapping, diseases, fraud and shipwrecks that frequently appeared in the press would have warned prospective emigrants of the numerous pitfalls and horrors that awaited the greedy, careless, foolish and unlucky, there was always enough good news to keep people dreaming of gold.

Ships for San Francisco
The number of ships and passengers bound for San Francisco increased dramatically; in 1851, 44 ships left Hong Kong for that port.[18] Ships began arriving in Hong Kong in large numbers to meet the demand. By 1854, we should remember, Chinese were also rushing to Australia where gold was discovered in 1851: Australia became known to the Chinese as 'New Gold Mountain' and the crunch on ships

intensified. Though the departures for Australia started modestly in 1853 with only 268 passengers that year,[19] during the first three months of 1854, 2,100 departed for Melbourne and 10,467 sailed for Australia between November 1854 and September 1855.[20] In response to the insatiable demand, European ships that had been condemned as unfit to carry cargo years before were bought at enormously high prices and fitted out for passengers.[21] Some of the vessels were reported to be old, filthy, rotten craft that had gone through their term of ordinary service, been used then for whalers and afterward abandoned.[22] The American Consul in Hong Kong observed in 1854, that 'the impossibility of finding vessels to transport those who wish to go is the only obstacle in the way'.[23] Would-be passengers competed with each other for ships in and around the China Sea which were wanted for North America and Australia, but no less for Havana, Peru and the West Indies. To make things worse, goods were competing with passengers for space on board. As the *Alta California* wrote in 1854:

> *Freights from China to this port are ruling exceedingly high, twenty six dollars per ton, for ordinary vessels, is freely given, but the number of passengers coming excludes a large amount of goods which other wise might be sent to this port.[24]*

A New Passenger Trade

The California emigration, which everyone at the time recognized as 'the mainstay of the colony',[25] gave rise to a new type of passenger trade in the China Sea. For many centuries, the main destination for Chinese emigrants had been Southeast Asia; they proceeded largely in Chinese vessels mainly sailing along the coast, and it was only after the 1850s that they were transported in large numbers by Western sailing vessels and steamers.[26]

Indeed, the large-scale transportation of Chinese passengers on Western trans-oceanic vessels started in the mid-1840s when the abolition of slavery by a number of European states, notably France, Spain and Britain, led to a demand for cheap Chinese and Indian labour for their colonies; Peru later became another prime importer of cheap Chinese labour.[27] This involved primarily contract/ indentured labour. For some destinations, particularly Havana, Demarera and Peru, conditions on board and in the final destinations were often so harsh that only through kidnapping or decoying and other deceptive means could men be found to fill the holds of ships that sailed there. Because of death, destitution, and above all the fact that their contracts did not provide for a return passage, many of these reluctant emigrants never returned to China.[28]

The discovery of gold in California, Australia and later New Zealand and British Columbia, attracted adventurers, labourers as well as entrepreneurs, from around the world, with the Chinese constituting only one block of this global migration. They represented a new type of passengers that shaped a new mode of oceanic transportation,[29] enabling Hong Kong to develop an infrastructure that would support its evolution into a world shipping centre.

Characteristics of the Hong Kong-California Passenger Trade

The most fundamental difference between early migrants to California and those destined for Peru and Havana, was that the former went voluntarily, even eagerly, and freely, as Governor Bowring described so emphatically, but it is a difference that cannot be emphasized enough. Many of the California-bound emigrants were fairly well-off. Besides paying for their own passage, they often brought with them a good quantity of clothing and other personal effects as well as cash to spend after their arrival in America. From the San Francisco Customs House records, we find that some of them also brought along merchandise for sale.[30] It should be remembered that migration of Chinese, whether inside or outside China, was a centuries-old phenomenon where men took calculated risks as they invested their fortunes in a journey to supposedly greener pastures, leaving their families and the familiar for the unknown. In their frenzy to share in the fabulous profits of the California discovery, Chinese Gold Rushers in the 1850s were continuing this tradition, eager to try their luck whether as traders or gold diggers, or by taking on jobs as cooks, house-builders, domestic servants – jobs forsaken by white men seduced to gold fields, or jobs created by the new prosperity. Far from being helpless pawns or captives, as we are often led to believe, the Chinese migrants bound for California and Australia were active agents, making decisions about their movements on many levels and strategizing their economic futures.

That the character of the emigrants shaped the nature of the passenger trade is clearly reflected by the behaviour of the shipping operators towards them as *paying customers* whose satisfaction was a major concern. Naturally, satisfied customers on one voyage would most likely travel again on ships managed by the same operators on their return voyage and future voyages. They would provide free advertisement by spreading the word about the quality of service to other prospective passengers. We can get an idea of how much this weighed on the mind of shipowners from W.M.Robinet's letter to the captain of his ship, the *Convoy*, bound for California in 1852.

Captain Meyer was urged to treat the passengers with great care.[31] 'Be generous with the water: give them the full gallon each per day. Be generous with provisions too.' If unfamiliar with Chinese habits, he could consult 'the Chinaman Voong', who would show him how to serve provisions, and what the men ought to have each day. To ensure order on board, Robinet advised him to 'apoint (sic) heads among the Chinamen with whom you will always understand and so they will control the rest of the passengers'. Of course Robinet was wary of any unwanted incident on board, and keen to avoid lawsuits that passengers might bring against the company that arose out of quarrels between them and

the crew after arriving in America. Any disharmony on board would be unwelcome, so Robinet was most eager to cultivate good relations with passengers. If they arrived 'contented', he figured, Meyer might get 'certificate from them of having been well treated so as to be able to get a good name to carry passengers in future'. It is not known if Robinet's farsightedness paid off on this occasion or not, but the acknowledgement passengers gave to good service was clearly a matter of great import to the ships' operators.

The certification of appreciation that Robinet was so eager to obtain from passengers was in fact becoming a new convention. When the *Euphroayne* arrived in San Francisco in July 1851, its Chinese passengers, through a notice in the newspaper, *Alta California*, thanked the captain for his 'kind treatment' and 'gentlemanly conduct'. They considered him a great sailor and gentleman and recommended him to all their countrymen while pointing out that the ship was well supplied with every comfort and convenience.[32] In the same month, Captain Drew of the *Lebanon* was thanked in a newspaper notice by a committee of 250 of his Chinese passengers.[33] To grant such acknowledgement – or not to grant it – was surely a sign of the agency of the free emigrant.

The convention evolved. At the end of their voyage from Whampoa to San Francisco in June 1852, the *Balmoral*'s Chinese passengers honoured Captain Robertson with a 'splendid ring, made of California gold' while the masthead of the vessel flew a 'magnificent silk flag' with the inscription in Chinese characters:

Presented to J.B. Robertson by 464 of his Chinese passengers who have experienced much kindness and attention from him during the voyage from Kwangtung to the Golden Hill.

The Chinese aboard the American ship *Persia* expressed their gratitude with a flag, reading 'Gratification to our race – Presented to Captain M.M. Cook, by Leong, Assing and others'. The same appreciation was shown by

Cantonese travellers on the British ship *Australia* with an inscription on their pennant assuring the captain that everyone of them had 'found a friend in you'. At Hong Kong, in 1856, Captain E. Scudder of the clipper *Ellen Foster* received a handsome Canton crepe flag from his Chinese passengers for his kindness. The Chinese merchants of San Francisco complimented Captain Slate for transporting seven hundred Chinese emigrants to that port without a single case of sickness or death in the summer of 1857.[34]

No wonder the captains and crews often preferred sailing the Hong Kong-California and Hong Kong-Australia routes! For although they might have been paid more when sailing to Havana and Peru,[35] the former routes were much safer, not to mention more gratifying, for them. As the nineteenth century Hong Kong historian, E. J. Eitel, observed, frequent mutinies occurring on the 'coolie' ships caused British skippers to eschew the Peruvian route.[36] In some cases, violence on board broke out even while the ship was still in port and the police had to be called.[37]

This picture is confirmed by the British Consul in San Francisco in 1858, who compared conditions on ships bound for California and for the Tropics. He emphasized that captains and crews on California-bound voyages found the Chinese passengers well-behaved – 'the easiest managed of any' – and the co-operative atmosphere on board enabled the crew to keep the decks clean and disease-free. Though occasionally one or two passengers died from sickness or other causes, these deaths were isolated incidents and not the result of poor sanitary conditions on the ship. Emigrants destined for the West Indies, on the other hand, he explained, being generally put on board against their wishes, or thieves out of the jails, posed a constant threat to the crew who were convinced that they would 'combine and try to take every vessel'. With the crews too afraid to venture down between the decks to enforce sanitary regulations, the deck became like 'a common sewer, causing a high incidence of sickness and disease'.[38] It is clear from the foregoing that the passenger trade on the different routes constituted significantly different types of activity.

Return Passage

Another feature of the California and Australia traffic distinguishing it from the others was that it was two-way traffic right from the start. Many of the ships arriving in San Francisco turned around for Hong Kong as soon as they had unloaded their cargo of goods and passengers from China. We saw how the return of a few Chinese as early as 1851 with their fabulous earnings triggered off great frenzy among their countrymen.[39] Other returnees followed. Later in the year the *Kelso* arrived in Hong Kong in October with 30 Chinese passengers, the *North Carolina* arrived in November with 17; the following month, the *Regina* and the *Flying Cloud* arrived with 24 and 3 respectively.[40] In October 1853, the clipper *Gazelle* left San Francisco with 350 Chinese for Hong Kong.[41] Of the early returnees, some had made enough money to return home for good while others intended to proceed again to California after having spent new year with their family.[42]

By 1856, the Reverend Speer, who was doing pastoral work among the Chinese in San Francisco, claimed that according to his 'careful investigations' there were about 40,000 Chinese men and 3,000 women in America; 9,000 Chinese had returned and 1,400 had died. By 1868, the number of Chinese in the United States was estimated at 61,000 with 46,000 departures and 4,000 deaths.[43]

One peculiarity of the California and Australia migration was that migrants returned to their native place not only when they were alive, but even when dead, the urge to return being honoured postumously. The traditional Chinese ideal to be buried in one's native village was a dominant one that molded much of their social behaviour. The practice among Cantonese, and the overwhelming majority of Chinese in California *were* Cantonese, of secondary burial enabled the

134

repatriation of human remains whether in the form of 'whole bodies', bones or spirits.c Most frequently, bones of deceased migrants were exhumed a few years after primary burial, cleaned and re-coffined, and then returned through Hong Kong for secondary burial in the native village. Very early on, Chinese merchants in San Francisco organized associations for their fellow-regionals to provide various forms of welfare, and repatriating bones was one of the most highly valued of their activities. The coffins enclosing bones and bodies were sent as cargo, freight ranging mainly from $7 to $10.

The earliest reported cargo of Chinese bones was despatched in 1855. On 14 May that year, the American ship, *Sunny South*, left San Francisco for China carrying the remains of 70 Chinese.[44] By 1858, it was a common sight to see 'cargoes of dead Chinamen' being shipped at San Francisco. It was reported in a San Francisco newspaper that the *Asie* which sailed in early 1858 took no less than '400 dead Celestials – untombed from their temporary resting places, and packed away in the most mercantile manner at $7 each'.[45]

Of the many Chinese native-place associations in San Francisco, one of the earliest was the Changhoutang, which was organized by natives of Panyu county. It first sent home a batch of 258 coffins in 1863, along with 59 spirit boxes; in 1874 it sent 858 coffins and 24 spirit boxes, and again in 1887, 625 coffins and 3 spirit boxes.[46] The activity of this one association gives us some idea of the scale of the traffic when we consider the many others that were doing the same thing.

It is not known who first thought of organizing such large-scale shipments of bones/bodies but it was certainly, from a business point of view, a very enterprising idea. Shipping bones became a welcome source of income for ships returning to China, and it must have made considerable impact on the freight business, at least in terms of a regular source of revenue. In 1870, by which time Chinese labourers were recruited in huge numbers to work on the railways, 9,000 kg of bones, the remains of 1,200 Chinese railway workers 'blasting their way through the Sierra's granite' were shipped home.[47] That would have represented, at $10 each, $12,000 in freight. The repatriation of bones from Australia, Canada and later New Zealand,[48] was also on a considerable scale, and it seems that this traffic, undertaken for Chinese Gold Rushers, who had the resources, became a model for Chinese communities in Southeast Asia and Peru later in the nineteenth century.

Long-term Impacts of the Trans-Pacific Passenger Trade

Voyages linking Hong Kong and California thus became regular, years before the first passenger line was established by the Pacific Mail Steamship Company in 1867.[49] This regularity had many implications. It reflected the consistency of the departure of Chinese from China as much as their return. It must have been a source of comfort for those so far away from home to know that a return passage was a certainty – and that of course induced more emigrants to wish to go. The regularity of the to-and-fro-traffic, moreover, helped to consolidate Hong Kong's position as a major Pacific port, so that when the Pacific Mail Steamship Co's line was formed, it was Hong Kong that was selected as the China Terminal.

The Gold Rush passenger trade had come at a critical moment for Hong Kong. Up to 1850, as mentioned, it had depended very much on one single trade, opium, and was struggling with competition from the newly-opened Treaty Ports, especially Shanghai for commodity trade and Xiamen for passenger trade.[50] As a whole new field of activity, the California and Australia passenger trade boosted Hong Kong's status and economy significantly. Eitel observed that 'Hong Kong continued to be the port from which all South China passengers, able to pay their passage, preferred to embark for foreign countries'.[51] That Hong Kong was a safe embarkation port seems to be widely recognized.[52] Apart from the Chinese Passengers Act, which we will examine below, the Hong Kong government also sought to eradicate emigration-related abuses such as 'coolie' barracoons (which were allowed to exist in Macao) used to detain, and even imprison, prospective emigrants,[53] and this must have been another welcome sign reassuring safety. In other words, individuals who desired a safe passage to California and Australia and were their own free agents, would choose Hong Kong as the embarkation port, partly for the safety it promised. Though Macao and Whampoa also sent passengers to San Francisco in the early years, by the mid 1850s, it was Hong Kong that completely dominated the California and Australia passenger trade. Macao, on the other hand, took over the shipping of Chinese to Havana and Peru. As for Whampoa, the disturbances created by the Taiping rebels, the Red Turbans, and others in the mid 1850s and eventually the Arrow War, drove Chinese as well as foreign businesses to Hong Kong.[54]

By 1939, over 6 million Chinese emigrants had embarked at Hong Kong for foreign destinations. The colony was indisputably the primary port for Chinese emigration, and the Gold Rush passenger trade, by laying the foundation of Hong Kong's passenger trade, was clearly one of the keys to this development.

The passenger trade was important in other ways. On one level these new shipping routes added new markets for commercial concerns, increasing the opportunities for capitalists of all nationalities to invest in different capacities, as we shall see. It is easy too to think of the many employment opportunities provided by the wide range of services necessitated directly and indirectly by the ships. On another level, which may seem too obvious to be worth stating, these routes helped to sustain the Chinese diaspora. Not only did ships provide the physical means for Chinese to travel across the ocean, a regular shipping service also helped them maintain relationships with their families and villages, to enable periodic returns to impregnate wives, to pay respects to parents and ancestors, to conduct business and to maintain their stakes in the intricate webs of

interests in the home community.[55] Ships also enabled their final return, when they felt satisfied with their earnings, or when they were too old and exhausted to work further. Even when dead, as we have seen, these ships carried their bodies or bones back for final burial. The maintenance of a thick and regular trans-Pacific traffic helped to sustain the Chinese diaspora by keeping alive the bonds between the migrant and the homeland, with Hong Kong playing the main bridging role. In the 1850s, the connections were mainly with North America and Australia, but from the 1870s, they extended to Southeast Asia, Central and South America, and the Indian Ocean too.

Once Hong Kong became the dominant port for Chinese emigration, other developments followed. It became the primary channel for the millions of dollars that overseas Chinese remitted to their native villages. It became the supplier of Chinese products from dried shrimps and dried fish to prepared opium and Cantonese opera for overseas Chinese consumers. In fact, one of the most long-lasting consequences of this traffic was the so-called California Trade (in Chinese, it was known as the 'Gold Mountain Trade'), which covered import/export, remittances and money-changing, insurance and shipping businesses between Hong Kong and America (as well as Australia, despite its English name).[56] California Traders were among Hong Kong's wealthiest and most influential merchants, and their guild one of the most powerful. As Hong Kong became the hub of commercial information, personal communication, business contacts, political propaganda and other political activities, its fortune became intimately tied up with Overseas Chinese even as the latter became increasingly dependent on it.

In addition, the California and Australia connections were significant in the context of the emergence of Cantonese merchants, late comers to the overseas business arena. Up to the mid-nineteenth century, Chinese who were active abroad, whether as merchants, sailors, artisans or workers, were primarily from

Fujian province or from Chaozhou prefecture in eastern Guangdong province, and these groups dominated the Southeast Asian market.[57] The Hong Kong-based traffic to California started a new pattern in which migrants originated from the Pearl River Delta, especially from the counties in Guangzhou prefecture.[58] The trans-Pacific Cantonese networks centered on Hong Kong were multi-layered, encompassing the migrants themselves, ships' owners and charterers, passage brokers, importers/exporters, insurers, bankers, regional associations and others involved in countless different ways.[59] Since, after one ethnic group dominated a field, it was difficult for others to break in, the Cantonese dominance in the trans-Pacific region expanded in the latter half of the 19th century, bringing about the emergence of what we might call a 'Cantonese sphere of influence'. This was a landmark development in the history of Chinese emigration.

I have often mused on this question. What might have happened if the California Gold Rush had occurred in 1839 rather than 10 years later, when Hong Kong was still an almost unknown island dotted with fishing and farming villages, when China was still generally closed to the western world, and a free-port under a foreign flag on its doorstep did not exist? By being the right place at the right time, Hong Kong was poised to become the centre for China's overseas passenger trade for the next century.

Business Organization of the Passenger Trade
The passenger trade to California was universally regarded as a wonderful money-making opportunity for individuals and firms and for Hong Kong as a whole. In July 1852, the Hong Kong newspaper *Friend of China* marvelled at the amount of business to which it was giving rise:

> *We find that the trade between China and California during the present year that it has given employment to eighty two vessels, averaging five hundred tons each, a total tonnage of say 43,000; and supposing that*

the number of passengers will have been at the rate of one man to two tons (a low estimate on the whole) we have an aggregate of 21,500. This again multiplied by $50 the average amount of passage money, shows a sum of $1,075,000 or, in colonial currency, £234,000 for the half year. The net estimated ship earnings out of this is four fifths £187,200, or say for a five months voyage all around, four guineas per ton, fast ships, of course, doing better than slow ones.

With 6 ships still on the berth, the newspaper predicted that the total number of emigrants for the first half year ending June could be 'safely stated at 25,000'.[60]

Eitel had a more straightforward way of calculating the revenue. If each of the 30,000 Chinese who went in 1852 paid $50.00 each, the total revenue in passage money would be $1,500,000.[61] In comparison, the colonial government's total revenue for the same year was only $99,638.

The Friend of China also examined the ships involved in the trade according to their nationality.

Table showing tonnage of ships according to nationality [62]		
Nationality of ships	*Number of ships*	*Tonnage*
English	41	26,071
American	17	8,738
Bremen	4	1,370
Peruvian	2	1,169
Portuguese	5	1,038
French	1	700
Dutch	1	570
Norwegian	2	569
Chinese	2	488
Spanish	1	484
Prussian	1	450
Hamburg	1	280
Equadorian	1	243
Danish	1	173
Hawaiian	1	161
Swedish	1	150

In 1851, the newspaper had been appalled that of the 21 ships that sailed from Hong Kong to San Francisco only 6 were British while American shipping was doing so much better.[63] Possibly the Americans were able to have a headstart due to their familiarity with the Pacific Ocean, partly from the China trade conducted by Boston merchants across this Ocean since the early 19th century, and partly through the whaling business. But now, in July 1852, the *Friend of China* had the satisfaction of seeing that, with 41 out of the 82 ships being British, they were leading the trade once more.

Even the Chinese sent a Chinese ship to California. The *Kam Ty Lee* departed Hong Kong on 4 January 1852 under Captain Knudsden, but unfortunately it was forced to put back on the same day it set sail on account of head winds, and never seems to have made another attempt.[64] In fact, from all accounts, these routes were monopolized by Western ships commanded by Western captains sailing under Western nautical protocol, although in time growing numbers of Chinese joined the crews.[65] The employment of large numbers of Chinese seamen on Western ships is another important historical phenomenon which deserves serious study.

In some ways, it is irrelevant to analyse national interests by looking at the flag under which the ship was registered. Partly, as is generally known, ships were registered under different flags for a variety of reasons, including that of convenience. Another reason for not taking this too seriously is that on any voyage, there were so many different parties engaged in the venture that simply by looking at the flag of the ship, the picture is incomplete, as will be shown.

Investing in Passenger Shipping
When news of the discovery of gold became certain, merchants of all nationalities in Canton, Hong Kong and Macao responded quickly to the bonanza. Those with existing connections with America, especially California, naturally stood to benefit most. Bush & Co, for instance, owned by the American merchant F.T. Bush, who acted as American Consul in Hong Kong from 1847,

was the consignee/agent for at least 5 ships sailing for San Francisco in 1849.[66]

On the California side, Frederic W. Macondray, an American ship captain who had had wide experience in the China Sea sailing the ships of the Forbes family and Russell & Co, in the 1830s and 40s (he was in charge of Russell & Co's storeship for opium, *Lintin*, between 1836-1838) and had recently settled in San Francisco, became very active in the new traffic. He operated as a commission agent for ships and for goods from China while trading in his own rights; he also became a major charterer of passenger ships between California and Hong Kong.[67]

Some of the early charterers/chartering agents/ships' consignees in Hong Kong were small firms, such as Murrow & Co,[68] which was heavily engaged in the California and Australia passenger trade In 1855, Murrow & Co. was the agent for two ships for California – the *Leonore* carrying 170 passengers and the *Sting Ray*, taking 301 – and two for Australia – the *Elizabeth Ellen* taking 240 passengers and the *General Blanco* taking 320. In the following year, the firm was agent to the *Taskina* which took 300 passengers to Adelaide and the *Tartar* which took 378 to Sydney.[69]

A few big companies also engaged in the traffic, among them the British company, Jardine, Matheson & Co. In 1855, the firm was the agent for at least four ships carrying a total of 1,218 passengers to Australia.[70] Among American firms, the biggest in China, Russell & Co, and Augustine Heard & Co, were active.[71] These and other companies acted as agents of ships, regardless of the nationality of the ships, chartering them to any destination, at least theoretically, to the highest bidder, regardless also of nationality.

One good example of this complexity of 'national' interests is the chartering of the *Caribbean* on a voyage to California in 1858. The agent for the vessel and captain was Jardine, Matheson & Co. The ship was chartered by Wohang, a Chinese merchant, whose Hong Kong agent was Russell & Co. In San Francisco, his agent was Macondray & Co.

and his broker was another American company, Edward & Balley.[72] The passenger trade from Hong Kong to America and Australia was truly an international business where different communities of merchants shared the profits and the risks.

Hong Kong's open port status certainly contributed to this cosmopolitanism. There was very little government interference in matters such as registration of ships. Registers were proofs of the nationality of vessels at the port and issued as such. Foreigners were permitted to own any kind of vessel and to employ them in any trade. The only constraint was the terms agreed upon by the parties in the bill of sales – a purely private contractual affair. Chinese inhabitants of Hong Kong possessing certain qualifications and finding security could obtain British register and sailing letters for vessels. There was no distinction between foreign, and British, built vessels[73] as far as the use of the port was concerned. These characteristics all made for a free, and free-wheeling, market.

The Chinese came in very strongly in this trade, as might be expected since most of the passengers were Chinese. As early as 1849, Kwanglee Hong was advertising itself in the newspaper as a broker for passage from Hong Kong to California,[74] and ever since then, Chinese brokers dominated the field. In the early days, it was common for a passage broker in Hong Kong to send out his agents to the mainland, and these on the payment of about $5 as bargain money gave to each prospective passenger a 'bargain ticket', sealed with the seal of the broker they acted for. With the ticket, the prospective passenger proceeded to Hong Kong, most probably by junk, where by showing the 'bargain ticket' and paying the balance of the passage money, he secured a passage to California. This was risky, of course, and there were cases where the broker received a shipload of passengers before ever a ship had been chartered or bought for the supposed voyage; or, as we shall find, he simply absconded.[75] But the gold fever was so intense that many felt the risk worth taking, and passage brokering thrived.

Chinese entrepreneurs also chartered ships for these routes, as we have seen, and even bought ships from European/American owners and employed European/American captains to run the ships for them. One of the first Chinese-owned ships to arrive in San Francisco was the *Hamilton*, which arrived in June 1, 1853.[76]

Some Chinese financed the front-players from behind the scene. For example, Tam Achoy, one of the wealthiest men in the new colony, was ready to finance charterers and individual passengers alike.[77] Chinese financiers were equally ready to lend money to foreigners, as in the case of Cheong Ahoy's loans to McCormick to buy and fix up the *Emma*. The *Emma*, formerly the *Countess of Seafield*, was towed from Pratas Shoal in 1855, sold by public auction in Whampoa and bought by a Mr. McCormick for around $3,000. Cheong first advanced him $1,000 to put the vessel in order. When the vessel was near ready, a further loan of over $5,000 was made to him.[78] Many levels of financial relationship between Chinese and foreign merchants had developed since the old 'Canton days' by which they made loans to each other – sometimes at usurious rates – and deposited funds with each other,[79] and the California passenger trade became only one more arena for such transactions.

On the San Francisco front, Chinese entrepreneurs were equally aggressive. In October 1853, A Choo chartered the clipper *Gazelle* for $8000; Captain Dolland and his American crew returned 350 Chinese to Hong Kong on A Choo's account.[80] Impressed by Chinese enterprise, and rather envious of it, the *Alta California* wrote:

> *Since the commencement of the trade between California and China, the latter people have imbibed some of our commercial ideas, and enter into maritime transactions with considerable alacrity...the Chinese merchants charter and freight vessels with the same spirit as the foreign merchant houses at Hong Kong.*[81]

Profits

Stories of huge returns in the passenger trade created excitement on both sides of the Pacific. The profits made on the *Potomac* in 1854, for instance, were made much of by the *Alta California*. A ship of 450 tons, the *Potomac* had been purchased in San Francisco by Mou Kee for about $5,000. The new owner spent ten thousand dollars on repairs and alterations, transforming 'an old hulk into a good ship'. At Hong Kong, she was subsequently sold for some $15,000. In the meantime, an extra deck was added to the vessel, and in a single voyage, 500 emigrants were taken on it to San Francisco, representing passage money to the tune of $37,000.[82]

To further illustrate the immense profits that were made, or expected to be made, we can refer to the *Libertad*, another foreign ship bought by a Chinese, Chook Sing, for the San Francisco route in 1854. The purchasing price for the Chilean barque was $30,000. She was expected to carry 536 passengers. In fact, she loaded 200 passengers at the rate of $52 and another 200, at shorter notice, at $62. This made a total of $23,800, so that the actual amount that Chook Sing needed to put up front was a mere $6,200! Even considering the many outgoings – provisions, water, crew wages, port facility charges, etc – that the owner would eventually have to make toward the voyage, it would still mean a very good return for the investment. Unfortunately, in this case at least, the profit did not materialize due to a fall-out between the owner and the captain, Captain Lund, who claimed that Chook Sing had not paid the balance of the purchasing amount as agreed, and therefore had forfeited the first payment of $2,000. Lund, as a result, took the ship out of Hong Kong harbour with 400 passengers on board, and their passage money as well. Before he could get away, however, he was arrested by the Vice-Admiral's man-of-war, as Chook Sing brought a lawsuit against him.

In fact, as in many other business ventures, while the profits were high, so were the risks, and the passenger business could go wrong in many ways.

But so long as the market was strong, ship owners and their agents could call the tune, as shown in the following case. In February 1856, J.Y. Murrow had started preliminary negotiations with Captain Dawson of the *Cornwall* to charter the vessel for a voyage to Adelaide for $12,000 or £3,000. The rate would be for passenger capacity only, i.e. the entire between-decks, about 12 feet of the poop, and the privilege of extending the poop some 22 feet. It was understood that the charterer would have the use for the voyage of all fittings and spare casks on board but to provide everything else. One third of the rate would be payable on signing the charter and the remainder before sailing.[83]

In the meantime, however, a better chartering offer came along, for the vessel to sail for Adelaide and Port Philip for $15,000 to carry emigrants and cargo, and the ship's agent, Jardine, Matheson & Co, decided that Murrow's offer of $12,000 was no longer good enough. Before closing the latter deal, however, it went back to Murrow to see if he would be willing to raise his offer for the passenger capacity to $12,800. Murrow decided to back out of the deal, lamenting that he could not compete with an offer that combined cargo and passengers.[84] In fact, with the atmosphere so frenzied, such haggling was a commonplace.[85] Of course, there were low seasons too, when the cost of chartering, passage and freight all fell accordingly, to the dismay of many.

Financing voyages

The financial aspect of the passenger trade was closely linked to the emerging import/export trade as well as to the many forms of remittances Chinese made from abroad. Increasingly, as the volume of trade between Hong Kong and these destinations – California, Australia, Canada and later Southeast Asia – grew, charterers were able to secure their payment for the charter through the sale of cargo they put on the ships. An excellent example of such a financial arrangement is demonstrated by the relationship between Charles Ryberg and

Augustine Heard & Co. Between 1863 and 1865, Ryberg chartered several ships from San Francisco to Hong Kong, regularly employing the firm as his Hong Kong agent/consignee. Right from the start, Ryberg tied his trading interests to shipping interests. The first ship he chartered was the *Derby*; he shipped wheat on it, consigning the cargo to the Chinese merchant Kwong Cheong Lung. He instructed Augustine Heard & Co.:

> *You will please to draw on them [Kwong Cheong Lung] to disburse the ship, the captain to be paid $3,000 according to charter. They will draw their own commission and expenses. Should there be any passengers on the ship you may advance the passage money on any goods shipped on board.*[86]

Thereafter, Ryberg regularly told Augustine Heard & Co to use the money it could collect from passage, inward freight or proceeds from sale of cargo on his own account to pay for various expenses connected with the charter, such as the consignee's commission and stevedoring, tugboats, surveying and other charges.

Like many other charterers, Ryberg also bought cargo in Hong Kong for sale in San Francisco with the proceeds of the Hong Kong-bound voyage, and besides Augustine Heard & Co, a number of Chinese merchants did this on his behalf as well. Rice was one of the main exports from Hong Kong to America, and at times the most profitable, no doubt as a result of the great demand for it among the growing Chinese populations there. Thus we find Ryberg on several occasions urging Augustine Heard & Co to buy 'Number 1 China Rice' for him and send it on the first available ship sailing for California.[87]

In turn, lumber, wheat and flour were the largest bulk exports from California and other West Coast ports. Ryberg started sending lumber on a small, experimental basis in 1863, and he wrote to Augustine Heard & Co.:

> *I have chartered the ship 'Midnight' for Hong Kong, and as I required some dunnage*

> *I have bought a small invoice of lumber which you will receive and dispose of. You will deduct the expense and commission and whatever balance there may be in your hands you will please transfer to Kong Chu Long as he has orders to buy goods for the ship 'Derby'.*[88]

The volume grew phenomenally. In April 1864, Ryberg sent 100,000 ft of lumber by the *Arracan* which he chartered, and another 100,000 ft by the *Oracle* a few months later.[89] In December that year, he sent 7-800 tons of flour and wheat on the *Midnight*.[90]

The passenger trade was therefore a great source of cash and credit that could facilitate many other transactions, and in turn, it was greatly dependent on other forms of trade and a wide range of commodities. These financial facilities, so vital in maximizing investment opportunities, became an integral part of the infrastructure for Hong Kong's passenger trade, an infrastructure that enhanced Hong Kong's special advantages as a centre for both passenger and cargo traffic.

Charles Ryberg apparently was able to thrive partly because of the very good relationships he enjoyed with Chinese merchants both in San Francisco and Hong Kong. At the time that he entered the chartering business, Koopmanschap & Co was one of the most active American firms in the chartering business, but as many of the San Francisco China houses were 'displeased' with that firm, Ryberg was urged by them 'to start an opposition'.[91] Being able to tap into the trans-Pacific network of Chinese firms was a great asset for him. He kept in close contact with Chinese firms and merchants in Hong Kong who kept him regularly informed of market situations. They assisted him in finding passengers, and one of his most trusted passage brokers was Cum Cheong Tye, an 'old friend' who was also a major charterer in his own right.[92] This was why, when Ryberg first approached Augustine Heard & Co, he was able to assure it of 'fast sale' of passage. He apparently knew many long-time Chinese merchants in San Francisco, including another 'old friend' of his, Ah Mook, who had been there since 1849. Ah Mook, who had a great deal of influence among the Chinese, was also Ryberg's business partner, so that when he returned to Hong Kong in 1865, Ryberg's Chinese contacts in Hong Kong were strengthened.[93] Keeping standing accounts with a number of Chinese firms, Ryberg instructed Augustine Heard & Co that any time his funds with it ran low, it could draw on these firms. These trans-Pacific networks, whether among Chinese and foreigners, among Chinese themselves, or foreigners themselves, and most of the time, it was an intricate mixture of all three, were the keystone to Hong Kong-California commercial interaction and they became extremely powerful over time.

In fact, at one point, Ryberg even entertained hopes of organizing a company with Chinese merchants to run a permanent passenger line between San Francisco and Hong Kong. He discussed the matter with Augustine Heard & Co, asking about commissions it would charge him to procure passengers etc, while not forgetting to remind it to make its terms as low as possible.[94] However, a permanent line was never established by him and his Chinese friends, and when one did come about in 1867, it was operated by the Pacific Mail Steamship Company.

Interestingly too, Ryberg's rivalry with Koompanschap & Co did not seem to have done the latter unnecessary damage. Nor did the rivalry last. Koopmanschap & Co continued to be active in the business, and in 1865, Ryberg even co-chartered two ships for Hong Kong with this firm, the *Marmion* in April and the *Sacramento* in October.[95]

The California/Australia passenger trade was of course not all rosy. Even though it was very profitable, and devoid of much of the violence, abuses and fraud that pervaded the indentured labour trade, serious problems did arise. These problems are illustrated in the case of the *Sultana*.

The **Sultana** case[96]

In April 1852, a British Ship, *Sultana* of Bombay, owned by a Parsee merchant, Kamesa H. Ahmed, was contracted to take passengers to California for a sum of $25,000, with a clause for demurrage after the rate of $200 per diem, and a penalty of $8,000 if the charter was violated. $18,500 was paid in Guangzhou by Yung Hee, the charterer, to Kamesa, with the remaining $6-7,000 yet to be paid. By early July, 570 passengers had boarded, but the charterer absconded, and naturally the ship's captain refused to go.

The passengers were the main victims, of course, but the shipowner and captain, were in an unenviable position themselves. One problem was that the ship was not only due to carry passengers; it was also committed to taking cargo. Being the one who had signed the bills of lading, Rice, the ship's master, was sued for the delay by Murrow, Stephenson & Co, shippers of the cargo, and sent to jail. In the end, the shippers complained so bitterly about the filth the passengers were causing to their cargo that Kamesa had to purchase it out and out. As the passengers, who were allowed by the owner to stay on board, became increasingly agitated about their fate, they became a source of fear for the crew. The Captain himself, fearing for his life, refused to sleep on board

Despite an attempt by several of the 'headmen' of the passengers to raise enough money to make a second contract with the owner so that the ship would sail, after much haggling and mismanagement, this deal fell through too, and the passengers were forced off the ship. A long legal battle ensued, with the passengers desperately trying to retrieve at least some of the passage money they had paid as well as compensation for loss of personal effects during the fracas when they were thrown off. One of the passengers, Koo Ahee, for example, besides losing his $63 passage money, also lost a box which contained clothing, money and bedding worth $25, plus $25 in cash to pay his expenses upon landing in California. Some of the passengers, having lost everything and unable to return to their native village, committed suicide.

Most of the passengers were unable to claim anything back due to the fact that the Hong Kong courts could not reach Kamesa who decided to remain in Guangzhou. In desperation, they wrote to the Governor of Hong Kong, hoping he would intercede, but to no avail. They tried to sue Rawle, Drinker & Co, the ship's agent, but this firm did not take over the management of the ship until 42 days after the charterer absconded and had not handled any of the money, and therefore could not be held responsible. The case was finally dismissed in January, 1853 leaving everyone, except the charterer, frustrated and out of pocket.

The passengers were certainly, in most cases, victims, but not always at the hands of an absconding charterer. In fact, just around the time of the *Sultana* case, another vessel, the *Sultan* refused to let four of its ticketed passengers on board, claiming that the ship was already full, and intended to sail off without them. Taking the charterer's agent to court, the passengers were able to reclaim their passage money and maintenance, but not the personal effects and money that they alleged to be on board.[97]

The Chinese Passengers Act

The emigration trades might be lucrative, but the grave abuses they gave rise to prompted various parties in Britain to attack the inhumanity involved. As political activists harangued the London government, often equating the 'coolie trade' with the slave trade, British Consuls on the China coast were made to report on the conditions of the trade, especially the notoriously barbarous traffic from Xiamen to Havana. Pressure on the London government to introduce regulations increased, but in Hong Kong, support for free trade, i.e. no government interference, was strong.

Up to late 1853, when the Home government finally applied the Imperial Passengers Act to all the colonies, the only

legal restraint Hong Kong shippers faced was the American Passenger Act of 1848, which mainly aimed at regulating ventilation, cleanliness, and number of passengers.[98] This Act was rarely enforced, and there were shocking cases of violation that got dismissed by the court, as Gunther Barth and Robert Schwendinger point out.[99] Ships' captains and owners, however, were not unmindful of the law's existence and tried to comply with it, however half-heartedly. At least most of the time, they tried not to break it too brazenly. For instance, when Robinet shipped ten passengers over the legal limit on the *Convoy* in 1852, he took care to remind Captain Meyer that they should be reported as crew members. Moreover, Meyer should make sure that when surveyors came on board in San Francisco they not only measured the between-decks but also the orlop deck so as to maximize the deck space for calculation. Meyer was also instructed to persuade the inspectors of the 'light and good ventilation of the area'. As a fall back, if he judged it necessary 'to give small sum to pass' then he was authorized to go ahead and pay the bribe.[100]

Likewise, Charles Ryberg, when discussing the possibility of chartering a ship from Hong Kong to San Francisco in 1864, reminded Augustine Heard & Co of the legal restrictions. The number must not be exceeded, he wrote, 'as I think the officials will be rather strict this summer'.[101] Thus the Act did to some extent serve as a deterrent to reckless overloading. American legislation in the late 1850s also succeeded in tightening the enforcement of the Act. The objective, however, in this case was not to improve passenger conditions but to limit Chinese immigration.

Hong Kong's merchants met the Imperial Passenger Act with dismay. In broad brush, this Act regulated the fitness of ships, the number of passengers and the quantity of provisions, and required the inclusion of a surgeon, medicines and medical instruments on a voyage. The number of passengers was limited both by tonnage and space: one person to every two tons and 15 clear superficial feet;

regulations governing the use of deck-space could be interpreted as making it illegal to carry passengers in the orlop deck. Governor Bonham, writing to the Colonial Office, made it clear that even though he had proclaimed the Act in compliance with London's orders, he could not strictly enforce it, for if he did, all the ships would resort to other ports. This, he warned, would mean the worst of both worlds – the ships would be beyond any interference by British authorities and Hong Kong's business would suffer.[102]

In the meantime, however, the government of Victoria, Australia, which, as a colony, was also subject to the Act, responded more positively to it, and by 1855, it was enforcing the Act with great enthusiasm, fining several captains whose ships carried more Chinese passengers from Hong Kong than it allowed.[103] According to some, this vigour was a measure to limit the number of Chinese immigrants, now seen as a 'calamity' by the citizens of Melbourne.[104] In one extreme case, the *Alfred*, according to Melbourne's Acting Immigration Officer, left Hong Kong carrying $192^1/_2$ persons over the legal limit according to the passenger-to-tonnage ratio, and his scathing charges against the incompetence of Hong Kong's Emigration Officer for allowing this to happen led to some acrimonious correspondence between the two governments.[105]

Amid the general opposition to the Act, one man in the Hong Kong government who did support it was William Caine, the Lieutenant Governor. As soon as Governor Bonham left Hong Kong at the expiration of his term, Caine wrote to the Colonial Office in May 1854 to criticize Bonham's inaction, exposing the many abuses of the trade that needed immediate action. Seeing it as the only way to put the emigration trade under at least a modicum of control, he appointed the Chief Police Magistrate, J.W. Hillier, to act as Emigration Officer[106] to enforce the Imperial Passengers Act. But Caine himself soon realized that the Act was 'unnecessarily stringent', and he wrote to the Colonial Office to explain why certain stipulations were not strictly observed.[107] In

doing so, he was in fact reflecting the most determined objections among Hong Kong's merchants.

In a letter to the Colonial Secretary in January 1855, several of the leading firms aired their grievances against the Imperial Passenger Act. While they conceded that specified and proper regulations for the protection of the emigrants were necessary, in classic style, they dismissed the Act as 'proverbially inapplicable' to Hong Kong. They were pleased that in the past, the Emigration Officer had exercised 'a wise discretion', but made it clear that they objected to more rigorous enforcement of the provisions in the future. In particular, they objected to rating a ship's passenger capacity according to her tonnage. With different nations using different ways to measure tonnage, this method was arbitrary – the difference in tonnage arrived at could amount to as much as 40 or 50% – and open to dispute. In view of this, the merchants suggested, the clear deck room forming the apartment for passenger accommodation should be the only basis for deciding passenger capacity. To the authors of the letter, the crux of the matter was this: if there were such strict limitations of numbers imposed in Hong Kong, the port would be unable to compete with adjacent ports *not* subject to the Passengers Act, from which more passengers could be freely carried.

Another anomaly in the Act, they pointed out, was the medicine chest it specified:

An European medicine chest is perfectly superfluous in a Chinese emigrant ship as the Chinese much prefer their own. The surgical instruments specified in the Hong Kong proclamation of December 1853 are also useless unless a surgeon accompanies them, neither one nor the other being procurable.

They claimed that the ships they had sent to California and Australia had delivered their emigrants with so few casualties that they had no hesitation in stating that out of many thousands of emigrants, the deaths had not amounted to $^1/_2$ per cent.[108]

The Governor forwarded these and other criticisms of the Act to the Colonial Office, which, after much deliberation, finally decided that 'an ordinance framed on the spot would work far better in Hong Kong than an Imperial Law which has been gradually moulded into its present shape by experience derived from English ports'.[109] Thus, the Chinese Passengers Act was enacted in December 1855, and proclaimed in Hong Kong in early 1856.[110] According to it, as far as Hong Kong was concerned, all ships carrying more than 20 Chinese passengers from Hong Kong on voyages longer than 7 days' duration were required to obtain clearance from the Emigration Officer. Only when he was satisfied that every provision had been fulfilled could the ship leave port with his certification.

The Act clearly made a number of concessions to the merchants. The orlop deck issue, which they had complained about on many occasions, was resolved by its omission. Measurement to determine number of passengers was to be based entirely on deck area not tonnage.[111] In addition, each Chinese passenger was allowed only 12 superficial feet rather than 15 feet, as allowed in the Imperial Act, thus increasing significantly the carrying capacity of any vessel.

One addition in this Act was to require the Emigration Officer to interview each passenger before sailing to ensure that he understood the terms of the contract, if any, and that he knew what the ship's destination was. Such a measure was obviously aimed at the worst abuses of the contract labour trade, such as kidnapping and decoying, and however apathetic the Emigration Officer might be when administering it, it did add to Hong Kong's general safety as an embarkation port. The Chinese Passengers Act was clearly a compromise between the British government's need to uphold humanitarian principles on the one hand, and the need to enable the employment of cheap labour for its colonies, maintain Hong Kong's prosperity and keep British shipping competitive, on the other.

Before they had time to digest the implications of the Act and the concessions made, some shippers in Hong Kong reacted to it by fleeing, by taking their ships out of the harbour. But some of them were seized in port by the Rear-Admiral's ships and charged.

The *Levant*, a Hawaiian ship, chartered by Cheong Ahoy for Australia, was one such ship. When he realized that new rules would apply, he decided to despatch his ship with its load of passengers from Macao, which was *under* 7 days' voyage away. But the Governor heard of its intention to go to Australia, and the ship was seized.

The Friend of China was appalled by the whole episode. It felt sorry for the passengers of the *Levant* who were trapped in Hong Kong and loitering about on shore. They had lost at least half a year's earnings in passage money, and, the newspaper observed in May, three months after the seizure, that even if the vessel was allowed to sail 'tomorrow', she would be unable to make her voyage against the changed monsoon. It sympathized with Cheong Ahoy and criticized the high-handedness of the government which imposed a fine of 100 pounds for the ship's 'apparent *intended* evasion of the law.' Nor was that all. The newspaper estimated that other court charges would amount to £300 or £400 sterling at the least, while the crew's wages during the three months' detention could not be less than $2,000. Add to this over $3,000 of provisions eaten by detained passengers or spoilt and the loss of the vessel's services, the 'total infliction' would be about $10,000 – the outside value of the vessel herself.[112]

Other ships evaded the law by under-reporting the number of passengers, and though they managed to clear the port 'legally', immense scandals broke out when the truth was discovered. One stark example was the *John Calvin*, which was certified leaving Hong Kong in 1856 with 81 passengers on board, and yet when it arrived in Havana, 110 emigrants were reported to have died! Another offender in the same year was the *Duke of Portland* which left with 332 emigrants, and arrived in Havana 150 days later with 128 passengers fewer, these having died of fever or committed suicide. Interestingly, when *John Calvin*'s captain was judged guilty and fined £1,000 by Hong Kong's Attorney-General, the major firms, including Jardine, Matheson & Co., Dent & Co., Gibb, Livingston and Gilman – but not Lyall, Still & Co, the charterer – jointly petitioned the Secretary of State for the Colonies to remit the penalty, and it was reduced to £50 as a result.[113] Such a combination of commercial forces shows clearly that there were vital common interests to be defended.

The British government, embarrassed by the international outcry and worried that such tragedies would further discourage much-needed Chinese labourers from going to the West Indies, put pressure on Hong Kong to enforce the Act more firmly. In addition, as we saw, the Hong Kong government acted promptly to eradicate any barracoon that was uncovered. As a consequence the passenger trade to Peru and Havana disappeared from Hong Kong almost completely to concentrate in Macao instead. Now that associations with the abuse-ridden indentured labour trade were being gradually eradicated, free emigrants must have felt more confident when choosing Hong Kong as the port to embark for California or Australia, and on their way home, the port to disembark.

Things also improved with the regulation of brokers. One of the worst problems in the trade, dishonest passage brokers, was not addressed by the Chinese Passengers Act, and it took another two years before a local ordinance was passed to deal with it. Under this ordinance, no person was to act as a passage broker without having entered into a bond and obtained a licence. In 1857, the bond was fixed at $5,000.[114] This might have created dissatisfaction among charterers and owners of vessels, but it represented much needed protection for passengers, and in the long run helped to further enhance Hong Kong's reputation as a safe emigrant port. There was another important effect. The requirement for brokers to obtain security and a licence in Hong Kong, thus making Hong Kong's

brokers more creditable, at least in principle, might have further drawn the business from Guangzhou and Whampoa.

The tussle between the Home government and the Hong Kong government continued, with the Colonial Office from time to time introducing new strictures which the Hong Kong Legislative Council, whose unofficial members were all merchants with shipping interests, struggled to resist. For example, in 1858, the Colonial Office introduced a provision for hospital accommodation on board; the Legislative Council accepted this, but made it possible through a local ordinance to allow the space appropriated for the hospital to be included in the measurement of the capacity for passengers.[115] In other words, the inclusion of a hospital would not reduce the number of passengers to be carried.

Another point that the Hong Kong merchants were keen to revise was the provision for a surgeon on board. In view of the local realities, they felt it would make more sense to employ a Chinese medical practitioner and carry a different scale of medicines and surgical instruments.[116] They argued that English or American surgeons were hard to find, but the implication it seems was that Chinese doctors were cheaper.[117] In any case, a Chinese doctor was perfectly adequate, claimed George Lyall, a British merchant active in shipping, at a Legislative Council meeting in 1858.

> *Where a Chinese medical practitioner* only *had been in charge on a Free Passengers Ship to and from California and Australia,* [he explained] *the average number of deaths has been but one in a thousand.*[118]

It was also likely that the Chinese, who generally had greater faith in Chinese doctors and Chinese medicine, preferred this arrangement too.[119] The provision for a Chinese doctor (as a substitute when an English one could not be employed) was finally made in Ordinance 12 of 1868.[120]

Given the general apathy and inefficiency of Hong Kong's emigration officers in the nineteenth century and the many vested interests in the business, the Chinese Passengers Act, along with its later amendments, fell far short of perfect enforcement. And yet, on the whole, apart from some outrageous cases of violation, it did provide a modicum of protection and safety all round. There were captains who kept scrupulously to the letter of the law. For example Captain Winchester of the *Caribbean*, whom we encountered earlier, despite pressure from the charterer, refused to carry more passengers than permitted, realizing that now, with the Act in place, things were different.[121] Moreover, prospective emigrants, at least the literate ones, were able to read for themselves in the newspapers and *Government Gazette* the provisions of the ordinances. Even though justice in Hong Kong was often meted out arbitrarily,[122] it must have been comforting for emigrants to know that such laws existed and that they had recourse to them. It must have provided a sense of certainty for those facing a long journey filled with uncertainties, and persuaded them to make Hong Kong the embarkation/disembarkation port of their choice.

Caine was right, after all, in predicting that legal strictures might drive some of the business away, and 'Yet it may well be doubted whether the additional protection and comfort afforded to the passenger by an effective surveillance will not render the colony more attractive to emigrants'.[123] Both because of *and* despite the law, the Gold Rush passenger trade remained rooted in Hong Kong and became the basis for the development of other routes and a range of auxiliary activities.[124] On balance, it is fair to say that legislation saved the passenger business from its worst excesses and ended up enabling it to function more effectively and vibrantly.

Conclusion

The California Gold Rush changed the world. As one of the most recent books on the subjects claims, it was a 'seminal event in history, one of those rare moments that divided human existence as before and after'.[125]

The Gold Rush changed Hong Kong's history too. When it was first annexed as a British colony, few would have imagined that its prosperity would one day rest, in large part, on the traffic of tens of thousands of Chinese leaving their homes to travel across the oceans, and on their way back. Pottinger might have wished Hong Kong to be a great entrepot of goods, but he would never have envisioned it as an entrepot of people.

The Gold Rush came at a fortuitous moment, and the passenger trade it engendered played a definitive role in Hong Kong's history. The Island had a few basic advantages, including its fine harbour, its free port status and its closeness to the Pearl River Delta, but merchants of all nationalities combined to seize the moment, capitalizing on the advantages to make Hong Kong a commercially effective emigrant port. Legislation, although vigorously contested by the mercantile community at first, proved to be another key ingredient in the infrastructure of a great port, an infrastructure with its legal, administrative, financial, commercial, political and social aspects. The passenger trade, enmeshed in a dense and multi-layered web of commercial interests, personal and familial ties and cultural ideals, became a major catalyst in Hong Kong's development. In terms of Chinese migration, it provided the physical link to give coherence to the Chinese diaspora, beginning with the Cantonese communities in the Old and New Gold Mountains and later assuming global dimensions and thus helping to centre the colony in the Overseas Chinese world. In more general terms, emerging at a crucial juncture of Hong Kong's history to lay the foundations, the Gold Rush passenger trade played a vital but much overlooked role in Hong Kong's evolution as an international hub and world city.

Notes and references

1   William Speer, *The Oldest and the Newest Empire:China and the United States*, (Cincinnati, 1870), 2 vols, Vol 1, 486; Henry Anthon Jr., Vice-

Consul to Peter Parker, Chargé d'Affaires for the United States, Canton 25 March 1852 in *The United States and China Series I. The Treaty System and the Taiping Rebellion, 1841-1860*, (Wilmington, 1973-) 21 Vols, Vol 17, *The Coolie trade and Chinese Emigration*, 151-2.

2   Bonham to Newcastle, 13 June 1853, #44 in *Hong Kong Blue book 1852, 130-39 and 136-7*. The Hong Kong government did not keep very accurate records of emigrants partly because of general negligence and inefficiency. Up to 1856 when the Chinese Passengers Act was enforced, there was no need for inspection of ships or to report on their passengers and even after its enactment, a certain amount of under-reporting by ships' captains was common. Speer's figure for 1852 was 'over 18,000' (Speer, 486) and the figure given by Persia Campbell Crawford, quoting Governor Low of California was 20,000; Persia Campbell Crawford, *Chinese Coolie Immigration*, (London, 1923), 34.

3   Many works have been written about Chinese migration, but Kenneth Pomeranz in *The Great Divergence: China, Europe and the Making of the Modern World Economy*, (Princeton and Oxford, 2000) puts it in a global context, making the story all the more fascinating.

4   The interesting thing is while many books have been written about Chinese emigrants in America, almost nothing has been written about how they got there and the ramification of the passage. One exception is Russell Conwell, who provides a charming eye-witness account of the process in *How and Why the Chinese Emigrate, and the Means they Adopted for the Purpose of Reaching America* (Boston and New York, 1871) but he does not deal with the business organization involved. Some works such as Corinne K. Hoexter, *From Canton to California: The Epic of Chinese Immigration* (New York, 1976) do not mention Hong Kong at all. Gunther Barth's *Bitter Strength: A History of the Chinese in the United States* (Cambridge, Mass, 1984) which is a very detailed study, does provide much information about the ships but does not do so in the context of Hong Kong's development. Besides he is too anxious to condemn the barbarity of the emigration, especially of those who exploited the emigrants, or opposed their entry into America, to provide an objective picture of what was going on. Michael Hunt, *in The Making of A Special Relationship: The United States and China to 1914* (New York, 1983)

discusses the business ties between Chinese and American merchants that played a role in the emigration, but he provides few details about the passenger trade, and the discussion is framed in the context of Sino-American relations. Robert J. Schwendinger's *Ocean of Bitter Dreams: Maritime Relations Between China and the United States, 1850-1915*, (Tucson, Arizona, 1988) provides some interesting insights on the passage, but tends to overgeneralize and is rather careless on details, especially in his eagerness to demonstrate what a bad deal the Chinese emigrants were getting.

5   Bush to Webster, April 11 1851: Despatches from US Consuls in Hong Kong, 1844-1906.

6   Bowring to William Molesworth, 6 October 1855: #147 Great Britain, Colonial Office Series 129. 'Original Correspondence, Hong Kong' [hereafter CO129]/52, 108-114.

7   Bowring to Edward B. Lytton, 22 October 1858: #141, CO129/69, 332-336. By this system, the emigrant paid a fraction of the ticket money to a broker and then repaid the outstanding sum over a period of time.

8   Barth, *Bitter Strength*, 68.

9   Minutes of Meetings of the Legislative Council, *Friend of China*, 20 October 1858.

10 *Hong Kong Register*, 28 September 1848.

11 *Friend of China*, 6 January 1849.

12 *Friend of China*, 13 December 1848.

13 *Alta California*, 6 January 1851.

14 *The Friend of China* predicted in 1849 that making houses in frame for San Francisco would become Hong Kong's main industry. (*Friend of China*, 19 December 1849); Bonham to Newcastle, 13 June 1853, #44 in *Hong Kong Blue book 1852, 130-39 and 136-7*.

15 Speer, *The Oldest*, 486.

16 *Alta California*, 9 May, 1851.

17 *Xia'er Guanzhen*, Volume 1: 1 (1853).

18 Eitel, *Europe*, 273.

19 Eitel, *Europe*, 274.

20 Elizabeth Sinn, 'Emigration from Hong Kong Before 1941: General Trends' in Ronald Skeldon (ed),. *Emigration From Hong Kong: Tendencies and Impacts*, (Hong Kong, 1995), 11-34.

21 Caine to Newcastle, 4 May 1854: #11 CO 129/46, 16-22.

22 Speer, *The Oldest*, 487.

23 Anthon to Parker in *The United States and China*, Vol 17, 151-2.

24 *Alta California*, 28 June 1854, reprinted in *Friend of China*, 23 August 1854.

25 George Lyall, Minutes of the Meeting of the Legislative Council, *Friend of China*, 20 October 1858.

26 See Felipe Fernandez Armesto (ed), *The Global Opportunity*, (Aldershot and Brookfield, Vt, 1995) for descriptions of Chinese ships and migration in earlier centuries.

27 See Sinn, 'Emigration from Hong Kong'.

28 See Robert Irick, *Ch'ing Policy Toward the Coolie Trade, 1847-1878*, (Taipei, 1982) for a very detailed study of the trade to Havana and Peru; for the Chinese in Peru, see Watt Stewart, *Chinese Bondage in Peru: A History of the Chinese Coolies in Peru 1849-1876*, (Westport, Conn:, 1970). According to one gory account, when Chinese labourers working on the guano islands of Peru died, they were simply left to rot amid the bird droppings, and when the guano was sold, their rotten remains were sold along with it! (*Zhongwai xinwen qiribao*, 8 April 1871).

29 Much more is written about the ships sailing for California from Europe and the East Coast of America. In fact, the literature, both primary and secondary, is massive. See for instance, John Haskell Kemble, *The Panama Route 1848-1869*, (Columbia, S.C, 1990) and James P. Delgado: *To California by Sea. A Maritime History of the California Gold Rush* (Columbia, S.C., 1990). Unfortunately, there is almost no first-hand account of the voyages from China to California, Australia and Canada by Chinese migrants themselves. Barth cites accounts of European travellers but they are filled with Eurocentric biases (See Barth, *Bitter Strength*, 70-71). For a brief but useful description of the new steerage passenger trade necessitated by mass trans-oceanic migration, see Bernard Ireland, *History of Ships*, (London, 1999), 98-99.

30 The San Francisco Customs House records are in the Bancroft Library, University of Berkeley.

31 Robinet to Meyer, 3 February 1852: Volume 541, Augustine Heard & Co. Collection II [hereafter Heard II], deposited in the Baker Library of the Harvard School of Business. This volume consists of outbound letters by W.M. Robinet, December 1850 to 1853, some in English and others in Spanish, and a note on the volume indicates that it is not clear how this letter book ended up as part of the Augustine Heard & Co Archive. Robinet, who was born in Peru of an English father but claimed to be a US citizen, had come to China in late 1850, moving between Whampoa, Macao and Hong Kong. Before that,

he was in San Francisco where he made a number of business contacts which proved very valuable. After this voyage, he sold the *Convoy*, and devoted himself almost entirely to shipping Chinese to Havana. He later set up his company, W.M Robinet & Co. in Hong Kong. His life as a maverick is nicely summed up in *China Mail*, 6 November 1858.

32 *Alta California*, 4 July 1851.

33 *Alta California*, 22 and 26 July 1851.

34 Barth, *Bitter Strength*, 74-75.

35 Crawford, *Chinese Coolie*, 105.

36 Eitel, *Europe*, 273.

37 See the Captain's account of the violence on the *Duke of Portland*, in the Parliamentary Paper entitled 'Copies of any recent Communications to or from the Foreign Office, Colonial Office, Board of Trade, and other Department of Her Majesty's Government, on the subject of Mortality on board the "Duke of Portland", or any other British Ships, Carrying Emigrants from China', reprinted in *British Parliamentary Papers* (Shannon: Irish University Press, 1974-) [hereafter *BPP*] volume IV, 'Chinese Emigration', 415 – 434, at 424-425; the case is also reported in 'Copies of Recent Communications to or from the Foreign Office, Colonial Office, Board of Trade, and any other Department of Her Majesty's Government, on the subject of Mortality on board British Ships carrying Emigrants from China or India', in *BPP* IV, pp. 459-493.

38 W. Lane Booker, British Consul at San Francisco, to the Earl of Malmesbury, 3 July 1858, enclosed in Foreign Office to Colonial Office, 21 August, 1858: CO 129/70, 283-292. Booker's despatch also includes the 'Memoranda of Rules' observed on board several of the British ships – *Mooresfort, Caribbean and Leonides* – which are revealing.

39 *Alta California*, 9 May 1851.

40 *Friend of China*, passim, 1851.

41 Barth, *Bitter Strength*, 60-61.

42 *Xia'er guanzhen*, vol. 2:1, 1854.

43 Speer, *The Oldest*, 487.
When a migrant died and his body could not be found, his spirit was summoned in a ritual and deposited in a box, called the spirit box, which would be shipped back to China for reburial.

44 Chen Yong, *Chinese San Francisco 1850-1943: A Trans-Pacific Community*, (Stanford, 2000), 105,

45 'San Francisco Prices Current and Shipping List', February 4, extracted in *Friend of China*, 3 April

1858.

46 See Elizabeth Sinn, 'In-between Places: The Key Role of Localities of Transit in Chinese Migration', presented at the Association for Asian Studies Annual Meeting, Washington D.C., 4-7 April 2002.

47 Mark O'Neill, 'Quiet Migrants Strike Gold at Last', *South China Morning Post*, 14 February 2002.

48 For a very good description of the return of bones from New Zealand, see James Ng, *Windows on a Chinese Past*, (Otago, 1993), 4 volumes, Volume 4 Chapter 1D 'Burial Customs'.

49 For the history of the Pacific Mail Steamship Co., see John Haskell Kemble, *A Hundred Years of the Pacific Mail Steamship Company*, (Newport, Va, 1950). A huge archive of the company is deposited at the Huntington Library and I am especially indebted to Dan Lewis and Mario Einaudi for helping me navigate through it.

50 For instance, in July 1852, 8-15,000 contract labourers were being processed for shipment in Xiamen. (Schwendinger, *Ocean of*, 29) Xiamen continued to dominate the older emigration routes to Southeast Asia, and for a few years in the 1850s the trade to Havana, but it never became an international passenger port of the same status as Hong Kong. By the early twentieth century, Hong Kong became the major transshipping point for Xiamen passengers, both inbound and outbound.

51 Eitel, *Europe*, 344.

52 Writing in 1865, a Guangzhou Chinese newspaper, while discussing emigration-related kidnapping cases, commented that most of the kidnapping took place in Macao; in Hong Kong, British law was very strict and in Guangzhou, officials kept a close eye on things as well. (*Zhongwai xinwen qirilu*, 9 October 1865.

53 Eitel, *Europe*, 344.

54 An interesting account of the troubles faced by foreign merchants and their gradual withdrawal from Whampoa is given in Boleslaw Szczesniak, *The Opening of Japan. A Diary of Discovery in The Far East, 1853-1856 from the original manurscript in the Massachusetts Historical Society By Rear Admiral George Henry Preble, USN*, (Norman, 1962).

55 Adam MacKeown's insightful article on Chinese emigration gives an excellent account of how the emigrant's connections, real and symbolic, with the home village were sustained. See 'Transnational Chinese Families and Chinese Exclusion, 1875-1943', *Journal of American Ethnic Studies*, Volume 18:2 (Winter 1999), 73-111. See also Madeline Hsu's excellent work, *Dreaming of Gold, Dreaming of Home: Transnationalism and Migration Between the United States and South China, 1882-1943*, (Stanford, 2000) in which she depicts the many ways Chinese Americans maintained two homes – spiritual, emotional and material.

56 Before the Gold Rush, some of the conventional 'China goods' such as silk, tea, matting, etc, were being exported from Hong Kong for American consumption, but with the passenger trade, very different products were also shipped specifically for Chinese consumption.

57 See Ng Chin Keong, *Trade and Society: The Amoy Network on the China Coast, 1683-1735*, (Singapore, 1873); James Chin Kong, 'Merchants and Other Sojourners: The Hokkiens Overseas', (Ph.D. Thesis, University of Hong Kong, 1999); Jennifer Cushman, *Fields from the Sea: Chinese Junk Trade with Siam During the Late 18th and Early 19th Centuries*, (Ithaca, N.Y, 1993); Anthony Reid, (ed), *Sojourners and Settlers: Histories of Southeast Asia and the Chinese*, (Sydney, Australia, 1996).

58 A brief description of the distribution of the different county groups overseas is given in Sinn, *'Emigration from'*, at 35-36.

59 For discussions of Hong Kong's role in bridging China and China overseas, see Sinn, 'In-between Places'; Sinn, *'Tongxiang Associations and the Centering of Hong Kong in the Chinese Diasporic World'*, paper presented at the "Repositioning Hong Kong and Shanghai in Modern Chinese History" conference, University of Hong Kong, 11-12 June 2002; Sinn, "Hong Kong's Role in the Relationship between China and the Chinese Overseas", in Lynn Pan (ed), *Encyclopedia of Chinese Overseas*, (Singapore, 1998), 105-107.

60 *Friend of China*, 23 June 1852.

61 Eitel, *Europe*, 259.

62 *Friend of China*, 23 June 1851.

63 *Alta California*, 17 Aug 1851.

64 *Friend of China*, 10 January 1852; *Alta California*, 13 March 1852; Later records show Kam Tay Lee (Chinese) captained by Atay sailing from Manila to Hong Kong, so it is likely that it stayed closer to home rather than tried to cross the Pacific again.

65 Schwendinger, *Ocean of*, passim; also Pacific

Mail Steamship Company crew lists at the Huntington Library.

66 These were *Mariposa, Honolulu, Pacifico, Evenline and Gazelle*; in 1850, he was agent for the *Cornwall and Ann Welsh*, also bound for California (*Friend of China*).

67 Ryberg to Augustine Heard & Co., 27 April 1865, 15 July 1865, 28 July 1865, September 1865. 19 *October* 1865, 28 October 1865. The letters are part of the Augustine Heard & Co. Collection II (Volume LV-1, F 52; Microfilm Reel 303) in the Baker Library. For Macondray, see also *One Hundredth Anniversary of Macondray & Co 1848-1948,* (Manila: s.n., 1948?) and Elizabeth Grubb Lampen, *The Life of Captain Frederick William Macondray 1803-1862,* (San Francisco, 1994).

68 Y.J. Murrow, a Welshman born in 1817, had come to China in 1838 and joined the old Guangzhou firm of Jamieson, How & Co. Later he set up in commerce on his own account in Hong Kong and Guangzhou; he operated his own company, Murrow & Co., but also at some point joined with James Stephenson, another active charterer, to form Murrow, Stephenson & Co. In Hong Kong's history, he is best known for being editor and owner of the *Hong Kong Daily Press* from 1858. See G.B.Endacott, *A Biographical Sketch-Book of Early Hong Kong,* (Singapore, 1962), 148-149.

69 *Friend of China*, 1855, 1856.

70 *Friend of China*, 1855. They are *Resolution* (315 passengers for Port Philips), *Thomas Fielden* (423 for Melbourne), the *Nile* (173 for Melbourne) and *Cornwall* (307 for Port Philip and Adelaide).

71 For a history of the firm, see Stephen C. Lockwood, *Augustine Heard and Company, 1858-1862: American Merchants in China,* (Cambridge, Mass, 1971).

72 Jardine, Matheson & Co. to Russell & Co, Hong Kong, 25 August, 1858 (p525, JMA/ Letter Book C14/7); Jardine, Matheson & Co. to Russell & Co, Hong Kong, 27 August 1858 (p.2, JMA/ Letter Book C 14/8); Jardine, Matheson & Co to Russell & Co, Hong Kong, 8 November 1858 (p.40 JMA/ Letter Book C 14/8). These documents are in the Jardine, Matheson Archives at Cambridge University Library.

73 Anthon to Webster, (consul to Secretary of State), 8 August, 1855: Despatches from US Consuls in Hong Kong, 1844-1906.

74 *Friend of China*, 20 June 1849.

75 Caine to Newcastle, 4 May 1854: #11 CO 129/46.

76 Barth, *Bitter Strength*, 60-61.

77 For example in the *Sultana* case, Tam Achoey acted as surety for $20,000 for the passengers who, after the charterer absconded, intended to collect enough money to pay the shipowner so that the ship would sail. (*Friend of China*, 7 August 1852).

78 *Friend of China*, 1 December 1858.

79 Jacques Downs, *The Golden Ghetto: The American Commercial Community at Canton and the Shaping of America's China Policy 1784-1844,* (Bethlehem Pa & London, 1997), 86-89.

80 Barth, *Bitter Strength*, 60-61.

81 *Alta California* 23 June, 1854, reprinted in *Friend of China*, 23 August, 1854. See also Barth, *Bitter Strength,* 61.

82 *Alta California* 23 June, 1854, reprinted in *Friend of China*, 23 August, 1854; see also Barth, *Bitter Strength,* 61.

83 Murrow to Jardine, Matheson & Co, 7 February, 1856, letter #450/ JMA. (Microfilm Reel #134).

84 Murrow to Jardine, Matheson & Co, 13 February 1856: Letter # 4509 / JMA (Microfilm Reel #134).

85 More examples of such negotiation can be found in the Jardine, Matheson Archives.

86 Ryberg, San Francisco to Augustine Heard & Co, Hong Kong, 25 May 1863, Heard II.

87 Ryberg, San Francisco to Augustine Heard & Co, Hong Kong, 14 January 1865, 6 April, 1865.

88 Ryberg, San Francisco to Augustine Heard & Co, Hong Kong, 6 July 1863; see also 19 April 1864.

89 Ryberg, San Francisco to Augustine Heard & Co, Hong Kong, 5 April, 1864, 27 October 1864. See also Thomas R. Cox, *Mills and Markets: A History of the Pacific Coast Lumber Industry to 1900,* (Seattle, 1974) for a study of the relationship between the lumber trade and ship chartering between Hong Kong and the American West Coast.

90 Ryberg, San Francisco to Augustine Heard & Co, Hong Kong, 18 July 1865.

91 Ryberg, San Francisco to Augustine Heard & Co, Hong Kong, 25 May 1863.

92 Ryberg, San Francisco to Augustine Heard & Co, Hong Kong, 6 July 1863.

93 Ryberg, San Francisco to Augustine Heard & Co, Hong Kong, 27 April 1865; 27 September 1865.

94 Ryberg, San Francisco to Augustine Heard & Co, Hong Kong, 6 July 1863; 19 April 1864, Heard II.

95 Ryberg, San Francisco to Augustine Heard & Co, Hong Kong, 6 July 1865; 19 October 1865. Cornelius Koopmanschap was himself a fascinating character. He was born in the Netherlands and went to California during the

Gold Rush, where he began as an importer of China goods. He went to Hong Kong and China several times, to recruit labour and to build up his chartering business. His greatest impact was in bringing huge numbers of Chinese into America, especially for the Union Pacific Railroad. See Barth, *Bitter Strength*, 191-193.

96 *Friend of China*, 7 August, 11 August, 14 August, 20 November 1852 and 12 January, 1853.

97 *Friend of China*, 7 July and 14 July, 1852.

98 For the full text of the American Passenger Act, see *Friend of China*, 25 February 1852.

99 For example, the *Libertad*, which sailed from Hong Kong to San Francisco in 1854 carrying 560 passengers when the limit was 297. The Chinese were without water the last six days of the voyage and 100 died, and the captain as well, before reaching the Golden Gate. Schwendinger, *Ocean of*, 67. Also 67-68 for other cases. See also Barth, *Bitter Strength*, 72-73.

100 Robinet to Meyer, 3 February 1852: Volume 541, Heard II.

101 Ryberg, San Francisco to Augustine Heard & Co, Hong Kong, 13 January 1864.

102 Bonham to Newcastle, 6 January 1854: #4, CO 129/45, 22-23.

103 *Friend of China*, 20 January 1855.

104 Hillier to Mercer, 3 September 1855, enclosed in John Bowring to Lord Russell, 14 September, 1855: # 140, CO 129/52, 61-80.

105 Letters enclosed in John Bowring to Lord Russell, 14 September 1855: # 140, CO 129/52, 61-80. Part of the reason for the discrepancy was that the Melbourne official was using the one passenger to two ton ratio to calculate the number of passengers permissible and the different ways of calculating tonnage led to disagreement as to the actual capacity of the vessel. Another discrepancy was that passengers were being carried in the Orlop Decks, which was in breach of the Act. But there were many real oversights by the Hong Kong Emigration Officer leading to the remarkable overloading. But the main factor was however, that the Hong Kong Emigration Officer had no intentions of following the strictures of the Act, which he felt was unnecessarily stringent. It was he who accused the Melbourne government of being anti-Chinese.

106 Caine to Newcastle, 4 May 1854: # 11, CO 129/46, 16-22; approval for the appointment given by Colonial Office in Colonial Office to Bowring, 29 August 1854: CO129/45, 26.

107 Colonial Land and Emigration Office to Herman Merivale, Colonial Office, 26 April 1855: CO 129/53, 302-308.

108 Letter to Mercer from Dent & Co., Lindsay & Co., J. F. Edgar, Lyall, Still & Co., John Burd & Co., Y.J. Murrow, William Anthon & Co., Gibb Livingston & Co., Wm. Pustau & Co., 11 January 1855, enclosed in #3273, CO 129/55, 100-106.

109 Colonial Land and Emigration Office to Frederick Peel, 15 September 1854: CO 129/48, 187-190.

110 The Act subjected vessels from any port in Hong Kong, and every British ship carrying from any port in China or within 100 miles of the coast thereof, more than 20 passengers being natives of Asia on voyages of more than seven days' duration, to the inspection of an Emigration Officer, no vessel would be permitted to sail without a certificate of clearance from him. From the economic point of view, one of the most important provisions was passenger-to-space ratio: the Act was modelled on the Imperial Passengers' Act, but while this provided 15 ft for each adult passenger, 12 superficial and 72 cubic ft was considered sufficient for Asiatics. It also stipulated the items and quantity of provisions, the scale of medicines and small stores and equipment for each vessel. To eliminate kidnapping, decoying and other forms of deceit and coercion, the Emigration officer was to ascertain that each passenger understood where he was going, and understand the nature of the contract of service which they had made.
The Act was accompanied by a schedule of the duration of voyages to different places, and this was regularly revised. In 1856, the voyage to California by sailing ships was deemed to be 100 days from October to March and 75 days from April to September; in 1858, the durations were revised as 76 and 59; for steamers they were 52 and 44.
Ordinance 12 of 1868 made any Chinese medical practitioner, who was qualified to the satisfaction of a Colonial Surgeon, eligible for the office of Surgeon of a Chinese Passenger Ship. In 1870, Ordinance 1870 permitted the governor to grant exemption from the operation of the Passenger Act, provided the passengers proceeding would be Emigrants and under no Contract of Service whatever.

111 See Letters enclosed in Bowring to Lord Russell, 14 September 1855: # 140, CO 129/52, 61-80 for the case of the *Alfred*.

112 *Friend of China*, 21 May 1856.

113 A full account of the *Duke of Portland* and *John Calvin* cases are given in two parliamentary Papers; see note 36. For the letters regarding the remitting of the fine, see 484-485.

114 Ordinance no 11 of 1857: 'An Ordinance for Licensing and Regulating Emigration Passage Brokers', *Hong Kong Government Gazette*, November 1857, 3-4.

115 Ordinance no. 6 of 1859.

116 Colonial Land and Emigration Office to Herman Merivale, Colonial Office, 26 April 1855: CO 129/53, 302-308.

117 Minutes of Legislative Council meeting, *Friend of China*, 20 October 1858.

118 *ibid.*

119 Letter to Mercer from Dent & Co., Lindsay & Co., J. F. Edgar, Lyall, Still & Co., John Burd & Co., Y.J. Murrow, William Anthon & Co., Gibb Livingston & Co., Wm. Pustau & Co., 11 January 1855, enclosed in #3273, CO 129/55, 100-106.

120 A clear summary of the amendments to the Chinese Passenger Act up to 1872 is provided in a notice dated 11 November 1872, *Hong Kong Government Gazette*, Volume XVIII: No. 47 (16 November 1872), 483-486.

121 Jardine, Matheson & Co. to Russell & Co, 27 August, 1858 (p.2, JMA/ Letter Book C 14/8)

122 For an insightful analysis of the early history of the rule of law in Hong Kong, see Christopher Munn, *Anglo-China: Chinese People and British Rule in Hong Kong 1841-1880,* (Richmond, Surrey, 2001).

123 Caine to Newcastle, 4 May 1854: #11 CO 129/46, 16-22.

124 For the physical development of Hong Kong, see T.N. Chiu, *The Port of Hong Kong:A Survey of its Development,* (Hong Kong, 1972). Given the importance of the shipping trade and auxiliary businesses, it is a pity that no serious scholarly work has been devoted to them. For more popular works, see Austin Coates, *Whampoa: Ships on the Shore,* (Hong Kong, 1980) and *Robin Hutcheon's Wharf: The First Hundred Years,* (Hong Kong, 1986).

125 H.W. Brands, *The Age of Gold: The California Gold Rush and the New American Dream*, quoted in *New York Times*, B7, 19 August 2002.

*Raft of logs alongside **M.V. Clytoneus** at Tanjong Mani, Rejang River, Sarawak, 1954*

(photo: Alston Kennerley)

*Ships party from **M.V. Clytoneus** setting off in the motor lifeboat to play a football match at the local sawmill, Tanjong Mani, Rejang River, Sarawak, 1954*

(photo: Alston Kennerley).

China Seas: Some Maritime Reminiscences

Edited by Alston Kennerley

A conference devoted to British maritime activity in a particular region was bound to attract people whose earlier careers, at sea or in shore employment connected with shipping, had taken them to that part of the world. In making time for an unstructured workshop or brainstorming session, the Conference organisers were amply justified as their call for ad hoc contributions received a full response. Indeed, twice the time allocated could have been filled. The session was recorded and I am indebted to Kathy Davies, Secretary to the Keeper of Merseyside Maritime Museum, who also took notes during the session, for her transcription. Early in the planning, Captain Roger Parry, who led the organisation in Liverpool, solicited written contributions through the Swire Association, which includes people who served in ships of the Hong Kong based company Butterfield and Swire, while I approached the Nestorian Association of former Blue Funnel Line staff. Only a small part of this material was presented in the session, but in compiling this paper I have included more substantial extracts. The contributions selected fall into three groups: experiences on the China coast during the 1950s and 1960s; Borneo and timber cargoes; escape in World War II and from Vietnam. Each contribution is allowed to speak for itself, though with clarification where it seemed helpful inserted between square brackets. However I have not included material unless it specifically relates to the China Seas.

The interpretation of China Seas adopted here stretches from Japan in the north to Malaya, Indonesia and Borneo in the south. It includes all the coastlines and islands bounding the part-enclosed China Seas. Reminiscences can of course be extremely wide ranging. They have the potential to be rewarding to historians specialising in almost

any field, and can draw attention to issues and episodes of importance, which would otherwise be lost to sight. In technology, for example, very little is recorded of how particular cargo handling operations were carried out. Rather more of social conditions experienced by seafarers is on record, but there is little of the surrounding context, especially of ships in port overseas. Indeed, many practices that are routine, common knowledge to those involved at the time, remain unrecorded and soon lost with the passage of time.

Merchant ships in communist Chinese ports in the 1950s and 1960s

Captain Goddard's recollections aboard SS Sudbury Hill

[*Sudbury Hill* was carrying a cargo of scrap iron from Manchester to Kobe, departing Manchester 18 March 1959, arriving Kobe, Japan, 2 May 1959.[1] It was not a happy ship and relations between the apprentices and the first mate were particularly bad. Goddard was senior apprentice.] The ship moored to buoys in Kobe harbour and discharged into barges, a surprisingly time-consuming business as the scrap was semi-sorted in the holds prior to unloading. The 'old man's' waning popularity fell several notches, when after the long voyage out, he only arranged for one shore boat each day and cut everyone's advance of pay in half. As Kobe in those days was renowned for its bars, girls and cheap shopping, this parsimony did little for his popularity or towards making a happy ship. On Sundays at least we had some respite, as we were able to convince the Chaplain from the Missions to Seamen of our religious fervour and desperate need to attend church. The Chaplain threatened to report the 'old man' [to the owners in London] if an additional boat was not provided on Sundays for us to go to Church, a move that infuriated the 'old man' and forever endeared the Mission to me. We found that the Mission chapel was also used by the local British community in Kobe, so the Sunday morning service also proved to be a friendly social gathering as well. They also took us under their wing so after church us 'poor starving apprentices' plus some of the junior officers were whisked off to various homes for a good square meal and pleasant conversation.

On completion of our discharge at Kobe (18/5/59), we sailed in ballast to Dungun, an anchorage port on the north east coast of Malaya where we loaded iron ore from barges for Hirohata on the Inland Sea of Japan. Much of our time southbound in ballast was spent in the holds repairing the damage from the scrap and preparing them for the iron ore. It was a tiring, hot and dirty business. [This included '…caulking bilges, a monotonous, and in this weather, extremely unpleasant job…', that is sealing the cracks between the heavy boards covering the bilges] The 'old man' extracted his revenge for the church boat in Kobe by ordering us three apprentices to each write a long letter to a school in London that had apparently 'adopted' the ship. [The British Ship Adoption Society linked ships with schools which followed ship's progress through maps and other data coming from the link person aboard ship who was often the master. The school would be visited when on leave. Resentment was common among apprentices forced to join in the correspondence.] After a heavy day's work what little spare time we had was taken up with our studies and correspondence course, so letters to a school had scant attraction for us. [Part of the apprenticeship contract was that apprentices should be taught the business of a deck officer. This was often fulfilled through a correspondence course from the Merchant Navy Training Board or one of the nautical colleges. This was part of the study for the first professional qualification, the government Certificate of Competency as a Second Mate of

a Foreign-Going Steam Ship.] Under dire threat of awful retribution, we finally produced the most ill spelt, ungrammatical garbage it was possible to devise, which resulted in a stoppage of our shore leave back in Japan. This later proved to be no real hardship as Hirohata turned out to be a grubby steel works in the middle of flat drab landscape so nobody bothered to go ashore anyway.

Whilst at anchor off Dungun we were given the job of going over the side on painting stages to repaint the ship's draft marks and load lines. It was a pleasant passtime in the tropical sunshine with the stages low enough for us to sit with our feet in the water – until we noticed several long repulsive sea snakes swimming past. Nick [one of the other apprentices] later claimed he thought the Mate had gone for a dip and was swimming past to check we were working. We finally decided that the snakes weren't ugly enough to be the Mate. However our stages were raised in record time and the painting abandoned… In fact they were never done before the end of the trip as going over the side in China was high on the list of forbidden activities…

[The Sudbury Hill was now chartered to carry mainly coal from the northern Chinese port of Chinwangtao (first loading on 20 July 1959) to Shanghai. There were eleven visits to Chinwangtao to load coal. Other ports visited while under this charter were Hong Kong (stores), Pasuo (iron ore), Tsingtao, Yulin Kang, Dairen (bulk maize and sawn timber). The charter came to an end in February 1960.] From Hirohata we proceeded with a pilot westbound through the Inland Sea and out across the Yellow Sea to China, where we were chartered to the Chinese government for employment on the coastal trade for an, as then, indeterminate period. It proved to be a rotten trade that further compounded the low morale already reigning on board the Sudbury Hill. Thus started what was probably the most miserable time of my life at sea, some 8 months on the China coast. In Chinese ports cargo work, whether it be loading or discharging, continued around the clock, accompanied by the ceaseless rumbling roar from the ship's steam winches, the 'Clark Chapman symphony' [referring to the winch maker]. It was music we could well do without as we often vainly tried to sleep to the accompaniment of ten winches thundering away throughout the ship. Down the holds and ashore on the wharf, ant-like hoards of coolies were exhausted by the discordant blare of Chinese martial music played over loudspeakers. It was even worse than the winches…!

By today's standards the methods of loading were virtually stone age. On the wharf gangs of coolies enveloped in dust shovelled coal out of rail trucks into closely woven rope cargo nets to be lifted aboard by the ship's derricks. In the hold the coal was tipped out and the empty net lifted ashore again to be replaced by a full one. Each lift weighed about one and a half tons though frequently the Chinese would overload them causing breakages in our derrick runners and guys… Before long we became expert at translating the creaking of our gear or labouring of our winches into the probable degree of overloading of the lifts. Since any instructions to the coolies to reduce loads were totally ignored, we normally resorted to immobilising the winches by shutting off their steam supply. This always produced an uproar from the Chinese and threats about our 'non co-operation' from the resident commissar.

During the winter months up north we became aware of another problem, when it was noticed that the coal was actually steaming as it was shovelled out of the rail trucks. It then became the apprentice's job to take the temperature of the coal in the trucks using a thermometer 'borrowed' from the ship's medicine chest. If the temperature was over 70°F we would refuse to load the coal from that particular truck until it had been spread on the wharf and cooled down. This of course created absolute chaos and reduced our loading rates dramatically, to the fury of the Chinese. Their attempts to ignore these instructions were frustrated by our engineers shutting off the steam to immobilise the winches again. The apparent awkwardness on our part was actually based on sound reasoning and safety, as, over a period of time, wet, poor-quality, coal could heat up through spontaneous combustion and either ignite or give off an explosive gas, thus becoming a danger to the ship…

One of the greatest annoyances experienced on the China coast was the 'inspection'. The authorities insisted on this procedure both on arrival and prior to departure, which meant four inspections every round trip. The officers and crew would be mustered on deck under armed guard regardless of the time of day (or night!) or weather conditions. We would all be counted and individually identified against the crew list, and would then wait while more armed guards would search the ship for exotica like anti-revolutionary material, American spies, stowaways, dissidents or any other subversive material their fevered imaginations could dream up. One trip a map of the world in the radio office was confiscated because Tibet, recently invaded by Chinese troops, was marked in a different colour from China; on another occasion our charts showing Taiwan with the old name of Formosa were removed. Carefully hoarded and much-read magazines supplied by the mission in Kobe, were nearly all confiscated within the first few weeks.

As winter approached and the weather became progressively colder, our Indian crew grew increasingly morose and unwilling to work. This meant that more and more jobs were pushed onto us three apprentices, including one that we had a particular dislike for, removing the ship's rails abreast the hatches prior to commencing cargo work and replacing them again before going to sea. Heavy sections of rails some ten or twelve feet long were secured in position with nuts and bolts. These had to be removed prior to dragging them clear… not an easy job in the middle of the night with temperatures well below zero and fingers freezing within gloves… It was an operation that left us covered in grease, coal and rust plus aching muscles as it took our combined efforts to move the rails in and out of position. One night in Shanghai we slipped on the ice in the scuppers and lost a section of railing overboard. The mate made us get a length of line and a grapnel to hook the rail back off the river bed, which we managed to do but not before we had been arrested by armed guards for illegally trying to take soundings… To overcome this problem, like so many others, we had to write a confession, apologising for our actions against the People's Republic of China. This would later be translated, no doubt with various embellishments, and published in local newspapers…

One of the greatest frustrations we lived with was the uncertainty of our future and when we would be released from the misery of the coal run. In the various ports we visited there was little to go ashore for except the government run Seamen's Clubs. There we could have a meal and a beer if we had any money to spend, which wasn't very often as the 'Old Man' was forever cutting back on the money we, or any one else, requested. The Clubs were generally pretty drab places reserved for foreign seamen as we were not encouraged to mix with or talk to the local Chinese. We were subjected to a great deal of propaganda promoting Chairman Mao and the communist way of life, all of which we rejected with derision. As a consequence most of our trips ashore were confined to visits to other overseas ships at nearby berths in the hope of picking up any books, magazines or food.

One success we achieved after some six months of endeavour, was the opportunity to visit the Great Wall of China which was only a short drive north of Chinwangtao. In spite of the grey day it was a delight to get away from the ship and the port area, and venture out into rural China. Six of us plus an uncommunicative driver all jammed into a venerable car for a bumpy trip over rough roads to the Wall. The few people we saw, including troops, were all hard at work in the fields, ignoring the strange sight of a car load of foreigners chugging past. We finally arrived at the most eastern gateway in the Wall. It had been restored, although on each side the Wall stretched away into the distance in varying stages of decay. Nevertheless we were tremendously impressed at the thought of this structure that ran for thousands of miles across northern China.

During our time at sea between ports we were able to listen to the latest pop music and news from American armed forces radio stations in Japan. Reception was generally poor, but at least we felt we had a link with the outside world and of course it was infinitely preferable to the screeching of Chinese music on the local stations. In port we were forbidden to listen to our radios which were often impounded by the authorities.

As time wore on and the winter weather closed in we experienced severe cold in the northern ports with temperatures dropping down to 24 degrees below freezing. We waddled around the ship wearing our entire wardrobes on our backs. The fire main on deck froze solid and the heavy steel pipe split in a dozen places. The rigging and fittings were festooned with icicles giving Sudbury Hill the appearance of a floating Christmas tree. We had to take special care of our winches to ensure they were not immobilised by the cold as steam quickly turned to water and froze when they were stopped. Normally the winches were kept turning slowly during breaks in cargo work, which didn't please the engineers who had to tour the deck and keep an eye on them. Usually this was a job for the Indian greasers, but due to the low temperatures, our crew had long since refused to turn out for all but the most essential duties… On our arrival at our final call in Dairen we found the intense cold had frozen the spray around our bows and the anchors were solid in the hawse pipes. Our anchors could not be let go so we had to steam round in circles waiting for tugs to come out and take us into our berth. Later when we shifted ship we steamed around in circles again, this time with our steering gear jammed up with ice.

12 December 1959. Hsing Kiang. [quoting from Goddard's diary] 'When we arrived the cabins were searched, the mate's especially,

which he said was literally stripped. The annoying thing about these searches is that the guards don't know what they are looking for. They just say it is regulations. Yesterday morning there was one of the security police walking about the cabins just looking around and reading letters, etc. Don and I caught him up here and got really sarcastic with him. He gave us a long oration about how good China is and how decadent the Western world was. It was an absolute farce. He got really angry before we'd finished and stalked off in a high temper. When we sailed at 4 am this morning the same guard came aboard for the muster and denounced the ship for being uncooperative, unfriendly and an enemy of the people, which was greeted with loud cheers. The agent in Shanghai claims we are the worst ship on the coast. Hsing Kiang is a new port (opened 1952) at Taku, just below Tientsin. It would look more cheerful in the middle of Siberia so I didn't bother to go ashore. The weather especially up north is atrocious, the temperature barely rises above 40 degrees Fahrenheit, and the wind is bitter. I've invested in a fur hat with flaps that I can pull down. Its very warm. Christmas this year promises to be a grim affair; the only food we've got is the muck the Chinese supply, most of which is bad or half bad. The 'old man' has been going round other ships in port asking if they can let us have any stores for Christmas, but so far he hasn't been successful… We spent Christmas in Shanghai, or rather most of it as the ship sailed that night. I spent the entire day on cargo watch so I was the only one who remained sober. By the time I'd finished I was covered in coal dust so it was rather a black Christmas for me. Most of the mob were too busy getting drunk to worry about meals…'

Alston Kennerley[2]: episodes in communist Chinese ports in the 1950s

By the time of my first visit to a communist Chinese port, in the summer of 1953, the communists had a complete grip on the country. In that period, these ports were the only ones throughout the Far East where it was

safe to leave one's room unlocked. Most of my experiences would have been common to any western ships trading to China, including the blaring Chinese songs and exhortations to the workers, which went on day and night whilst alongside. For most Blue Funnel ships, the impact of the communist regime was felt during a preliminary visit to Hong Kong where the master was briefed on what was to be expected, how to handle the officials and asked to make a report on a return visit. For ordinary members of the crew, it meant getting rid of all magazines, books and anything else which might decry the regime, in preparation for the ship inspection lasting several hours on arrival, when petty officials poked their noses into every nook and cranny, while the whole crew was lined up on deck regardless of the weather. The process also involved a medical inspection, and the ship's radio room was sealed up, along with personal radios.

My first run-in with the system, normally an innocuous enough incident, involved a piece of dunnage. At Taku Bar aboard the *Alcinous*, the four middies (apprentices) were shifting dunnage in a 'tween deck while cargo was being worked in the lower hold.[3] Probably we were laying it ready for loading. Some how a piece slipped from the stack and fell below. No one was injured, but the accident stopped the ship for twelve hours while officialdom ran its course. It probably involved an abject apology from the master.

In the spring of 1954 aboard the *Glenlogan* (Glen Line but wholly owned and manned by Holts), we loaded a full cargo of soya beans at Dairen.[4] Alongside, compared with being at anchor at Taku Bar, we middies were able to get a run ashore. Most ports had a state seamen's club, where the principal attractions in a dingy building were communist literature, table tennis, beer and Chinese food. Perhaps it was here where we took a free coach tour, mainly around communist Chinese prestige initiatives such as factory estates. We certainly wandered around the town, but there was little of interest and not much in the shops. However, we did all purchase pale blue

Chairman Mao cotton caps, with cardboard peaks which collapsed in the first downpour of rain. Of course it was my other purchase which caused a fuss at the dock gate. This was a copy of the 1931/32 Official Shippers Guide, issued by Osaka Shosen Kaisha, which weighs in at seven pounds. At some time it had been used to conceal jewellery, the holes being punched out of the pages. It was confiscated at the gate, and I thought I had lost it for good, but the master returned it after we had sailed with a comment about the trouble it had caused him.

Two years later as fourth mate of the *Glengarry*, we were loading in Shanghai – tins of frozen egg white come to mind. Normally a junior officer was in charge of the deck during loading and would expect to give orders directly at each hatch or through the foreman of the stevedores.[5] However, this was not the case in communist ports where orders could only be passed through the duty communist official who did not understand what was going on. Standing by No. 3 hatch on my first period of duty in Shanghai, I heard a voice saying in English 'Don't look at me, but if there is anything you want done, just speak to no one in particular and I'll make sure it happens'. Fortunately I caught on, and was soon found muttering to myself things like 'it would be much better if cargo mats covered the cargo in the after end'. Later I found out that the man had been a foreman stevedore in the 'old days', working many a Blue Funnel ship, but was now having to survive as a common labourer.

Things were much the same when I went up to Whampoa, the port for Canton, at the end of 1958, as third mate aboard the *Atreus*.[6] It's a dramatic run up the Pearl River from Hong Kong during which, on duty on the bridge, I was charged with noting the positions of navigation marks, surreptitiously so as not to be noticed by the bridge guards, basic navigation data being something that the British authorities needed to up-date charts. The run ashore here was to the huge state department store, open only to foreigners, with payment in sterling or dollars. With much better prices than in Hong Kong some of the crew lashed out. The chief

engineer blew £70 on a sculptured Chinese carpet, which was probably worth many hundreds back in the UK.

Captain Richard Woodman:[7] Tsingtao, 1962
I recall that strictures on the China coast, particularly, were taken to extreme lengths e.g. the word 'Formosa' had to be blacked out on every chart; no 'Formosa' Strait, just 'Taiwan' Strait. Chinese ports were the only ports where we were particularly directed to carry out flag etiquette extremely carefully. As you know, a merchant ship flies the mercantile ensign of the country she's in. These were taken down on the whistle, at sunset, and hoisted every morning at 08.00 which meant that all the midshipmen [apprentices] had to turn out and the junior officer, usually the fourth mate, had to officiate at this ceremony. One of the reasons was, of course, that any dishonour to the Chinese flag attracted the process where you had to write a letter of apology to the population of China, in its entirety. If you accidentally dragged the courtesy ensign on the deck, for instance, and were seen doing so by the guard of the Red Army, you were reported and in very hot water. So, if you had the job of hoisting or lowering the Chinese courtesy ensign, rather than the Red Duster or the Company house flag, or the Company Jack, it had to be done very carefully. Just as it must not touch the deck, when hoisted in the morning it had to go up with a matchstick in the slipknot so you broke it out smartly, in one go.

One abiding memory was of Tsingtao in 1962, on the *Glenearn*.[8] It had been a German treaty port – the *Emden* made her famous cruise from there in the First World War[9] – and the skyline was dominated by the former Lutheran cathedral: we also passed what had been the old German naval base on the way in. We were allowed ashore, never a guaranteed privilege, and I remember walking down a back street of the town and seeing an old man sitting outside a house on a typically Chinese stool about six inches high. He had, at one side of him what looked like a paint kettle and on the other side a bundle of twigs. In his hand he held a penknife and he was making matches, dipping them in, presumably, phosphorus or something dreadful in the paint kettle. It just struck me, that image of the patience of China. It has always remained in my mind.

As to the rumour of spying, which occasionally got out of hand, there was a sort of notion that we were obviously 'agents of the west' and it was quite paranoid. In the 1970s, during the Cultural Revolution, and after I had left the Company, there were a number of Blue Funnel officers taken off their ships and I have been in correspondence with some of them in an attempt to get their stories. One was held ashore for a very long time. He was a Royal Naval Reserve officer and the son of a famous Second World War submarine commander. He was also a very interesting individual. My own encounter with this aspect of a visit to China occurred in 1961 aboard the *Glenfruin*.[10] Midshipmen used to have to keep logs and I kept mine assiduously and illustrated it with sketches and drawings, for a bit of fun. I remember on the way up the Whang Pu River to Shanghai, we passed the forts at Woosung where a new-looking Chinese Destroyer was berthed. Without giving the matter a second thought, I drew a sketch of the wretched thing. Perhaps to my good fortune, the Chief Officer, who was notionally in charge of our education, used to collect these log books in once a week to make sure we were keeping them properly. Having sighted and signed them he gave them back. During the course of that same morning he called for the logbooks and must have thumbed through them, because we had just arrived in Shanghai when came along to the half deck, absolutely steaming, with my name on his lips. 'You B.F. idiot. You could have the ship impounded. Tear this page out immediately!' I had to deface my precious log book because I had committed a terrible and potentially disastrous gaffe.

Fraser Stuart, Shipmaster, Retired.[11]
Experiences in China, 1947 to 1968
Early in 1947 I was a first year apprentice on Shell tanker, *Naninia*, anchored at the Yangtze bar light vessel awaiting a pilot.[12] I was on anchor watch with the Chief Officer who drew my attention to what looked like a bundle of old clothes in the water. 'A body,' he said, 'I am surprised we have not seen more with all the turmoil going on ashore'. We berthed at the Shell wharf at Pudong and because of the unrest there was no shore leave. Inflation was rampant but surprisingly local traders were allowed on board eager to trade curios for cigarettes. The carvings were not very good but we all wanted a souvenir from Shanghai, the 'Paris of the Orient'.

My interest in China lay dormant until 1952 when I was Third Mate on the tanker *Goldmouth*.[13] The Master, Captain Elwyn Jacob, had spent many years in the far east including the inter-war years with Asiatic Petroleum Company tankers on the Lower and Middle Yangtse. He sensed my interest and described his life in China: snipe shooting on the Yangtse delta, summers in Cheefoo and winter skiing in Japan. Unfortunately, I did know enough to ask him about the Upper Yangtse, which, much later, became my main interest. He gave me one piece of advice, 'get your master's ticket [certificate of competency] and get out of tankers'. I did that in 1957.

My next visit to China was as Chief Officer of *London Breeze*, a cargo ship.[14] Late in 1958 we loaded coal at Dairen. We berthed at night and the lights on the coal berth were like red-hot nails, a characteristic of most Chinese ports at this time. The Harbour Inspection Authorities, very tall north Chinese dressed in padded winter uniforms, were very intimidating. The whole business of mustering all hands on deck, seamen's books and passports, and searching the accommodation took about three hours. Our Radio Officer was a young Canadian-born Chinese who had been looking forward to his first visit to China. When asked by the authorities what was his nationality, he said, 'Canadian'. They told him in no uncertain terms he was Chinese. The poor lad was so shocked he paid off in Hong Kong and vowed never to go back to China.

There were occasions when the Chinese authorities tried to be more friendly. In

Chinwantao we were invited by the Seamen's Club to a circus but were very embarrassed to see the locals being removed from the front row seats to accommodate us. In Whampoa in 1959, after a period of anti-British/American demonstrations, we were invited to five nights of Peking opera to foster British/Chinese relations. I was never a fan of Chinese opera. The Radio Officer did his best to explain the story without much success, and the music and singing did nothing for me.

In 1962 occurred one of the most satisfying experiences I ever had in forty years at sea. I came into Shanghai as Master on a rather elderly Empire boat, *Hong Kong Breeze*, chartered to load bagged rice for Colombo. As we came up the river we had to turn round to berth head down river.[15] The pilot asked us to let go the starboard anchor, which we did. Either the current was underestimated, or we were carrying too much way. The cable parted and we lost some of the chain and the anchor. However, we came alongside, without difficulty. After we had berthed and the authorities had left, I had a look at the spare bower anchor which was secured to the forward mast house. Not surprisingly on a twenty year old ship, second or third hand, it was solid with rust. I realised that without a second anchor the ship was no longer seaworthy, and that the insurance on the cargo and any other expenses the Chinese decided to impose (and they would!) would be for the owner's account. I discussed the situation with the Chief Engineer, and we agreed that the whole deck and engine-room crew equipped with oxyacetylene burning gear, sulphuric acid, chain blocks and seven pound hammers, would start work the next morning.

Shortly after this I had a visit from the charterer's superintendent, Captain Zhee, a very tall north Chinese, who spoke very good English. I mentioned that that we had lost an anchor and I hoped that the ship chandler would get a replacement from the shipyard. Of course, he did not think this would be a problem. Next morning, we got busy and by late afternoon the moving parts on the anchor

were free, and the anchor was manoeuvred to the bow and secured to the cable. Eventually loading was completed and as we were ready to sail, Captain Zhee came on board: 'Captain you have a problem. You have only one anchor so your ship is unseaworthy, and the insurance of the cargo will be for Owner's account. You will also require two pilots and two escort tugs for the river passage'. I really savoured the next bit. I asked Captain Zhee to come with me down the jetty and along to the bow. I pointed to the anchor: 'What is that?' He was thunderstruck; his eyes bulged and he managed to say, 'How did you do it? Who helped you?' I could not resist saying that it was just a simple task for good seamen. And really it was, but I did enjoy the end result. I met Captain Zhee some time later at an off-hire survey after time charter and he had remembered. 'Lost any anchors recently?', he asked. 'No', I replied, 'I have not been in Shanghai'. He did smile.

From 1963 to 1966 my ship, *Thames Breeze*, was time-chartered to Sinofracht, the Chinese Government.[16] We loaded general cargo in Shanghai and Whampoa for Singapore, Conakry in Guinea, Dakar, but mainly Havana. We then loaded bagged sugar for China via the Panama Canal. Relations between Cuba and USA at this time were rather strained and the Panama Canal authorities, including the pilots, treated us like social lepers. The only time the pilots spoke to us was to give the necessary orders.

My last call at China was on the *Sydney Breeze* in 1968, to discharge bagged urea from Japan to Tsingtao, which I consider one of the nicest cities in China.[17] I had a bicycle on board and I was allowed to go anywhere I wished. From Tsingtao we went to Chogjin, North Korea, to load coal for Japan. I had never been to North Korea and the Japanese charterers were equally ignorant, so I just followed the same procedure as for entering China. We arrived off Chongjin at daylight and after berthing were boarded by a large contingent of very grim looking officials who immediately accused me of entering a prohibited area which could result in serious consequences. After a very long and detailed inspection they said that as a result of my actions there would be no shore leave. With tongue in cheek, I asked them not to penalise the officers and crew for my mistake. Away they went to consult their superiors. They came back after dark, to say that in view of my apology we could all visit the seamen's club until 2200 hours. I went out of curiosity. They were showing a film about how they won the war against the imperialist US and their running dog lackeys, and the only things for sale were books of Korean stamps. The place was worse than Dairen in 1958. We did not get any mail and apart from the seamen's club there was no entertainment. However, food was very cheap and very good, and the business people I had to deal with as master were honest and reliable – I liked them.

China was not a seafarer's most popular country to visit. I was very disappointed to learn from a friend at Baoshan in 1982 that the Chinese pilots, who were given access to the officers' smoking room, stole CDs and other things. This would not have happened in the past.

Timber cargoes in Borneo in the 1950s and 1960s

Jonathan Parkinson.[18] Sarawak, 1960
I refer to 1960 when I was hired in London to go out as a very green 20 year old into the shipping business, to Sarawak in the north coast of Borneo, which may be known to some of you as the 'Land of the White Rajahs.' For anyone who is a philatelist you may have seen stamps of the various Brooke regimes. There were three of them. The last one, Vyner,[19] sold Sarawak to Britain in 1946. So much damage had been caused during the war and, of course, the politics of the area had altered too. So it became a colony[20] – the British Empire was still expanding in 1946.

The Borneo Company, by whom I was employed, had been set up by some of the first Rajah's[21] friends in 1856 to help him develop the country and the Borneo Company[22] had pretty well 75% of the business of Sarawak, of which shipping was an important part.

Kuching, the Capital of Sarawak, is just 400 miles east of Singapore. So it gives you a rough idea of the area, and Sibu, still further east, was the centre of the big trade which developed after the war in Sarawak, the ramin [tropical hard wood] timber business – and some gentlemen I've spoken to here from Blue Funnel have been there in their youth.

Sibu was an extraordinary place, 48 miles from the sea at the head of the Rejang River delta. Larger deep sea ships could not come that far up. They anchored near the mouth of the river about ten to fifteen miles upstream at a suitable bend in the mangrove swamps: nothing on either side except mangroves stretching for miles and miles; flat as a pancake. Tanjong-Mani was the name of the anchorage, and this was where I worked for two and a half years. Sibu was fairly civilised. We came down either by longboat, a hollowed out tree trunk with sides built up with planks, painted in the Company colours, predominantly light blue, and flying the Company flag. There was an atap [woven leaf] roof to protect tuan's (master's) head from the beating sun, and from the rain for that matter, and a 40 horsepower Johnson on the stern. We were agents for Johnson outboard motors, so we always used those. There were speedboats available too, but the longboats were more comfortable on a 48 mile run up and down the river. You could sleep or idle away your time. In the speedboat the trip was frequently rather bumpy and any wash of passing Chinese launches made for an uncomfortable ride. There were no roads outside the immediate vicinity of the small towns, so all traffic, passengers and freight, went by river.

If you left Sibu at six in the morning, which was the time the Chinese pilot, Captain Lo, picked up deep sea ships at the mouth of the Rejang River, by the time they had come up and anchored at Tanjong Mani then you had done your 48 miles downstream. The idea was that as the ship anchored you came around the bend and, hopefully, the Chinese coolies in their houseboats – two-deck Chinese launches with normally four or five gangs of men –

would appear roughly at the same time. If you were even more fortunate, Chinese lighters, laden with timber, were there ready for the ship, too. The idea was, if you had done your homework, everything coincided. The ship arrived; you arrived; the coolies arrived, and the cargo arrived at more or less the same time. I must say that one was never let down by those very hard working people.

On the ship, formalities were very simple. The Customs officer from the Sarawak service, you, as agent, and your clerk lived on board as guests of the of the steamship company. The coolie houseboat launches tied up alongside, and likewise the lighters, too, tied up alongside the appropriate cargo hatch. Union purchase – you know the system – was the method used to load the cargo using the ship's derricks, and after about three days work all the sawn timber, some in bundles and some as loose planks, would be loaded.[23] One then waited for the next flood tide so that the ship was pointing downstream, off you went again, the ship to her next port, usually Singapore, and us back to Sibu or on to the next ship anchored close by.

There I was, as I say, for about two and half years of my earlier period of learning the business of a shipping assistant. On average I suppose I spent about twelve days each month on the ships in the middle of the swamps. As may be imagined, at the time it could be tedious, especially after a couple of years, nevertheless I count myself fortunate to have experienced a little of those days when there was, well, an element of romance still present in the business.

Captain Richard Woodman at Tanjong Mani

Can I add to this? At Tanjong Mani which I visited frequently in various ships, in addition to the houseboats alongside with four or five gangs on board, they also came down with their own cook and the cook had a couple of assistants and they used to set up, on a dunnage base, built on the well deck, a fire and galley of their own on which the rice boilers

were brought aboard. The big problem, of course, was to make sure there was always a fire hose running on the metal deck underneath this dunnage platform because we didn't actually want the ship to be set on fire, particularly as she contained timber! One more thing, about the timber trade. It was carried on extensively: Blue Funnel ships lifted a lot of timber out of various Borneo ports during the period I was there, in the early '60s, and in a kind of interested look back to the period discussed elsewhere in this book, we used to go to one island in the middle of a very deep bay on the Pacific coast of Borneo, called Darvel Bay. There was no formal port and we used to take the ship to an anchorage off a tiny island called Bohihan, which was not much more than a dot on the Admiralty chart. In order to navigate in and out of the place, Blue Funnel had produced its own chart and the chart was picked up from the agent in Singapore, and every time a Blue Funnel ship went there, it was expected to take some soundings, or do a bit of triangulation to add to the stock of common knowledge. I've no idea if anyone goes there today, but the point about this anchorage was, instead of the timber being sawn as it was at Tanjong Mani and coming down from the sawmills in lighters, it was dragged out from the adjacent jungle from logging camps situated all the way round Darvel Bay. The logs were Ramin logs of anything between five and eight to sometimes ten ton lifts. The logs were floated into the various creeks, swamps and rivers around the Bay and contained in a sort of 'corral' of lighter logs which were stapled and chained together. These log 'corrals' were then towed by chugging tugs for distances of perhaps 20-25 miles and anchored around the anchorage at Bohihan. Once a certain amount had been collected and the news signalled to Holt's agents at Singapore, a ship would be ordered to proceed to Bohihan. So you arrived and your cargo was all waiting for you around this little Bay, and dragged alongside, and loaded from there.

Dr Alston Kennerley at Tanjong Mani
I loaded there on five occasions during the 1950s. Approaching the entrance to the Rejang River was always a little uncertain owing to the low lying land and the unreliablilty of the lights on the navigation marks. Radar echoes were simply reflections of the edges of the mangrove. At Tanjong Mani there were no navigation marks, so for anchor marks we had to go ashore and whitewash suitable bits of mangrove and in the evening the apprentices were quite often sent out in the ship's boat to hang oil lamps there, so we could tell whether or not we were dragging the anchor. The sawn timber came in all shapes and sizes, the smallest pieces being strapped in bundles. Consignments could be quite small and one was separated from another in the ship's holds using coloured tapes. We also loaded logs which reached the ships side afloat in rafts. They were greasy with river slime and had to be hosed down once lifted clear of the water. Manoeuvring them down in the holds was very dangerous. Often weighing several tons, extra purchases were needed to drag them still slippery with water to the selected location.[24]

On one occasion there, we got up a team to play football against the local sawmill team. I think the sawmill owner was keen on this, but the apprentices were bulldozed into it.[25] When we arrived at the sawmill, we discovered that the pitch was made of sawdust and that our opponents were playing in bare feet. We had managed to cobble together some boots and other kit, so we had this rather hair-raising match against people used to the climate and were we glad when it was over and they produced the bottles of chilled Tuborg [Danish beer] to cool us down! This was one of the few places where the apprentices and junior officers got plenty of lifeboat handling experience.

Escape episodes

Captain Tom Willows: M.V. Phrontis escapes from Singapore in 1942[26]
[Tom Willans joined the *Phrontis* (NMSO, Nederlandsche Stoomvaart Maatschappij

Oceaan, or Dutch Blue Funnel), in Birkenhead in 1941, as a midshipman (apprentice).[27] The ship was intended for the Far East via the Atlantic Ocean, Panama Canal and Pacific Ocean. The sinking of HMS *Repulse* and HMS *Prince of Wales*, caused a detour to Australian ports where supplies for Singapore were loaded. Proceeding south and west around Australia, and then via the Sunda Straits, she was finally approaching Singapore] '…just north of the Banka Strait we observed nine planes; the alarm was raised and hands manned the Hotchkiss guns – how idiotic and futile. We were to see many more Japanese planes flying around Singapore without hindrance, not even a puff of smoke from an exploding shell fired by A.A. guns was seen.

So we arrived in Singapore Western Roads on February 1st [1942], which coincided with the dismantling of the Johore Causeway [linking Singapore Island to the Malayan mainland]… For some considerable time *Phrontis* stayed at anchor until a small launch approached flying the White Ensign: at least someone was taking notice. Ultimately [came] a change of anchorage to the Eastern Roads. It was during this operation the first might of the Japanese air force was observed, 27 planes in formation and making a symmetrical arrow (9x3).

During our stay these sightings became the 'norm'. Sometimes it was a bombing raid, others for a general reconnoitre or demoralising exercise when thousands of leaflets were dumped onto the island. I did manage to retrieve one which depicted a young mother holding a child with a caption: 'Please come home daddy, mummy and I are very lonely without you…'

Both East and West roads were virtually devoid of shipping, the odd Straits Steamship and KPM [Koniglijke Paketvaart Maartschappij] being the only ships present… neither was there the [normally] omnipresent sampan, small junk or motorboat… Throughout there was no sighting of any plane, civil or military, taking off from the airport – there was an overwhelming feeling of foreboding…

165

Bombing in the main took place during the hours of daylight. The powers that existed in charge of port operations decided that the ship should berth before sunset and commence discharging operations immediately. Bear in mind that the dockside labour force had ignominiously retreated to the jungle. Alongside, our doubts were quickly dispelled when a major of Transport Command announced that a detachment of JATS (apparently a nondescript Indian regiment who had deserted/mutinied) would work on board. Meanwhile ship's personnel would be ashore with wheelbarrows conveying the discharged cargo into the appropriate godown [dockside cargo warehouse]. The crew (Chinese) had not been considered for cargo duties as their services on board were positively vital…

Eventually the JATS appeared on the quay and spent hours arguing about the prospect of becoming stevedores before attempting to board. Our cooks had been prepared to have gallons of strong tea available… Teaching someone who just wasn't interested to drive an electric winch was difficult; in reality then by the time some sense was drilled into them it was time to knock off. Singapore Harbour rules prevailed. So the following morning to the anchorage and that evening alongside again… The following night a special dispensation was granted to work cargo throughout the hours of darkness. Commencing proved a hazardous period with guys of derricks and runners breaking. Using our standing derricks in the swinging mode proved easily the best mode: it was slow and still difficult for our new stevedores. Apart from deck officers all went ashore to manoeuvre huge two-wheeled barrows: they proved unwieldy and difficult to handle… After a short time one's thirst needed quenching. Initially bottled apple juice and thence a more palatable Australian brew quenched our thirst… Next day *Phrontis* stayed alongside completely idle….

[This was the period when Singapore residents became desperate to get away on any ship leaving, social order began to break down, and looting became widespread.] A day or so later around noon, a rather large force of bombers attacked Keppel Harbour [Singapore's main commercial port area]; needless to say there was little we could do apart from finding a wall near the godown which may afford protection. News about the fate of the *Talthybius* [bombed alongside in Singapore on 12 February 1942, in which Willows had spent the previous three voyages, and he now went over to help out] was quickly relayed…[28] Some of the ship's officers had their gear ashore and ready to be transported to Connell House [a residential club for Merchant Navy personnel]; at least they would have a roof over their heads. Transport remained a problem. Eventually I found a Fordson tractor suitably hooked to a trailer. I was more than conversant with Fordsons as my father had a couple on the farm, but like all implements used in agriculture they had built-in problems. Starting up was the first as petrol had to be used for a period for heating the combustion chambers before turning over to paraffin. Petrol was ultimately acquired from the Talthybius and we were in business. However, those who could leave had to stay and my effort… failed.

Some ten days after arriving at Singapore, we sailed. However, before the ship's company knew about our departure, cars by the score were making their inexorable way down to the ship. Indeed it was thought prudent to haul up the gangway and have an orderly embarkation, and with strict instructions to give priority to the elderly, women and children. No one [of the crew] was officially to give up his accommodation, actually we middies did give way and eventually the correspondent associated with *The Times* slept on the settee. I have no idea how many souls clambered up the gangway, and like ourselves they had no idea about our destination. They had but one thing in mind: 'leave Singapore'. Eventually we did sail to the south with the possibility of seeking the haven of Batavia [now Djakarta in Indonesia]…

Sailing was [at] 1700 hours with departure through the Eastern entrance. En route we

166

noticed that the *Talthybius* had moved into Empire Dock [a tidal basin] – there was no sign of anyone aboard. As quickly as possible the pilot disembarked, but there was some conflict at the bottom of the gangway as another evacuee fought for the platform… the sampan had no hope of gaining the gangway… As quickly as possible maximum revolutions were produced, the hull began to shudder and the three masts whipped dangerously, derricks were almost whipped out of their crutches, sparks and soot shot into the air… Shell [petroleum company] had been ordered to fire all their oil installations, hence Pulo Bukom [the island to which ships went to refuel] was a blazing inferno as we passed….

And so *Phrontis* headed south towards Tanjong Priok (sea port of Batavia), and at a very much reduced speed. At least no longer did sparks exhaust from the funnel… Departing the Durian Strait, course was set for Sinkep Island to arrive at dawn to anchor off Sparrow Fart. There four lifeboats were lowered into the water and duly tested for water tightness. From our passengers/evacuees, volunteers were called upon to man these boats, in order to land on Sinkep Island and procure vegetation to camouflage the ship – a tall order. Imagine trying to decorate the funnel some 50 feet above the boat deck. It was attempted. The volunteers did a marvellous job. In spite of raiding the carpenter's shop, cutting tools were at a premium, just an odd saw and the axes belonging to the boats… Possibly the Sinkep saga was the ship's salvation. One solitary plane did fly over and caused a little consternation. The same evening anchor was raised and course set for Tanjong Priok… We berthed at NMSO's own berth the following day… From Batavia (Tanjong Priok) we sailed for Melbourne.[29]

Captain Overland: M.V. **Poyang** *rescues Vietnamese refugees in 1981*

[In 1981 Captain Overland was in command of the *Poyang* trading between Hong Kong, Singapore and the South Pacific Islands.[30] She was owned by Swires' China Navigation Company. The incident involved Vietnamese refugees picked up in June 1981] At that time some owners were very reluctant for their masters to pick up refugees because of the great difficulty of finding a country that would accept them. We were lucky in that we were on course for Hong Kong in a Hong Kong registered ship.

[The account is a paraphrase from a China Navigation Company document, a copy of entries made in the official log book of the M.V. *Poyang* bound from Singapore towards Hong Kong, on Monday 29 June 1981 at noon on board in position Latitude O7° 10'N Longitude 108° 22'E (about 300 nautical miles south east of Saigon). At 1110 Cadet Wong Ting Yuen (No. 11 on the ship's articles [crew agreement] and Acting Third Mate) sighted two small boats on the port bow. At 1125 Wong Ting Yuen reported to Captain Overland that he had seen many people on one of the boats waving frantically. The Captain altered the vessel's course to return and investigate, and he manoeuvred the engines so that the vessel was alongside the boat at 1155. An English-speaking person, Mr Willy Ho came on board up the pilot ladder and stated that there were 43 persons on the small boat including 12 children, and that they were refugees from Vietnam. Mr Ho informed the Captain that they had left Vietnam on June 23 (some six days previously) and also that most of the persons in the boat were suffering from the effects of seasickness. They had run out of food and water on the previous day. The ship's crew lowered the gangway and all the refugees boarded safely. The refugees all stated that the other boat was empty and that the occupants had already been rescued. At 1213 (after a delay of about three quarters of an hour) the vessel proceeded on course to Hong Kong. Messages were sent to all ships (prefixed CQ) , and to the authorities at Hong Kong and Singapore regarding the now derelict boats. The refugees were weak and exhausted but otherwise in comparatively reasonable health. A few persons required first aid for minor ailments, details as per ship's Medical Log. A tally of the refugees showed that there were 17 men, 13 women, 6 boys and 6 girls. Details of this incident were cabled to owners, Hong Kong agents and the Marine Department, Hong Kong. A list of the refugees was appended. Both were endorsed (on 8 July 1981): 'for Superintendent Mercantile Marine Office, true copy of this log entry' and signed by the Captain and officers.

[Another document, also paraphrased, on China Navigation Company paper, typewritten on M.V. *Poyang*, is a report: Voyage 11 Singapore to Hong Kong: Rescue of Vietnamese Refugees. Much of the opening content is similar to the official log book entry, after which it describes the handling of the refugees on board]. The refugees were accommodated in the crew's mess room and were given food and hot drinks. The ship provided them with mattresses, blankets and pillows, and the port side of the mess room became their sleeping quarters. The third mate and cadets provided them with lifejackets. Some were spares and others old stock. By five in the afternoon they were all washed and dressed in a variety of clothes provided by the ship's officers and crew. The children were now all fast asleep. Next day, Tuesday 30 June 1981, the Captain interviewed the English-speaking refugee, Willy Ho (Ha Due, born 30 December 1964), and Nguyen Duy Hung (born 1 September 1948), an ex naval officer. They explained their escape from Vietnam. They sailed from a small village on the Mekong River delta located at 09° 52'N 106° 31'E. They possessed a US Navy chart of the South China Sea but no compass or navigation aids. Their express intention was to be picked up by a ship, as their boat was not capable of a sea voyage and they carried little food or water. On Saturday 27 June a large fishing boat approached them and to their horror they realised the boat contained armed Vietnamese pirates. They all panicked and threw their identity papers overboard, and two young men swallowed their gold rings. The pirates robbed them of all their possessions, their few valuables and Vietnamese money. The pirates refused to give them any food or water. From Friday to Monday, the day of their rescue they steered East towards the rising sun, but mostly drifted. All their food and water was used by Sunday afternoon and by the next day they thought they had no chances of surviving. This additional information was cabled to the Marine Department Hong Kong in answer to their questionnaire. The Captain reports that the refugees came mostly from the Saigon area. They all stated that the main reasons for leaving Vietnam were denial of basic human rights and government persecution of South Vietnamese. On Wednesday (1 July) the Captain reports that all the refugees continued to improve physically. On morning sick parade there were only headaches and head colds probably caused by the ship's efficient air conditioning. At 1520 that day the vessel was granted permission to enter Hong Kong and the next morning (Thursday 2 July) at 0636 she came to anchor in the Western Quarantine Anchorage. At 0700 Customs and Port Health officials boarded and at 0820 the Immigration Department officials boarded. [In his covering letter Captain Overland reports that the man at the top of the refugee list, Willy Ho, was their leader due to his good English. He wrote to the Captain about 18 months after the rescue by Christmas card saying that most of those rescued were in San Francisco and being offered various jobs and assistance in finding homes. However the next of the ships on the same trade route as the *Poyang* also came across a boatload of people but only found two alive out of about thirty.]

The Escape and rescue of a buffalo

'Buffalo Rescue at Sea' was the headline of a piece that appeared in the *South China Morning Post*: the crew and lifeboat of M.S. *Han Yang* off Indo-China took part in a dramatic rescue of a buffalo at sea last Thursday, while the ship was on her way from Bangkok to Hong Kong. (In those days, and right into the '70s, live buffaloes were imported to Hong Kong in substantial numbers). The ship was carrying over 300 buffaloes to Hong Kong when she was off the Indo-China coast. One of the animals broke loose and jumped overboard. The ship was immediately put about and the lifeboat lowered. Although the buffalo was swimming strongly away from the ship, the officer in charge of the lifeboat took it in tow. After a rope sling had been passed around the animal it was heaved on board. Thanks to the prompt rescue, the buffalo was none the worse for its adventure. The *Han Yang*, belonging to the China Navigation Company Limited, arrived here on Sunday. She leaves tomorrow, for Chilung [Taiwan]. A covering letter reports that all was not quite how it was reported in the newspaper and how they were enjoying their drinks, and the launching of the lifeboat took x minutes, where x equals 'considerable!' There was also reference to awnings rigged above the afterdeck to afford some protection to 300 standing passengers, mainly students for the passage from Hong Kong to Chilung, and return passengers during the busy holiday period in August to September. *Hang Yang* had a special licence, either to carry 380 buffaloes, or 380 standing passengers!

Conclusion

That the recollections included here were amenable to grouping under three themes was a matter of coincidence rather than advance direction, though it may say something about common experiences. Together they offer an insight into the diversity of maritime experience, and it is to be hoped that, through reading them former 'China Seas' hands will be encouraged to write up their own experiences. The experiences of British merchant seafarers in far eastern waters need to be matched with those of the army of British ex-patriots who worked in the maritime service occupations in China Seas ports: ships agents, merchants, pilots, harbour officials, customs, marine surveyors, and so on. Social historians increasingly recognise the value of memoirs and diaries, though they often have to trawl many volumes when pursuing particular themes. Of course they make judgements about the reliability of memory,

and comparisons between one source and another will from time to time raise questions.[31] But the value of new information in personal recollections far outweighs this disadvantage.

Notes and references

1 *Sudbury Hill*: managers Counties Shipping Ltd; built as a Fort boat in Canada 1943-7; gross tonnage 7,140.
2 Alston Kennerley served as a midshipman (apprentice) and deck officer with Blue Funnel from 1951 to 1961, when he obtained his Master's Certificate (foreign-going). After reading history in Wales and a course in education, he became a lecturer in navigation and later maritime history at Plymouth. He retired in 2000. He has published extensively, mainly papers on the history of nautical education and on seafaring welfare.
3 M.V. *Alcinous*: managers Alfred Holt & Co; built 1952; gross tonnage 7,799.
4 S.S. *Glenlogan*: owners Glen Line Limited; built 1943 in the USA (a Sam boat); gross tonnage 7,313.
5 M.V. *Glengarry*: owners Glen Line Limited; built Copenhagen 1939 but before delivery fell into German hands. Holt's recovered her in 1945; gross tonnage 9,199.
6 M.V. *Atreus*: owners China Mutual Steam Navigation Co. Ltd, Managers Alfred Holt & Co.; built 1951; gross tonnage 7,800.
7 Richard Woodman joined Blue Funnel in 1960 serving as apprentice and deck officer. He joined Trinity House in 1967 and has commanded several of its lighthouse tenders. Now writing full time, he is the author of many historical novels and of works on maritime history.
8 M.V. *Glenearn*: owners Glen Line Limited; built 1938; gross tonnage 9,869.
9 *Emden*, a German light cruiser of 3,600 tons, was the best known surface raider of the First World War (1914-18).
10 M.V. *Glenfruin*: owners China Mutual Steam Navigation Co.Ltd.; built 1948 as *Astyanax*, reverted to *Astyanax* 1962, broken up 1972; gross tonnage 7,645.
11 Fraser Stuart served as an apprentice and junior deck officer with Shell Tankers between 1947 and 1957, gaining his Master (foreign-going) Certificate in the latter year. He spent a year with the Union Steamship Company of New Zealand, and then between 1958 and 1969 he

served as master with Manners Navigation of Hong Kong. He then had a spell ashore first as Djakarta representative of Manners Navigation, and then as Training and Safety Officer with the Aberdeen Trawler Owners Association. He returned to sea from 1973 to 2000, serving as master successively with World-Wide Shipping, Hong Kong, Sanko Steamship Company, Tokyo, and Ropner Shipping/ British Steel Corporation.

12　M.V. *Naninia*: owners Anglo Saxon Petroleum Co.Ltd; built 1946 as *Empire Macmahon*; gross tonnage 8,166.

13　M.V. *Goldmouth*: owners Anglo Saxon Petroleum Co.Ltd.; built 1927; gross tonnage 7446.

14　M.V. *London Breeze*: owners John Manners Co., Hong Kong; built 1954 as *Welsh Trader*; gross tonnage 7,897.

15　M.V. *Hong Kong Breeze*: owners John Manners, Hong Kong; built 1943 as *Caxton*; gross tonnage 7,140.

16　M.V. *Thames Breeze*: owners John Manners, Hong Kong; built 1953 as *Ripley*; gross tonnage 7,343.

17　M.V. *Sydney Breeze*: owners John Manners, Hong Kong; built 1949 as *Trelevan*; gross tonnage 7,119.

18　Jonathon Parkinson was born in Trinidad in 1939, and educated in Tonbridge. He was employed in the shipping business in Sarawak, the Bahamas, South Africa, Belgium and the USA. He is presently actively engaged in items of naval research, principally but by no means entirely involving the Royal Navy on the China Station.

19　His Highness Sir Charles Vyner de Windt Brooke, GCMG. Born: 30 September 1874. Died: 9 May 1963. Rajah from 1917 to 1946.

20　The Brooke family rule ended on 1 July 1946. In September 1963, Sarawak became a constituent country of the newly formed Malaysia.

21　The first Rajah was James Brooke. Born: 29 April 1803. Died: 11 June 1868. Succeeded by his nephew, Charles Anthoni Johnson. Born: 3 June 1829. Died: 17 May 1917.

22　Early in 1967 it merged with Inchcape Co. Ltd.

23　When rigged in the Union Purchase mode, one ship's derrick was plumbed over the ship's side, the other over the hatchway. Their cargo runners (lifting wires) were shackled together at the hook, Loading, a sling of cargo suspended from the hook overside was raised clear of the ship's rail under the derrick, then the load was gradually transferred to the other derrick and lowered down the hatch. Two winches provided the power. Unloading, the procedure was reversed. See also Note 24.

24　For the Blue Funnel approach to cargo handling and stowage see Alston Kennerley, 'Cargo Handling and Stowage: British Cargo Liner Practice in the 1950s, with Some Reference to Nineteenth Century Practice', in Stephen Fisher (ed), *British Shipping and Seamen, 1630-1960: Some Studies*, (Exeter, 1984), 86-109.

25　Jonathon Parkinson recalls that the manager was an Anglo-Burmese, Hector Soord, and his assistant, also Anglo-Burmese, was Warren Trinidad. The sawmill was known as Bukit Kinyau. Hector's son served for a short while as Midshipman in Blue Funnel.

26　Reproduced from The *Newsletter* of the Nestorian Association, No 5 (May, 2002), 15-18, with the permission of the Editor, Mr J.C. Hurst. This monthly newsletter has been produced for nearly 40 years. A full run may be found in the Maritime Archives & Library of Merseyside Maritime Museum. Most issues contain memoirs of former Blue Funnel staff, many relating to China Seas waters.

27　M.V. *Phrontis*: owners Nederlandsche Stoomvaart Maatschappij Oceaan, managers Alfred Holt & Co; built 1926; gross tonnage 6,636.

28　*Talthybius*: managers Alfred Holt & Co; built 1912; gross tonnage 10,254. Her crew escaped to Batavia in HMS *Ping Wo*, a small naval auxiliary. The ship was raised by the Japanese. At the end of the war she was found sunk in Maizuru Harbour, Honshu, Japan, raised again, made seaworthy and brought home with a cargo of scrap iron, after which she was sold for scrap. See S.W. Roskill, *A Merchant Fleet in War, Alfred Holt & Co., 1939-1945,* (London, 1962).

29　*Phrontis* survived the war.

30　M.S. *Poyang*: owners China Navigation Co.Ltd. (Butterfield & Swire) of Hong Kong; built 1973; gross tonnage 8,705.

31　For a discussion on evaluating autobiographies, letters and diaries see Michael Drake and Ruth Finnegan (eds), *Sources and Methods for Family and Community Historians*, (Cambridge, 1994), 105-7.

Britain, Macao, and Portuguese Ambitions in the South China Sea

G.H. Timmermans

The British presence in China Seas can be dated from the mid-seventeenth century, when early navigators called at ports in Malaysia and along the China coast.[1] In this they were preceded first by the Portuguese,[2] who opened the sea route to Asia in 1498, and then by the Dutch. In terms of the area called the China Seas, that British presence was consolidated in 1795 by wresting control of Malacca from the Dutch, who had, in turn, taken it from the Portuguese in 1641. Occupation of Malacca was crucial for establishing a dominant presence in this area, as control of is straits was, in effect, to dictate the traffic from the Andaman Sea into the South China Sea. For British ships to sail in China Seas did not, of course, require that control but the growth of British maritime power in this area was greatly enhanced by the occupation of parts of Malaya, and later Singapore (1819), as well as Hong Kong (1842).

British ships became a regular feature of China Sea traffic with the re-opening of Canton to foreign traders in 1685 and this developed into one of the most profitable branches of the East India Company's commerce. The tea trade, a significant sector in seventeenth and eighteenth-century British economics, motivated, in part, the development also of the opium trade, as the sale of one was needed to finance the purchase of the other. That, in turn, led to the so-called First Opium War (1839-1842), and the subsequent establishment of Hong Kong and opening of the treaty ports.

Hong Kong was, and probably remains, even after its return to China, the most tangible symbol of the British presence in this region but the development of British trade with China, and the rise of British maritime power in East Asia, began to develop two hundred years before Hong Kong's foundation. While this trade, maritime by nature, required only a

fleet of ships, it was greatly assisted by the Portuguese presence in the now largely ignored city of Macao.[3]

This paper will seek to address early Portuguese ambitions in China Seas as the first Europeans in this area and, at the same time, it will attempt also to demonstrate how the later British domination was crucially assisted, however unwittingly, by that Portuguese presence. The context of this paper is *British Ships in China Seas*, and if, as seems inevitable, this is to concentrate largely on China rather than the island archipelagos that define its southern reaches, the role of Portuguese ambitions as a precursor to British maritime power here must be addressed. Put simply, the Portuguese presence in Macao from 1557 to 1999 is a much greater achievement than might immediately be obvious. Its contribution to later British domination in this region is not always sufficiently appreciated.

Discussion of British activity in terms of the tea and opium trade almost always centres only on Canton and, after 1840, on Hong Kong, and the vital presence of Macao in this network continues to be neglected. It is consistently forgotten that British trade with China was made considerably easier because the British could base themselves in Macao out of the Canton trading season. As in so many areas in the tense relations between Europe and China, Chinese law was also uncompromising on the question of a foreign presence in Canton out of the trading season. That season usually ran from about September to late January/early February (Chinese Lunar New Year), whereafter all foreigners had to leave, and were then permitted to return only at the beginning of the new season the following September. Macao, about eighty miles down river from Canton, gradually developed into a British base where arrangements for trade and its management could continue uninterrupted. Without the convenience of Macao, the East India Company's supercargoes and other officialdom would all have had to withdraw to Calcutta, adding considerably to costs and seriously weakening management of the Canton trade.

All too often Canton is used as a convenient shorthand for Macao *and* Canton, but to do so is to ignore the important differences between the two: one under Chinese law and the other under Portuguese, and thus rather more hospitable to a British presence, though it was not without its tensions either. Foreign women were strictly banned from Canton, and while British and American women only began to arrive in Macao in the early nineteenth century, many British traders took Chinese mistresses in Macao. Even today, amongst the Macanese – the mixed race people of Macao – there are some families with distinctly British surnames.

China's relations with various European powers were never easy, largely because it had long regarded itself as the dominant power in Asia, and its interaction with foreign states was arranged according to this acknowledgement of its supremacy. This was something few European powers were willing to accept and the British consistently rejected it. China was, of course, humiliated in the Treaty of Nanking following the First Opium War, and the forfeiture of Hong Kong rankled until its return to Chinese sovereignty in 1997, and it is still invoked in the rhetoric of Chinese nationalism. But it has also to be acknowledged that Britain partly provoked war with China precisely to gain an offshore territory like Hong Kong, though initially they had planned to take territory further up the coast and closer to Peking. This request for an offshore territory was made during Lord Macartney's Embassy in 1793, and its denial by the Qianlong Emperor was cause to find other means of securing it. In essence, Britain wanted something like Macao, somewhere sufficiently close to the trading ports to make it a viable base, but somewhere also where extra-territorial powers and laws, beyond the reach of the Chinese mandarinate, could be exercised. Britain had used the cover of the Napoleonic Wars, and France's occupation of Portugal, to invade and occupy Macao in 1808. Portuguese dismay and Chinese fury put an end to that ill-considered gamble but Britain continued to strive for something like it, whence the importance of Hong Kong as part of war reparations in 1842.

Macao is unique in Chinese history as the only piece of Chinese territory ever to be loaned or bequeathed to a foreign power through negotiation and not as a spoil of war through 'unequal treaty'.[4] That the Portuguese succeeded in establishing a permanent settlement on the China coast by means other than conquest has not yet been adequately explained and this paper will not presume to offer such explanation either. It will, however, mention just some of the theories of how this came to be.

Like so many histories in recent years, Macao's has also been subject to different revisionist approaches and this has been motivated, in very large part, by the contesting ideologies of Portuguese post-colonialism and Chinese nationalism.[5] Macao offers an almost ideal case study of a contested space, with competing versions of history and foundation myths. Certainly, the topic 'the origins of Macao' has now become a stable for all publications devoted to the history and culture of this tiny city enclave.

Macao was handed back to China at the end of 1999 according to the same 'One Country, Two Systems' formula used for Hong Kong's return to Chinese sovereignty in 1997, with the most important differences being the protection of Portuguese as one of two official languages for fifty years, and the continuation of the Portuguese (Civil Code) legal system. In the run up to handover in 1999, as China's media and official scholarship began to take an interest in Macao (a place much neglected previously despite the nationalist rhetoric of anti-colonialism), the question of Macao's origins attracted increasing interest.

From the European point of view, the

uncontested historical 'facts' can briefly be summarised. The history of Portugal's opening the European sea route to India in 1498 and later occupation of Goa in 1510, and Portugal's subsequent domination of Indian Ocean maritime trade by replacing Arab and other Muslim-controlled commerce, is sufficiently well known to pass without any further comment. Portuguese Goa became the centre of the *Estado da India* – that nexus of European/Asian trade – and the viceroy ruled all of Portuguese Asia from this base. The conquest of Malacca by Afonso de Albuquerque in 1511 further strengthened Portugal's position, and again at the expense of the Islamic trading empire. The dividing line between Portuguese activity in India and in the Indian Ocean generally, and its somewhat separate activity in China Seas can be usefully located in the conquest of Malacca. The ramifications of the Portuguese conquest were felt also in China. Malacca had long formed part of the Chinese tributary system, whereby sovereign states paid obeisance to Chinese power and dominance through a complex system of diplomatic tribute, and after the Portuguese 'seized Malacca, the Chinese lost its prestige among the states in South-East Asia'.[6]

It was in Malacca that the Portuguese first came into direct contact with Chinese traders, about whom they had heard in India. China, of course, was already familiar to the European imagination from the writings of Marco Polo but it seems that Polo's use of the name Cathay may initially have confused any obvious connection between the two. Even before the conquest of Malacca, Vasco da Gama had brought Chinese Ming porcelain, purchased in India, back to Portugal, and it had sufficiently aroused the curiosity of the king, Dom Manuel I, that he ordered his representatives in Asia to:

> … ask after the Chijns, and from what part they come, and from how far, and at what times they come to Malacca, or to the places at which they trade, and the merchandise they bring, and how many of their ships come each year, and regarding the form and type of their ships, and if they return in the same year, and if they are wealthy merchants, and if they are weak men, or warriors, and if they have arms or artillery, and what clothes they wear, and if they are men of large build, and all other information concerning them, and if they are Christians or heathens, or if their country is a great one, and if they have more than one king amongst them, or if any moors live amongst them or any other people who are not of their law or faith; and if they adore, and what customs they observe, and towards what part does their country extend, and with whom do they confine.[7]

The king was obviously determined to gather a fairly comprehensive intelligence report and certainly after seizing Malacca, most of these questions would have been answered. Very shortly after that conquest the Portuguese made their first forays into Chinese waters, and it was Jorge Alvares who became the first European to reach Chinese soil by sea when he landed at Tamao in 1513. The precise location where he made landfall is still open to conjecture but it seems Tamoa was either present-day Lintin (in the Pearl River Delta) or another island close by. Alvares, in customary fashion of Portuguese explorers, erected a *padrao*, or stone cross, as a mark of Christian and Lusitanian conquest.

There is a certain naivety in that action, an assumption of European power and Christian right – raising a cross of conquest on Chinese soil – but its non-violence also reinforces the achievement of Portuguese involvement in the South China Sea, and more specifically in China itself. The period between Jorge Alvares' first landing on Chinese soil in 1513 and the establishment of Macao as a Portuguese settlement 1557, can be summarised as a series of hit and miss attempts to achieve in China what the Portuguese attained rather more easily in Goa and Malacca at the beginning of the sixteenth century. It is not clear when the Portuguese realised that military conquest – as in Goa and Malacca – was not an option, but certainly various attempts were made both to establish regular trade links with China from

Malacca and also to set up diplomatic relations with the Ming Imperial Court.

In 1517 Portugal sent Tomé Pires as diplomatic envoy to China but it was only in 1520 that he was allowed to proceed from Canton to Peking, and he was then delayed until 1521 waiting for the emperor to return from his southern capital in Nanking. This embassy was to prove as ill fated as most that followed. While Pires was struggling to meet the emperor, other Portuguese were launching small-scale raids along the China coast, and this ill-considered aggression led to Pires's imprisonment, along with his diplomatic suite, and they all perished in a Canton gaol. Thus this Portuguese piracy not only led to diplomatic failure but also poisoned early Portuguese-Chinese contact.

Pires, or some other member of the diplomatic suite did, however, manage to smuggle two letters out of the Canton prison. These documents, known as *The Letters from Portuguese Captives in Canton*, were the first written descriptions by Europeans, since Marco Polo, to describe Chinese life and they went some way also towards answering Dom Manuel I's many questions – about Chinese custom, costume, legal system, religious practice, etc. At the same time they are also full of useful military intelligence, suggesting which parts of the South China coast were most vulnerable to attack, descriptions of Chinese artillery, military strength, and other information all leading to the conclusion that the Portuguese were seriously considering the possibility of incorporating China into their expanding Asian empire.[8]

The historical timing of the Portuguese encounter with China is interesting in its own right, and is open to interpretation whether it was perhaps to Portugal's advantage that this contact occurred during the latter years of the Ming Dynasty, when the closed-door policy was a reality. The Ming Dynasty only finally collapsed in 1644 but it was already beginning to unravel and the closed-door policy was in part motivated by a desire to increase internal security. This fear of the outside world may, of course, have been to Portugal's advantage, and this idea needs to be examined.

The Pires Embassy was a disaster and it set the tone for the next thirty years of Portuguese-Chinese relations. In 1522 the Port of Canton was closed to foreign trade and the emperor banned all further contact with the Portuguese. In response to this Chinese refusal to trade, Martim Afonso de Melo Coutinho sailed defiantly up the Pearl River and various skirmishes ensued throughout 1522 and 1523. The Portuguese finally abandoned the Pearl River Delta area and traded further up the China coast, in much the same way that early English and Dutch traders would do in the seventeenth century. They managed to secure a base at Liampo, on the Yangtze River, and there they traded for the next fifteen years on an informal basis.

In 1542 the Portuguese, more by accident than design, landed on the Japanese island of Tanegashima, and this chance encounter is the catalyst that set in motion the beginnings of Portuguese prosperity in Chinese Seas. The Chinese emperor's insistence on isolationism had proscribed all trade between China and Japan and they soon realised that as middlemen between these two wealthy countries there were fortunes to be made.

The idea persists that the early European traders made their fortunes largely in the spice trade and, of course, this was a key part of Europe's economic relationship with East Asia. But this China-Japan trade, carried out by the Portuguese, is a precursor also of the later India-China country trade, for which opium was the basis. There is a dynamism in these Asian economies, and in this intra-Asian trade, beyond European control, even though Europeans often played a leading role, which is not always sufficiently emphasised in Western views on non-European economies.

In the late 1540s the Portuguese were expelled from their Liampo base and needing to supply the Japan trade – silk, porcelain, and gold into Japan in exchange for silver much wanted by the Chinese – they moved south to the Pearl River Delta again, this time to the island of Shangchuan. It was there that Francis Xavier, often called the Apostle of the East, recently arrived from Japan and hoping to convert China, died in 1552. He was, of course, followed by other Jesuits and their role in Portuguese trade and influence in Japan, China, and elsewhere in Asia, was of considerable significance in Europe's relations with the East, and in the histories of various Asian countries as well.

In 1555, for reasons which are not wholly clear, the Portuguese moved from their mat-shed settlement in Shangchuan to the small peninsula of *Ao-men* (Mandarin)/*Ou-mun* (Cantonese), where the temple of Ah-ma, goddess of seafarers, was already well established. It was from her name that *Ah-ma-gao* evolved into Macao.

Portuguese maritime ambition in the China Seas extended, of course, much further than Macao. The Japan route, where ships from Goa and Malacca called at Macao in order to purchase Chinese silks, porcelain and gold before sailing on to Nagasaki, became the mainstay of Macao's early economy. This trade was the foundation of Macao's early prosperity and it represents the greatest period of Portuguese trade in East Asia. Thus Dutch success in expelling the Portuguese from Japan lead to the collapse of Macao's economy and seriously effected Portuguese prosperity throughout Asia.

Portuguese maritime activity in China Seas included not only occupation of places like Nagasaki, and Timor, but also an extensive trade network between Macao and Mexico through Manila; between Macao, Siam and Cambodia; Macao-Macassar-Flores-Solar-Timor; and Macao-Macassar-Goa-Europe. This network made Macao one of the most important entrepots in Asia and Macao was, briefly, also an immensely wealthy city through this trade. Macao was sustained by this trading network after the loss of Japan, and it enjoyed later periods of prosperity as well, but the Japan years were, without doubt, its golden age. The entry of the Dutch into China Seas in the 1620s seriously curtailed Portuguese ambitions, and the subsequent arrival of the English as well meant that Portuguese power diminished still further, and survived only in Brazil, and in the African colonies.

This brief period of economic boom followed by slow decline with occasional recovery has been a consistent pattern throughout Macao's 445-year history but its existence as a Portuguese colony, until 1999, remains wholly peculiar. There are, as has been pointed out, contesting versions of how this came about, and historians, Portuguese and Chinese, as well as others, continue to offer their interpretations.

The long established and, until recently, received, version of Macao's foundation argued that the Portuguese arrived in Macao from Shangchuan only to dry goods damaged in a storm, and while there they assisted the local Chinese in driving away Chinese bandits and Japanese pirates (*wakos*). The problem of piracy in the Pearl River Delta has long been acknowledged and it is perfectly feasible that the Portuguese should have protected their own trade against this scourge. But whether a grateful Chinese officialdom then bequeathed Macao to the Portuguese, so to ensure their continued guardianship over the mouth of the Pearl River has become increasingly doubtful. Portuguese historians long claimed that Macao was formally given to the Portuguese traders but early English and other Western traders cast doubt on this, partly because there were no documents substantiating it, but, more importantly, because the Portuguese paid an annual land rent for the territory.[9]

Chinese historians, who have argued that there is no precedent for this arrangement in Chinese history, challenge this version. Acknowledging the early Portuguese presence, they claim instead that the Portuguese took advantage of corrupt officialdom, and were then obliged to pay this annual rental as a continued bribe, while the emperor was kept ignorant of this local arrangement. These rather simplistic interpretations have recently been challenged or developed and rethought by an emerging generation of Macao historians, now seeking to explain their city's own history away from the competing ideologies of coloniser and aggrieved colonised.

K.C. Fok, a leading historian of early Macao, has long argued that the Chinese authorities compromised their normal anti-foreign policy precisely because the China-Portuguese trade was too profitable to be ignored. The Portuguese arrival in Macao during the accelerating decline of Ming power was advantageous to the foreigners, as the imminence of Ming collapse precipitated an economic crisis and Peking was in urgent need of this new-found source of revenue. Fok further argues that the Ming feared the possibility of a Portuguese alliance with those threatening imperial power and so it was simple expediency to incorporate the Portuguese into a controllable system whereby they would be confined to a single area rather than left to maraud the coast of China along with other hostile groups.[10]

A young Macao historian, Wu Zhiliang, has recently proposed a controversial but interesting theory that Portuguese success in Macao derives partly from Ming dynastic needs. The Ming, he argues, were compromised by Portuguese conquest of Malacca and this weakened their potential relations with the Chinese but, at the same time, alerted Peking to the military strength of this hitherto unknown power. He has produced convincing evidence that the walls of Canton were considerably strengthened in the 1530s, precisely at the time the Portuguese were testing their strength along the Pearl River. Thus, along with Fok, he suggests that allowing them a foothold in Macao was a diplomatic means to accommodate but confine the Portuguese at the same time. However, Wu also suggests that the Jiajing Emperor's consistent failure to produce an heir was causing alarm in a dynasty already weakened by other factors, and the Portuguese trade in ambergris made them indispensable to the Chinese. Ambergris was thought to be a powerful aphrodisiac, improving vitality as

well as fertility, and this product was urgently sought by the imperial household. Again, Wu has produced evidence to support this idea in references to ambergris in Tomé Pires' *Suma Oriental* as well as other early Portuguese writing from China; and in Chinese sources he has located a specially created office of 'Imperial Commissioner For Ambergris Search'.[11]

The various approaches to the question of Macao's foundation are fully explored in works by Fok, Wu, and others. The point which needs to be made here is that there is no sufficient explanation for this creation of a Western city, where Christianity was rigorously practiced, and foreigners were allowed to live and work under the vigilant watch of the Chinese who only interfered when their laws were openly violated. Portuguese historians have tended to write of Macao in strictly Chinese and Portuguese terms but a number of Chinese historians have shown that traders of various nationalities congregated in Macao, and that it developed as a minor market from its convenient location close to Canton. They argue that Portuguese aggression eventually deterred others from visiting and this belligerence, while never leading to open conflict, ensured their monopoly of this peninsula. Whether this was then consolidated through bribery or other arrangements remains unclear.

Portuguese ambitions in China Seas were certainly extensive in the sixteenth century and stretched from Goa to Japan, including Timor, various Spice Islands, Malacca, and Macao. The Portuguese succeeded in opening trade relations with Japan but were ultimately defeated partly through their own sponsorship of the Jesuit enterprise but also because they failed to repel Dutch influence. The Dutch, in turn, tried to expel the Portuguese from Macao in 1622, but were defeated in a major battle, and it is likely that even had they succeeded in wresting control from the Portuguese, they would promptly have been trounced by the Chinese. China tolerated a Portuguese presence in Macao for reasons which cannot be adequately explained but another European presence would not be allowed, and hence also the expulsion of the Dutch from Formosa/Taiwan in 1683.

The loss of the Japan trade led to Macao's decline but that city flourished again, if on a lesser scale, once the Dutch, Swedish, Danish, and especially the British used it as a base for the Canton trade. In the eighteenth century the presence of the East India Company in Macao aroused some resistance from the Portuguese but it was also vital to the Macao economy and so was increasingly tolerated.

It was from Macao that Britain slowly established its trading supremacy in Canton and it was in Macao that the British settled in increasingly large numbers. They developed into a community who made a significant contribution to the non-mercantile life of Macao, in language study, in medicine, in art, and in education. They were the conduit for the Protestant missionary movement which, while viewed as a mixed legacy, must be acknowledged for its role in the development of modern China. Britain's contribution to the history of China has been marred because of the political fallout from Hong Kong and the treaty ports, but viewed objectively it was often positive. Equally, the British presence in Macao allowed the development of English Sinology concomitant with trading activity, and commerce and education developed to mutual benefit. The East India Company was in Macao because the Portuguese made it possible for them to be there, and it was a British desire to have something similar that led, ultimately, to the establishment of Hong Kong and British maritime supremacy in China Seas for much of the nineteenth and twentieth centuries.

Notes and references

1   The first English ships reached Macao on 27 June 1637, under the command of Captain John Weddell. See *The Travels of Peter Mundy in Europe and Asia, 1608-1667*, edited by Sir Richard Carnac Temple (London, 1919), and also Austin Coates, *Macao and the British 1637-1842*, (Hong Kong, 1988). An earlier English ship, the *London*, sailing under an English flag of convenience, reached Macao in July 1635 but it was chartered by the viceroy of Goa.

2   The history of Portuguese maritime activity in China Seas has been extensively studied by Charles Boxer and his various works in this area remain essential texts. However, one of the more interesting and important recent studies is Sanjay Subrahmanyam, *The Portuguese Empire in Asia 1500-1700*, (London, 1993). It is probably reasonable to say that Subrahmanyam has established himself as the leading contemporary historian, writing in English, in this area of historical research.
Numerous articles on Macao, as well as the history of the Portuguese in Asia, together with various other related subjects, are regularly published in *Review of Culture/Revista de Cultura*, a quarterly journal from the Cultural Institute of Government of the Macao SAR (ICM).

3   Macao is variously spelt as 'Macao' or 'Macau'. Both forms appear in English but the historical rendering has inclined to the end 'o' spelling in English while the Portuguese spelling is always with a 'u'. The Chinese State Council decreed in 2001 that the English spelling should now always be 'Macao' but this is still ignored by many, especially in both Hong Kong and Macao. This article uses Nanking and Peking, rather than their modern equivalents, only because these were the forms commonly in use in English during the period covered here.

4   The term 'unequal treaty' is used by the People's Republic of China to describe both the Treaty of Nanking in 1842, and the later Lisbon Protocol and Treaty of Trade and Friendship in Peking (1887-1888), whereby the Portuguese presence in Macao was formally recognised by China, and Macao, like Hong Kong, was bequeathed to its occupiers 'in perpetuity'.

5   It can reasonably be argued that Portugal, partly in response to its ignominious departure from East Timor, Mozambique, and Angola, has sought to redeem its colonial past in Macao. Prior to departing on 19/20 December 1999, Portugal spent considerable sums on public works and various monuments as part of a positive legacy of the Portuguese presence in Macao for nearly 450 years.

6   Wu Zhiliang, 'Ambergris and Opium in Macau's History', in *Macau on the Threshold of the Third Millennium*, Macau Ricci Institute Studies 1 (Macao, 2003), 59.

7   *Alguns Documentos do Archivo Nacionl da Torre do Tombo*, (Lisbon, 1892), 194-5. The translation here is based on Donald Ferguson's, cited in J.M. Braga, *The Western Pioneers and their Discovery of Macao*, (Macau, 1949), 60.

8   The Pires Embassy is discussed in detail, and often amusingly, in a chapter called 'Poor Pires', in Nigel Cameron, *Barbarians and Mandarins*, (Hong Kong, 1989).

9   One of the key histories of Macao in English remains C.A. Montalto de Jesus, *Historic Macao*, first published in 1902 and subsequently reissued in a new edition in 1926. This second edition questioned Portugal's fitness to continue governing Macao and this led to public burnings of the book in Macao. The 1926 edition was reissued by Oxford University Press, Hong Kong, in 1984, and it offers a thorough analysis of some of the Portuguese theories of Macao's origins.

10 See, for instance, Fok Kaicheong, 'The Existence of Macau: A Chinese Perspective', in *Macau on the Threshold of the Third Millennium*, Macau Ricci Institute Studies 1 (Macao, 2003), 13-38. Other works by Fok, on this same subject, are extensively cited in this article.

11 See Wu Zhiliang, 'Ambergris and Opium', 57-83.

'Africa to the British, East Asia to the Germans:' Germany's Rise to an East Asian Power

Lars U. Scholl

Despite a worldwide economic slowdown which seems to have hit Germany harder than other countries, Hamburg's port authorities in 2002 proudly reported record increases in port traffic, with more than five million containers (TEU) handled, a growth of fifteen per cent over 2001. No other economic sector enjoyed such growth. Two geographic areas were responsible for this development: the Baltic region, with its new potentials in the enlarging European Union (EU) and in the Russian markets, and the China trade, which created opportunities that are expected to reach huge dimensions in the future, according to Hamburg's minister of economic affairs, Gunnar Uldall. Indeed, this trend will likely receive an extra boost once China joins the World Trade Organization (WTO).

German car manufacturers like Volkswagen and economic giants like Siemens or Thyssen Krupp are investing heavily in the Chinese economy. Thyssen Krupp provided the expertise for the Shanghai Transrapid Maglev Line, the world's first high-speed commercial commuting system using state-of-the-art electromagnetic levitation technology. The Chinese and German Prime Ministers were aboard when the train made its maiden journey on 1 January 2003. These and other activities are a clear indication of the importance of China, with more than one billion potential customers, to Germany's export-orientated economy. They are, however, by no means of recent origin, since there has been German economic interest in China since the eighteenth century.

In this essay I will present an overview of German engagement in the China trade and outline the maritime dimension of these activities.[1] Although the paper is largely a synthesis, it draws on scattered and disparate sources that will largely be new to an English-speaking audience. I will begin with the first German vessel known to have returned from China in the first part of the eighteenth century. The different phases and changing rationale for sailing to China will be discussed, leading up to the engrossment of a strip of land in Tsingtao by the Imperial German Navy in 1897. This territory, which was meant to be a 'German Gibraltar' in the East, was the starting point for making inroads into the Chinese market and remained in German hands until it was taken by the Japanese in 1914.[2] German rule ended formally in 1919 when article 156 of the Treaty of Versailles forced the country to cede all its rights, titles and privileges in China. This interesting episode, however, will have to await a future paper. Likewise, there is no room here to deal with the German role in putting down the Boxer Rebellion, when the call 'Germans to the front' was made. While I have to refrain from touching upon these topics in this article, I will conclude by drawing attention to the hopes of Emperor Wihelm II for a rapprochement with England based upon the principle *Africa to the British and East Asia to the Germans*.

I. Tentative Approaches to China prior to 1789 : The Hanseatic Cities

Long before any German ship sailed to China it had been fashionable in bourgeois, aristocratic and mercantile circles to recount fantastic stories about China. Such tales, however, were often based more upon imagination than reality, and so little knowledge existed that it is often impossible to determine whether a ship sailed to China or only to India. This is because the sources often refer to East India when the destination of a vessel is given. One of these accounts is Eberhard Werner Happel's book *Der Asiatische Onogambo*, published in Hamburg in 1673. In the course of the seventeenth century Chinese porcelain found its way to Hamburg, most likely via Portugal, which had acquired Macao in 1557 and had close shipping connections with the German port.[3] In 1625 one fifth of all ships leaving the River Elbe were destined for Portuguese ports. Chinese or Portuguese chinaware, for example, came to the Hanseatic city either via this trade or through Sephardic Jews from Iberia and the Netherlands who had sought asylum in Hamburg. Such imports enriched a porcelain manufacture that had just begun to develop. *Chinoiseries* became a fashion, and artists painted pagodas, townscapes, Chinese arcades or strange trees, while Chinese characters appeared in operas or theatrical productions as exotic and distorted figures.

While it is possible to trace these indirect contacts with China in Hamburg and elsewhere, it is not as easy to pinpoint precisely the beginning and the exact nature of the first direct German engagement in the Chinese seas. This may have something to do with the monopoly which the British East India Company held in the China trade between 1773 and 1834. But the Chinese geographer Chen Lungiong mentions German trading vessels in Canton in 1730 in his book *Report on the Countries Bordering the Sea*. At the same time, a Hamburg-based French merchant named Karl Quentin Dumanoir suggested to the King of Prussia that he form a Prussian East India Company. Although such a plan never came to fruition, the suggestion must be seen in the context of Denmark's trade with China. In those days the Danish Kingdom stretched down to the Elbe, where Altona was a rival to Hamburg. Attempts to found a Danish East Asiatic Company in 1728 were successfully undermined by Britain, France and the Netherlands, but in 1732 King Christian IV signed the charter for the Dansk Asiatisk Kompagni (DAK) which renewed old trade links with China dating back to the seventeenth century.[4]

The first German vessel known so far to have returned from China, in September 1731, was the *Apollon*, which sailed under the Prussian flag.[5] British and Dutch diplomats in Hamburg tried to have the vessel and its cargo placed in quarantine. They advanced two arguments for their position: first, that no vessel was allowed to sail directly up the Elbe or to land Chinese cargo in Hamburg, thus avoiding the monopolies granted to their respective companies; and second, that this vessel sailed under no protection whatsoever. The magistrate refused to countenance these arguments and in his decision pointed to the freedom of the port of Hamburg. As a result, the cargo of tea and porcelain was put on display for ten days and then successfully auctioned for good prices. Although silk, tea and porcelain had been popular for some time, the German states were unable to compete with countries like Denmark, Britain and Holland. Still, there are reasons to believe that a private trade which paid tax to the state and duties to the Dutch East Asia Company existed. Some of these ships may have sailed to Canton from Altona/Hamburg. A second way of participating in the China trade involved the supply of silver provided by merchants and bankers in Hamburg when the DAK suffered from financial problems from 1760 onwards. While we can assume that there were many contacts with China during the eighteenth century, the first vessel we know with certainty that left Hamburg for East Asia sailed in 1787 and went at least as far as India. Another ship that entered the port of Hamburg in 1792 came from Canton, and some vessels may have sailed under foreign flags despite the fact that they were originally registered in Hamburg.

Looking at the Hanseatic sister city of Bremen, one of the first merchant-skippers to sail to China was Carl Philipp Cassel (born 1744).[6] He had served in the DAK and become one of its captains in 1769. Using the knowledge he had acquired, he founded a trading company which sent the *Präsident* to East Asia under the Prussian flag.[7] The same year the *Asia* sailed from Emden for the East. These operations, which seem to have been for reconnaissance in order to establish trade relations with China, ended during the Napoleonic wars.

The Royal Prussian Asiatic Company

Frederick the Great (1712-1786) succeeded his father as king of Prussia in 1740. He never intended to build a navy to protect his merchant fleet and even advised his successor to refrain from competing with the British, Dutch, French and Spanish.[8] Much of his thinking, energy and resources were directed towards rounding off his territory through conflict with Austria over Silesia. Nevertheless, he began to 'see the sea' after Prussia gained access to Stettin in 1720 and to Emden in 1744, although Prussia ideologically remained a continental and agrarian society. Frederick heeded the advice of his great grandfather, the Great Elector Frederick Wilhelm (1620-1688), who claimed that 'Seafaring and maritime trade are the most important pillars of the state because the inhabitants are able to secure their nourishment and subsistence both by the sea as well as by manufactories.' While a commission had decided in 1732 that Prussia did not need shipping companies since it had sufficient access to foreign tonnage and hence to foreign goods, Frederick emphasised a few years later that maritime trade with an indigenous merchant fleet would be quite profitable. When he died in 1786, Prussia's merchant fleet comprised 791 seagoing vessels, most of which were registered in East Frisia. These figures are a third lower than at the beginning of the 1780s, when Prussia profited from a boom during the American War of Independence.

It is not surprising that Frederick was as interested in overseas trade as the other west European countries. Following their example, he founded the Royal Asiatic Company in Emden in 1750/51.[9] From 1752 onwards several armed vessels sailed from Emden to China. This explains why Cassel in Bremen dispatched his vessels from Emden under Prussian protection. The company's vessel *King of Prussia*, a ship built in England, returned with silk, tea, porcelain and other goods to Germany. The auction in Emden was very profitable, a fact which was noted in

London and Amsterdam with dismay. Merchants of the East India Company in London went berserk when it became known that the vessel had been insured in London. Shouting *Emden esse delendam* (Emden has to be destroyed), Parliament in Westminster passed a bill forbidding the insurance of foreign ships trading with East Asia. In total, fourteen vessels sailed to China. When the war at sea between England and France erupted in 1755, significant damage was done to the Prussian company, which eventually collapsed in the course of the British-French colonial war between 1755 and 1763.

Several attempts to revive the company failed, and Frederick hoped that French merchants could establish new links with China. But their initiative ended with no success. Likewise, merchants sent several ships to Bengal, Batavia and China in the 1780s without lasting results. All these efforts were made with half-hearted support from the state administration. The civil servants in Berlin lacked the experience to foster Frederick's maritime aspirations, and continental affairs had still a higher priority than maritime trade. The allegedly privileged company never had real freedom to conduct its business; in reality it was a company directed from a capital that was far removed from the sea. In the end, all initiatives to establish maritime contact with China proved no more than a whim by a state that was more interested in its continental

*The **King of Prussia**, the first Prussian ship dispatched to China in 1752.*

interests, despite the fact that Prussia wanted to assume the leading role in the German foreign and overseas trade.

II. New Efforts to Revive the China Trade after 1815

The Hanseatic Cities
As soon as the Continental Blockade ended the Hanseatic cities of Bremen, Hamburg and Lübeck, now independent cities after the dissolution of the Holy German Empire, began to revive their maritime trade with East Asia and especially with China. It took some time to get together enough seaworthy ships for such a long voyage. Many vessels had been rotting away through enforced inactivity during the Napoleonic wars. Between 1816 and 1842 there were at least fifty-one vessels with cargo from China that entered the port of Hamburg. On average, three ships per year sailed from Canton to Hamburg in the 1820s, 1830s and 1840s. Later, up to 1871 fourteen or more ships annually arrived from China in the River Elbe. Direct relations between Bremen and China developed more slowly. In 1836 two vessels returned from China, and in 1837 and 1838 three ships sailed up the Weser. In the following years, four or five vessels per annum arrived at Bremen.

These figures are cloaked in uncertainty, however, because up to 1855 China, East India and Australia were lumped together in the statistics. Therefore it is impossible to determine if a ship that was dispatched to 'East India' sailed to Batavia, Australia or China. It is quite obvious, however, that these voyages were of a pioneering character and were based on speculative business expectations. Vessels could be loaded with cargo in Germany, and the captain or supercargo had to find buyers in various ports on the way to China. Customers and additional cargo of interest to the Chinese had to be found in East Asia. The volume of western goods consumed in China was limited compared to European demand for Chinese goods like silk, tea, porcelain or lacquer ware. The value of Hamburg's exports to China in 1837/38 amounted to 500,000 Mark banco

(£38,461), but the value of Chinese imports amounted to 1.3 Million Mark banco (£100,000). This imbalance increased over the next decade, so that in 1852 the ratio had more than tripled: exports totalled 541,750 Mark banco (£41,675) while imports exceeded two million Mark banco (£154,000). Before the 1880s this lack of balance changed little according to the statistics.[10]

What we will not find mentioned in the statistics, however, is the fact that smuggled opium remained the backbone of the European China trade. The importation of opium from India had been forbidden by Chinese authorities in 1776. Despite severe penalties on opium smoking, the trade continued and even increased in the 1820s and 1830s. Opium was considered contraband and was sold from depot ships at the port. When Emperor Tao-Kwang demanded the withdrawal of the opium ships in 1839, the British refused to comply. Some outrages on both sides led to an open war which was ended with the Treaty of Nanking in 1842. The import of opium continued and was finally legalized in 1858. The court in Peking never succeeded in suppressing opium imports because provincial viceroys encouraged the trade. Until 1842 Canton had been the only Chinese port open to foreign trade. As a consequence of the Treaty of Nanking four additional ports, Shanghai, Ningpo, Fu-chow and Amoy, were opened to foreign trade, and foreigners were allowed to enter the city of Canton. The opening of additional ports was very important because it terminated a monopolistic trade system in Canton. Formerly, only thirteen merchants, called *hong* or security merchants, were allowed to trade with foreigners in Canton. Before we look at the impact of the Treaty on trade with Germany after 1842, though, it is necessary to turn our attention to Prussia in the first decades of the nineteenth century.

The Prussian Overseas Trading Corporation
Although the Asiatic Company had ceased all its activities in 1757 when French troops

invaded East Frisia, Frederick the Great continued to foster economic growth by active state intervention. Although this is not the place to discuss the role of the public sector in the process of industrialisation, it is significant that Frederick founded the *Preußische Seehandlung* (Prussian Overseas Trading Corporation) in 1772.[11] This privileged state trading and financial institution controlled many state industrial enterprises, including mining, textile factories, merchant ships and, in the nineteenth century, a small fleet of steamships and tugs on the rivers Elbe, Spree and Havel. In 1784 the *Preußische Seehandlung* owned eleven ships, and Frederick encouraged Prussian merchants to seek direct business relations with America through it. While a commercial treaty was signed with the United States, it initiated more activities in Bremen and Hamburg to establish regular mercantile connections across the Atlantic than in Prussian ports like Emden or Stettin. The Napoleonic wars, however, brought everything to a halt, and in 1804 the shipping company was dissolved.

Five years after hostilities had ended a new and energetic director, Christian von Rother, revived the shipping activities of the *Seehandlung*. He was convinced that Prussia's negative trade balance was mainly due to a neglect of the maritime sector. As the vessels that sailed under Prussian flag in 1820 were old and unsuitable for overseas trade in tropical waters, he bought ships in North America and Bremen and ordered new vessels from German shipyards to be built according to American and British designs. An office was established in Stettin in 1824.[12] Since the *Seehandlung* had been involved in wholesale trade from its beginnings in the eighteenth century, he decided to expand this aspect of the business. He bought wool from sheep farmers, organized sales in Berlin and endeavoured to promote a revival of the linen industry by opening up new overseas market for cloth. Making use of the opportunities engendered by the recent independence of a number of states in South America, a vessel named

America was sent to Rio de Janeiro in 1822 with a cargo of linen worth 54,000 Taler (£8310). The ship returned the same year with coffee, sugar and cotton worth 50,000 Taler (£7690). In September 1822 a second ship was dispatched to New Orleans to buy tobacco and cotton. A third vessel, the ship *Mentor*, left Bremen for Valparaiso and Coquimbo to sell linen in Chile in December 1822. The voyage was continued via Honolulu and across the Pacific to China. In January 1824 the ship moored in Canton where its supercargo, Wihelm O'Swald from Hamburg, was able to sell Prussian fabric that caught the eyes of the *hong* and fetched good prices. Returning to Swinemünde in September 1824 it proved to impossible to sell 5000 boxes of tea. As a result, the tea had to be shipped to Hamburg, where it was very easy to sell or to auction the goods from Canton.[13] Apart from this unlucky incident the experiences were encouraging and resulted in further voyages. The most famous vessel was the ship *Princess Louise*, which sailed three times around the world between 1826 and 1834, calling at Canton each time.[14]

In total the *Seehandlung* owned in whole or in part ten ships between 1822 and 1848. In 1848/49 the *Seehandlung* altered its character and became a state bank. All maritime activities came to an end, and a broker in Hamburg was engaged to sell all the vessels. By 1854 the flag of the Prussian *Seehandlung* had disappeared from the oceans and the ports. However, the voyages of the *Seehandlung*'s vessels had paved the way for the establishment of regular trade connections with South America, East India and China. Prussian linens and woollens could be marketed profitably and the profit used to purchase colonial goods. These experiences were observed in the Hanseatic cities where the ships had been acquired and the crews and supercargoes recruited.

German Consulates in China prior to the 1840s
When it became clear that the China trade would be more than an occasional encounter

List of Hamburgh shipping f...

Arrived

No	Name of ship	Date of Entry 1856	Tonnage	Where from	Nature of Cargo
—	"Sta. Adorazion"		492	Hongkong	Sundries
—	"Mathilde"		202	do	do
—	"La Rochelle"		700	Shanghai	do
—	"Faust"		148	Hongkong	Opium
—	"Ceterprize"		120	Shanghai	—
—	"Congo"		340	Hongkong	Sundries
1	"Charles Ross"	Sep. 9	236	do	do
2	"Mathilde"	" 15	202	do	do
3	"Ceterprize"	" 30	120	Shanghai	do
4	"Alardus"	Nov. 8	378	Hongkong	Ballast
5	"Gustav"	" 22	186	Shanghai	Tea & Sundries
6	"Niederwald"	Dec. 20	302	Hongkong	Tobacco & do.
total	12 ships		of Tons 3426		

Hamburgh Consulate
Fonchoufoo. 31st December 1856.

List of Hamburg shipping for the year ending 31st December, 1856, Hamburg Consulate, Fu-chow.

with the *hongs* in Canton, the question was raised in Germany whether the trade required legal protection through consular missions in China. As early as 1787 an unnamed Englishman had acted as Royal Prussian Consul in Canton.[15] It remains obscure how he received this position, but it was very useful to have him to help circumvent the monopoly on the China trade held by the British East India Company. When Rother sent out the *Princess Louise* in 1824 he asked the supercargo Wihelm O'Swald to look for a German or Prussian 'individual' to take over the vacant Prussian consulate. This suggests that there must have been a person taking responsibility for German interests in Canton between 1787 and 1824. Although O'Swald was unable to find a suitable person, he suggested that a British citizen, Mr. Hollingworth, who was well respected, take over as Vice Consul. Similarly, from 1825 the Kingdom of Hanover was represented by a consular mission, and in 1829 the British

merchant John MacVicar became Hamburg's first representative. He presented his credentials to Howqua, the *hong* representative responsible for foreign trade with Europeans, who promised to give ships from Hamburg the same rights and privileges as were given to traders from other countries. An incident in 1830 shows how important a mission could be when a vessel of the *Seehandlung*, sailing under Bremen's flag, was only allowed to enter Canton harbour when flying the Hamburg flag. In the following years ships from Bremen often switched flags in Chinese waters and sailed under Hamburg's protection.[16]

MacVicar spent only a short period in China, so Hamburg appointed Alexander Matheson of the trading house Jardine, Matheson & Co as his successor. Matheson stayed in Canton until 1843, when he began to shift his engagement to the foundation of Hong Kong. As a result, he neglected his consular duties and the mission fell into disarray. But the importance of consular representation was repeatedly stressed. Indeed, the lack of protection and the fragmentation of German consular representation had been criticised by Hanseatic merchants in 1840. They pointed to the fact that only one quarter of German trade was handled by German ships and argued for a joint consular mission for all German states engaged in trade with China. This view was reiterated in 1846 in a memorial by German merchants in Canton and Hong Kong sent to Hamburg and Berlin. One of the authors was the German merchant Richard von Carlowitz, who had started business in Canton in 1846. He became later the consular representative for Prussia and Saxony and even later for the Grand Duchy of Oldenburg. Other German members of the Customs Union interested in the China trade had already voiced their belief that consulates in China were a necessity and had sent the Prussian economist Friedrich William Grube to China in 1844. Although it was obvious that it did not make sense to have representatives for each German state, the time was not yet ripe for this sort of cooperation. Free traders in Hamburg and Bremen opposed the protectionist policy of Prussia and the Customs Union.

III. The Post-Nanking Era, 1842-1871

Hanseatic Consulates

The opening of four additional ports and the acquisition of the Hong Kong Island by Great Britain as a result of the Nanking Treaty of 1842 changed the trade with China radically. New opportunities were immediately seized upon by European traders. The German economist Friedrich List compared the importance of the Treaty with the discovery of America. In Germany, and especially in the Hanseatic cities, there were high expectations, and a Bavarian newspaper reported that merchants throughout Europe were excited. Even the Germans, the article continued, who were always slow to grasp an advantage, moved to carve out their slice of the pie.

The Treaty soon had important negative consequences for Canton as trade was gradually diverted to ports in more navigable waters. This shift can be seen in the trade statistics over the next three decades. While in 1840 almost all Chinese exports were shipped through Canton, the port's share dropped to thirteen percent in 1870 while Shanghai's portion rose to sixty-three percent. As a consequence, German consulates were rapidly established (see table 1). In 1852 the Senate in Hamburg appointed Georg Theodor Siemssen as its next representative in Canton, and in 1855 he took over the same responsibilities for Bremen and in 1856 for Lübeck and the Grand Duchy of Mecklenburg-Schwerin. Siemssen was a most influential character, and he and his associates dominated consular representation in the 1850s and 1860s.[17]

All these appointments were initiated by Hamburg, and from 1862 the new consular missions were responsible for protecting the interests of all Hanseatic cities. Some consuls were chosen from the ranks of German merchant houses based in China, although sometimes British merchants were asked to serve in that capacity (see table 2). The most prominent Hanseatic merchant house was Siemssen & Co of Hamburg, and several consuls were chosen from among the partners in this firm. In Shanghai the English merchant Wihelm Hogg was appointed to represent the Hanseatic cities in 1852, while Prussia had its own consular mission. Between 1854 and 1859 his brother James Hogg held the office.

Hamburg consulates on the Chinese coast in the 1850s.

Table 1 German Consulates in China[18]	
Canton	1852
Shanghai	1852
Hong Kong	1853
Fu-chow	1856
Xiamen (Amoy)	1859
Shantou	1862
Tianjin	1863
Niuzhuang	1864
Danshui (Taiwan)	1865
Ningbo	1866
Dagou (Taiwan)	1866

on whether he deemed an extra agreement with China necessary to safeguard Hamburg's position in the Chinese market. He doubted the need of such a contract because the amount of trade did not justify such a step, especially since China extended every right granted to other nations to vessels from the River Elbe. Although this issue was raised several times during the next decade there was little need for action until England, France, Russia and the United States forced China to sign a more liberal trade agreement in 1858 and to open eleven additional ports.

The Senate in Hamburg ordered its consul, Ludwig Wiese, in Hong Kong to inquire if the Chinese government was prepared to sign a similar agreement with Hamburg because the most favoured-nation status no longer applied to the German states. Commercial rivalry between Europeans began to develop. There were a number of important commercial, political and legal reasons that made it desirable to enter into negotiations for a mutual agreement. When it became known that Prussia intended to send representatives to China and Japan to conclude trade and friendship agreements, the other German states asked Prussia for permission to

In the 1860s more merchant houses founded branches in China. Apart from Siemssen & Co one of the most prominent was the trading house of C. Melchers & Co in Hong Kong. The mother company was based in Bremen. Melchers not only looked after cargo of the company's own vessels but also served as an agent for other shipping companies. Before we turn our attention to the development of trade with China after 1842 it is necessary to look at an important diplomatic step which was taken by the German states.

The Friendship, Trade and Shipping Agreement of 1861/63

The Treaty of Nanking did not exclusively protect British interests. The rights given to Great Britain were also granted to other European countries and to the Hanseatic cities in a supplementary agreement signed in 1843. Nevertheless, the committee of commerce in Hamburg's parliament asked the German merchant Theodor Johns in Macao for advice

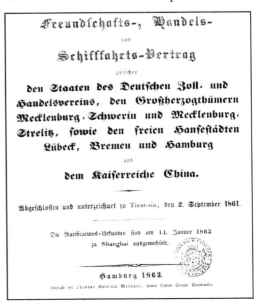

Title page of the Friendship, Trade and Shipping Agreement of 1861/63

join in. The expedition headed by Count Friedrich von Eulenburg, who was accompanied on his voyages to East Asia by several Prussian warships, ended successfully after long negotiations in 1861.[20] While Japan refused to include all German states, China extended all privileges to Prussia and all members of the German Customs Union, including the Hanseatic cities. The *Traité d'amitié, de commerce et de navigation entre les États de l'Association de douanes et de commerce Allemande* was signed in Tianjinn on 2 September 1861, and the ratification documents were exchanged in Shanghai in 1863. Copies were handed over to all twenty-two German states involved. The agreement devolved upon the North German Federation in 1867 and upon Imperial Germany in 1871. It remained in essence the basis of Sino-German relations until 1921. Despite the propaganda that celebrated the Eulenburg expedition as a diplomatic success, merchant circles in the Hanseatic cities were disappointed. Eulenburg had neither achieved any improvement with regard to their consular representation in China nor had he been able to open an economic entry into Japan. Without any support of the other European powers and the United States the expedition just managed to reach Prussian diplomatic and consular agreements for members of the Customs Union. The reaction in the Hanseatic cities was negative. It was criticised that Prussia had only shown interest in a political representation in order to reach the same status the other powers had in China. However, the governments in Hamburg, Bremen, and Lübeck thought it not opportune to refuse ratifying the agreements for nationalistic reasons.[21]

The Increase of Trade

In the aftermath of the Opium War, Hamburg's trade with China experienced an important upswing. In 1844 Hamburg and Bremen imported tea worth £120,000 of goods and ranked fifth in the China trade behind Great Britain, the United States, the Netherlands and Sweden. In 1847 only three vessels from Hamburg, Bremen and Prussia called at the port of Canton, but in the 1850s the increase was quite substantial (see table 3).

Between 1854 and 1861 no less than 384 German ships registered in Bremen, Hamburg, Hanover, Oldenburg, Schleswig-Holstein and Prussia called at Shanghai.[22]

Table 3 German ships in Canton, 1847-1859[23]				
	From:		*To:*	
	Hamburg	Bremen	Hamburg	Bremen
1847	3	3	–	–
1851	20	12	–	–
1855	23	6	21	6
1856	47	8	49	8
1857	–	–	–	–
1858	9	8	9	4
1859	40	7	40	11
Total	*142*	*44*	*119*	*29*

During the Second Opium War (1856-1858) trade ceased almost completely. However, in 1859 hostilities ended and trade returned to its previous levels. Since statistics are scarce it may be useful to see the figures for 1858. In the five ports open to trade 1440 foreign ships called, 696 British; 236 American; 180 German; and 117 Dutch. Half of the German ships came from Hamburg, putting the city into fourth position. In 1866, 871 British ships entered Hong Kong (542,622 register tons) compared to 234 ships from Hamburg (78,510 register tons) and 132 ships from Prussia (36,990 register tons). The tonnage of British ships was seven times higher than the tonnage of vessels from Hamburg.

Despite the fact that the Hamburg consulate also looked after trade from Bremen, a trade rivalry remained between the two cities. Vice-consul H. Krüger reported in his annual overview to Hamburg for 1866 that in Fuzhou calls by Bremen vessels had risen while the number of ships from Hamburg had declined (see table 4).

Table 4 German Ships Entering Fu-chow, 1855-1866[24]		
Year	From Hamburg	From Bremen
1855	14	–
1859	29	–
1864	22	1
1865	19	8
1866	8	13

A fire in 1868 destroyed the consulate and all the documents, so nothing is known about the following years.

What goods were exported from Germany to China? In the eighteenth century the German states had little to offer to the Chinese apart from silver, while in the early nineteenth century exports comprised cheap utility goods called 'sundries' by the Chinese. Later in the century woollen fabrics and cotton, sugar and other refined products, sewing needles as well as various iron and steel products and chemical products were sent to China. Products exported to Germany included not only silk, tea and porcelain but also spices, skins, furs, downs, perlmut, Nanking cotton and Chinese cinnamon. The latter was used both as a spice and a medicine. Germany's share in the export and import trade with China amounted to about one percent of total Chinese foreign trade,[25] while Great Britain controlled eighty percent in the 1860s.[26] Compared to Britain's share, German participation in the China trade was of limited importance.

Ships from Hamburg in the Chinese Coastal Trade

For years growing numbers of ships from Hamburg had called at Chinese ports. In the second half of the 1860s the calls stagnated and began to fall, as we know from Krüger's report. The decline he observed in Fu-chow was also characteristic of other ports (see table 5).

Table 5 German Ships Calling at Selected Chinese Ports, 1864-1870[27]

Year	Niuzhuang	Ningbo	Shanghai
1864	-	-	102
1865	-	-	63
1866	-	-	40
1867	-	-	33
1868	-	36	24
1870	-	-	12

This decrease was by no means a uniquely German phenomenon since it also affected other nations. There is a very convincing explanation for this. Many sailing vessels in the 1850s and 1860s no longer sailed between Europe and China but remained in Chinese waters and earned their revenues there. Tramp shipping along the Chinese coast developed into a profitable business not only between the treaty ports but also between Bangkok, Saigon, Macao, Manila, the east coast of Australia and Manchuria/East Siberia. Superior sailing techniques with more flexible rigs gave European vessels an advantage over Chinese junks with flat-bottoms, prominent stems and lugsails which were unable to cruise into the monsoon winds.[28] The junks could only make one voyage to the south in the north-easterly monsoons (October to April) and one return voyage (April to October) while European vessels were able to make several voyages in the same period. The smaller European ships, barques, brigs and schooners, with capacities between 200 and 300 tons, were quite useful in small bays and could also serve minor harbours (see table 6).

Table 6 Hamburg Ships in the East Asian Coastal Trade, 1851-1888[29]

Year	Number	Year	Number
1851	5	1865	75
1853	7	1867	56
1854	20	1868	45
1855	33	1871	43
1860	40	1879	30
1862	60	1883	18
1864	85	1888	9

There are three reasons for the decline after 1864. First, the Chinese were able to purchase European vessels and to engage western captains and crews. Between 1859 and 1866 Hamburg shipping companies sold fifty-eight wooden sailing vessels. They were happy to rid themselves of this old tonnage. The Chinese were able to enlarge their fleet from 469 vessels in 1870 to 6932 vessels with a tonnage of 4.3 million gross registered tons in 1879, a fifteen-fold rise in numbers and an increase of 145 times in tonnage. Ironically, however, by selling their old tonnage the Europeans fostered their own rivals. Second, Hamburg's consul in Niuzhuang reported home in 1867 that the Chinese had taken over the coastal trade because their costs were lower. They could buy goods cheaper than Europeans and could therefore sell them at competitive prices. In addition, the Chinese had begun to impede coastal trade in foreign hands. Third, the transition from sail to steam, in which the British leaders undermined the German position in the coastal trade, as the market report by the consul in Shanghai had forecast in 1869. His colleague in Canton repeated the view that Germany had done too little to protect its position by switching over to steamers.

At the end of the 1880s Siemssen & Co founded the *Chinesische Küstenfahrt-Gesellschaft*, and a second shipping company, the *Dampfschiffs-Gesellschaft Swatow*, founded by the Hamburg-based merchant house Dircks & Co, started business.[30] Germany held about fifteen percent of the coastal trade in the next decade, of which Hamburg had the largest share.

IV. China in the Focus of Imperial Germany

Economic Expansion

From the 1850s public attention in Germany began to focus on China and the Far East. Following Commodore Perry's expedition to Japan in 1854 and the Second Opium War the Prussian government decided to send Count Eulenburg to East Asia to establish diplomatic relations with China, Japan and Siam and to sign trade agreements. The Prussian navy escorting him wanted to look for possible coaling stations in China and in Japan, and the first depot was erected in Yokohama in 1867. There was talk of a *German Hong Kong* either on Formosa or elsewhere. In 1870 Chancellor Bismarck told the German envoy in Peking that a naval stronghold in China would be necessary to protect Germany's commercial interests. He emphasised, however, that he did not intend to engage in colonial expansionism in the Far East.[31] All he wanted was to lease a strip of land for commercial and naval needs. A colony, Bismarck argued, would require a strong navy which Germany neither had nor needed. Well into the 1880s Germany's aspirations in China were based upon an

overall consensus of commercial *laissez-faire* expansionism. This was to change very soon.

German shipping companies were doing extremely well alongside their British and American rivals without any problems arising from the lack of naval protection. It was known in commercial as well as in political circles that German ships dominated the Chinese coastal trade, and contemporary estimates in the 1860s concluded that three-quarters of all tramp vessels along the Chinese coast belonged to German shipping companies. Thus, there was little need for state intervention in East Asian waters in the first decade following German unification in 1871. The commercial prospects excited merchants and politicians like a *Fata Morgana*.[32] Yet for the moment the expectations of the 1860s and 1870s bore little resemblance to reality, as Germany's share in the Chinese coastal and overseas trade amounted to about 7.4 percent of overall tonnage (see table 7). Inner-Chinese political uncertainties, lack of Prussian initiative in economic terms after it had achieved political prestige in the 1860s and the slump in Germany in the second part of the 1870s were obstacles on the way to an economic expansion of Germany in the Chinese market. The lesson German merchants had to learn was that the Chinese market lacked the dynamic of the European market. It took some time before improvements were noticeable.

Table 7 Foreign Shipping in China, 1868-1902[33]					
Year	Tonnage (Millions)	UK	Germany	US	Japan
1868	6.4	52.2	7.3	35.0	7.3
1872	8.5	46.8	7.2	41.1	7.2
1882	12.6	85.7	7.0	1.3	7.0
1892	22.9	84.4	6.4	0.3	6.4
1902	44.6	60.4	16.2	1.1	16.2

To safeguard and extend its position was high on the list of German priorities. As early as 1871 the recently established Deutsche Bank opened branches in Shanghai and Yokohama, although the Shanghai operation had to be closed in 1875. Notwithstanding this closure and other drawbacks, German merchants and shipping companies could now operate in Chinese waters with the support of a central government of a united country. They had become the agents of national rather than Hanseatic or regional interests, but they had to wait for new developments before the overseas trade to China got into the swing again.

The Beginning of Liner Services to China
Two important factors helped to intensify links with the Far East. The opening of the Suez Canal in 1869 shortened dramatically the time it took to sail to China. In 1752 the *King of Prussia* needed six months to sail to Canton, and 100 years later it still took four to five months for a modern sailing ship to reach China. But from 1869 onwards it took a ship only six weeks. A new era in shipping to the Pacific and to Chinese waters had begun, and the situation was further improved when a telegraphic cable to Hong Kong was completed in 1871. Rapid transport and communications brought China much closer to Europe. An additional factor that had an important impact on trade was the advent of steam. Although the transition from sail to steam was much slower in the German merchant marine than in Britain, an early German steamer, the *Sedan*, owned by the Hamburg shipping company J.C. Godeffroy & Son, called at the port of Shanghai in 1871. The slow transition to steam, however, resulted in a temporary decline in German trade with China. The number of ships declined in the 1860s, although the carrying capacity rose gradually. Hamburg suffered less than the other German ports (see table 8).

Table 8 Hamburg Trade with China, 1860-1900[34]		
Year	*Entrances from China*	*Clearances to China*
1860	14	21
1865	14	22
1870	11	14
1875	16	21
1880	24	29
1885	26	30
1890	34	30
1895	27	31
1900	43	64

Unfortunately, the statistics provide only the absolute figures of vessels to and from Hamburg involved in the China trade. It is, however, safe to assume that gross registered tons more than doubled over the period. The twelve ships in 1873, for example, had a capacity of 12,000 gross registered tons, while the twenty-seven vessels in 1895 were about 55,000 gross registered tons. Since it took two decades before the last sailing vessel left this trade, my estimate is very conservative. Hamburg's shipping companies were slightly faster in the making the transition from sail to steam and were therefore able to lessen the effects of the decline of German shipping during the period. From the 1880s onwards the stagnation was overcome and the German fleet managed to regain lost ground.

The Kingsin Line
Plans to found the *Deutsche Dampfschiffs-Rhederei zu Hamburg* were already circulating in Hamburg in the years before the Franco-Prussian War in 1870/71. The founding fathers had envisaged a tramp shipping company that would operate in European waters. One of the firms behind this project was the merchant house of Wm. O'Swald, already known to us from the activities of the supercargo Wihelm O'Swald in the service of the *Seehandlung* in the 1830s. This house, with much experience in the trade, managed to find cargoes for China. As a result, the five vessels of the new shipping company, which was later called the Kingsin (Golden Star) Line, were dispatched to East Asia and never sailed in European waters. Occasionally passengers were carried, but in general the ships sailed regularly with cargo and the post to China. Once the freight was unloaded the captains had to seek return cargoes in various Chinese ports.

A round-trip voyage lasted approximately six months. Only three to five vessels served as liners, while the other ships remained in Chinese waters for between two and four years during the 1870s. While trade was attractive in the Far East, the regular line between Hamburg and China was a money-losing proposition. In 1879 the shares of the joint stock company had to be amalgamated in the ratio of 3:2. But business improved during the 1880s. In 1884 more than 20,000 tons were shipped in each direction, while five years later 70,000 tons were shipped outward and 60,000 tons homeward. After fifteen years the Kingsin Line had become a profitable shipping company.[35]

But in the process the reputation of the Kingsin Line suffered with regard to regularity, and this prevented it from winning a subvention for postal services in 1886. Despite the fact that a German rival had begun to operate between Germany and China with the help of public money, and despite the fact that the British P&O Line and the French *Compagnie des Messageries Maritimes* received state subventions, the Kingsin Line survived because there was enough potential in the trade. The Rickmers Line, another German entity, was already engaged in the tea trade in the 1860s when it discovered that rice was a product that could be processed in the company's own mill in Bremen.[36]

Both companies came under pressure when the North German Lloyd won the shipping contract and joined the China Homeward Trade Conference. They stayed outside the cartel and fought against considerable difficulties. The Kingsin Line was pushed out of the direct China trade and could no longer sail to Shanghai, leaving Hong Kong as the only port of call at on the route to Japan. In 1897 the Kingsin Line joined the conference and was allowed again into the port of Shanghai. But the following year the line was forced to ask for a merger with the Hamburg-America Line (HAL), whose energetic director Albert Ballin had discovered the politically and economically promising country in the Far East.[37] From time to time the HAL had sent vessels to China since 1856 but had never really viewed China as a target for the expansionary business concept that Albert Ballin had drafted in order to lift the HAL to the top rank among world shipping companies. On 25 February 1898 the HAL opened a monthly cargo service to China after

the Rickmers Line had started a similar line in 1896. Before entering into a ruinous rivalry the shareholders of the Kingsin Line accepted the take-over initiative by the Hamburg-America Line in March 1898. The shipping company went out of business immediately.[38]

Imperial Mail Steamship Service to the Far East (1886–1898)

For many years after unification Chancellor Bismarck opposed the acquisition of overseas possessions despite calls for the establishment of a colonial empire. In 1871 he declared that, 'for Germany to acquire colonies would be like a poverty-stricken Polish nobleman providing himself with silks and sables when he needed shirts'.[39] Ten years later he still ruled out the option of imperialism while he was chancellor. For Bismarck there were several positive aspects in eschewing colonies. In case of war, all efforts could be concentrated on defending German frontiers in Europe, while overseas possessions would need naval protection – and he thought a navy was unnecessary. Moreover, he feared that his system of alliances could be endangered by disputes over distant colonies. But Germany's commercial and shipping interests expanded in the 1870s in Africa, the Far East and the Pacific, and it became increasingly impossible for Bismarck to ignore appeals from the mercantile community. To give one example, when the Hamburg-based merchant house Godeffroy ran into financial troubles in Samoa in 1878, Bismarck tried to organise assistance in order to avert the danger of the company's stations falling into the hands of English creditors. Nonetheless, when the Samoa Subsidy Bill was defeated in the Reichstag in 1880 it was the banker Adolph von Hansemann of the Discount Company who, much to Bismarck's relief, raised the money to secure the firm's survival.[40]

As a result, Bismarck gradually changed his mind on colonial policy. In 1881 he presented a memorandum to the Reichstag stating that:

> *In reorganizing the German export trade, the basic principles will include – and this is an urgent necessity – the establishment of a*

191

regular freight service between Germany and overseas sales markets.[41]

In the debate it was pointed out that France spent about 20,000 million Marks per annum for her merchant marine's postal services while Great Britain paid about thirteen million Marks in postal subsidies to her shipping companies, in addition to sums allocated by the colonies. Bismarck warned that under these circumstances German shipping and trade could not develop satisfactorily. On 12 May 1881, when a supplement to the Sino-German Trade Agreement of 1861/63 was discussed, he said that the decline in the China trade could only be reversed by active merchants and shipping companies. As long as foreign ships handled the greater share of German exports, new markets in China could not be won without adequate and regular steamship services.

Until 1871, when the Kingsin Line began operating in the China seas, there had been no direct steamship service from Germany to Asia and to a large extent German trade went indirectly through the ports of London and Amsterdam. Only sailing vessels, which were decreasing in number, maintained direct German trade with Asia. Running mail and freight services on routes well frequented by five British, six French, one Austrian and four Italian subsidised shipping companies was not a lucrative business for any German shipping company unless the government was prepared to grant subsidies.[42] One of the main opponents of subsidies was the founder of the North German Lloyd, Hermann Heinrich Meier, who was a member of the Reichstag in 1881. Only three years later this liberal free trader had changed his mind and had become an advocate of subsidisation when under-secretary Heinrich von Stephan, organizer of the German postal system, was given the task to prepare a bill for the Reichstag in 1884.

Much had happened in those three years. Two colonial associations had been founded in 1880 and 1882 which put pressure on the chancellor, and the colonial enthusiasts increased their efforts to rally public opinion to their cause. Alliances with Russia, Austria and Italy between 1879 and 1882, and a brief rapprochement with France in 1884, gave Bismarck an ideal opportunity to pursue what now had become his colonial aims.[43] In April 1884 he placed the establishment of the Bremen merchant Adolf Lüderitz in South West Africa under imperial protection. He acted the same way on the coasts of the Cameroons, Togoland and in northern New Guinea, where he came to an agreement with Great Britain concerning colonies in the Pacific. Moreover, the Congo Conference was held in Berlin in 1884/85.

The fact that Bismarck presided over an international gathering to determine the future of a vast region in central Africa added to his prestige and showed the world that Germany had definitely entered the ranks of the colonial powers.[44]

Germany had joined the scramble for colonies or what – a few years after Bismarck had been dropped by the Kaiser – was seen as

A poster advertising the Imperial Mail Steamship Service to the Far East, c1910.

the last chance to get 'a place in the sun.'

Under these circumstances the 'Act Relating to Mail Steamship Links with Overseas Countries' was passed by the Reichstag in 1885, but the margin in favour of subsidies was small. Subsidised lines to East Asia and to Australia passed while a line to Africa was scuttled.[45] The North German Lloyd was the only German line capable of meeting nearly all the requirements laid down in the Act: a monthly liner service to the Far East with ships that sailed at an average speed of twelve knots; the times of the passages precisely specified; and the ships deployed had to be of the same quality as the mail steamers of other nations operating on these routes. New ships had to be built on German shipyards. When Meier and Bismarck signed the contract worth 4.4 million Marks annually the North German Lloyd undertook to maintain for a period of fifteen years the following mail steamship services:

Bremerhaven to China via Colombo, Singapore and Hong Kong to Shanghai, with an additional service from Hong Kong to Japan and Korea;
Bremerhaven to Australia, with an additional line from Sydney to the German colony islands of Tonga and Samoa; and
Trieste to Alexandria to link up with lines from the Far East and Australia.

On 30 June 1886, the *Oder*, a converted Atlantic steamer, opened the line to the Far East, and a fortnight later the *Salier* inaugurated a service to Australia. Within the next eighteen months six newly-built vessels came into service. The first years were very disappointing and ended with losses which had to be met by profits made on the North Atlantic (see table 9).

In the decade from 1886 to 1896, 44.3 million Marks in subsidies were paid, yet the North German Lloyd still lost 5.25 million Marks. There are several explanations for this initial disaster. The *Oder* stranded in the Indian Ocean in 1887 and was a write-off, while the *Preussen* had to stay in quarantine when a smallpox epidemic broke out on the way to Australia in 1886. More important than these accidents was that the managers in Bremen had misjudged the ratio of cargo to passengers, and there was not enough room for freight. The clauses in the mail contract were detrimental to a flexible reaction by the shipping company and hence were economically damaging. The North German Lloyd, operating successfully on the North Atlantic, had to learn this the hard way on the route to the Far East and Australia before money could be earned. Meier had been right when he said to shareholders in 1885 that 'Although we don't want to entertain all to sanguine hopes concerning the profitability of the new lines, we are still firmly convinced that we will come out on top'.[47]

Nothing but honour was gained initially, but in the long run the company secured a decisive share of future markets in the Far East. In 1898 the postal contract with the Reich was prolonged for a further fifteen years with modifications that had proved necessary in order to run the services economically. The following year the North German Lloyd bought a subsidiary fleet of twenty-five former British vessels for feeder services in East and South East Asia and the Pacific. It is clear that by this time the original goals sought through the creation of subsidised lines were achieved, as exports to China increased about nine-fold and imports increased about three-fold (see table 10).

Table 9 Losses of the Imperial Mail Steamship Service to the Far East and Australia[46]

1887	1,753,361 Marks
1888	60,000 Marks
1889	266,000 Marks
1890	1,500,000 Marks

Table 10 Cargo and Passengers Carried by the Subsidised Lines, 1886-1890[48]

Year	Total Freight (tons)	Total Passengers
1886	34,000	3,000
1895	124,214	10,995
1890	71,303	6,793
1900	299,273	17,956

In the meantime a German cruiser division had sailed into Jiaozhou Bay and captured the small port of Tsingtao in 1897. Following the British example the German Empire pressed the Chinese government to sign a lease for the bay in a so-called 'unequal contract' for 99 years. Imperial Germany had made the decisive step to achieve Great Power status in East Asia. Now the nation had an opening into the Chinese market for industrial goods like railway material and armour, while its shipping lines were returning with rice, tea, silk and raw materials, such as ores and wood. Although the German colony was under the aegis of the Imperial Navy Department and military interests dominated over commercial, the North German Lloyd was quite happy with the new situation.

The acquisition of a territorial base, the founding of the Shandong Rail and Mining Company, the involvement of German capital and German intellect in the development of China and the very great significance of the coal deposits at last coming within the German sphere of interest surely demonstrate the need to create closer links between Chinese ports and Germany.[49]

Conclusion

For more than 150 years German shipowners, shipping companies or state-sponsored reconnaissance expeditions had been engaged in business in the China seas. From individual encounters with the Far East the most prominent Hanseatic cities and Prussia became involved and tried to facilitate trade by establishing consulates and signing trade agreements with China. The first merchant houses founded branches in the Far East. Although the volume of trade in terms of turnover was modest, there was a growing interest in Chinese goods like tea, silk and porcelain. In the age of sail a regular shipping service comparable to the Dutch and British East India companies never came into being. Even after unification, when the Reich took over much more responsibility for German foreign trade, the private Kingsin Line was unable to sustain regular departures in either direction. Only when Chancellor Bismarck gave up the hitherto dominant free-trade position under which Germany wanted 'trade and not dominion' was a new policy pursued. Germany acquired colonies and began to seek her 'share of the cake'. Since the flag was followed by trade, subsidised steamship services were favoured by the Reichstag. Finally, a German Gibraltar or Hong Kong paved the way for new trade opportunities in the vast Chinese market. But Tsingtao was first of all of military interest to the Kaiser and his advisors after it had been decided that Germany wanted to be a Great Power with colonial possessions. Since the Kaiserreich did not have a navy that was able to protect its interests in the Far East, Kaiser William fostered the idea that Germany could work with Great Britain Germany to achieve this goal. One of the turning points was the war between China and Japan over Korea in 1894. The government in Berlin was afraid that other powers could make use of the turmoil and take possession of land in China while Germany sat on the sidelines. The German foreign secretary, Marschall von Bieberstein, therefore told his British counterpart that Germany was prepared for a joint intervention to restore peace if Britain would assist in Germany's attempt to acquire colonies in the Far East. Although nothing followed this first move, the idea of cooperation with London prevailed in Berlin during the next few years. The British ambassador in Berlin, Sir Frank Lascelles, reported to his government in 1898 that Kaiser William 'wished to be friendly with Great Britain, to gain her alliance and to work hand in hand with her'.[50] At the farewell dinner following the funeral of Queen Victoria, William II even advocated a Pax Teutonica when he declared that:

> I believe that the two Teutonic nations will, bit by bit, learn to know each other better. We ought to form an Anglo-Teutonic alliance…with such an alliance not a mouse could stir in Europe without our permission.[51]

Against the background of his desire for a rapprochement with England, Emperor William developed a plan to divide the world according to the motto: *Africa to the British and East Asia to the Germans*. In a private audience he told Lascelles that:

> *The Germans had not proved successful colonizers among the barbarous tribes of Africa, and He should now try them in the Far East and in China where they would find a form of civilization at all events superior to the savages in Africa…He considered that His best policy was to be on friendly terms with us, and if we wanted German East Africa, to be able to retire gracefully without waiting to be 'kicked out'.*

William left the impression that he intended 'to direct his attention to Asiatic rather than to African Colonization'.[52]

Despite Admiral Sir E. Seymour's call *The Germans to the Front* during the campaign to punish China in the wake of the Boxer Rebellion, Anglo-German cooperation in the Far East had only limited value. In 1900 Germany for the last time came to an agreement with Great Britain concerning Samoa. Great Britain withdrew its claims to any port in the islands in exchange for compensation from Germany in other parts of the world. But as early as 30 January 1902 Britain found a new ally in the Far East and entered into an alliance with Japan. With the naval race beginning in Europe, and with the decision to build battleships, it became chimerical that Germany would be able to defend her political, colonial and economic interests in China in case of a military conflict between the great powers. Before the East Asia Squadron under the command of Admiral Graf Spee was destroyed in the battle at the Falklands in December 1914, the Japanese had accepted the German surrender of Tsingtao.

Notes and references

1 I would like to thank the organizers and the participants of the conference 'British Ships in China Seas' for their useful and helpful suggestions. Students at Bremen University listened to a shortened version of this paper on 28 January 2003 and shared with me their knowledge of 'Europeans in East Asia and in the Pacific.'

2 Michael Salewski, 'Die preußische und die Kaiserliche Marine in den ostasiatischen Gewässern: Das militärische Interesse an Ostasien,' in Hans Martin Hinz and Christoph Lind (eds.), *Tsingtau. Ein Kapitel deutscher Kolonialgeschichte in China 1897-1914*, (Berlin, 1998), 76-83.

3 Bernd Eberstein, *Hamburg-China. Geschichte einer Partnerschaft*, (Hamburg, 1988), 18–25.

4 Eric Gøbel, 'Danish Companies' Shipping to Asia (1731-1807),' in Jaap R. Bruijn and Femme S. Gaastra (eds.), *Ships, Sailors and Spices. East India Companies and their Shipping in the 16th, 17th and 18th Centuries*, (Amsterdam, 1993), 99-120.

5 Bernd Eberstein, 'Kaufleute, Konsuln, Kapitäne: Frühe deutsche Wirtschaftsinteressen in China,' in Hinz and Lind (eds.), *Tsingtau*, 49-60.

6 Dagmar Bechtloff, 'Bremer Kaufleute im Asienhandel während des 19. Jahrhunderts,' in Hartmut Roder (ed.), *Bremen-Ostasien. Eine Beziehung im Wandel*, (Bremen, 2001), 44-53.

7 Peter Hahn, 'Carl Philipp Cassel 1742-1807,' in Hartmut, *Bremen-Ostasien.*, 53-67.

8 Lars U. Scholl, 'Die Schiffahrt,' in Jürgen Ziechmann (ed.), *Panorama der Fridericianischen Zeit*, (Bremen, 1985), 641-647; and Scholl, 'Flotte und Seeschiffahrt,' in William Treue (ed.), *Preußens großer König. Leben und Werk Friedrich des Großen. Eine Ploetz-Biographie*, (Freiburg, 1986), 113-118.

9 Victor Ring, *Asiatische Handelskompagnien Friedrichs des Großen. Ein Beitrag zur Geschichte des preußischen Seehandels und Aktienwesen*, (Berlin, 1890).

10 Eberstein, *Hamburg-China*, 26-61.

11 Wolfgang Radtke, *Die preußische Seehandlung zwischen Staat und Wirtschaft in der Frühphase der Industrialisierung*, (Berlin, 1981); Radtke, *Die Preußische Seehandlung* (Berlin, 1987); and Werner Vogel (ed.), *Die Seehandlung. Preußische Staatsbank*, (Berlin, 1993).

12 Heinz Burmester, *Weltumseglung unter Preußens Flagge. Die Königlich Preußische Seehandlung und ihre Schiffe*, (Hamburg, 1988).

13 Elisabeth Kuster-Wendenburg, *Entdeckungsfahrten im Auftrag Preussens. Der Bremer Kapitän Wendt 1802 bis 1847*, (Delmenhorst, 2002).

14 Stefan Hartmann, 'Unternehmungen der preußischen Seehandlung in der ersten Hälfte des 19. Jahrhunderts am Beispiel des Schiffs PRINZESSIN LOUISE,' in Oswald Hauser (ed.), *Vorträge und Studien zur preußisch-deutschen Geschichte* (Köln, 1983), 87–150; and Lars U. Scholl, 'Die PRINCES LOUISE der Königlich Preußischen Seehandlungs-Societät. Zwei unveröffentlichte Dokumente,' Deutsches Schiffahrtsarchiv, IX (1986), 117-122.

15 Eberstein, *Hamburg-China*, 62-112.

16 Eberstein, 'Kaufleute, Konsuln, Kapitäne,' 53.

17 Eberstein, *Hamburg-China*, 70-80.

18 Eberstein, *Hamburg-China*, 70-80.

19 Compiled from, Eberstein, *Hamburg-China* 62-112.

20 Michael Salewski, 'Die Preußische Expedition nach Japan (1859-1861),' in Salewski, *Die Deutschen und die See. Studien zur deutschen Marinegeschichte des 19. und 20. Jahrhunderts*, (Stuttgart, 1998), 54-67.

21 Udo Ratenhof, *Die Chinapolitik des Deutschen Reiches 1871-1945. Wirtschaft – Rüstung – Militär*, (Boppard, 1987), 25-50.

22 Max Peters, *Die Entwicklung der deutschen Reederei seit dem Beginn des 19. Jahrhunderts bis zur Begründung des Deutschen Reichs*, 2 vols., (Jena, 1905), II, 13.

23 Eberstein, *Hamburg-China*, 32.

24 Eberstein, *Hamburg-China*, 98. See also Hermann Wätjen, 'Die deutsche Handelsschiffahrt in chinesischen Gewässern um die Mitte des 19. Jahrhunderts,' *Hansische Geschichtsblätter* LXVII/LXVIII (1942/1943), 222-250.

25 Chi-ming Hou, *Foreign Investment and Economic Development in China, 1840-1937*, Unpublished MA University of Cambridge, 1965, 228 ff.

26 Arthur Sargent, *Anglo-Chinese Commerce and Diplomacy*, (Oxford, 1907), 142 ff.

27 Eberstein, *Hamburg-China*, 167.

28 Frank Stielow, 'Deutsche Küstenschiffahrt in chinesischen Gewässern,' in Roder (ed.), *Bremen-Ostasien*, 188-190.

29 Walter Kresse, *Die Fahrtgebiete der Hamburger Handelsflotte 1824-1888*, (Hamburg, 1972), 186 and 247 ff.

30 Eberstein, *Hamburg-China*, 171.

31 Salewski, 'Die preußische und die kaiserliche Marine,' 78-79.

32 Hans-Ulrich Wehler, *Bismarck und der Imperialismus* (4th ed.), (Munich, 1969), 194-206.

33 Hou, *Foreign Investment*, table 16.

34 Compiled from Eberstein, *Hamburg-China*, 384-386

35 Kresse, *Fahrtgebiete der Hamburger Handelsflotte*, 245-255.

36 Arnold Kludas, *Rickmers. 150 Jahre Schiffbau und Schiffahrt*, (Herford, 1984).

37 Otto Mathies, *Hamburgs Reederei 1814-1914*, (Hamburg, 1924), 112-116

38 Arnold Kludas, *Die Geschichte der deutschen Passagierschiffahrt. Vol. I: Die Pionierjahre von 1850-1890*, (Hamburg, 1986), 156-162.

39 Quote taken from Wihelm Otto Henderson, *The Rise of German Industrial Power 1834-1914*, (London, 1975), 224.

40 Wehler, *Bismarck*, 215-223.

41 Susanne Wiborg and Klaus Wiborg, *The World is our Oyster. 150 Years of Hapag-Lloyd*, (Hamburg, 1997), 75.

42 Christine Reinke-Kunze, *Die Geschichte der Reichs-Post-Dampfer. Verbindung zwischen den Kontinenten 1886-1914*, (Herford, 1994), 23.

43 For a detailed discussion of Bismarck's motives see Wehler, *Bismarck*, 412 ff.

44 Henderson, *Rise of German Industrial Power*, 227.

45 Arnold Kludas, 'Deutsche Passagierschiffs-Verbindungen in die Südsee 1886-1914,' in Hermann Joseph Hiery (ed.), *Die Deutsche Südsee 1884-1914*, (Paderborn, 2001), 156-176; and Christian Ostersehlte, 'Der Reichspostdampferdienst des Norddeutschen Lloyd,' in Roder (ed.), *Bremen-Ostasien*, 215-220.

46 Kludas, *Geschichte*, 176.

47 Wiborg and Wiborg, *Our World*, 77.

48 Dieter Glade, *Bremen und der Ferne Osten*, (Bremen, 1966), 88.

49 Wiborg and Wiborg, *Our World*, 120.

50 Peter Winzen, 'Zur Genesis von Weltmachtkonzept und Weltpolitik,' in John C. G. Röhl (ed.), *Der Ort Kaiser Williams II in der Deutschen Geschichte*, (Munich, 1994), 216.

51 Röhl (ed.), *Der Ort Kaiser Williams*.

52 Röhl (ed.), *Der Ort Kaiser Williams* 217.

Some early examples of the activities of British aircraft carriers in Chinese waters between the Wars.

J. M. Parkinson

The Background

The first attempts at naval aviation were made before the Great War broke out, and *Jane's Fighting Ships* for 1919 shows the Royal Navy as having nine aircaft carriers, of which only *Hermes*, which was not completed, had been designed as one from the start. The others had begun life variously as merchant vessels, a battleship and a light cruiser. Those in service during the war had flown off planes for reconnaissance, gunnery spotting, bombing and attacking enemy aircraft, and while everything was a little makeshift they did well enough to make it clear that naval aviation had a future, possibly a very important one. By looking at the micro-level of the daily life of a carrier in the inter-war years, this paper seeks to show how the Navy developed its ideas of what carriers were good for and how they should do it.

On Monday morning, 3 November 1924 HMS *Pegasus*,[1] 3,300 tons (Commander Henry C. Rawlings, DSO, RN) secured to No 4 buoy in Victoria harbour, Hong Kong. Four Fairey 3D seaplanes in the ship were carried for the purpose of taking aerial survey photographs of British colonies in the Far East. The first flight by carrier-borne aircraft at Hong Kong was made on 4 November 1924. Machines 'A' and 'Z' left the ship at 0830, the former returning at 0920, and the latter some time afterwards without the time being noted.[2] Flight Lieut. G. E. Livock DFC, is recorded as piloting one of these aircraft,[3] having taken off from the waters of Kowloon Bay along with his fellow-pilot. Subsequently it was felt that inside the harbour itself the waters were dangerously congested with junk traffic so *Pegasus* shifted to Tolo Harbour in Mirs Bay. It was from this anchorage that the first aerial survey of the Colony had been carried out.

On Monday, 1 December 1924, His Excellency Sir Reginald Stubbs[4] became the first Governor of Hong Kong to inspect his territory from the air. He arrived onboard *Pegasus* at 0945 and boarded aircraft 'Z', which left the ship at 1000 and returned at 1006, so it was an extremely short flight. Sir Reginald left the ship at 1020 but unfortunately any remarks which he may have made do not appear to have been recorded.

The first aircraft carrier in any Navy of the world to be laid down and launched as such[5] was HMS *Hermes,* the ninth ship of this name to serve in the Royal Navy. On Wednesday, 17 June 1925 at 1815 hours[6] she weighed in Spithead to proceed to the Mediterranean at the start of her second commission.

Meanwhile, on 30 May 1925, an unfortunate incident had taken place in Shanghai. The International Settlement police, under British command, had fired on a group of demonstrators outside some Japanese-owned cotton mills and a number had been killed. Briefly, since the spring of 1921 the Soviet Communists, inspired by reports from their agent, Hendricus Sneevliet, known as Maring,[7] had been working to infiltrate the Chinese nationalist organisation, soon to be known as Kuomintang, which Dr. Sun Yat-sen was endeavouring to build up. This process of infiltration included funding and advice. In October 1923 Maring had been succeeded by the Soviet agent Michael Grusbenberg, better known as Borodin.[8] On 16 June 1924 Dr. Sun[9] had opened the Whampoa Military academy near Canton. The first Superintendent of this Academy was Chiang Kai-shek who was very well aware of Soviet motives, and had warned Dr Sun accordingly. Nevertheless, Dr. Sun chose to be guided by Borodin and selected as his policy 'Allying with Russia and tolerating the Communists.'

Following the death of Dr. Sun in March 1925, many runners emerged in the race to fill his position. These included warlords who hardly had the broad nationalistic picture in mind. Beside local power and authority, their principal interest lay in filling their pockets. Communist activity thrived in these conditions of domestic chaos and unrest. On 23 June, within a month of the incident at Shanghai, the whole business was exacerbated by another incident which occurred opposite the foreign concession area of Shameen Island at Canton. British and French forces opened fire on demonstrators who were protesting against the earlier episode at Shanghai, and again a number were killed. There is little doubt that the demonstration in Canton had been organised by Borodin since he had been delighted by the earlier misadventure in Shanghai and had worked hard to take advantage of it. It is clear that at Canton the first shot, which had provoked return fire, had been fired by an agitator.[10] From a commercial point of view the consquences of the incidents at Shanghai and at Canton were catastrophic, including as they did the great anti-British boycott of 1925, which was thoroughly well-organised, especially in the South of Canton.

Hermes was ordered from the Mediterranean to the China Station. Her new Captain, Cecil P. Talbot,[11] spent Friday 10 July 1925 in London, preparing to cross overland to join the ship at Malta. At the Admiralty he received a short briefing:

> *…and was informed of the Chinese situation. Strikes and anti-foreign riots, instigated by Bolshevik Russia, are going on over China, principally directed against the British. Women and children have been evacuated from Shameen, the international settlement of Canton, where the situation is about the worst. But the Chinese and Russians are known to be working on a fort[12] halfway up the river between Hong Kong and Canton, which would be in a position to prevent the passage down stream of our river gunboats now at Canton, and so isolate them and the Europeans there.* Hermes' *aircraft may possibly be the answer to this fort.[13]*

At Malta on 15 July Captain Talbot duly

assumed command and took *Hermes* east, arriving at Singapore on 5 August, and leaving the same afternoon. In the vicinity of the Paracel Islands a typhoon warning was received, but fortunately, although several downpours were experienced, with winds up to Force 6, there was no need to alter course. However as she neared Hong Kong on Sunday 9th the rain fell so heavily that the ship could only be navigated by dead reckoning. Consequently Captain Talbot hauled her around to the South East until the weather cleared. Even so, as she approached the Colony that night it was at slow speed and through deluges of rain. Fortunately, early on Monday morning the visibility did improve, and Waglan light to the South East of Hong Kong was sighted. At 0705 she secured to No. 18 buoy in Victoria Harbour.

Having made the obligatory calls ashore, and received a number of return visits, on Tuesday evening, 11 August Captain Talbot noted in his diary that:

> *The situation in the coast and river ports of China is still most difficult. Russian Bolsheviks have almost complete control in Canton, and no one has any idea what the outcome will be.*

Hermes *goes to work*

That Friday, 14 August, while Captain Talbot was on board *Hawkins* dining with the C-in-C, Vice Admiral Sir Edwyn Sinclair,[14] news was received of an overdue British steamer. On a voyage of only about 300 miles from Hainan Island to Hong Kong it appeared that SS *Yueying Wa*[15] was already five days overdue. This led to the first non-military use of search aircraft from the ship. Here is the sequence of events:

At 0730 the next morning, 15 August, two Fairey 3D aircraft[16] fitted as seaplanes, flew off to inspect the coast and nearby islands, flying as far as about 130 miles south west of Hong Kong. Unfortunately no trace of the missing ship could be found.

Early on Saturday, 22 August four officers from *Hermes* took passage to Canton in the

British-flag steamer *Tung On*,[17] returning on Sunday afternoon. On Tuesday, six officers proceeded in the same ship on another overnight visit to Canton. In spite of the boycott on trade with British interests, no unpleasant incidents occurred. Throughout this period frequent seaplane flights were undertaken, mostly on exercises. However Captain Talbot did record that on Friday, two machines went up at the request of the G.O.C. with an army officer in one, and flew up and down the Chinese frontier several times. On another occasion he noted that aeroplanes dropped three live bombs for practice, presumably a rare event as it merited special mention in his diary.

Between Monday, 7 and Friday 11 September *Hermes* steamed the short distance to carry out gunnery and other exercises in Mirs Bay. The change of air too was rather pleasant. Below decks she was always a very hot ship and during the humid summer many members of her company had been adversely affected. Captain Talbot, commenting on 16 September:

> Went up the Peak in afternoon to see our officers and men at the Sanatoria and Mount Austin Barracks who are there, to the number of about ten officers and fifty men, to recuperate from the dreadful heat in this ship.[18]

There was some excitement on 26 September as at 1900 hours a police launch apprehended a small steamer laden with some 150 'Red' Chinese soldiers who were endeavouring to escape from their victorious enemy in the eastern part of Kwangtung Province. This steamer was made secure to a buoy near *Hermes*. Throughout the night an armed motorboat crew stood by in *Hermes*, and at intervals one of her searchlights was trained on the steamer.

On Sunday 4 October two reconnaissance seaplanes went up in an attempt to intercept an un-named Russian steamer reported to be laden with ammunition for Canton. Naturally the Peking government wished to board this vessel prior to her arriving to discharge. In the event after an hour or two the machines were recalled as it had been learned that the ship in question already had arrived at Canton.

Two Chinese cruisers arrived in port on 10 October, the 'Double Tenth'.[19] Early the next morning, Sunday, aircraft from *Hermes* were involved in further contraband patrols:

> Carried out seaplane patrols at 6.30am and 1.30pm to the South West of Hong Kong to try to locate two Dutch ships reported to be bringing guns and ammunition to the Red government at Canton; the two Chinese cruisers are here with the object of intercepting them. The afternoon patrol found one ship which may be one concerned – the Chinese ships went in pursuit on receipt of our information.

Similarly on the 12th: 'Carried out the same seaplane patrols as yesterday, and put the Chinese cruisers on to one or two ships'.

On Saturday, 31 October 1925 Sir Reginald Stubbs left the colony to proceed on leave prior to taking up his new position in Jamaica. Captain Talbot arranged for some aeroplanes to escort his P&O liner as she left port bound for Singapore and home.

At 0600 hours the following morning the new Governor, Mr Cecil Clementi,[20] arrived from Ceylon in the P & O's SS *Kalyan*.[21] She was escorted to her buoy by seaplanes. Unfortunately at about 0640 aircraft number 47 flew into the slipstream of the formation leader and from about 900 feet went into a spin into the harbour. Happily, in the last fifty feet or so, her pilot managed to flatten her out before she crashed into the sea and so the three occupants[22] were not severely injured.The wrecked aircraft, 9774 Fairey 3D, was found by sweeping on Monday afternoon, and at 1815 was hoisted up onto the flight deck.

Also on the Monday, Captain Talbot was kept busy in a meeting with the C-in-C and Commodore. Admiral Sinclair had received word from the Admiralty that any work carried out ashore at the Kai Tak airstrip by men of the Royal Navy or RAF was in contravention of the terms of the Washington Agreement of 1921–1922, Article 19 of which stated that the United States of America, the British Empire, and Japan agreed to the status quo with regard to fortifications and naval bases in their respective territories and possessions over a huge area in the East and Pacific. Hong Kong fell within these boundary limits, thus it was thought possible that work at the airstrip could be construed as amounting to an improvement in the fortifications of the Colony. Fortunately the problem was overcome since initially, on 24 January 1925, the airport had been opened for civilian purposes. The facilities at Kai Tak could also be used by aircraft disembarked from visiting Royal Navy carriers.[23]

The following Monday, 9 November, at 0600 hours *Hermes* slipped from her buoy and proceeded up the coast to Amoy. She had a dirty bottom so that in order to make twelve knots Captain Talbot had to order revolutions corresponding to fourteen. At 0945 the following morning she anchored off Kulangsu, the island in Amoy harbour on which the foreign community resided.

'Showing the Flag' and developments ashore

During the morning the British consul, Mr W.M.Hewlett,[24] came onboard for an hour to discuss preparations for the Armistice Day remembrance arrangements in readiness for the following day, receiving his salute of seven guns on his departure. At 1300 *Hermes* shifted and anchored in the Northern part of the inner harbour, 'with just swinging room'. Here she saluted the Chinese republic with twenty-one guns and a Chinese gunboat returned the compliment. That evening, Captain Talbot held a dinner party onboard to which Mr Hewlett and various other British officials from the Concession and port, including Mr Bessell, the Commissioner of Customs, were invited.

Promptly at 0900 on Wednesday 11 November, *Hermes* landed her Ceremonial Marine and Seamen platoons. The ceremony at 1100 commenced with a short open-air service

on the recreation ground after which the guard marched past the assembled group of Allied Consuls and Chinese officials. Subsequently much other entertainment took place, which for the ship's Captain only ended at 0200 on the following day.

As a result of the anti-British boycott, the atmosphere ashore in many Chinese ports could be rather strained. Happily, in some of the smaller ports such as Amoy, restrictions had been relaxed relatively early on. Therefore one can appreciate Captain Talbot's annoyance when, on 12 November:

> The boycott on British ships and goods at Amoy was re-instituted today on account of a fool of an Englishman hitting a Chinese student with his stick to clear him out of his way, and knocking him down when he protested.

Hospitality ashore and in the ship continued at a vigorous pace. Meanwhile it became clear from local press articles that members of the ship's company in *Hermes* had made a favourable impression on the Chinese community. The town's Boycott Committee issued orders that although the anti-British boycott was to remain in effect it was not to apply to *Hermes*: everything required by the ship was to be supplied. Naturally it is also possible that the ever-pragmatic Chinese merchants of Amoy were aware of the considerable purchasing power of such a number of men.

That Saturday, 14 November, a rumour circulated ashore that the 'Red' military forces were about thirty miles away and closing on Amoy. Fortunately on the following day, although numerous refugees could be seen arriving in the town, it became apparent that the first news of 'Red' military success had been somewhat exaggerated. Nevertheless even this small example serves to illustrate something of the uncertainty of life in China at the time. Such news would be unsettling enough for those living in Concession areas at the coast, but much more so for those posted hundreds, even thousands, of miles inland.

On Monday *Hermes' visit* to Amoy came to an end. Prior to departure, and as a token of their appreciation for her visit, the British Community presented *Hermes* with a silver loving cup mounted on a plinth. At 0815 she commenced to unmoor, and at 1005 steamed from the harbour in pouring rain. By 1550 the following afternoon she had returned to her buoy at Hong Kong. Following a Defence Meeting, held ashore on Tuesday, 24 November, the Governor and Mrs Clementi together with their three children and His Excellency's ADC, returned to the ship for lunch with Captain Talbot. In the afternoon, Mr Clementi went up for a short flight. The following morning *Hermes* entered Taikoo dry dock for the long-awaited cleaning of her bottom which was 'very foul'. The work was completed quickly, and by 0850 on Saturday, 28th, she was back at her buoy.

In December there was a noticeable increase in the amount of operational flying as opposed to merely exercising. Some shooting incidents had occurred on the border with China and troops, in one case a company of 2/5th Punjabis had been forced to return fire, killing a number of Chinese. A daily air patrol of the frontier was instituted. On Monday 7th, Mr Clementi himself went up in one of those patrol aircraft. With the Governor airborne no chances were taken, his machine being one of a formation of five. On Wednesday the same week Captain Talbot went up to witness bombing practice on a suitably rocky island. Four bombs were dropped from 4,000 ft and two hits achieved, as he noted dryly 'Rather to my surprise'.

On 14 December Captain Talbot noted in his diary that at the end of November the Admiralty had ordered *Hermes* to prepare to return to the Mediterranean. However, as soon as Mr Clementi heard the news he protested to the Colonial Office with the result that the departure was postponed. The remaining few days leading up to the period of Christmas festivity passed busily but fortunately, as regards warlike activity, quietly. Through the holidays there was a great deal of hospitality both in the ship and ashore. This included a

dance for the men of the fleet which was given by Lady Clementi[25] on Tuesday, 5 January 1926.

At 1115 on 7 January Lieut E.B. Carnduff in Flycatcher No 9888 crashed into the sea at the head of Kowloon Bay. His engine stopped while he was flying down wind at low altitude. Fortunately the depth of water was only five feet and he was not injured. The wrecked machine was recovered during the following afternoon.

On Wednesday, 13th *Hermes* slipped and proceeded to sea, first to act as target for submarine exercises, and later to exercise her own high angle gunnery. She spent the night in Mirs Bay, exercised again on Thursday, and returned to her buoy that afternoon.

This leisurely pace at Hong Kong continued through until the end of the month. Various farewell parties, dances and sporting events were held, and on Sunday, 31st forty eight ratings embarked for passage to Malta. Finally at 0805 on Monday, 1 February *Hermes* slipped for Jesselton in North Borneo, Labuan and Singapore where she arrived on 12 February, reaching Malta on 15 March 1926. Her duties in the Far East had endured for barely eight months and it was anticipated that she would remain in the Mediterranean until the end of her commission. She was succeeded on the China Station by *Vindictive*,[26] Captain Ronald Howard.

The narrative above gives a glimpse of the customs and traditions of Empire which on occasion demanded much formality. Naturally it was both courteous and necessary for each Captain, RN to meet and to become known to senior officials at each colony. Nevertheless, shortly after his arrival at Hong Kong but having already called at Aden, Trincomalee and Singapore, even Captain Talbot felt constrained to comment in his diary on Monday, 17 August 1925 'Returned some calls ashore in forenoon and received others; there is too much of it.' In addition, the amount of entertainment hosted both ashore and in the ship was very considerable indeed. On the other hand a great deal of sport was played, particular efforts being made in this regard so as to involve all members of the ship's companies. To modern eyes it is possible that the few months of the ship's deployment in the Far East might appear to have been leisurely. Carrier-borne naval 'air' was a new feature on the China Station[27] which had proved itself: the Governor of Hong Kong was enthusiastic to the extent of going to the trouble to arrange for *Hermes* to remain available until her replacement arrived. In the circumstances it is clear that the routine followed was within the accepted norms of that imperial era.

From his position as Superintendent of the Whampoa Academy by October 1925 Chiang Kai-shek had felt powerful enough to launch five of his armies against local opposition in the South of China. The several warlords in the region had not been strong enough to compete and within a month Chiang had achieved success. These victories require explanation. It was the custom that when warring factions met only the minimum amount of actual combat should take place. Negotiations were entered into and discussions held, a process by which the two 'generals' involved would ascertain who was the more powerful. Once each was sure in his own mind how the land lay, then the weaker would withdraw discreetly. Naturally while these negotiations were taking place various defections from one side to the other would tend to occur. Bribery was normal as was any amount of duplicity. When fighting did take place, however, then behaviour was frequently barbaric. It is worth noting that early in 1926 Chiang's armies totalled a modest 85,000 men and of these only some 60,000 possessed rifles.[28]

Matters become more serious: the return of Hermes

Having secured his position and authority in the South, Chiang found himself ahead in the race to succeed Dr Sun. He had become a prominent figure in the leadership of the left wing of the Kuomintang. Now was the time to plan the next step towards the unification of China, his march to the North. If achieved this would fulfil one of the dreams of his late mentor, Sun Yat-sen. However he continued to be the object of considerable personal opposition and behind the scenes much manoeuvring for power continued. Although inspired by individuals, as a body it was the Communists who were the disciplined group. Chiang was well aware of this intrigue and remained uneasy, not surprisingly since at the time two separate attempts were made on his life.

At 0300 on 20 March 1926 he acted. Twenty five Communists, including all Soviet advisers, were placed under house arrest. His coup was a success since it had been entirely unexpected. At a stroke Chiang became the unchallenged leader of the Kuomintang. However he did not overplay his hand. He was conciliatory enough to continue a close relationship with Borodin. The Soviet Communists were simply put in their place as advisers. By mid 1926, his plans made and with his party position as secure as was possible, Chiang had started his armies moving to the North. With a mixture of indoctrination, so that his men knew the cause for which they were fighting, and harshly strict discipline, his forces achieved a series of spectacular successes. In that peculiarly Chinese manner described above, those whom he was about to conquer, clearly seeing the way the wind was blowing, frequently defected from their own warlord of the moment and joined Chiang's forces. His troops were astounded to find themselves being paid regularly. Equally unusually, instead of pillaging and looting as they advanced, the armies paid their way.

Between 30 August and 5 September the SS *Wanhsien*[29] incident took place in the Gorges. It was a complicated affair to do with smuggling, local warlord power struggles, funds obtained by extortionate warlord taxation, and attempts made by Chinese 'soldiers' to illegally board British river steamers for passage, there being no alternative in the Gorges but to travel by river. In the course of regaining possession of the ship, three officers and four ratings, all of the Royal Navy, were killed by rifle fire from men of the warlord Yang Sen.

This affair, taken together with much other uncertainty, including the progress towards the Yangtse basin being made by Chiang, caused the Admiralty to order *Hermes* back from the Mediterranean to the Far East. On 7 October, while *Hermes* was at Singapore on return passage to Chinese waters, Wuhan fell to the advancing Kuomintang forces. This success was impressive as the warlord hitherto in charge had been Wu Pei-fu, a more capable man than was usually the case. For Chiang Kai-shek, celebration of the 'Double Tenth' in 1926 will have had special meaning.

Hermes reached Hong Kong on 11 October. RAF stores were landed at Kowloon, but otherwise she remained at her buoy, exercising seaplanes regularly.

Although not yet mentioned, one other aspect of Naval life on the China coast involved piracy. During the following month *Hermes* was to be involved in a modest way in one such affair The SS *Sunning*[30] was pirated off Chilang Point to the South West of Swatow at 1600 on 15 November 1926. *Sunning*, Captain J. Pringle, had sailed from Shanghai on 12 November and had called at Amoy on the 14th. She had been scheduled to carry a large amount of bullion but, as was the precautionary custom, at the last moment this consignment had been switched to another vessel. At 0930 on 15 November she had sailed from Amoy bound for Hong Kong. In common with most coastal steamers of the day she was fitted with steel anti-piracy grills around the bridge superstructure and she was also carrying four Hong Kong Police guards. In spite of these precautions the pirates, who had boarded the ship at Amoy as ordinary deck passengers, managed to penetrate the grill gate which gave them access to the bridge. The guards and ship's officers were overpowered and the latter forced at gunpoint to steer a course for Bias Bay, the pirates' lair a short distance to the East of Hong Kong. Leaving a few of their own guards on the bridge, the remainder of the pirates then proceeded to ransack the cabins and cargo searching for valuables and for the bullion they believed to be there.

That night *Sunning* was passed by the company flagship *Anhui*.[31] In the normal course of events the junior ship should have signalled her respects to the Commodore. This she neglected to do and fortunately the pirates were not acquainted with this example of maritime etiquette. The Commodore suspected that there were problems onboard *Sunning* and radioed for assistance. In addition during the night the officers in *Sunning* managed to overcome the pirate guards on the bridge and regain control. The story goes that the first pirate guard had been hit over the head with the ship's lead-weighted sounding line. The blow must have crushed his skull. Other pirates in the vicinity then were dealt with. In retaliation the remainder of the gang set her on fire.[32] When the blaze started to get out of control the majority of the pirates escaped in lifeboats leaving the crew and passengers, together with some of their own colleagues, to continue to fight the fire.

Meanwhile it so happened that at 0630 on the 15th *Hermes* had proceeded from Hong Kong to Mirs Bay, which lies between Hong Kong and Bias Bay, to carry out exercises. As the C-in-C was to state in his subsequent report:

> *Para 5.* **Hermes** *at anchor in Mirs Bay, was ordered at 0929/16 to send aircraft to search the coast in the vicinity. Two machines were promptly sent up and the ship proceeded towards Bias Bay at 1000.*
>
> *Para 7. Some machines from* **Hermes** *were also detailed to search for missing boats and ordered to closely investigate junks if a derelict ship's boat was seen.*[33]

In addition the sloop *Bluebell*, 1,200 tons (Commander G. C. Muirhead-Gould, DSC) was ordered to close the scene. In the event it was she who came up with *Sunning* in the morning and closed to render assistance. She also managed to capture some of the pirates although one deliberately drowned himself in order to avoid capture. Later *Sunning*, a smouldering wreck, was towed back to Hong Kong. She was rebuilt and in February 1927 re-entered service.

At 0800 on Saturday, 8 January 1927 the new C-in-C, China Station, Vice Admiral Sir Reginald Tyrwhitt,[34] who had travelled out from England in the P & O's SS *Morea*, hoisted his flag in the light cruiser *Despatch*, 4,850 tons (Flag Captain D.B. le Mottee). From Hong Kong Sir Reginald immediately sailed to Shanghai.

Meanwhile, Chiang Kai-shek's Kuomintang army had been advancing steadily from the South. After their capture of the tri-city Wuhan they began to work their way eastwards towards those two important cities closer to the mouth of the Yangtse, Nanking and Shanghai. However, this being China, there was always an abundance of intrigue. By no means did all those who professed to support Chiang fully agree with the degree of power which, by now, he had assumed for himself. In addition, although the Communists had had their wings clipped, they were not quiet. Strikes were organised and, a common tactic, continuous efforts were made to play upon Chinese xenophobia. Frequently those Chinese who did business with the 'foreign Imperialists' were forced to pay protection money.[35] On 3 January 1927, only some twelve weeks after the occupation of Wuhan by Chiang's forces, serious anti-British troubles occurred at Hankow, the city within Wuhan wherein the foreign settlements were situated. Many foreign residents, particularly families and dependants, wisely moved from the interior of China towards important centres such as Shanghai. In London in January 1927 the Conservative government of Stanley Baldwin decided to heed protests and demands from British merchants and administrators in the East. Considerable arrangements were made to reinforce the garrison at Shanghai.

During January and February 1927 *Hermes* spent most of the time at her buoy in Hong Kong harbour but with occasional short periods in Mirs Bay to exercise her gunnery and to carry out other drills. In the usual manner while at her buoy continuous exercises were carried out with her aircraft. As one would imagine, the harbour was extremely busy as, in addition to the normal traffic, there were large numbers of military transports and many other chartered vessels passing through on their way to or from Shanghai. The Kuomintang forces steadily made their way towards that city. SHAFORCE, as the reinforced body was known, troops were positioned in such a manner as to defend the International Settlement. Naturally their terms of reference did not include the Chinese city, and nor was it desirable that they become involved.

On 21 March, while on passage from Hong Kong to Swatow, SS *Hop Sang*[36] was pirated. Fortunately she was released quickly and subsequently reached Hong Kong at 1400 on Tuesday, 22 March. However, it was decided by the authorities that a punitive raid should be launched immediately. As the Rear Admiral was to report to the C-in-C:

At the request of H. E. the Governor of Hong Kong the punitive measures planned against the pirate villages of Bias Bay were put into effect on Wednesday, 23.3.27.[37]

Captain Calvert in *Frobisher* was given overall command of the small operation and various boats and men were made available by warships at Hong Kong, including *Hermes*. At 1907 on the 22nd *Frobisher* slipped[38] and in company with *Delhi* and *Marazion* steamed into Bias Bay where they arrived at 0210 the following morning. Care was taken to lower the starboard anchor as quietly as possible and then the men commenced to disembark. In the interim *Hermes* slipped from her buoy at 2200 and anchored in Bias Bay at 0436 on the 23rd. At 0340, also on the 23rd, *Marazion*, a small minesweeper, took a number of boats in tow and proceeded into Fan Lo Kong harbour, and at 0550 the Landing Force disembarked. At 0600 *Hermes* launched seaplanes which were used to carry out an aerial reconnaissance over Fan Lo Kong. From 0700 men of the Landing Force commenced to demolish the village of Hoi Chau. This was accomplished rapidly, and at 1015 the boats began to re-embark the force.

By 1330 all men of the Landing Force had re-embarked in *Frobisher* who returned to Hong Kong where she secured back to her buoy at 1825. *Hermes* had returned a short while earlier, at 1658. No casualties had been incurred on either side and the raid did little to curb the activity of the pirate gangs. However the Chinese authorities, such as they were, had been shown that if their hand was forced then the British could and would take action. Certainly they would not merely sit back and do nothing.

In the Yangtse basin Chiang Kai-shek and the Kuomintang army continued to enjoy success. The Chinese city of Shanghai fell on 22 March, and Nanking followed on 24 March 1927. Unfortunately when his 6th Army entered Nanking, elements amongst Kuomintang troops had attacked and looted the premises of foreign commercial companies, Consulates, and Roman Catholic Missions. Six foreigners were killed and many others subjected to gross indignities. This was the 'Nanking Incident' which provoked an immediate reaction by the West, including a short naval bombardment. However, *Hermes* was not involved.

Chiang was no lover of the foreign presence in China but neither did he support this undisciplined behaviour. Upon his arrival at Nanking he quickly, and ruthlessly, restored order in his 6th Army. In April he resolved to take the most important step of further establishing his authority over the Communists. On the 11th secret orders were issued to his supporters that on the following day they were to disarm many hundreds of Chinese Communist troops at widely scattered centres throughout Southern China. In Shanghai the Communists offered some resistance and in addition to fighting back they endeavoured to organise a general strike to take place on the 13th. Chiang and his allies had out-manoeuvred them, however, and neither effort succeeded. On the contrary, a purge followed and many Communists in Shanghai lost their lives, a figure as high as five thousand being mentioned.[39]

At the time the British Consul-General in Shanghai was Sir Sidney Barton.[40] Here follow excerpts taken from his political report for the quarter ending 30 June 1927:

> At the end of March the local situation was in a very uncertain state. Chiang Kai-shek had declared war on the Communists and begun to break their power, without however carrying the process to a successful conclusion. It was not long however before the Military Authorities manifested their determination to be masters in this area. On 11 April concerted attacks were made on all the known rendezvous of the armed labour organisations, and this was followed up by vigorous repressive measures during the next few days with such effect that at the end of a fortnight these organisations had either been completely broken up or had gone underground. The Communist General Labour Union was declared to be dissolved, and a newly created officially sponsored anti-Communist 'Federated Association of Labour Unions' installed in its place.[41]

It is apparent that the Communist methods were not wholly guided by idealism. Sir Sidney continues:

> Although the strength of the Communist Labour Union and of the 'Workers Supervisory Corps' was broken, so thoroughly had the fear of them been instilled into the labouring classes that the latter allowed themselves to be influenced by it even after the power of these bodies to do them harm had gone.

Later in the same report Sir Sidney gives an illustration of another aspect of The Comintern's work. He describes attempts which were made to produce a feeling of discontent and of class hatred amongst the rank and file of the British military. Also there were British Indian troops within SHAFORCE and in addition to the distribution of Communist propaganda amongst British troops 'Cases have occurred where Indian troops were approached direct by their fellow countrymen.'

Otherwise, those Chinese in power were, as usual, desperate to increase the sources and amount of income:

The energies of such civil administration as can be said to exist are concentrated on the collection of revenue. Forced loans, blackmail, and increased taxation in every form have been in evidence since the arrival of the Nationalist authorities.

This coup of 12 April 1927 marked the split between Chiang Kai-shek and the Chinese Communists. As the result of a visit to Moscow in 1923, Chiang knew that ultimately the Communists had but one aim. In due course they were to defeat him and on 8 December 1949 cause him to go into exile in Taiwan. However, in April 1927, and for the foreseeable future, he appeared to hold the upper hand.

On Tuesday, 26 April *Hermes* slipped from her buoy and proceeded alongside the quay at Whampoa Dockyard. The next afternoon she embarked two flights from Kai Tak, 401 and 440, together with ammunition and RAF stores and on Thursday she weighed for Woosung at 0847.

It was not a straightforward voyage up the China coast. On several occasions fog came down. Sometimes she was able to maintain her progress, merely slowing, sounding her siren, and posting additional lookouts, but at other times the visibility was so restricted that her Captain was forced to anchor. Eventually she crossed the bar at the mouth of the Yangtse and proceeded upstream to anchor off Woosung at 0018 on Monday 2 May. It was while at anchor off Woosung that a very young member of the ship's company came across one sad consequence of life in China during these years of civil war. As Mr E.G. Clark relates in his memoirs:

I am on watch as sideboy on the quarter deck when I am ordered to remove a dead body that has jammed under the gangway. I get a boat hook and go down the gangway and stand on the tidespar, the timber that is fixed diagonally from the ship's side. The tidespar is meant to fend off anything floating down the river. In this case the body has come up

and become jammed. I push down with the boathook which promptly goes right through the torso and I get the full flavour of the stench. I did free the body but I should have used a broom. When I got back in-board I found I was reported for going over the side without a lifeline, thus endangering my life. I soon learned.[42]

Between 0620 and 0905 the spare aircraft and bombs from Hong Kong were disembarked into lighters which had been towed the fourteen miles down from Shanghai. As soon as this operation was complete the tug and lighters cast off and at 0912 *Hermes* weighed for Hong Kong, securing back alongside at the Whampoa Dockyard at 0930 on Thursday, 5 May. On Saturday hands were employed in embarking seaplanes.

In the interim the Governor of Macao had become concerned at the presence of a concentration of 'Reds' in the hills overlooking his territory on the west bank of the Canton River estuary.[43] Consequently he requested the Governor of Hong Kong to arrange for a demonstration of air power. This request was approved and passed to the Navy, and to the Captain of *Hermes*. He in turn ordered Lt. Commander (O) E. W. Woodruff to carry out the patrol. Three Fairey 3D seaplanes of 440 flight were used and at 1000 on Thursday 12 May they took off and thirty minutes later arrived over Macao. Aeroplanes still were so unusual that considerable curiosity was aroused:

The appearance of the seaplanes over Macao caused a great deal of interest amongst the Chinese population, and a large number of these had flocked to the housetops to get a better view of the machines.[44]

The visit and the aerial patrol passed off very satisfactorily and with mutual assurances of goodwill. The three machines duly took off from Macao to return to Hong Kong, an event which was witnessed by the Portuguese Governor and his family who embarked in a launch to observe their departure at 1700 that afternoon. At 1750 they alighted safely alongside *Hermes*.Between 31 May and 2 June

Then at 1150 the following morning she weighed for Wei-Hai-Wei. On passage along the coast full power trials were carried out, 25.5 knots being achieved. She anchored off Liu Kung Tao[58] at 1607 that afternoon.

A later model of Fairey aircraft, the 3F,[59] was by now being operated by the ship. The then Flying Officer Angus Macmillan relates that there had been a design fault in that when fitted with floats for use as a seaplane there was a tendency for this model of aircraft to break its back. *Hermes* was the first ship to fly the 3F in this configuration and on 19 June Mr E.O. Tipps from Fairey Aviation arrived onboard to look into the matter. He recommended that certain structural wires be replaced by struts, which solved the problem. Unfortunately in the meantime another, unconnected, fatal accident occurred on Wednesday, 20 June. Whilst engaged in dive bombing practice, Lieut Raymond Arthur Aldridge RN, of No 403 Flight, flying Flycatcher No 9661, pulled out too abruptly, the wings of his machine parted company with the fuselage, and he went straight into the sea. His funeral took place on Friday, 22 June.

Two days later *Hermes* sailed for Chingwangtao, a port at the head of the Gulf of Chihli close to where the Great Wall reaches the sea at Shanhaiguan. The harbour was used for the export of coal from British-owned mines some sixty miles inland. Good overnight rail facilities existed for visitors who wished to travel to Peking (Beijing). The heavy cruiser *Berwick* and the sloop *Magnolia* were already there and there was no further space available alongside so from Monday 25 June until Sunday 15 July, *Hermes* lay off at anchor. From 16 to 30 July *Hermes* was back at anchor at Wei-Hai-Wei. On the 18th her diving party were able to make themselves rather useful by removing a target towing wire from the propeller of the RFA *Francol*.

Some three years had elapsed since the first arrival of *Hermes* in Chinese waters, providing a corpus of experience from which we may summarise a number of the ways in which she was able to provide a unique service to the C-in-C, and to the Colonial authorities.

1. Aerial border patrols, with army personnel embarked as might be required.
2. Aerial photography – surveying.
3. Aerial contraband patrols.
4. Demonstrations of 'air power' to Allies: 'showing the flag'.
5. Piracy search and reconnaissance patrols.
6. Sales demonstrations on behalf of British aeroplane manufacturers.
7. Search for overdue British merchantmen.
8. Spotting cruiser gunfire.
9. Standing by for possible evacuation of British citizens. Had an emergency arisen then her aircraft would have been most usefully employed.
10. Transport of RAF stores, ammunition and aircraft.
11. VIP ceremonial escort.

The importance of one of the duties of HM ships in Far Eastern waters, the protection of British interests, is very clearly shown by the figures in respect of merchant shipping traffic at the greatest port of them all, Shanghai, in 1928:

(a) Number of ships by Nationality (excluding small local craft)

Chinese	4,472	40.16%
British	3,054	27.42%
Japanese	2,210	19.85%
American	648	5.82%
Norwegian	277	2.49%
German	156	2.49%
French	105	0.94%
Others	214	1.92%
Total	11,136	

(b) By tonnage, however, there is a considerable difference in this distribution:

British	32%
Japanese	27%
American	15%
German	8%
Chinese	5%
Norwegian	3%
Others	10%

(c) In the publication no figures are given for foreign export trade but inbound foreign trade for the whole of China, not just Shanghai, in

1928 was carried in these proportions by tonnage:

British	33.90%
Japanese	31.42%
Chinese	9.46%
American	8.60%
Others	16.62%

(d) Likewise on the China coast the British were dominant. The entire coastwise trade was carried in the following proportions by tonnage.

British	37.60%
Chinese	30.12%
Japanese	23.05%
American	2.32%
Others	6.91%

By value, the entire coastal trade amounted to 55.57% of China's total trade, so it can be seen that the coastal trade alone was very considerable.

In August 1928, *Hermes* left Wei-Hai-Wei and proceeded to Woosung and Shanghai, returning to Wei-Hai-Wei on 14 September. On Thursday, 18 October she weighed to return in a Southerly direction to Hong Kong. The following evening she passed 17.8 miles to the East of the North Saddle lighthouse in the Chusan archipelago. Her uneventful voyage was enlivened on Sunday, 21 October when at 0845 she altered course to close SS *Kwangse*,[60] ashore on Ping Rock, South of Foochow. She had been on passage from Swatow to Shanghai when misfortune had struck. However at 1101 *Hermes* was informed that her assistance was not required after all and so she resumed her passage. Apart from short intervals spent in exercising at sea or in Mirs Bay she remained at Hong Kong from 22 October to 29 November 1928.

An important event in the world of aviation occurred on 18 November, when the Far East Flight arrived and landed at Kai Tak. Air Order 1691 dated 12 May 1927[61] had led to the formation of the Far East Flight. In 1927 the most Eastern RAF establishment was located at Karachi. In their four Supermarine 'Southampton' class[62] flying boats the RAF

pilots involved had left Felixstowe on 14 October 1927 and reached Karachi on 18 November. Subsequently they had made their pioneering journey, with many stops en route, as the safe maximum range of their machines in still air was only 500 nautical miles,[63] to Singapore and Melbourne. On 15 September 1928 they had returned to Singapore. The side trip from Singapore to Hong Kong and return was to last from 1 November to 11 December 1928.

By a nice coincidence, the second-in-command of the flight was Squadron Leader Gerald Edward Livock, DFC, the same officer who in November 1924 had made the first flight at Hong Kong, from *Pegasus*. In the meantime considerable progress in aeronautical equipment had been made. Here he is describing his arrival at Hong Kong by air. They are crossing from Salomargue Bay, North Luzon in unpleasant conditions:

> *Most of the way across we had a cross wind from the North East of almost gale force. The clouds were at a thousand feet, and there were frequent rain squalls. Flying an accurate course was misery on account of the bad bumps, and it gave me the shivers every time I looked down at the sea below us We had hoped to sight the Pratas Reef halfway across but didn't see it, although a strip of shallow water suggested that it was not far away to the North. As we approached land we were relieved to pass over a large merchant ship, which, we assumed, must be on her way from Hong Kong to Luzon. Shortly afterwards a Fairey 3F from the carrier* Hermes *arrived to escort us in. Of all the long flights I have made I think this was in some ways the most remarkable. The four of us had been in the air for nearly eight hours, out of sight of land and flying in very poor conditions.*[64]

Conclusion

From these few abbreviated notes we see something of the manner in which early, and very modest, British naval air power began to

British Minister, Sir Claude MacDonald. Between 1916 and 1922, as acting Consul-General in Chengtu, Szechwan Province, had undergone some astonishing adventures. Consul at Amoy:1923-1927. Consul-General, Nanking:1927-1931. KCMG:1 January 1931. Consul-General, Hankow: 1931-1935. Retired 2 September 1935. *Foreign Office List* and *Who's Who;* Coates, *China Consuls,* 424-427.

25 His Excellency had been knighted in the New Year's Honours

26 9,750 tons. Once intended to be the cruiser *Cavendish,* but launched on 17 January 1918 and completed on 21 September 1918 as a carrier. Between 1923 and 1925 re-converted as a cruiser but with a hangar forward of the bridge and capable of handling six seaplanes. From 17 August 1937 used as a Cadet training cruiser. Six 7.5″, three 4″ A.A. and smaller guns. Six 21″ T.T., four above water and two submerged. 29 knots. In January 1946 sold for scrapping. *Jane's;* R. D. Layman, *Before the Aircraft Carrier,* (London, 1989), 62-66.

27 The sad story is outside the scope of this paper, but remember that since 1 April 1918 the Royal Naval Service and the Royal Flying Corps had combined to form the Royal Air Force. In consequence, as has been seen, many of the Fleet Air Arm pilots were RAF personnel, as were the maintenance crews. There is no doubt that much focus on the development of air power thereby was lost to the Royal Navy. As just one example of the application given to the subject in the U.S.N consider the following: 'Meanwhile in California Admiral J.M.Reeves continued to train his US Navy air squadrons vigorously. For five weeks from early July 1928 Commander J.H.Towers took *Langley* CV-1 to sea each weekday and in that short period a total of 945 landings were made onto her flight deck. Ninety four new Naval pilots were qualified'. In neither the USN nor IJN was Naval 'air' ever released from Naval control and development. Author's notes for *'The Life and Times of* HMS *Hermes 1923-1942,* 79.

28 Brian Crozier, *The Man Who Lost China,* (London,1977), 84.

29 868 grt. Built in 1922 by Yarrow & Co Ltd, Glasgow for China Navigation (Butterfield & Swire). Fitted with especially powerful engines to enable her to navigate the rapids and strong flow of the upper river. She spent the war years in Chungking and in 1948 was sold to Chinese owners. John Swire & Sons, *The China Navigation Co Ltd.,* (London, 1992), 19-21.

30 2,555 grt. Built in 1916 at Taikoo Dockyard, Hong Kong for China Navigation (both Butterfield & Swire companies). On 17 August 1936 wrecked at Junk Bay, Hong Kong by the effect of a typhoon. Subsequently sold for breaking up. John Swire & Sons, *The China Navigation Co Ltd,* 57.

31 3,494 grt. Built in 1925, also at Taikoo Dockyard. Placed on the Straits-China route. At Mila on 10 December 1941 damaged by Japanese air attack but escaped to Australia. In February/March 1942 ran military equipment from Australia to the Philippines. In 1946 returned to her owners. On 16 June 1950, with 700 passengers onboard, struck a Nationalist mine at Swatow. Holed in engine room but beached. There further damaged by air attack. Wreck sold to the Moller Group who re-floated her in August and towed the hulk to Hong Kong arriving on 3 September 1950. Subsequently broken up. H. W. Dick and S. A. Kentwell, *Beancaker to Boxboat,* (Canberra, 1988), 92 and 94.

32 John Swire & Sons, *The China Navigation Co Ltd,* 57; Harry Miller, *Pirates of the Far East,* (London,1970), 168-174.

33 PRO ADM 116/2502. Report 1427/1034 dated 24.11.26.

34 Reginald Yorke Tyrwhitt. Born:10 May 1870. Died: 30 May 1951. As Commodore, Destroyer Flotillas in the North Sea, well known for his vigorous prosecution of the war against Germany during WW1. DSO:1916. KCB: 1917. Rear Admiral: 2 December 1919. C-in-C, East Coast, Scotland: 30 1923-1925. Vice Admiral: January 1925. C-in-C, China: 8 November 1926 – 1 February 1929. Admiral: 27 February 1929. GCB: 1929. C-in-C, The Nore: 16 May 1930-33. Admiral of the Fleet: 31 July 1934. *Navy Lists* and *Who's Who.* See also A.Temple Patterson, *Tyrwhitt of the Harwich Force,* (London, 1973),

35 Brian Crozier, *The Man Who Lost China,* 98.

36 2,149 grt. Built in Glasgow in 1901 for Indo-China S.N. Co Ltd (Jardine Matheson & Co). On 11 March 1937 wrecked while on passage from Takao to Keelung, Formosa. Dick & Kentwell, *Beancaker to Boxboat,* 29.

37 PRO ADM 116/2502. Report dated at Hong Kong, 23.3.27. Miller, *Pirates of the Far East* has a brief account of the punitive action on page 175.

38 PRO ADM 53/77643. *Log book,* HMS *Frobisher.*

39 Edgar Snow, quoted in Crozier, *The Man Who*

Lost China, 103.

Dick Wilson, *China's Revolutionary War* (London, 1991), 17, suggests a much higher figure. David Bergamini, In *Japan's Imperial Conspiracy,* (London, 1971), 355 also gives a figure of 5,000 Communist deaths.

40 Born: 26 November 1876. Died: 20 January 1946. St Paul's School. Joined the China service in 1895, aged 18. Barrister-at-Law, Middle Temple: 1910. Service in Wei-Hai-Wei, Peking, Tientsin, Shanghai, then back to Peking. Consul-General, Shanghai: 1922-1929. In 1929 transferred to the diplomatic service and appointed Minister to Abyssinia: 1929-1937. KBE: 1926. KCVO: 1930. GBE: 1936. *Foreign Office List* and *Who's Who.*

41 PRO FO 228/3640.

42 *A Working Life,* (Printed privately, 1996), 10.

43 Established by Portugal in 1557, a minute territory about six square miles in extent. For the early history of Macao, see Glenn Timmerman's paper elsewhere in this volume. The presence of the Portuguese in their small enclave was tolerated by China until its return in December 1999. See also C. R. Boxer, *The Portuguese Seaborne Empire 1415-1825,* (Carcanet, 1991), 63; also Om Prakash: 'The Portuguese in the Far East 1540-1940' in Anthony Disney and Emily Booth (eds) *Vasco da Gama and the Linking of Europe and Asia,* (Oxford, 2000).

44 PRO ADM 116/2510 S.N.O, Hong Kong. Letter C.47 dated 31 May 1927, paragraph three.

45 2,604 grt. Built at Taikoo Dockyard in 1920 for China Navigation (Butterfield & Swire). On 12 December 1941 scuttled at Hong Kong. Subsequently raised by the Japanese occupying power and in May 1942 renamed *Tosan Mare.* On 22 August 1945 mined and sunk near Shimonoseki; Dick & Kentwell, *Beancaker to Boxboat,* 90.

46 Beaufort Scale, Force 11: Storm. Wind in mph: 64-73, or km/h: 103-117. 'Widespread damage; very rare occurrence.'

47 4,850 tons. Completed: June 1919. Six 6" plus smaller guns. Twelve 21" T.T, 28.5 knots. Re-armed with five 5" D.P guns during WW2, which she survived. *Jane's.*

48 7,050 tons. Launched: 9 October 1923. Ten 6" plus lighter guns. Six 21" T.T. Two catapults and two aircraft. 34.5 knots. Survived WW2. *Jane's.*

49 Early in April, two hangars had been erected on Shanghai racecourse. Initially aircraft had been supplied by HMS *Argus,* but these were later replaced by RAF aircraft shipped from England.

The ship herself was laid down as the proposed Italian merchant vessel *Conte Rosso,* but was acquired by the Admiralty on the Beardmore stocks and launched on 2 December 1917 as an aircraft carrier. 14,450 tons, six 4" A.A plus four 3-pounder guns. 20 knots. First commissioned on 14 September 1918 by Captain Humphrey H. Smith, DSO, the first flush deck carrier in the Royal Navy. In the mid 1920s served with the Atlantic Fleet. From 17 January 1927 under the command of Captain A. R. Palmer, and later that year spent several months on the China Station prior to returning to the Atlantic Fleet. Into Reserve from 7 May 1930. *Navy Lists*; Chesneau, *Aircraft Carriers of the World,* 89-90; Vice Admiral H.H.Smith, *A Yellow Admiral Remembers,* (London, 1932), 318.

50 2,284 grt. Built at Newcastle-upon-Tyne in 1904 for Indo-China S N Co Ltd (Jardine Matheson& Co). 11 December 1941 scuttled at Hong Kong. Later salvaged by the Japanese occupying power and in February 1943 re-named *Nissho Maru.* 17 July 1945 mined and sunk off Yawata, the important pig iron producing centre in North Kyushu. Dick & Kentwell, *Beancaker to Boxboat,* 30.

51 PRO ADM 116/2502.

52 Born: 1881. Died: 20 December 1958. Midshipman: 15 January 1897. Early China Station service both as a Midshipman and Lieutenant Gunner. Promoted Commander: 30 June 1913, and spent most of the Great War as Commander in, respectively, the pre-dreadnought *King Edward VII* and the dreadnought *Emperor of India.* Captain: 30 June 1918. From 1921 service on the Yangtse in command of *Bee* and as Chief of Staff to RAY. In command of *Hermes* from 14 August 1926 to 2 December 1927. Rear Admiral on the Retired List: 9 October 1929. Vice Admiral: 8 May 1935. From 16 September 1939 rejoined active list. Service in Liverpool, *Eaglet II,* then from 11 June 1942 in *Fortitude,* parent ship Ardrossan but for duty across the Firth at Lamlash, Isle of Arran. *Navy Lists* and *Who's Who.*

53 7,552 grt. Built in 1913 for Alfred Holt & Co, Liverpool. (The Blue Funnel Line). In 1952 sold for breaking up after forty years of service. *Lloyds Register.* The Ocean Steam Ship Company was registered on 11 January 1865. With Alfred Holt's first three ships, *Agamemnon, Ajax* and *Achilles,* each 2,280 grt, began what became the greatest line of steam ships plying between

Europe and the Far East. Francis E Hyde, *Blue Funnel*, (Liverpool, 1957), 1 and 19; Malcolm Falkus, *The Blue Funnel Legend*, (London, 1990), 96.

54 PRO ADM 53/78832. *Log Book*, HMS *Hermes*.

55 Letter to the author dated 1 April 1996.

56 HM Queen Victoria was born on 24 May 1819.

57 Today Memorial Day is the last Monday in May.

58 Being the island on which the base facilities were located. These were largely recreational in nature. The Chinese town of Wei-Hai-Wei itself is on the mainland opposite the island.

59 Depending on the Mark, loaded weight between 5,300 lb (2,404 kg) and 6,301 lb (2,858 kg). Maximum speed between 130 and 135 mph (209 – 217 km/h). Endurance from three to four hours. A total of 352 3F machines of different marks were produced for the Royal Navy. Taylor, *Fairey Aircraft*, 144-166.

60 1,985 grt. Built in 1898 by Scott & Co, Greenock for China Navigation (Butterfield & Swire). She was not salvaged so there on Ping Rock she became a total loss. Dick & Kentwell, *Beancaker to Boxboat*, 84.

61 PRO AIR 27/1214.

62 Machines S1149, S1150, S1151 and S1152. Open cockpit biplane. Five crew. Early models fitted with two 470 hp Napier Lion engines, but subsequently more powerful engines were introduced. Cruising speed: 83 mph. G. R. Duval, *British Flying Boats and Amphibians 1909-1952*, (London, 1966).

63 G. E. Livock, *To the Ends of the Air*, (London, 1973), 137. This was the first flight made by RAF machines through to Singapore. A sector margin of safety was essential. In normal operational circumstances the range of the aircraft was 770 miles, with an absolute maximum of 930.

64 Livock, *To the Ends of the Air*, 163. Note however that the sector distance is only some 460-500 miles.

*The **Ariel** of 1865, built by Robert Steete & Co for Shaw, Lowther & Maxton of London. Dimensions 197.4 ft x 33.9 ft x 21.0 ft and 853 tons.*

The Tea Clippers, 1849 - 1869

David R. MacGregor

The heyday of the tea clippers lasted a mere twenty years from the repeal of the Navigation Laws in 1849 until the opening of the Suez Canal in 1869, and yet they have captured the imagination to an excessive degree. Although ships had been built to sail moderately fast in earlier years, it was largely to participate in illegal or questionable occupations, such as privateering and smuggling, or for carrying valuable cargoes liable to damage such as fruit or opium and as Post Office Packets. The clipper ship era properly began with the discovery of gold in California in 1848 and the race to carry gold prospectors out there resulted in an explosion of shipbuilding activity in the United States of America. The discovery of gold in Australia in 1851 gave further impetus to clipper ship building, in this case in Great Britain.

Trade with China was controlled by the East India Company until 1834 when it lost its monopoly, though after this date trade remained restricted to Canton. After the seizure of opium by the Chinese authorities in 1839, hostilities erupted and a British force was dispatched with the result that the Treaty of Nanking was signed in 1842 at which Hong Kong was ceded to Great Britain and the ports of Canton, Amoy, Foochow, Ningpo and Shanghai were opened to free trade. Of these 'Treaty Ports' Canton remained the most important until 1853 when it was found that at Foochow tea was available for shipment earlier than elsewhere, and this soon became the most popular loading port for the crack ships. The anchorage was off Pagoda Island in the Min River, some 22 miles from the outer bar; if no tug was available local tow boats had to be used. Shanghai, already an important port, was close to the estuary of the great Yangtsze Kiang River, and so not far from the sea. Following the second Anglo- Chinese War, the Tientsin Treaty of 1858 opened up trade on the Yangtsze by which the port of Hankow, 586 miles above Shanghai, exported tea.

Four crops of tea were said to be gathered from the bushes which were grown on small holdings; the first was picked in April and was of the highest quality. The first teas were shipped from Foochow at the end of May or during the first two weeks of June. Black tea mostly went to England and green to America. The clippers deemed capable of making the fastest run home were the ones usually picked to sail first. In most of the business relations with the Chinese, British and other firms employed a local manager known as the *compradore* (from the Portugese word *compra* to 'buy'), whose astuteness frequently earned his employer a fortune or else saved him from disaster. Telegraphic communication between England and China only began towards the end of the 1860s and Grant's Trans-Mongolian Line took between ten and nineteen days to deliver a message in 1870. A year later a submarine cable was in use, routed via Gibraltar, Suez, Aden, Bombay, across India, Singapore and Hong Kong. The charge for twenty words was then £7.[1]

It would be wrong to assume that every vessel sailing out to China or loading there for a port in the United Kingdom was automatically a clipper, but without such a sobriquet no ship could expect to obtain good freight rates. Advertisements in newspapers tried to outdo each other with descriptions which might result in business, often citing the length of a fast passage. In 1861 the *Stornoway* was described as 'this far-famed yacht-built clipper and regular trader'.[2] She was ten years old at the time. Commenting on the newly-arrived tea clipper *Fiery Cross* at Melbourne in 1855, after a maiden passage of 81 days from Liverpool, a newspaper called her 'a smart and race-horsey looking ship'. Possibly carrying copies of such reports to impress loading brokers and consignees, she managed in 1857 to obtain the high freight rate of £6 6s per ton of tea.

The repeal of the Navigation Laws in 1849 permitted ships of any nationality to take cargoes to London from the Far East, and the first American ships to enter the British tea trade did so in 1850 by carrying cargoes to London. Gradually the desire to drink the new season's tea brought about intense competition to be the first ship to reach London with the aromatic commodity. Beginning in 1856 and stimulated by what was fast becoming a race, the first ship to reach London with the new season's tea was awarded thereafter a premium of £1 per ton.

Ships were always looking for ways to obtain a paying cargo on their return passage after delivering the outward one, and an opportunity now presented itself. Due to the discovery of gold in Australia in 1851, many ships diverted to carry out gold prospectors from the United Kingdom sailed on to China, seeking cargoes. Among them were American ships which in their turn had got rid of the gold prospectors they had carried around Cape Horn to San Francisco from New York and Boston, and had crossed the Pacific, hoping to load tea in China for either New York or even London. So the British ships were now faced with unexpected competition and to their chagrin found that American ships could usually command a higher freight rate

Before proceeding further, a word must be said about what constitutes a 'clipper'and to justify such a description a vessel should possess the following characteristics:

(1) A fine lined hull
(2) An emphasis on streamlined appearance
(3) A large sail area
(4) A daring and skilful master.

In a fine-lined hull, naval architects and shipbuilders exerted their individual skills and no two men agreed on the ideal combination of the form of the midship section as well as that of the entrance and run. In the China tea trade,

speed in light winds was needed and good weatherly qualities, so that some ships were given such a great rise of frame that a special cradle was fashioned to support the hull on the launching ways before it was fully afloat. By contrast, the *Annandale*, built the following year at Annan on the Solway Firth, possessed a full midship section with fairly flat floors, but this was compensated by having a long narrow hull with an exceedingly sharp entrance and run. A long hull had greater potential for speed than a short one and iron hulls readily achieved these proportions. However they were never popular as it was said that condensation occurred and spoiled the tea.

Ships that were of excessively sharp form, with a long fine entrance and run, and whose hulls were exclusively designed for speed and in which cargo capacity was sacrificed, were termed *extreme clippers*. Other ships less extreme in form might be *clippers* and those with fuller hulls, yet with pretensions of sharpness, were *medium* clippers. Those of extreme form were also referred to as *full bloods* or *crack ships*.

As the shape of the hull defined in the *lines plan* is an important part of the clipper definition, it must be pointed out that only ships whose plans or models have been examined can be assigned undisputed clipper status, although there will be many others whose pedigree accords them the unequivocal definition of clipper, and it is under these constraints that the term 'clipper' is employed here. Historically, the *lines plan* consists of the sheer elevation, the half breadth plan and the body plan, ideally drawn to the same scale; but this was in the days before computerised design and the greater flexibility of the newer system.

The second clipper characteristic was a streamlined appearance in which there were no heavy stern windows or quarter galleries and the trail boards which sprang from the base of the figurehead were not too cumbersome. Nevertheless armed warriors with swords outstretched, and nymphs with golden tresses frequently adorned the bows of

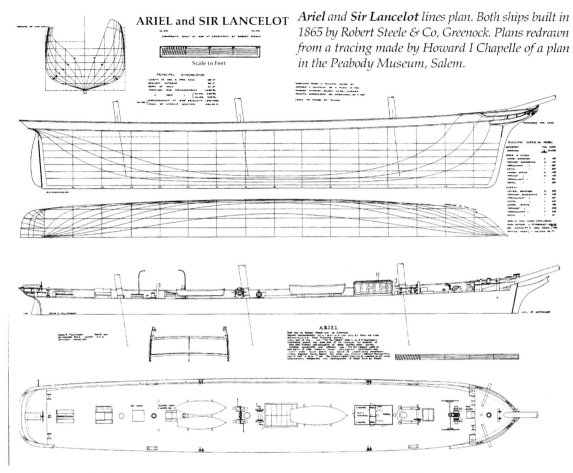

ARIEL and SIR LANCELOT

Ariel and *Sir Lancelot* lines plan. Both ships built in 1865 by Robert Steele & Co, Greenock. Plans redrawn from a tracing made by Howard I Chapelle of a plan in the Peabody Museum, Salem.

tea clippers. The desire of achieving an unbroken sheer line was sometimes carried to absurd lengths as in the Aberdeen clipper *Black Prince* where the headroom at the after end of the forecastle was reduced to only five feet, thereby avoiding an unsightly break to the sheer line.

Towards the stern, the accommodation could be in a deckhouse surrounded by a low deck which did not rise above the rail, which is an arrangement to be seen in the *Cutty Sark* today. Alternatively a raised quarter-deck, placed three feet or so below the main deck level, provided an unbroken sheer line. The heavy cumbersome channels which protruded outside the ship's hull and on which the lower rigging was set up were able to be removed as iron wire replaced hemp for the standing

rigging. The size of ships usually ranged from 500 to 900 tons; larger than this forced them to spend over-long filling their holds with tea. The two principal exceptions were vessels built before 1848 and American-built ships.

In the matter of sail plans, it was normal for studding sails to be set on booms which extended beyond the yards on the fore and main masts and by which means the sail area could virtually be doubled. In addition, skysails could be carried on each mast above the royals, and above them moonsails as sported by the Sunderland clipper *Maitland*. Sails such as these together with ringtails and *Jamie Geeens* were known as *flying kites*.

The fourth clipper characteristic and possibly the most important was the daring and skill of the master and his untiring zeal in driving his ship along under all conditions of wind and weather which required unusual stamina found in all too few captains. Not least was the ability to know which courses to steer to find fair winds, which was often a closely-guarded secret. The works by the American hydrographer, Matthew Fontaine Maury, first published in 1847, provided sailing instructions throughout the world.

An example of driving a ship hard is taken from a passenger's diary aboard the American-built extreme clipper *Lightning* when under British ownership on a passage from Liverpool to Melbourne. The entry dated 7 July 1854 reads in part:

> *10pm. Top gallant sails not taken in although the blocks 18 inches above the lee rail are frequently under water – the deck is on an angle of 45° to 50°…The second mate whose watch it is, says 'Now this is what I call carrying on'.[3]*

The majority of the tea clippers were built either in the north of England or in Scotland at Aberdeen and Glasgow. In the 1850s, the crack ships were mostly built at Aberdeen by Alexander Hall & Sons; in the 1860s it was from shipyards on the Clyde between Glasgow and Greenock that the fastest clippers were launched. In the Sunderland area, the brothers John and William Pile were responsible for the majority of the clippers in these two decades. At Aberdeen we are fortunate to have half-models of several of Hall's clippers, but for those built by Walter Hood not a single one exists with the exception of *Thermopylae*. On the Clyde, there are examples from the yards of Robert Steele, Charles Connell, Alexander Stephen and John Scott in the form of models or plans. Two naval architects also produced designs: Bernard Waymouth designed *Leander* (1867) and *Thermopylae* (1868); William Rennie designed six clippers.

Some of the ships built at the end of the 1840s had all the hallmarks of clippers, particularly those launched at the port of Aberdeen and of these it was the *John Bunyan* which obtained some fame when her passage from China, made in 1850, was compared with that of the larger American clipper *Oriental*. Both ships took 99 days on the passage to London, and the British ship, leaving in January 1850, had the north-east monsoon in her favour but had to sail a greater distance from Shanghai, or about 850 miles more, whereas the American ship only had to sail from Whampoa, yet had the monsoon against her, because she left in August the same year. This at once indicates the difficulties of comparing performance in clipper ship races when not only the season but also the port of departure has to be taken into account.

Another ship built in 1848 was the Aberdeen clipper *Reindeer*, constructed by Alexander Hall and measuring 328 tons new measurement. A surviving half-model in the Glasgow Museum of Transport shows that she possessed the long forward-raking stem known as the 'Aberdeen bow' which evolved as a means of reducing the register tonnage. A reduction was useful as numerous expenses were directly related to tonnage. It is worth noting here that between the years 1836 to 1854, a system of measuring a ship to determine her tonnage attempted to obtain some internal dimensions and if, on comparing the pre-1836 figure (known as *old measurement* or *o.m.*) with that operating 1836-1854 (known as *new measurement* or *n.m.*), a smaller tonnage by the new rule would indicate a finer-lined ship. Plans and half-models generally confirm this.

The development of the raking Aberdeen stem in the 1840s stimulated clipper shipbuilding and many of Hall's ships and those of other builders who copied him were built on this model, but the hull-form varied from one vessel to another. The *Stornoway*, which he built in 1850 for Jardine, Matheson & Co, is often looked on as the first real British tea clipper, and her fastest homeward passage was probably 104 days made in 1851 between Whampoa and London and against the monsoon. An indication of how important the master was to a ship's performance can be gauged by the passages of the *Chrysolite* when

Anthony Enright was in command. He had already done a round voyage in *Reindeer* to China and back and now in his new ship made four homeward passages from China averaging 105 $1/_4$ days against the monsoon; however, her next four from China, under Alexander McLelland averaged 135 days, also against the monsoon. What a difference! Enright continued a successful career by being master of the large American-built clipper *Lightning* for four voyages to and from Melbourne, and then returned to the China trade as master, first of the *Highflyer* and then of the *Childers*.

The *Cairngorm*, built by Hall in 1853, was an extreme model with dimensions of 193.6ft x 36.6ft x 20.2ft and tonnages of 939 *n.m.* and 1246 *o.m.* and cost £15,434 which is about £700 less than the original cost of *Cutty Sark*. Described as the *Cock of the Walk* she made some fast passages under Captain Robertson. On her maiden passage in 1853, she was partially dismasted in the North Atlantic and put into Lisbon for repairs. Continuing her passage, she took the incredibly short time of only 72 days to Hong Kong. Her fastest homeward passage from China lasted 91 days in 1858-59 between Macao and Deal.

Another extreme clipper built in 1853 was the *Lord of the Isles* constructed of iron by Scott & Co on the Clyde with a tonnage of 691, an overall length of 210ft and a breadth of 27.8ft, which resulted in a long, narrow hull, and she soon obtained a reputation as an extremely fast ship. On her maiden passage it was claimed that on one occasion she sailed 428 miles in 24 hours; if true, this would easily be the longest day's run ever performed by a British-built sailing ship. Another similar-sized iron clipper built on the Clyde in the same year which was described as a 'yacht of large tonnage', was the *Gauntlet*.

To construct a long narrow ship in timber rather than in iron was the problem faced by the wooden shipbuilder, John Nicholson, whose son, Benjamin, at the age of twenty in 1854, was responsible for the *Annandale* with proportions of 7.13 beams-to-length. Her

dimensions were 226.9ft x 28.5ft (inside) x 18.5ft and tonnages of 1131 *o.m.* and 759 *n.m.* Lines taken off the half-model show a long hollow entrance, a long hollow run, not much deadrise and virtually no sheer. But the timbers required to retain her shape were massive for her size, and occupied valuable cargo space. The master claimed a noon-to-noon run of 381 miles and a maximum speed of 18 knots on her maiden passage. She only once brought back a tea cargo and that was in 1859-60 with a passage of 117 days to Plymouth from Whampoa.

So the years went by. More clippers were built, but the owners had to look at the costs continually to ensure they were getting a proper return on the capital invested. In the 1850s, Alexander Hall was charging from £14 to £18 per ton for wooden ships, the amount varying on the classification assigned by Lloyd's Register. During the early years of the Australian gold rush, there was so great a demand for ships to take goods out to the goldfields that clippers could obtain a freight of £6 per ton; if they then crossed over to China and loaded a homeward cargo of tea at £5 per ton, they might clear the initial cost of the ship in one or two voyages. Extreme clippers which could carry only a little more cargo than their own register tonnage were good money-spinners under boom conditions, but after the end of the Crimean War, when there was a glut of ships on the market and all freight rates plunged down, life was not so rosy for them. Instead, medium clippers which could carry twice their register tonnage were the sort of craft that earned their keep. It has been estimated that the clipper *Lothair*, built 1870 of 794 tons net, on a voyage to Hong Kong and back in 1873-74, incurred expenses of, say, £3,000; outward freight was £2,000, homeward freight at £3 per ton was £3,300; this resulted in a profit of £2,300.[1]

The three examples cited above indicate the great variations in design continually appearing as new ships were launched, but as the decade progressed experimentation became less common. The continual reduction of the import duty charged on tea, gave steady encouragement to build new clippers. By 1863 it had fallen to 1s 0d which was approximately half what was levied ten years earlier. However, the number of fast passages made from China against the monsoon were far fewer in the 1850s than they were in the next decade.

The prevalence of the south-west monsoon in the China Sea, which blew from May to the end of September, meant that the ships which left with the new season's tea had to beat down to Anjer against the wind through the poorly charted and dangerous China Sea. This tested them to the limit and inevitably lengthened their passage times, and ships which could make the entire passage from a port in China to one in England in under 100 days were considered of superior quality. Most ships sailed southwards down the China Sea, passing the Paracel Islands, then down towards Borneo, through Gaspar Strait to Anjer where they reported, and thence into the Indian Ocean. Another route, known as the Eastern Route took ships to the eastward of the Philippines and through a maze of islands past Timor and into the Indian Ocean. From either of these, the course lay towards the Cape of Good Hope and northwards up the Atlantic towards the coast of Brazil, near Cape San Roque, and eventually picking up the north-east trades which would take them to the mouth of the English Channel. The distance between Shanghai and Hong Kong was approximately 900 miles and Foochow was more or less equidistant between the two; the distance from Foochow to Anjer was some 2800 miles, but ships could never sail a direct route. The entire passage from Foochow to London was about 14,000 miles.

Only three passages of less than 100 days have been found prior to 1860 for British ships that had to sail against the south-west monsoon. In 1856 *Spirit of the Age* took 99 days from Whampoa to Deal; in 1857 *Fiery Cross* took 99 days from Foochow to London, but she passed Dartmouth 94 days out; in 1858 *Robin Hood* took 99 days from Foochow to London. It was in this year that *Fiery Cross* loaded tea at

the high rate of £6 6s per ton. It should be noted that this *Fiery Cross* was wrecked in the China Sea in 1860 but was replaced immediately by another ship of the same name. The *Robin Hood* (1856) was one of Hall's faster and more successful ships.

The number of homeward passages of less than 100 days made during monsoon did increase somewhat during the 1860s, but it was the few exceptionally fast ones of less than 95 days which were particularly noteworthy. Although the numbers of clippers in the trade increased in this decade, the majority of ships were still taking 100 to 130 days on the passage from China to England. The *Cutty Sark*, for instance, never a made a passage back in less than 100 days, and her three fastest, all made from Woosung to London, were 110 days in 1870 and again in 1871, and 109 in 1876. If attempting to compare a passage from, say, Foochow, where the full bloods were accustomed to load before the opening of the Suez Canal, then a week or so would need to be deducted, but this starts to become hypothetical. Perhaps *Cutty Sark* never made a fast passage home from China because at that time she did not have a skipper possessed of sufficient drive and daring. Later, when carrying wool home from Australia, the reverse was the case under Captain Woodget, who was not afraid to carry sail and made many fast passages.

Of record passages made against the south-west monsoon, the palm goes to the *Sir Lancelot*, (Captain Richard Robinson), which left Foochow on 17 July 1869, passed Anjer on 7 August and was off the Lizard on 10 October, 84 days after leaving the river Min, passed Dungeness two days later and docked in London on 14 October, 89 days out. The *Thermopylae* (Captain Robert Kemball) took 2 days longer, but her passage was also remarkably fast. It is worth reading what James MacCunn, owner of *Sir Lancelot*, wrote of his ship in a letter dated 13 Nov 1869:

> It was very gratifying to find this noble ship passing through the Downs on 13th Oct last, being out 88 days from Foochow anchorage,

a performance never before accomplished against the monsoon. All the other ships were signally defeated, Thermopylae *by two clear days. All the rest were 'no-where'. Even the passage of some of the steamers was equalled.* [his dates do not quite agree].[5]

Some other unusually fast passages made against the monsoon were as follows: 96 days made by *Titania* in 1869 from Woosung to Deal; 93 days made by *Titania* in 1871, Foochow to London.; 96 days made by *Spindrift* in 1868, Foochow to London. Several passages of less than 90 days were made with the aid of the north-east monsoon, of which that by the *Zingra* in 85 days from Shanghai to Liverpool in 1863-64 appears to have been the quickest. She was built at Sunderland in 1861 with a tonnage of 486 and on this short passage did not carry tea but 2,100 bales of cotton.

The most celebrated race home from China took place in 1866 with *Fiery Cross*, *Ariel*, *Serica*, *Taeping* and *Taitsing* crossing the bar at Foochow in that order between 29 and 31 May. *Ariel* loaded 1,230,900 lbs of tea at a freight rate of £5 per ton. The ships were very evenly matched. When approaching British waters, Captain Keay of the *Ariel* thought he was well ahead of the others and was horrified to discover on the morning of 5 September that *Taeping* was close astern. Both ships raced up the English Channel all that day and night, sometimes logging 14 knots, with studding sails set, and both took their pilots and tugs almost simultaneously off Deal, early on 6 September, 99 days from Foochow and docked that day. *Serica*, sailing up the Channel along the French coast, managed to dock in London on the same tide as the other two. *Fiery Cross* docked two days later and *Taitsing* a further day later. Prices of tea fell on the market with so many clippers arriving simultaneously – nine more got in that week – which was a deplorable thing from the tea dealer's point of view.

With the start of the 1860s, there was less experimentation with hull-form and fewer extreme clippers until the end of the decade. The yard of Robert Steele at Greenock produced a range of fine tea clippers, the earliest for which a plan exists being the *Falcon*, built in 1859 with a tonnage of 794. She possessed fine lines with evenly balanced ends and a fair amount of deadrise, and from her successful design stemmed the whole range of clippers which they built, totalling fourteen ships in the years 1859-1869.[6]

The construction of ships with iron frames and wooden planking had been tried in the 1850s at Liverpool and London and some were built for the China trade, but it remained for Alexander Stephen of Glasgow to realize its advantages and organize its acceptance, not only by owners and builders, but more importantly by the classification society, Lloyd's Register. Stephen worked strenuously on the project throughout 1861 and in October he got Lloyd's consent to build ships that could be classed up to 15 years A1. The advantages were that an iron frame removed all the heavy structural timbers which occupied so much space in a wooden ship, thus increasing stowage capacity; it removed the cost of docking an iron ship at the end of each voyage to scrape and paint the bottom; and it permitted wooden planking to be used which could be copper sheathed. Unfortunately the cost rose about £2 per ton compared with a wooden ship. Lloyd's Register was alarmed at the rush to build clippers in this way and until 1867 classed them as 'experimental' and predicted that they would have short lives. How wrong they were! The first tea clipper produced by Steele in this new mode was the *Taeping*, built in 1863.

Perhaps the tea clipper par excellence was the lovely *Ariel*, launched by Robert Steele in 1865 to the order of Shaw, Lowther & Maxton of London, with dimensions of 197.4ft x 33.9ft x 21.0ft and 853 tons. This was a typical size for a tea clipper of the 1860's. Unusually, she was flush-decked although there was a monkey focs'sle for working the anchors, and a grating for the helmsman to stand on; otherwise the crew got wet feet if they were down to leeward. Also built in the same year by Steele, apparently from the same set of plans, was the *Sir Lancelot* with virtually similar measurements, although her deck plan varied as she had a raised quarter-deck.

It is a strange fact that the last three years of the 1860s should have witnessed the construction of six extreme clippers for the tea trade, at a time when freight rates were in decline and the return on invested capital would have been shrinking, and what prompted the determination to order these ships is not clear. Bernard Waymouth designed *Leander* and *Thermopylae*, Charles Connell designed and built *Spindrift*, William Rennie designed *Norman Court*, Alexander Hall designed and built *The Caliph*, and Hercules Linton designed and built *Cutty Sark*.

Nowadays the clippers *Thermopylae* and *Cutty Sark* are often linked together for some inexplicable reason, but in the days of the China trade this was not the case. Admittedly they did have very similar measurements, but then what ships did not. On the three parts of *Thermopylae's* maiden voyage, a record was established on each of the three sections: London to Melbourne 63 days in 1868-69; Newcastle NSW to Shanghai 31 days 1869; Foochow to London 91 days in 1869. This voyage was much discussed at the time and the track chart pasted inside many a log-book. Her eleven tea-laden passages averaged 106$\frac{1}{2}$ days.

A few clippers were built for the tea trade after the Suez Canal opened in 1869, but the trade had changed by then. The ships continued to race each other home, but gradually economies had to be introduced. The iron frame of the composite tea clipper *Ambassador* may still survive on the beach at Punta Arenas; if so, she would form an interesting comparison with *Cutty Sark* as both were built in 1869. The latter was built by the unknown Clyde-side firm of Scott & Linton which went bankrupt during her construction and she was completed by Denny Bros. In spite of this inauspicious start, she has had a long eventful life and survives today at Greenwich as a reminder of, and living witness to, the days of the tea clippers.

Notes and references

1   *Hong Kong Times and Daily Advertiser*, 4 July 1873.
2   *Mitchell's Maritime Register*, 6 July 1861.
3   Diary of John Fenwick, 14 May to 31 July 1854, copy loaned the author by the late John Lyman.
4   David R. MacGregor, *The Tea Clippers, their History and Development 1833-1875*, 2nd ed, (London, 1984), 18.
5   Jardine Matheson Archives no 10677, Cambridge University Library, Letter to Jardine Matheson & Co from James MacCunn, dated 19 Nov 1869.
6   MacGregor, *Tea Clippers,* 118.

From *Agamemnon* to *Priam*: British liner shipping in the China Seas, 1865-1965

Malcolm Cooper

The leading ship of Alfred Holt's first class of purpose-built steamships, which sailed to China in 1865, was called *Agamemnon* after the King who led Greek forces in the Trojan War. Almost exactly one hundred years later, Holt's chose the name of the Trojan King *Priam*, who had held Troy against the Greek army, for the lead ship of what was to prove the firm's last class of conventional cargo ships. A brief comparison of the specifications of the two ships reveals how far marine technology had advanced in the intervening century. Eighty percent longer, and over one hundred percent wider than her predecessor, *Priam* had between five and six times the carrying capacity of the first Agamemnon. Her Burmeister & Wain nine-cylinder diesel engine could drive her far greater bulk through the water at just over twice the speed of the older ship's two-cylinder compound steam engine.

This huge increase in cargo carrying capacity, however, was not the product of any technological revolution. Rather it was the end result of a century of evolution, a process which, while attended by numerous technical innovations, was basically a matter of successive relatively small increments in size and speed, and in carrying capacity and fuel efficiency. The two major revolutions in technology that did occur are actually the beginning and end points for this paper. *Agamemnon* was one of the earliest products of the first revolution, the interaction of metal construction and steam propulsion to produce ships capable of operating economically over long distances on regular schedules. *Priam's* life was brought to a premature end by the second revolution, this time the introduction of containerization, which rendered existing ships obsolete in a manner possibly even more complete than the fate visited on the tea clippers of a century before. *Agamemnon*,

pioneer though she was, actually served her owners for thirty-five years. *Priam*, in many ways the culmination of a century's progress and experience, was destined to be sold out of service after only twelve.

This paper then is built around a story of slow progress. Much of this progress was led by ships of Alfred Holt and Company's Blue Funnel Line, the premier British operator on the China sea routes throughout the century between the clipper and the container ship. Other companies, however, played their part. In the last third of the nineteenth century, it was often Holts' smaller competitors, particularly McGregor Gow's Glen Line and Thomas Skinner's Castle Line, which appeared to be setting the standard in size and speed. Holts have actually been criticized, both by their partners at the time, and by historians afterwards, for being over-conservative in ship design. Similarly, in the second and third decades of the twentieth century, it was other firms that took the lead in the introduction of the motorship. Finally, some of the finest ships introduced by Blue Funnel in the last third of its century of dominance, notably the *Glenearn* class of 1938-40 and the *Priams* that brought the era to an end, were produced to meet threats posed by other firms. All this notwithstanding, Blue Funnel remained the dominant player on the scene. This was partially because a durable mixture of entrepreneurship and financial strength always kept them in a position to respond to both competitive challenge and changes in trade pattern. It was also due to the firm's unwavering adherence to the highest standards of marine engineering, which usually ensured that Holts' ships were better built and more efficient than those of their rivals. Paradoxically, even the firm's conservatism sometimes worked in its favour, saving it from the expensive mistakes of innovators, and allowing it to deploy carefully-husbanded financial reserves to make large investments in competitive tonnage when a particular mix of size and technology had proved its worth.[1]

The development of British liner shipping during Holts' century can be broken down into a number of reasonably clear phases. During the period from the mid-1860s to the mid-1880s, the technological pace was set by the rival Glen and Castle lines, which generally built the largest and fastest ships and in the second decade always won the annual race to bring the first China tea cargoes of the season home to the UK market. Holts, however, built up a far larger fleet and far greater financial strength, and were left in a position of dominance when competition began to flag, partially due to the decline of the tea trade on which it had been too heavily dependent. From then until the closing years of the century, this dominance drifted slightly, but at the end of the period the arrival of a new generation and the availability of years of accumulated retained capital allowed the firm to embark on a huge programme of re-building. Ships doubled in size and carrying power in little more than a decade, and by the outbreak of the war, Holts were in possession of a bigger and more competitive fleet than ever before.

The First World War obscured the arrival of an innovative challenge in the form of the motorship, championed by the old rival Glen Line, now part of the huge Royal Mail empire. The early motorships, however, were not a clear financial success, and the Royal Mail challenge failed through a dangerous mixture of over-investment and poor trade conditions. Although Holts made a small concession to new technology in replacing fairly modest Great War losses, it was able to survive the 1920s and 1930s and to enter another war which would cause it far more severe casualties with an ageing but still competitive fleet. The Second War also concealed a step forward, this time through the final adoption of motorship technology. The *Glenearn* class of 1938-40 were arguably the finest examples of

large, fast cargo liners to be built anywhere in the world in their day. It was entirely typical of Holts that they should appear after a decade of steady development of the type by other owners. It was also indicative of the company's primacy that they were actually built for its former rival Glen, which had been taken over after the collapse of the Royal Mail group.

The *Glenearns* were to remain amongst the elite of the China route for almost their entire service lives. With its position if anything strengthened by the war, which temporarily removed its most dangerous foreign rivals, Holts' huge post-war rebuilding programme featured ships attempting to achieve economy within the limits of accepted design and involving little by way of innovation. This fleet saw the company through two decades, where the biggest threats to the business came not from competitors but from political upheaval in the Far East. At the end of the period, however, competitive pressure began to re-assert itself with other firms, both foreign and British, making significant steps forward in size and speed. Holts responded with two splendid classes of ships, the more traditional *Glenlyons* and the more revolutionary *Priams*. These ships, however, appeared in the shadow of containerization, and the era of the conventional cargo liner came to an end with none of the new ships more than halfway through what might otherwise have been their normal economic lives.

It was the opening of the Suez Canal in 1869 that really made the steamship a successful competitor to the clipper ship on the China Sea route. This said, the arrival of Alfred Holt's steamships in the trade actually pre-dated the opening of the canal by almost four years. The self-designed compound steam engines that powered Holt's first trio of China ships made the vessels an economic proposition even on the long haul around the Cape of Good Hope. The successful survival of sailing ships on other long sea routes until the closing years of the century, and the unimpressive record of other steam ventures on such routes does, however, suggest that the venture might not have made the progress it did had the Canal not quickly cut some 3,000 miles off the route. Until further improvements in efficiency arrived, most notably the triple expansion steam engine in the mid-1880s, the steamship was really only viable on ocean routes with large passenger flows and subsidised mail contracts.

The opening of the Canal was not an undiluted blessing to Holt's fleet. While it greatly increased the potential profitability of his sailings, it also brought a number of new steamship operators on to the route. While the new steamships brought the era of the tea clipper to a rapid close, the competition between the new vessels rapidly became every bit as fierce as it had been in the age of sail. By the mid-1870s there were already signs of over-capacity, and it was no accident that before the end of that decade, the China route was to witness some of the first attempts at protecting market share through the formation of shipping conferences.

The early growth of the Blue Funnel fleet was very impressive in terms of numbers. The three pioneer ships of the *Agamemnon* class were followed between 1868 and 1871 by the seven-strong *Diomed* class, in 1872 by the four-strong *Patroclus* class, and between 1875 and 1877 by another seven ships of the *Stentor* and *Sarpedon* classes. None of the new ships, however, represented anything of an advance in speed or size over the early trio, indeed most were actually smaller and slower. A further large group of ships built in the 1880s followed the same pattern, despite the fact that by the mid-1870s competitors were emerging who aimed to break down Blue Funnel's early dominance through steady increases in both speed and carrying capacity.

Most of the new steamship owners brought into the China trade by the opening of the Suez Canal quickly faded from the scene, condemning ships with names reminiscent of the clipper age like *Galley of Lorne* and *Lord of the Isles* to other less demanding trades. Three British firms did succeed in making long-term inroads into the market. One of these, Jenkins'

Shire Line never really emerged as a front-line contender. Despite being one of the first firms to undertake an extension of the service to Japan, it remained largely content to earn a living at the lower end of the market and operating a fleet that always had to depend on a relatively high proportion of chartered tonnage.[2] The other two, McGregor Gow's Glen Line and Skinner's Castle Line, posed much more dangerous threats to Blue Funnel.

These two firms originated in Glasgow, although both moved their base of operations south to London in the mid-1870s. McGregor Gow were relative newcomers to shipowning and had only owned five sailing ships and a composite steam brig in the half decade before they built their pioneer steamship *Glengyle* in 1871. Skinner, on the other hand was well-established, not only in ship-owning but also in the China trade, where he had built up a fleet of almost 20 tea clippers during sail's last splendid decade on the route. Skinner in particular brought an appetite for speed with him from the earlier phase of his career, but both firms followed a policy of introducing progressively larger and faster vessels in complete contrast to the course taken by Blue Funnel. This trend culminated in 1883 when each firm introduced a two-funnelled flyer (McGregor Gow's *Glenogle* and Skinner's *Stirling Castle*) some 50 per cent larger and faster than the unspectacular plodders that the Holt brothers were still adding to their far larger fleet.[3]

The different choices in technology made by the major protagonists in the first decade and a half of the China trade's steam age represent one of the most interesting inflection points of the entire century covered in this paper. The Holts were heavily criticized at the time, particularly by John Swire, their influential agent in the Far East, for their conservatism.[4] This criticism has to a greater or lesser extent been echoed by modern historians. There is no doubt that Glen and Castle were, quite literally, making all the running, their apparent primacy being marked by the fact that one firm or the other won the annual race to get the first tea cargo of the season back to London in every year between 1874 and 1883. These triumphs, however, were not necessarily attended by commercial success. Skinner's *Stirling Castle*, the largest and fastest of the early iron compound-engined ships, was an expensive failure. Her two record-breaking tea passages not only failed to provide returns adequate to cover inflated capital costs, but also effectively bankrupted her owner. Skinner gave up after two years of ruinous operation and the ship herself was sold to Italian owners to spend most of her career carrying emigrants to North and South America. McGregor Gow survived, but as early as the late 1870s were sufficiently concerned that their thoroughbreds might prove uneconomical to experiment by buying a smaller and slower vessel off the stocks.[5]

There were three problems with what might in retrospect be seen as the premature pursuit of size and speed. In the first instance, the compound steam engine, while offering huge gains in efficiency over earlier single cylinder power plants, could still only produce high speeds at the cost of massive cylinder sizes and huge coal consumption. While steam could pay dividends on short routes or on a relatively conservative size/power combination, it really required subsidization through mail contracts or large and relatively remunerative passenger flows to prosper elsewhere. North Atlantic passenger liners and P. & O. mail steamers on the Far East run benefited from just this sort of support, but it was not available to most cargo liners.

In the second instance, the tea cargoes on which Skinner and the other advocates of speed built their China route steamship companies proved too weak a foundation for commercial success. Skinner in particular was really attempting to extend the clipper commercial model into the age of steam. While early season tea cargoes were still attracting high freight rates in the 1870s and early 1880s, they could not alone meet the higher capital costs of a steamship whose high season homeward tea passage might, even on a all-

embracing definition of voyage time, account for only a quarter of the business year. Trade conditions were generally difficult in the Far East trades from the mid-1870s, and with both import and export trades still in a fairly uneven state of developments, all owners were soon struggling to find cargoes outside of the tea season. Starved of trade on the London berth, Skinner actually formed an alliance with Cardiff coal interests to provide what are only likely to have been loss-making outwards cargoes for his ships. McGregor Gow's Glen liners spent an increasing amount of time making short-haul tramping voyages in the Far East to provide out of season employment.

The final problem was that the tea business did not prove a long-lasting source of even seasonal revenues. By the mid-1880s Indian tea was driving its older Chinese rival into a distant second place in European and North American markets. The collapse of the business was rapid and almost complete. The annual tea race had still fascinated the maritime world when *Stirling Castle* was pounding her way homewards in 1883. Only a few years later, the arrival of the first tea steamer scarcely merited a mention, and the rates had fallen so low that the trade press proclaimed the China tea trade to be 'finished'.

Thus while John Swire might be proclaiming 'ruin' when McGregor Gow's *Glenlyon* beat Holts' *Ulysses* home from Foochow by a week in 1880, the latter was the more enduring recipe for success. There can be little doubt that the small and relatively slow Blue Funnel ships lagged behind the pace of technological development, and it is probably fair to say that in their later years the Holt brothers were unduly conservative in their design and building policies. Nonetheless, the fact remains that they handed over to their successors a large and profitable concern with the financial reserves not only to buy out a newer and more dangerous competitor (China Mutual) but also to fund an almost complete re-building of the fleet in the years around the end of the century. By this time, Skinner was in his grave and his firm with him, while a second generation of McGregors and Gows were casting about desperately for new routes or new investors to keep their ailing business alive.

Steel hulls and the triple expansion steam engine arrived in the China trade in 1886-7. The immediate impact was not dramatic, indeed Holt's were so unimpressed with their first attempt at the new recipe that they actually reverted to the older technology until the early 1890s. Nonetheless, these two innovations did open the doors to building much larger ships and powering them at competitive speeds without ruinous fuel bills. By this time, changing trade patterns were making such ships not only viable but necessary. The early years of the steam era had to a certain extent been an extension of the preceding age of sail, with relatively homogenous cargoes, mostly low in bulk and high in value, being carried between a limited number of terminal points. Gradually, however, this pattern had broken down under a wide range of influences, not least of which were the progressive disruption of the China market, the rapid industrialization of Japan, and the economic development of other areas of the Far East, stretching from southeast Asia to Korea and Russia's Pacific coast. Ultimately these developments required that liner shipping become more flexible, with vessels equipped to call at a longer and longer itinerary of ports and carry a wider and wider mix of cargoes.

At the beginning of the 1890s, the British steam fleets competing in the China seas would still have been recognizable to someone who had sailed with them two decades before. Many of the original vessels were still in service, including all of the early Holt ships to survive marine hazard. By the end of the decade, the picture had changed completely. No single class of ships epitomizes this transformation, but the scale and nature of the change can be understood from the milestones in the long-delayed modernization of the Blue Funnel fleet. The four-ship *Ixion* class of 1892 measured 3,600 tons gross on a length of 355

feet. They were followed in 1894-5 by the six-ship *Orestes* class, measuring 4,650 gross tons on a length of 390 feet. In 1896 the four-ship *Prometheus* class increased gross tonnage to 5,500 and length to 420 feet, and in 1899-1900 the nine-ship *Idomeneus* class extended them further to 6,750 tons and 440 feet. Finally in 1901-2, the four ship *Peleus* class stretched gross tonnage to 7,450 and length to 455 feet.

There were two particularly interesting features of this reasonably rapid increase in size. First of all, increasingly powerful and efficient engines allowed for maintenance of the established ten knot service speed. Secondly, the total cost per vessel only increased over the period from £50,000 to £65,000. These were roughly the same levels of capital costs incurred in building the ships of the late 1860s and early 1870s. The three pioneer ships of the *Agamemnon* class of 1865 had cost an average of just under £52,000 per vessel. *Glenartney*, the most successful tea steamer of the early 1870s had cost £55,000 in 1873, and *Glencoe*, one of the fastest vessels of the second half of that decade had cost £63,000 in 1879. These vessels were all less than half the size of the Blue Funnel ships being commissioned at the end of the century. Even making adjustments for the higher speeds of the Glen vessels, the new generation of ships were providing roughly double the overall carrying capacity for roughly the same capital outlay.[6]

Having soared in little over a decade, ship size achieved a plateau from which it was not to make any real further progress for several decades. Some larger ships were built, both by Holts and their competitors, but these were actually intended for longer routes. Holts entered the UK-Asia-trans-Pacific service as a result of their takeover of China Mutual, by which time their surviving British flag direct rivals, Glen and Shire, were also experimenting with extending voyages to the west coast of North America. Ships intended to serve only China and other east Asian destinations remained of a size comparable with the ships built around the turn of the century. The large

Perseus class, whose 19 members were built between 1908 and 1916 were, for example, almost identical in size to the *Idomeneus* and *Peleus* classes of 1899-1902. From the early years of the twentieth century, the debate on competitive improvements in ship design was once again to move largely into the fields of speed and fuel efficiency.

The competitive landscape in the China Seas changed around the end of the century in one other critical dimension. The rivals of Blue Funnel in the late nineteenth century had been relatively small British firms based solidly in the tradition of Victorian family entrepreneurship, with only China Mutual, arguably the most dangerous of the early rivals, being built on a wider capital base. Holts took over China Mutual in 1902, but otherwise the firm's expansion was based on building up its own fleet from its by now considerable retained capital reserves. Elsewhere, however, the shipping world was being convulsed by two almost simultaneous developments: the concentration of British liner shipping into a small number of very large groups, and the emergence of serious foreign competition. By 1911-12, both Shire and Glen, the two surviving competitors from the 1870s had been taken over by Lord Kylsant's sprawling Royal Mail Group, which was seeking to diversify beyond the Atlantic where most of its component companies operated. By the same time, another large group, assembled around the turn of the century by John Ellerman, was also probing into China waters, this time from a base of operations that had already made it a considerable force in the Indian Ocean.[7]

Foreign competition from industrial Europe, particularly in the guise of Germany's large diversified shipping groups, also made dramatic inroads into eastern shipping markets in which the red ensign had been hitherto almost unchallenged. The German-led European challenge touched almost all of Britain's liner trades. In the Far East, however, the foreign threat also emerged at the other end of the trade routes. Most western liner

companies did not have to face serious reverse competition until after the Second World War. In the Far East, the rapid growth of industrial Japan produced a far earlier threat. Indeed, such was the strength of the largest Japanese shipping concern Nippon Yusen Kaisha that it was able to gain admission to the London berth of the Far East freight conference as early as 1898 (the same year, coincidentally, that the second of the large German shipping groups Hamburg-Amerika joined the first, Norddeutscher Lloyd, in the Far East trade).[8]

Japanese competition was originally launched with second-hand vessels, most of them bought from the British firms now being competed against. By the turn of the century, however, Japanese firms were equipping themselves with new modern ships (most of which continued to be built in British yards up until the Great War). Germany's shipyards, and those of other competing European nations like Holland and France, were building vessels as advanced as those originating on the Clyde, Mersey or Tyne by the 1890s. Blue Funnel was better placed by home geography to face their challenge than were its British rivals. The west coast Liverpool berth was not as open to foreign intervention as the London and east coast berths of firms like Glen, and Holts were not as dependent on continental import and export traffic as the east coast firms, which had been calling at Dutch, Belgian and German ports since the 1890s. Foreign competition, in fact, was one of the main factors that forced the small independent British operators into the arms of large groups like Royal Mail.

Royal Mail ownership had the potential to transform the competitive situation within the British-flag portion of the China Seas trade. When first Shire and then Glen fell into Kylsant's hands, Blue Funnel was probably in as strong a position relative to its British rivals as it had ever been. Its China Seas fleet was large and modern, supported by an extensive network of local agents and feeder services, and operated at the centre of a wider route network reaching to Australia and the west coast of North America. Shire and Glen at the time of their takeovers owned only a dozen ships between them, half of them obsolescent. Kylsant, however, had considerable access to capital and the energy to mobilize it to considerable effect. While his impact on the Group was ultimately to be disastrous, there is no questioning the fact that he created a large modern fleet in a very short time.

Glen and Shire, which were effectively combined as one business from the time of the Royal Mail takeover, received a significant injection of new tonnage. The considerable investment involved never really produced the threat to Blue Funnel that it had seemed it might. The choice of vessels, while sometimes innovative, was not always best fitted to the requirements of the trade. The modernisation plan itself was dislocated by the war, as a result of which Glen (into which Shire was effectively merged) emerged with a badly unbalanced fleet. In line with the experience of the other group companies, the ships themselves were too expensive and so stretched the balance sheet that ongoing modernization was all but impossible. Finally, the centre of Royal Mail activities remained very much in the Atlantic, and the Glen fleet was run almost entirely independent of it without any access to the synergies that such a large combine should, in theory at least, have offered.[9]

The first moves made by Royal Mail to revitalise the Glen-Shire combine revolved around the steamship. Three fairly standard medium-size cargo steamers were purchased off the stocks to provide an immediate injection of new tonnage. They were followed by three pairs of large steamers (four ships for Shire and two for Glen), designed explicitly to operate on a service stretching out across the North Pacific and roughly equivalent in size to the similarly large Blue Funnel *Bellerophon* quintet of 1906 built for the same service. Both classes of ships introduced twin-screw propulsion to the route, but the real innovation came from Royal Mail in the war years when it brought motor ships into the Far East service.

The Glen Line, under Kylsant's guidance

became the major early user of diesel propulsion in the British mercantile fleet, operating the largest number of motorships of any British company at the beginning of the inter-war period. Unfortunately, neither Kylsant nor Glen were particularly well-served by their initiative. Built at the peak of wartime inflation, the new motorships were even more expensive than might otherwise have been the case and would have struggled to cover their capital costs under all but the best trading conditions. Equally important, the power-weight ratios of the early marine diesels were far less impressive than those being achieved by the 1930s and 40s, and the new ships were not dramatically more efficient than the more modern coal-powered steamships. They also tended to be on the slow side, with top speeds not dramatically above the 10 knot standard employed in the Holt steamships of the early 1890s.[10]

Between 1915 and 1924 no fewer than fourteen large motorships joined the Glen fleet. By 1924, however, only eight were actually in service, and only six of these were still in company ownership a decade later. Of the early departures only one was a war loss, the other seven being disposed of (largely to other companies within the group) because they did not meet the demands of the service. Indeed, Glen, which had acquired four of the unremarkable pre-fabricated War Standard 'N' type steamers to meet immediate post-war demands, actually kept several of these vessels in its fleet in preference to some of its motorships.

Blue Funnel lost 18 of its ships in the war, less than a quarter of the 83-strong fleet with which it had entered hostilities. These losses, while heavy, were much less severe than those suffered by other owners, particularly those whose ships spent a greater part of their time in the European waters to which the first U-Boat war was largely confined. The 12 ships lost by the rival Glen-Shire fleets represented a much higher proportional loss, indeed the Glen Line itself actually had only one of its seven-strong pre-war fleet still afloat under its colours when the war ended and had also lost three of the new ships built during the war. As a result, the modernisation of the Glen-Shire fleet was severely dislocated and the post-war challenge to Holts' primacy never really emerged. Holt, on the other hand, faced a relatively more manageable rebuilding challenge, one that was helped by the fact that the capital expenditure programme started in the 1890s had continued to roll forward through the first decade and a half of the twentieth century. Many of the ships produced in the latter period were still to be in service when the Second World War commenced.

The durability of the Blue Funnel fleet is worthy of some consideration. The normal economic life of British front-line liner tonnage in the age of steam was roughly 20 years. A large part of the Blue Funnel fleet served far longer. All three vessels of the pioneering *Agamemnon* class of 1865 remained in service between 33 and 35 years. The average fleet life of the three members of the *Prometheus* class of 1894 that survived the First World War was 29 years. The five large ships of the *Bellerophon* class delivered in 1906 were all still in service when the Second World War broke out 33 years later, and the three ships to survive that conflict were finally broken up in 1948 at the venerable age of 42.

One of the reasons why Holt ships lasted so long is that the company's building activities were heavily concentrated in two periods immediately after a significant step forward in merchant ship design. After the arrival of the compound-engined iron steamship in the late 1860s and early 1870s, and after the rapid increases in size and power of its triple-expansioned steel successor in the decades either side of the turn of the century, ship design and capability entered something of a plateau. Ships built during the periods of change thus remained competitive as long as their hulls and engines could be maintained in good condition, without new developments threatening premature obsolescence. It was the maintenance of hulls and engines, or to be more precise, their design and maintenance,

that provided the other key to Blue Funnel longevity. From its very beginnings, Blue Funnel devoted higher than average amounts of time and care to engine and hull design, and built its ships to a far higher standard than required by either Board of Trade or Lloyd's regulations. Hulls were more heavily built and engines better maintained than was normal even elsewhere in a British liner shipping sector which was commonly recognised as the world leader in marine excellence. Holt ships were built to last, and last they did.[11]

A long and profitable economic ship life was not, of course, simply a matter of design and maintenance. Only a minority of nineteenth century sailing ships survived long enough to be hulked or sent to the breakers. Most fell victim in some way or other to the sea. The combination of metal construction and steam-power greatly improved survivability, but even in the late nineteenth century ship losses were still relatively high. This was certainly the case in the early days of the China steam trade when the poor marking of often treacherous Chinese coastal waters added an extra threat to the normal perils of wind and weather. While it was the expensive failure of *Stirling Castle* that ended Thomas Skinner's challenge in the China Seas, his firm was also crippled by a series of wrecks, collisions and founderings that accounted for six of his eleven steamships in just under a decade. Even the Holt brothers, who could never have been accused (as Skinner was) of risking a ship in search of a fast passage, suffered occasionally, actually losing three ships in under a year in 1875-6. Generally speaking, improving navigational aids and greater ship size had reduced losses by the early part of the twentieth century, although risks still remained. The Glen Line actually lost as many vessels to marine hazard during the four years of the Great War as it had during the previous four decades. With only occasional exceptions, Holts' safety record was excellent, indeed when *Menestheus* was lost to explosion and fire in 1953 she was the company's first peacetime marine casualty in 36 years.[12]

British shipping operating in the China Seas in the age of steam was seldom entirely free of external disruption. In the half century after 1865, China itself was convulsed both by sporadic local warfare and occasional foreign interventions. Towards the end of this period, the Boxer Rebellion and the Russo-Japanese War caused more severe if relatively short-lived dislocation of trade. Similarly the two decades after 1945 saw the political geography of the region transformed by the forces of communism and post-colonial nationalism, a process that completely changed the competitive economics of the shipping business in favour of new locally based companies and against the long-time European-based incumbents. The latter developments would ultimately do at least as much to bring Holts' century to an end as the advent of containerization. Between these two periods, however, British shipping was exposed to equally dramatic, and far more destructive pressure as a result of three events of global rather than regional significance – the two world wars and the Great Depression that came between them.

Of the three, the First World War was the least damaging in direct terms, although as we have already seen, it did hit some of Blue Funnel's smaller competitors far harder in percentage terms than it did the Liverpool firm itself. This was partially a product of the fact that the Great War was largely a European war. The Central Powers military presence was largely extinguished in Africa, Asia and the Pacific in a matter of months, and with the exception of a handful of commerce raiders, the naval threat to shipping was confined to home waters, the eastern Atlantic and the Mediterranean after the end of 1914. The losses that did occur took place either near the beginning or near the end of normal commercial sailings, or because the ship in question had been taken into government service. The waters of the Far East were relatively safe, and with government control of shipping never as complete as it would be in the second war, most ships spent a fair amount of time there.

Where the Great War was more damaging was in its consequences for shipping costs. A potent mixture of wartime inflation, heavy shipping losses, artificial tonnage shortages produced by trade dislocation, and speculative attempts to capitalise on growth in asset values quite literally pushed new and second-hand ship prices through the roof. One set of examples must suffice to illustrate the scope of this price explosion. The Glen Line purchased the steamship *Glenearn* off the stocks for £60,500 in late 1913. In 1919 the firm paid between £250,000 and £265,000 each for four War Standard steamships which were only 20 feet longer than the earlier vessel. In May 1915, Glen paid £171,000 for *Glenartney*, the first of its large motorships bought within a month of completion for a sister group company. In 1919, the slightly smaller *Glenade* cost £380,000 to build. Finally, the four 9,000 ton motorships of the *Glenogle* class cost a staggering £620,000 each to build in 1920-2.[13]

The shipowners who were prepared to pay these prices were driven by two considerations: the need to replace losses to resume full peacetime service before competition eroded traditional route dominance, and the belief that the end of the war would herald in a prolonged period of trade prosperity. The second of the global shocks to hit the shipping industry, the Great Depression, thus compounded the damage done by the first. With the concern to rebuild quickly proving premature and expectations of prosperity entirely misplaced, many owners were left with hopelessly stretched balance sheets and no real chance of generating the levels of revenue need to cover inflated depreciation and interest charges. The Royal Mail Group was ultimately the largest casualty of these developments, and one of the incidental results of its collapse would be the transfer of its Far Eastern shipping assets to the rival Blue Funnel.

Blue Funnel was immune neither to the war-inspired inflation in shipping costs nor to the subsequent sharp depression in trade. While losses had not been severe as a proportion of total fleet size, there was still a considerable need for replacement tonnage both for casualties and for surviving vessels built in the 1890s. The new ships were expensive, the large 11,400 ton *Achilles* completed for the trans-Pacific service in 1920 cost £545,000, but Holts had the advantage of large financial reserves and insulated themselves to a certain extent against future asset deflation by using some of the windfall gains of the short-lived post-war boom in freight rates to make large early write-downs on recent investments. Overall, the company managed an adequate degree of fleet renewal while living within its considerable financial means. As a result, when trade conditions deteriorated severely in the early 1930s, the company's balance sheet was strong enough to stand the strain, and the fleet, still featuring a high proportion of pre-war vessels, was modern enough to soldier through the difficult years without significant reinforcement.[14]

Holt's 1920s building programme featured a number of 10,000 ton ships intended for the trans-Pacific trade and some even larger cargo-passenger ships destined for the Australian route. The vessels built for the basic China service, however, were only slightly larger than their pre-war predecessors. The largest single class, the 8-ship *Eumaeus* class of 1921-23, were typical in basic hull layout at 460 feet in length and 7,700 gross tons. The company did undertake a certain degree of experimentation with propulsion, employing triple expansion, quadruple expansion and steam turbines in different classes. In 1923, it finally built its first motorships, and thereafter all but a few of the new ships it added to its fleet were diesel powered. Inter-war new building virtually came to a stop with two groups of motorships built in 1930-31, the four ships of the 6,700 ton, $11^{1}/_{2}$ knot *Maron* class and the five ships of the 7,700 ton, 14 knot *Agamemnon* class. The only significant groups of ships to come under Holt control from then until after the Second World War did not sport the famous blue and black funnel of the parent company, but the red and black of its long-time rival the Glen Line.

The full details of Holts' 1935 rescue of the Glen Line from the wreckage of the Royal Mail Group are outside the remit of this paper. The basic factors underlying Glen's problems and Holts' enduring financial strength have already been touched on. Holt acquired Glen's 10-ship fleet for £650,000, only a fifth of its pre-acquisition book value, and not much more than the building cost of one of the 9,000 ton motorships Glen had crippled itself in building in the early 1920s. The ships acquired were generally larger and slower than their Blue Funnel equivalents, and only six were retained in service. The other four were quickly sold, three of them for scrap, and replaced with four Blue Funnel ships transferred to Glen colours to maintain the combined Glen and Shire East Coast conference rights until a more comprehensive modernisation could be undertaken. A comparison of the ships leaving and joining the Glen line during this reorganisation provides one last interesting insight into the merits of Blue Funnel design. The three ships sold for scrap, one of which was a motorship, had all been built between 1914 and 1916, the vessel sold for further trading was another motorship built in 1920. The four ships drafted into replace them had all been built between 1917 and 1923 and on paper should have been only marginally more modern. All, however, were capable of 14 knots and both built and maintained to far higher standards. While the Glen motorship *Glenamoy*, completed in September 1916, was fit only for the scrapyard in 1936, Holt's steamship *Elpenor*, completed only four months later and drafted in as a replacement, would continue to sail for one company or the other until 1952.[15]

Holts did not make any additions to their own China fleet between 1931 and the Second World War. Progressive replacement and upgrading in the 1920s had left Blue Funnel well equipped to capitalise on the improvement of trading conditions that began in 1935. Investment was concentrated on the newly-acquired Glen Line, whose east coast home berth had always been far more vulnerable to competition, and whose rather slow fleet was facing increasingly pressure from modern vessels introduced by German and Japanese competitors in particular. The planned revitalisation of Glen took the form of the eight-ship *Glenearn* class, the first of which entered service in December 1938. These 9,000 ton, 480 foot, 18-knot twin-screw motorships have a fair claim to being the finest products of British inter-war marine engineering. Offering the highest possible combination of power and speed, they were superior to any similar vessels on the route and among the best of a distinguished group of fast cargo liners introduced by various British companies in the shadow of the Second World War. As such, they represented just as prominent landmarks in the development of the China seas liner as the *Agamemnons* of 1865 or the large steamers of the turn of the century, and like both previous classes they were destined to remain competitive and profitable throughout their long lives. Unlike their predecessors, however, their arrival was almost immediately overshadowed by war – indeed only half the class had actually entered commercial service before the Second World War broke out.

The Second World War, the third global catastrophe to disrupt the middle years of Holts' century, was far more destructive to China shipping than its predecessors. The conflict itself was truly global in reach and the war against merchant shipping was waged with a wider and more potent range of weapons. The combined Blue Funnel/Glen fleet lost ships to mines in the Bristol Channel, to German submarine attack in the Gulf of Mexico and off the Gold Coast, to Italian motor torpedo boats in the Mediterranean, to German surface raiders in the Indian Ocean and to Japanese aircraft in the Philippines. Blue Funnel lost as many ships in 1942 alone as it had in all of the Great War, and the whole group's losses for the entire period totalled 44, excluding another 8 lost while being managed on behalf of the government. Beyond the scale of losses, the second war also differed from its predecessors in that the entire far eastern

trading base of the company was lost to Japanese conquest and occupation for more than half the conflict.[16]

When the Second War ended, the Blue Funnel Group had lost just over half its fleet. The rebuilding challenge was even more severe than the losses suggested. Of the 87 ships with which the Group had entered the war, no fewer than 28 had been built before or during the First World War. Those of this older group that survived, their usefulness further eroded by hard war service, could not be expected to remain economical far into peacetime. Indeed, as the Blue Funnel fleet had not been bolstered by any new tonnage after 1931, it would be fair to expect that almost all surviving vessels would have to be replaced within a decade. Paradoxically, the much smaller Glen Line subsidiary was actually in far better shape. Despite almost constant use in the most dangerous conditions, six of the eight new *Glenearn* class ships survived the war. With the two losses replaced by vessels laid down during the war, the eight-ship fast service from east coast ports, originally intended to be complete in 1940, finally became a reality in 1948 after post-war refits and reconstructions were completed.

Rebuilding the Blue Funnel fleet was a much larger and more prolonged process. After the First World War, Holts had not followed most of the remainder of the British liner industry in buying government war-built standard ships as replacements. The ships in question had been designed as all-purpose general cargo carriers, and, even leaving aside the issue of the inflated prices at which they were sold, were never likely to represent adequate additions to a liner fleet. Given the scale of losses, and the reduced capacity of the British shipping industry to produce new purpose-built tonnage, there was no real alternative the second time around. In addition, the terms of purchase available were much better than they had been after the Great War, and the ships bought represented reasonable value in a sense that the purchases made by other firms 25 years before had not.

Interestingly enough, Holts still did not buy any standard British-built ships. The acquisitions the firm made came entirely from the huge fleet of ships mass-produced between 1942 and 1945 by the United States. In 1947, Holts bought six of the 15-knot Victory class and eight of the 11-knot Liberty class. While the Liberties in particular were far below the standards and specifications the company would normally have required for its fleet, they did provide the necessary immediate injection of tonnage. The Victories actually enjoyed two decades of company service. The Liberties generally provided about a decade of solid if unspectacular service before sufficient purpose-built vessels could be introduced to allow them to be sold.[17]

The main replacement effort did revolve around ships designed by the company to meet its own exacting standards. There were, however, some interesting features of these vessels which distinguished them from the products of Holts' previous major building programmes. Only a small percentage of the new buildings, the four-ship *Peleus* class of 1949-50 and the similarly sized *Helenus* class of 1949-51, were really ships built up to the highest standards of speed and carrying capacity. Steam-turbined vessels capable of 18 knots (and actually the first steam ships built for the company since the mid-20s), these vessels were intended to spearhead the services to the Far East and Australia respectively. The bulk of the replacement ships, however, were far more modest vessels, 15 knot ships of decidedly unoriginal design, described accurately by one of the firm's own managers as 'merely work-horses wrapped around the maximum single-shaft diesel power obtainable in the late '40s and early '50s.' These ships, known generically as the 'A' class represented an attempt to produce reliable tonnage as cheaply and as quickly as possible to bring the fleet back up to strength. No fewer than 21 of them were completed by 1954, making them easily the biggest single class of ships the firm ever built.[18]

Both Blue Funnel and its Glen subsidiary had in fact embarked on a deliberate two-tiered strategy. Each operated a premium service built around very fast and modern vessels, the *Peleus* and *Helenus* classes of the former and the reinforced *Glenearn* class of the latter. Each supported this with a secondary service, initially provided by pre-war survivors and ex-Victory or Liberty ships, which were gradually replaced by 'A' class ships as the 1950s wore on. The latter provided critical mass at reasonable cost, thus supporting market position within a competitive environment which did not at the time require an entire fleet of fast vessels. This model appears to have worked well through the first decade and a half of full peacetime operation. That it did so was, however, partially due to the weakness of competition. Most traditional rivals entered peace without any fleet to speak of, and potential British rivals were facing rebuilding programmes at least as challenging as Holts' own, often without the same financial resources. The situation only began to change in the late 1950s, when the German and Japanese fleets began to replace the second-hand ships with which they had restarted their businesses with new tonnage, and when Scandinavian and other British owners also started to challenge the Blue Funnel/Glen monopoly on speed at the top end of the market.

Holts' century had begun with the firm being challenged by faster ships put into the water by other British owners. It was somehow fitting that it should begin to move towards its end with another British challenge built around speed. As if to complete the circle begun by McGregor's Glens and Skinner's Castles more fully, the new threat also emerged from a Scottish company with a Scottish naming tradition. While competition from foreign fleets was also beginning to bite, it was really the appearance of fast ships wearing the colours of Leith's Ben Line that triggered the building of what was to prove Holts' last generation of conventional cargo ships. The Ben Line had actually been a participant in the China trade right through the age of steam, but it had generally been content to operate on a small scale at the lower end of the market with ships of utilitarian design and capabilities. This strategy began to change in the mid-1950s with the introduction of the 10,000 ton, 17-knot *Benreoch* class. These ships, capable of competing with the best Blue Funnel had to offer, were reinforced at the beginning of the 1960s, by the 11,300 ton, 20-knot *Benloyal* class, vessels clearly superior to their rivals. The Ben challenge found its final form in the mid-60s with the arrival of the 12,000 ton, $21^1/_2$ knot *Benledi* class.[19]

As an east coast line, Ben posed a more immediate threat to Glen than to its Blue Funnel parent. By the early 1960s, the splendid thoroughbreds of the *Glenearn* class were, in any event, entering their third decade and beginning finally to be overtaken in technological terms. The first Holts response was therefore the four ships of the *Glenlyon* class, ordered in 1960 and completed in 1962. These 11,900 ton ships were the largest yet built for the group, and with a service speed of 20 knots, easily the fastest. With speeds continuing to edge up, and with Japan's NKY also introducing vessels capable of more than 20 knots, further ships were required and in 1964 an order was placed for eight 12,200 ton 21 knot ships, four each for Blue Funnel and Glen.

The new ships, known as the *Priam* class in Blue Funnel and the *Glenalmond* class in the Glen Line were really the first vessels to deviate from the tall centre section funnel profile that had made Holts' ships unmistakeable since the 1890s. In every sense they represented the very latest in marine technology and design, and were truly superior, at least at the time of order, to all the other ships deployed on the China route. Their history, however, was to be brief and unhappy. It began with a series of cost and time over-runs in the builders' yards. Holts had been sufficiently concerned about the already manifest problems of British shipbuilders to order two of the eight vessels from Japanese yards. Their concerns proved well-placed. The two Japanese vessels were built in 12 months; the best British performance was 16 months and two ships actually took more than two years to complete. This sorry tale was symbolic of the plight of an industry which was to collapse even more quickly and more completely than the ship-owning companies it served. It cost Holts more than just time and money. Given the rapid technological pace of the time, it meant that ships designed to be the best were often matched, or even exceeded in performance by the time they entered service.[20]

The *Priams*, however, were not really doomed by the disorganisation of their builders but by a change in the very nature of the liner business that cannot have been foreseen at the time they were first designed but was already beginning when they entered service. Containerisation, beginning on other routes in the mid-60s had effectively taken over the Far East liner trades by the early 70s. Coming at a time when many conventional services were already being cut back under pressure from shipping companies set up and supported by Far Eastern governments, it brought a rapid end to the careers of even the newest conventional ships on the China Seas routes for which they had been designed. The eight *Priam*/*Glenalmond* ships left their designed service in 1972 after only six years. They survived another six in company colours on other routes in a series of joint ventures with other conventional cargo ship owners, but in 1978 four were sold en bloc to Asian owners and the rest soon followed. 1978 also saw the Glen Line disappear as a ship-owning entity in the general contraction of Holts' shipping interests. Blue Funnel itself survived into the late 1980s operating a variety of types of tonnage, but Holts' century as the pre-eminent operator of liner tonnage on the China Seas routes had really come to an end in the early 70s.

Notes and references

1 Holts' Blue Funnel Line has been better served by historians than most British shipping companies. F. E. Hyde, *Blue Funnel: A History of Alfred Holt & Company of Liverpool 1865-1914*, (Liverpool, 1957) remains a seminal work of maritime business history and covers the first half of the firm's history in impressive detail. M. Falkus, *The Blue Funnel Legend. A History of the Ocean Steam Ship Company, 1865-1973*, (London, 1990) is a definitive study of the entire period of ship-ownership. J. Clarkson, B. Harvey & R. Fenton, *Blue Funnel Line*, (Preston, 1998) presents an excellent collection of photographs of the company's ships and a wealth of information about their careers. D. Haws, *Blue Funnel Line*, (Torquay, 1984), while occasionally unreliable on points of detail, is nonetheless a comprehensive history of the fleet.

2 For brief histories of the Shire Line see W. A. Laxon, *The Shire Line*, (London, 1972) and D. Haws, *Glen and Shire Lines*, (Hereford, 1991).

3 For the Glen Line see Haws, *Glen and Shire Lines*; E. P. Harnack, *Glen Line to the Orient*, (London, 1970) and M. Cooper, 'McGregor Gow and the Glen Line: The Rise and Fall of a British Shipping Firm in the Far East Trade, 1870-1911, *Journal of Transport History*, 3rd Series, Vol 10, (1989), 166-79. Skinner, like many of the shipowners whose businesses did not survive the nineteenth century, has yet to receive the attention of modern historians.

4 Merseyside Maritime Museum, Ocean Steamship Co. Papers, OA 300/A & B, Correspondence between Alfred Holt and John Swire, 1875-1881.

5 D. R. MacGregor, *The China Bird: The History of Captain Killick and One Hundred Years of Sail and Steam*, (London, 1961), 185-8; Cambridge University Library, Jardine Matheson Papers, Correspondence between A. C. Gow & Co. and Jardine Matheson, 1872-1881.

6 Falkus, *Blue Funnel Legend*, 96, 111-6; Hyde, *Blue Funnel*, passim; Haws, *Blue Funnel Line*, 57-61; and Merseyside Maritime Museum, Glen Line Papers, OA113, Steamer Costs and Earnings, 1871-98.

7 E. Green & M. Moss, *A Business of National Importance: The Royal Mail Shipping Group, 1902-1937*, (London, 1982), 21-40; J. Taylor, *Ellermans: a Wealth of Shipping*, (London, 1976), 55-8.

8 W. D. Wray, *Mitsubishi and the NYK 1870-1914: Business Strategy in the Japanese Shipping Industry*, (Cambridge, Mass, 1984), 293-340.

9 Green & Moss, *A Business*, 41-90.

10 A. S. Mallett & A. M. B. Bell, *The Pirrie-Kylsant Motorships 1915-1932*, (Coltishall, 1984); Merseyside Maritime Museum, Glen Line Papers, OA361, Notes by C. McGregor.

11 Hyde, *Blue Funnel*, 172-181.

12 Falkus, *Blue Funnel Legend*, 312-6.

13 Merseyside Maritime Museum, Glen Line Papers, OA639 & OA981-3.

14 Falkus, *Blue Funnel Legend*, 171-234.

15 Merseyside Maritime Musuem, Glen Line Papers, OA639; Falkus, *Blue Funnel Legend*, 232-4; Green & Moss, *A Business*, 181-3.

16 For a full description of the Holt companies experiences and losses during the Second World War see S.W. Roskill, *A Merchant Fleet in War: Alfred Holt & Co, 1939-45*, (London, 1962).

17 Falkus, *Blue Funnel Legend*, 260-2.

18 *ibid*, 262-7.

19 For a brief history of the Ben Line see G. Somner, *Ben Line*, (Kendall, 1980).

20 Falkus, *Blue Funnel Legend*, 327-32; Clarkson et al, *Blue Funnel Line*, 156-162.

The China Seas in the Container Era

John Roberts

The past forty years have seen changes in world shipping and ports that surely equal and perhaps surpass those of the nineteenth century, which at thxe time seemed so dramatic. This chapter will examine the impact of the container revolution on shipping in the China Seas region up to the present, including the British involvement which earlier chapters have amply demonstrated for earlier periods. It will focus on trade between China Seas locations and other parts of the World, especially Europe, container shipping services to the region and the scale of British participation. The changes brought about by containerization, have affected all sectors of shipping operations, and imposed world wide or global standards, of which the most obvious is the modern container itself.

In the new language of container ports and shipping, the container is a strong metal box of standard 8 feet by 8 feet cross-section, and standard lengths of 10 feet, or 20 feet or 40 feet. For purposes of comparison the 20 feet long unit has been adopted and the term twenty feet equivalent unit (TEU) is in common usage. Special corner castings allow one container to be locked to others above or below, or secured when placed on lorries or railway wagons. These serve also as lifting points for quayside container gantries and for straddle carriers. General purpose containers have lockable doors at one end and can be 'stuffed' with any cargoes up to the limits of their dimensions. There are also a variety of special containers, including those for the carriage of refrigerated and liquid cargoes. To understand the magnitude of the change from 'conventional' shipping, it is necessary to review the main features of the powered ship era up to the 1960s.

In the nineteenth century revolution, wind propulsion gave way to power, building ships using wood gave way to building in iron and then steel, and powered mechanization was introduced to cargo handling Ports had to respond to the ever increasing size of ships, more frequent voyages and growth in trade, by expanding and renewing their facilities, and migrating to more suitable locations. For river ports the last generally meant down stream. Matching these developments were changes in many related areas such as communications, finance, ship owning, management, ship design and navigation. By the mid-twentieth century the prevalent ship types concerned with cargoes, were tankers, tramp ships and cargo liners. Despite some modest growth in ship size, the maritime world had absorbed the changes and had for some decades (ignoring war) been settled in a relatively stable system. This was as true for China Seas shipping and ports as other parts of the world. Following World War II, maritime industries invested heavily in new but conventional shipping, and ports were reinstated to cater for them. As in the inter-war years, tankers and tramp ships carried oil cargoes or homogeneous dry bulk cargoes (such as grain, minerals, coal), as charters demanded. Scheduled services were left to the cargo liners which carried a great mix of manufactured goods and raw materials in much smaller consignments. A great many of these smaller shipments needed some form of packaging if they were to survive the journey from shipper to consignee without loss or damage.

In the past some standard forms of packaging had evolved such as the amphora of the ancient world and the barrel, with its different sizes, significant from medieval times into the twentieth century. Barrels were used for anything: beer and butter, nails and naptha, soda and sugar. By the twentieth century there were many new forms. Bags, bales, cartons, cases (wooden boxes), crates, drums, in a variety of sizes, had one thing in common: they were of a size and weight capable of being manhandled. Together with commodities and goods which traveled unpackaged, these were the 'break bulk' cargoes which required individual handling, not only in and out of ships, but at every stage of their, in China Seas terms, lengthy journeys. Loading and unloading ships took time and in the 1950s cargo liners were spending half their voyage time in port. Their officers became expert at the complex stowage created by the mix of commodities, loading and discharging ports. The use of dunnage, typically cheap timber of 3 x 3 inches or 6 x 1 inches and, in China Seas ports, woven mats, was a critical element in break bulk cargo stowage. It consolidated the stow and protected the cargo from a variety of forms of damage.

At the heart of modern containerisation is the concept of through transport from inland origin, via inland waterway, rail or road to port, the sea passage, and from port via inland waterway rail or road to inland destination. It was not a new concept. The railways, in particular, had pioneered through transport on short sea passages from the late nineteenth century. In some cases whole trains went by sea, in others there was transshipment to ferries in port. Large, rail-compatible, lift on/lift off steel framed wooden boxes were developed to speed the handling, about half the volume of a modern standard container unit. Their use in long sea passages does not seem to have been anticipated.

The need to speed up cargo handling using mechanical handling devices, was recognized. In the fifties commodities such as timber, previously handled as individual pieces were strapped into large bundles, requiring power handling in and out of ships, and the pre-slinging of bundled cargoes increased efficiency in , for example ship turn-round times. Palletisation came in the same period, pointing the way but handling at ship side was not eliminated except in ro-ro (roll on/roll off) operations (mostly short sea passages). These

developments, and the early stages of containerization, were for a time called unitization. At a much larger scale was investment in another through transport concept, the lighter (or barge) aboard ship systems (LASH, Seabee, Bacat), which were pioneered, as the container was, by American interests. These systems offered some advantages over containers being suitable for ports with river hinterlands, but were not suited to land transport networks. In the final analysis it was the needs of the continental scale American rail network which drove the adoption of the standard container, ultimately world wide.

From the late 1950s the most noticeable changes in ships were the increasing sizes of tankers, and the introduction of new specialist vessels, notably bulk carriers. In the search for economies of scale, each new batch of orders for these types seemed to be for larger vessels. Tankers became super tankers, then very large crude carriers (VLCC) and then ultra large (ULCC). Eventually ships of a quarter million and even a half million tons were built. There was more specialization in ship types, examples being liquid gas carriers and car carriers, and of course the container ship itself. Although containers could be and were carried on conventional cargo liners, they were physically incompatible, and from the beginnings of containerization, it was recognized that specially designed ships were required. A container represented a 'heavy lift' on conventional ships, geared to the union purchase handling system lifting less than two tons at a time, and could only be carried on deck or in the square of the hatch. In all such ships remaining space was suited only for break bulk cargos. Even the earliest container ships were of necessity very much larger than conventional ships, in order to contain the vast cellular structures into which containers were slotted when loading.

There was the same problem in ports. Break bulk cargo berths with adjacent godowns (a China Seas term) or warehouses, were similarly incompatible with container operations, for which special heavy lift handling gear was required. The new technology demanded vast new deep draft container berths, with huge flat, uninterrupted container marshalling areas, and container gantries of a size many times larger than any such earlier structures. On shore, had to come the new massive mobile container lifting device, the straddle carrier. All this could achieve greatly improved turn-round times, providing the records and documentation could keep pace. It was no coincidence that the computer was beginning to come into its own, and would replace the manual/paper systems in use since the dawn of international trade. This was not just for the benefit of the shippers, port authorities, customs services, ship records, and consignees. The safety of the ship itself depended on knowing what was in each container, where it was loaded and what it weighed. The weight affected the stability of the ship, and the complex calculations involved, which in break bulk ships occupied many hours of officers' time when planning and supervising the stow, needed computer systems if the time scale was not to be seriously affected. Indeed, the whole stowage task moved almost completely from the ship to the container terminal operator, in the new world of container shipping. The stowage of the cargo in the container now became the responsibility of the place ashore where the container was 'stuffed', and container ships had no need for many tons of loose dunnage.

Finally it must be noted that nothing to do with shipping is immune from the impact of international events. In the context of the container revolution in the Far East, the status of the Suez Canal was to have a significant impact. The closure of the waterway between 1967 and 1973 was at first considered to be permanent. It led to reduced route capacity and to the need to build more conventional cargo liners, or to continue with the development of the container system. The latter was chosen, and the UK / Europe to Far East container trade developed at least ten years earlier than originally planned. Holt's

Priam class ships were thus made prematurely redundant. The re-opening of the Suez Canal changed route capacity again, this time increasing it. Initially the third generation container ships could not make the transit. However, encouraged by the World Bank, the canal was dredged to enable the largest container ships to pass through. Initially this led to over capacity on the route and reduced freight rates, but these were factors which encouraged trade.

East Asia liner trades

World economic activity has grown immensely since conventional cargo ship days, but overseas trade has grown much faster than economic activity, while trade using scheduled container services, still known as the liner trade, has grown faster still.

Table 1 Westbound East Asia to North Europe Trade, 1965 & 2001

	1965	2001
Total assessed in 1967 study	173,500	
Allowance for areas omitted from 1967 study	26,500	
Total westbound trade (1,000s)	200 TEU	3,725 TEU
Increase in trade 1965 to 2001 (multiple)		18.6
Sailings available to UK trade shippers per week	3.5	23
Increase in sailings 1965 to 2001 (multiple)		6.6

Sources: 1965: OCL Feasibility Study, 1967; 2001 P&O Nedlloyd data (estimate).

Typically this has been by a multiple of three times gross domestic product (GDP), and amounts to about eight or nine per cent per annum over the last ten years. As an example of this, the Westbound peak leg of the Far East to North Europe trade has grown about nineteen times in volume since 1965. This means that for every 'bill of lading ton' of 40 cubic feet (the measure of volume at the time), there is now a 20 foot container load equivalent (TEU) (today's normal measure). It also means that if the same type of ships were used now as then, there would be nineteen times as many

241

required, together with the port facilities to handle them (Table 1). Although some container trades have grown more quickly and some more slowly, the growth trades have included East Asia at one end of the route or the other, and the area has expanded significantly in economic terms (Table 2). The base overall volumes have increased about fifteen times since 1973. By then most major trades had been containerized, but many minor ones had not. Hence the data has been adjusted to take this into account, with the effect of muting the East Asia data whose growth would otherwise have appeared even more spectacular. It should also be noted that the number of transshipments, especially in East Asia, had, by 2000 also increased considerably.

Table 2 Relative Importance of East Asia in Liner Trades, 1973 & 2000. Container throughputs at terminals

	1973 %	2000 %
East Asia	20	39
Europe	34	24
North America	28	15
Rest of World	18	22

Source: *Containerisation International Yearbook*, with estimated corrections to allow for trades not containerized in 1973, and high levels of transshipment in East Asia in 2000. Note: Overall growth in World throughputs in 2000 equals 1973 x 15.

Table 3 The World's Largest trades in 2001 (two way flow) in million TEU

East Asia/N. America (USA, Canada, Mexico)	10.9
Intra-Asia	10.5
East Asia/Europe inc. the Mediterranean area	8.7
Europe including Mediterranean/N. America	4.4

Source: As Table 2.

The current significance of East Asian liner trades is shown in Table 4, where of the top four, the three largest involve East Asia and account for 42 per cent of all liner trades. The fourth is significantly smaller than these, but the four together account for half the World's liner trade. Further, the China Seas are the location for the World's five leading container ports: Hong Kong, Singapore, Pusan, Kaohsiung and Shanghai, making the area far busier in these terms than in earlier periods. Even though the largest container ships on Far East / Europe trade have about thirteen times the capacity cargo liner shipping had in the 1960s, the average container ship is nothing like so large, being only about four times larger than a 1960s conventional vessel. There are many more ships at sea than formerly, especially when the number of Asian feeder vessels (not in the intra Asia data) is added.

Table 4 Comparative Importance of East Asian Areas in 1965 & 2001. Shipments from Ports in the Westbound East Asia/Europe Trade

	1965 %		2001 %
Japan	35	China	31
Hong Kong	20	Hong Kong	20
Malaysia	16	Japan	12
Singapore	10	Indonesia	6
Philippines	6	Thailand	6
Other	13	Other	25

Source: As Table 2. Note: Cargo shipped from Hong Kong today mainly originates in south China. Other areas today include Korea, Taiwan, Malaysia, Vietnam.

Within the East Asian region, there have been major shifts in cargo movement (Table 4). The 1960s must be considered unusual owing to the isolation of China, which was probably greater then than it had been for perhaps 100 years. Today China is more fully engaged in World trade than ever before. Another change affects Japan. In the 1960s it was a major exporter of all kinds of finished manufactured goods and was almost the World's workshop. That is no longer the case today. In the 1960s Malaysia was still a major exporter of raw materials such as natural rubber and plywood, which were carried in cargo liners. Now its wealth is based on natural gas, manufactures and palm oil. Palm trees have replaced rubber trees. Palm oil, previously carried in cargo liners, is no longer a liner cargo. Although Hong Kong appears to hold the same proportion, in 1965 cargo was made in Hong Kong itself, whereas today most shipments originate in the Shenzen Province of China and outside the current Hong Kong area. One area that has not changed as much as others is the Philippines, which has declined to one per cent of shipments. This may be compared with Vietnam, which has increased from a negligible proportion to 4 or 5 per cent of shipments.

Container Shipping Services

Table 5 A Conventional 1960s Cargo Liner in the Far East/Europe Trade compared with container Ships of the 1970s and the present

	Pembrokeshire	Liverpool Bay	PONL Shackleton
Build year	1967	1972	2001
Length over all (metres)	171.8	289.6	299.9
Beam (metres)	23.7	32.3	42.8
Draft (metres)	10.2	13	14
Capacity	693000 cu.ft. (c. 600 TEU)*	2300 TEU (later 3043)	6805 TEU
Speed (knots)	21	26	24.5
Round Voyage time (days)	120	65	56
Routed via	Cape	Cape	Suez Canal
Approx time in port (days)	57	15	12.5
Annual one-way capacity (TEU)	1800	14,600	44,200

Note*: *Pembrokeshire* was a conventional liner and could carry 150TEU of containers.

Source: *Containerisation International*.

The trade analysis has shown that the conventional systems of the 1960s would have been wholly inadequate for today's volumes of cargo. That was a period of searching for solutions to growing problems, particularly the need to reduce the time ships spent in port. The container revolution was the outcome. It produced a secular change in which all the contributing elements had to adapt more or less at the same time, to enable the new system to work. The comparison in Table 5 shows the impact on the ships themselves, while those on the Far East / Europe route provide the best example as that was where the largest liner vessels were, and still are, placed.

The *Pembrokeshire* was a *Priam* class vessel placed by Alfred Holt & Co. in their Glen and Shire Line service from the United Kingdom east coast and north European continent to the Far East. The *Liverpool Bay* class ships were the world's first Panamax (the limit of the Panama Canal) container ships built for the new container ship consortium, Overseas Containers, in which Holts had a stake. P & O NedLloyd *Shackleton* represents the result of the following 30 years of evolution and growth. The most significant item of data in Table 5 is the time in port. Containers speeded up cargo working rates ten to fifteen times initially, while maximum ship size increased five times in a very short space of time. Since then the largest ships have further increased three times in size, the same ratio at which container ports have improved working rates.

These rapid changes produced innumerable operational problems at all levels. Even though container terminals were still being built, such problems affected the ships and port operations less than they did the infrastructure underpinning the whole business of trade. Shippers had to be induced to understand that export cargo had to be delivered much earlier if it was not to be left behind. Most of the business transactions were on letter of credit terms, and shippers were used to receiving their 'shipped on board' bills of lading (cargo documentation) as soon as the ship departed. But with so many more documents to issue at the same time, weeks and months passed before teething troubles were overcome. At a different level were the needs of the large numbers of truck drivers congregating in the terminals. In the original planning there was no provision for refreshment facilities or even public conveniences. Since this first container revolution (the second has been identified with the 1980s), there has been concern that increasing ship size must pose problems ashore. But compared with the original situation, absorbing changes in scale has been a matter of evolution, and the impact relatively easily assimilated. Change there has been, most noticeable in the general improvement in services. In 1965 there were about fifteen direct sailings to the Far East each month, where as now there are 23 per *week*, an increase of six or seven times as many. Including feeder services, the range of destinations served is much wider. If a shipper wants to send goods inland it is much less difficult than it used to be. Likewise, the range of logistical services, some completely innovative, is much wider. Examples include packaging, bar-coding and goods confirmation as well as inland transport.

Table 6 Far East/Europe Trade freight Rates per TEU		
	1967	2002 (first quarter)
	$	$
East bound	590	601
West Bound	540	1073
Profit/loss	139	loss

Source: 1967 as Table 1 (profit was probably somewhat exaggerated); 2002 *Containerisation International* index of freight rates.

The processes of gradual evolutionary improvement on all fronts has meant that the costs of freight movements in real terms are a fraction of what they used to be. The advantages of e-commerce in enabling much more direct communication between lines and customers should produce many more savings in the future. But while real costs are much lower, this is even more true of freight rates in 2002, which were at levels below break even in several trades, including Far East/Europe (Table 6). Competition is much stronger, especially from East Asian based lines. Freight conferences, so significant in the conventional liner era in setting common rates for member liner companies, are much weaker, while the influence of non conference operators has become very important, resulting in more volatile freight rate fluctuations. These are

rapidly influenced by supply and demand factors. Only a year earlier, freight rates were much higher and yielded reasonable profits. The supply and demand factor also meant that peak west-bound leg rate was priced much higher than that of the east-bound leg in 2002. By way of comparison the nominal price of a car has increased about ten times since 1967, while the freight charged on a Far East/Europe container load has less than doubled. This in itself is, of course, a reason for the expansion of trade. Another reason for lower costs and prices, is that, despite the increase in price competition between lines since the 1960s, there has been more co-operation between them through running joint services in a cost-effective manner.

Table 7 Grand Alliance: Far East Main Line Call Ports
Japan: Sendai, Tokyo, Yokohama, Shimizu, Nagoya, Kobe
Korea: Pusan; Taiwan: Kaohsiung
China : Qingdao (Tsingtao), Shanghai, Ningbo, Xiamen (Amoy), Yantian, Shekou, Hong Kong
Thailand: Laem Chabang (nr. Bangkok); Singapore; Malaisia: Port Klang (Swettenham)
Indonesia: Tanjung Priok (Jakarta)

Source: *Containerisation International.*

The 1960s container revolution gave great impetus to what were called 'consortia', because individual traditional liner companies were unable to finance and run container services on their own owing to the large amounts of capital required by the new system. Container ships were much larger and more specialized and significant investment was also needed for the new container terminals. Today, through growth, mergers and other aspects of consolidation, shipping lines might just be able to do so again on their own, but they do not choose to go down that avenue because the standards of service and frequency now demanded would be costly to meet without co-operation. These advanced service standards include, despite the large amount of container feeder servicing provided, the need for a wider range of direct port calls (Table 7). For cost and marketing reasons, this is hard to achieve economically without an adequate spread of partners. Alliance, the modern term for joint services in which ship space is shared between three or four lines, achieves significant cost savings by deploying a large fleet over two or three of the largest trades, with vessels sized to suit requirements.

Britain and Present Day Container Shipping and Terminals

The ranking of the twelve leading container lines by capacity is presented in Table 8. The British involvement is represented by P&O NedLloyd, which is half Dutch, the Canadian, though UK-based, CP Ships Group, and some operators which have some UK or Isle of Man registered ships. Its proportion might seem meagre until it is realized that its share would still place Britain in the top half of the list. Reference to Table 9 offers a more detailed view of British involvement in the Far East. Further, of the former traditional liner companies not listed, Blue Funnel/Ocean (now named Exel) is still heavily involved as the World's largest logistics operator, and through movements by air and sea as forwarders (not running ships). Ben Line runs ship agencies in Japan and elsewhere. The British presence is still influential.

Because East Asia's trade is now so widespread, operating effectively there today involves providing a full range of offices in all areas, and other logistical services inland to deal with cargoes from, for example, Chongqing (Chungking), reputedly the World's most populous city and 1000 miles inland from Hong Kong. This might be seen as the modern equivalent of British companies running steamers up the River Yangtze in the past. For a global player, such as P&O NedLloyd, there is a need to cover many Asian trades. Shipping companies are not like airlines which are confined to routeing everything and everybody through a single country hub. They

Tokyo Bay *at Hong Kong, 5 September 1972, the first container ship call.*

Arafura*, built 1970.*

Osaka Bay*, built 1972.*

Oriental Bay*, built 1989*

*P&O Nedlloyd **Shackleton**, built 2001.*

Papuan Chief, *built 1991.*

Shenkou Container Terminal, Shenzhen.

Table 8 The leading World liner Companies, 2002			
Operator	Fleet TEU	World share % of TEU	Nationality
Maersk / Swedish Lloyd + Safmarine	772,203	11.7	Danish
P&O NedLloyd	413.808	6.2	Anglo Dutch
Mediterranian Shipping Co.	388,935	5.9	Swiss
Evergreen Group	384,381	5.8	Taiwanese
Hanjin/Senator	308,295	4.7	Korean
COSCO	238,295	3.6	Chinese
APL	236,363	3.6	Singaporean
CMA-CGM Group	220,931	3.3	French
NYK	196,305	3.0	Japanese
Mitsui / OSK Lines	188,419	2.8	Japanese
CP Ships Group	181, 327	2.7	Canadian
UK K Line	172,814	2.6	Japanese

Source: *Containerisation International.*

Table 9 British Companies in East Asian Trades	
P&O NedLloyd	Half British; world No. 2; global network
China Navigation	John Swire & Sons; several local & Far East/Australia/N.Zealand services
Bank Line	Weir Group. Calling at New guinea, Indonesia, Singapore
Sea Consortium	British owned; Singapore based feeder co; E.Asia/India/Middle East/Med
CP Ships	Canadian but UK based; share in Far East/Europe and Pacific trades
Maersk Line	Danish; World No. 1; has UK arm
Evergreen	Taiwanese; World No. 4; has UK arm

Source: *Containerisation International*

really can and do operate globally. P&O NedLloyd provides seven sailings a week from the Far East to Europe (five to UK and North Europe), but it also provides ten sailings from the Far East to North America, about fourteen separate East Asia services to and from other areas of the world, all weekly, and various intra Asia sailings.

Yet another area of important activity is the operation of container terminals, which are now an international business. P & O Ports (a separate arm from the shipping combine) is ranked fourth in the world in this field. The Swire Group owns a major share in two terminal companies in Hong Kong and south China.

Table 10 British Involvement in Container Terminals in East Asia

P & O Ports Container Terminals
    Qingdao, Shekou (China); Laem Chabang (Thailand)
    Manila (Philippines)
    Surabaya (Indonesia)
    Vostochny (Russian Far East)
Non-container facilities in China, Philippines and elsewhere
Swire Group;
    Major shares in Hong Kong terminal and Shenshen (China)

Source: *Containerisation International*

Container operators were involved in the management and development of container terminals from the start, creating not only new facilities in existing ports, but totally new ports. Indeed ports became globalised alongside container shipping. Just as in shipping the scale and finance demanded partners, so in terminals the investment demanded collaboration. In any case container operators were making the running, and needed to ensure all the new systems needed in a terminal were provided. The rapid creation of terminals, the increase in the scale of container shipping and operations and the advent of new container locations in the very short time from the original initiative, has

meant that ports are forever watchful of the changes and especially competitors, lest their market positions be undermined. In the race to keep abreast of developments speedy new investment in terminal facilities and services is essential. The civil engineers designing and building terminals and upgrading the water site are driven by the ship designers and builders producing the latest shipping.

In the discussion of such a new system as container shipping, it is easy to lose sight of the human element aboard ships as well as in ports. Port labour is universally local, except perhaps at management levels. Containerisation has displaced the large numbers of comparatively low skilled manual labourers needed to handle break bulk cargoes. It uses instead small numbers of much more skilled people to drive container handling equipment. Employment is lost to the port, except to the extent that containers are stuffed locally. Aboard ship, manning has, over the past forty years been subject to many other pressures, of which cost cutting through reduced crew sizes and employment of third world seafarers on lower wages must be the most significant. While just over half of P&O NedLloyd's owned fleet operate under the British flag, there is no guarantee of purely British manning. The same is true of the other container fleets, noted above, as having some British connections. True, it is likely that masters will be British but junior officers and whole crews are likely, for example, to come from the Philippines. However, it must be kept in mind that in the 1950s many conventional cargo liners trading to the China Seas, carried substantial Asian crews. In Holt's ships all the engine room ratings were Chinese, and a significant proportion of the deck and catering ratings, though all the deck and engineer officers were British. Such patterns were true of other British companies running ships to East Asia. An analysis of crew agreements for the period would be revealing. Nevertheless, there is no doubt that the numbers of United Kingdom based British seafarers at all levels, to be found aboard ships in the China Seas, is now significantly reduced.

Conclusion

 This chapter has brought British Shipping in the China Seas into the twenty first century by offering an overview of the impact of containerization on the region and on British shipping trading to the area since the late 1960s. The treatment is by no means comprehensive. Indeed the topic is not amenable to simplistic approaches, given the radical nature of the changes and the global dimensions involved. But enough has been said to indicate the significance of the advent of the container age, and to demonstrate something of part played by British interests. The overview of conventional break bulk cargo liner operations offered an essential context without which containerisation cannot be appreciated. For a fuller treatment of its history, reference should be made to the seminal study by the late Professor Frank Broeze. It must be borne in mind that many other forms of shipping not discussed here have throughout the past forty years continued to operate in China Seas waters, so that this chapter by no means offers a comprehensive picture.

Bibliography

Frank Broeze, *The Globalisation of the Oceans: Containerisation from the 1950s to the Present,* (St. John's, 2002).

Mark L. Chatwin, et al., *Ocean Container Transportation: an Operational Perspective,* (London, 1990).

A. D. Couper, *The Geography of Sea Transport,* (London, 1972).

Malcolm Falkus, *The Blue Funnel Legend: a History of the Ocean Steam Ship Company, 1865-1973,* (London, 1990)

Shin Goto, 'Globalisation and International Competitiveness: the Experience of the Japanese Shipping Industry', in David J. Starkey & Gelina Harlaftis (eds.) *Global Markets: the Internationalisation of the Sea Transport Industries Since 1850,* (St. John's, 1998), 355-384.

Alston Kennerley, 'Cargo Handling and Stowage; British Cargo Liner Practice in the 1950s with Some Reference to the Nineteenth-Century Practice', in Stephen Fisher (ed.), *British Shipping and Seamen, 1630-1960: Some Studies* (Exeter, 1984), 86-109.

Roy Pearson & John Fossey, *World Deep Sea Container Shipping: a Geographical, Economic and Statistical Analysis,* (Aldershot, 1983).

For much of the detail of containerization, reference must be made to shipping periodicals, and especially to their supplements and regular status reports. The main examples are *Containerisation International* (and its *Yearbook*); *Fairplay International Shipping Weekly*; *Lloyd's List*; *Lloyd's Shipping Economist*; *Lloyd's Maritime Asia*. There are also some useful websites on container shipping and port organizations.

Canton and Macau: early Chinese images of the European settlements

Patrick Conner

Canton

The latter stages of the sea route to Canton are perhaps better documented pictorially than any comparable location in the Far East. Four sites stand out: Macau; the narrows of Bocca Tigris (modern Humen) some 30 miles to the north; the anchorage at Whampoa (Huangpu), ten miles further up river; and the foreign Factories at Canton, another ten miles beyond. For nearly a century (and in some cases more), these locations were repeatedly depicted by Cantonese artists working for clients from Europe and North America, adapting their style, medium and presentation to suit the requirements of these Western visitors.

What are we to make of these topographical pictures, painted in a semi-Western manner by Cantonese artists? For much of the eighteenth and ninteenth centuries, such 'export' pictures (including portraits, interiors, subject pictures and studies of natural history as well as port scenes) were the only Chinese pictures to be sent back to Europe and North America on a regular basis. In the late eighteenth and ninteenth centuries, as classical Chinese painting began to be taken seriously in the West, 'export' pictures tended to fall out of favour with collectors and academics alike. Then in the last 30 years of the twentieth century a fresh interest has been taken in the genre, stimulated by publications and by exhibitions, some in Europe but most in the United States. The study of Chinese export painting is still a young subject, however, and some basic questions have still to be addressed, one of these being 'how far did early Chinese port scenes depend on Western prototypes?'

The artists and artisans of Canton enjoyed a reputation (which was built up over several centuries) as skilled imitators. Whatever new pattern, medium or technique might be required by Western speculators, as being acceptable to Western tastes, the Cantonese studios seemed able to supply it, whether in porcelain or lacquer, ivory or painted paper. European engravings were often brought out to Canton, where the studios would reproduce the image not only on porcelain but also in the form of reverse-glass paintings, or even oil paintings on canvas. Yet it was the unanimous opinion of visitors that the Chinese artists were completely deficient in imagination; they were skilled, even slavish copyists, it was felt, but incapable of invention. Even 'export' views of the Pearl River – the straits of Bocca Tigris, and the anchorage at Whampoa – may have been derived from European engravings; it has recently been proposed that the most familiar compositions of those places were based on engraved illustrations published in 1773 by Carl Gustav Ekeberg.[1]

But what of the classic emblem of the China trade, the view of Canton itself, with the foreign 'Factories' or 'hongs', ranged along the river? Were these, too, based on specific Western prototypes? Here we may offer a tentative 'no'. It is a defining quality of all 'export art' that the artist or craftsman adapts his artefact to suit the tastes of the foreign consumer. But 'export' paintings of the Canton Factories seem to have evolved, at least until 1825, without the intervention of particular models or engravings or artists from the West.

It may be useful to analyse a typical (although unusually large) example of an 'export' painting of the Factories (see inside front cover). It can be dated to the period 1790 to 1794, as the transitional *tricolore* (largely white, but with red and blue motifs) flies above the French Factory. At first sight we scarcely recognise this as a Chinese painting. It follows Western practice in its medium (oils on canvas), its marshalling of subject-matter, and its use (albeit not quite consistent) of single-point perspective.

On the other hand the picture is quite unlike anything that a European *vedutista* would have conceived. Not only are the windows, the pediments and the porticoes evidently depicted by an artist who was unfamiliar with the traditions of Western architecture; the entire composition is that of an animated diagram rather than a topographical scene in which a sense of recession is achieved by the interplay of foreground and background elements. To Western eyes it must have appeared precise, lucid, pleasantly animated, and yet fundamentally alien. Perhaps it was this combination of qualities which appealed to Western clients; for this kind of view of the Factories remained popular for some fifty years, despite the fact that the Cantonese studios were certainly capable of producing more 'Europeanised' views of the same subject – and occasionally did so.

The limited, even austere palette seen in this picture may be due to the fact that the Cantonese studios had only recently begun to use oil paint. Earlier (and contemporary) views of the same scene are painted in the traditional Chinese medium of gouache, with a predominance of the blue-green, greys and pale warm brown that are seen in the oil painting. The earliest depictions of Canton that we would characterise as 'export pictures' take the form of handscrolls, up to eight metres long, Some (such as the scroll in the Göteborg City Museum) adopt a single viewpoint, generally opposite the Factories, so that as we look in either direction, the suburbs and countryside become less and less distinct. Others, like the scroll in the British Library, adopt a succession of viewpoints along the river: these cover the dozen miles from lower Whampoa to western Canton on a scale of about thirty inches per mile.

Thus we can trace a sequence of development. It is likely that the first topographical scrolls to reach Europe displayed scenes of Canton and its neighbourhood without concession to Western taste; one such 'non-export' scroll is in the Chinese Pavilion at Drottningholm Palace, Sweden.[2] As the Factory site was gradually transformed into a series of Western-style façades, with verandahs and in some cases porticoes, it became more distinctive and pictorially interesting, at least to the foreign visitors. Scrolls in an 'export' style, a style which Cantonese painters might first have experienced in the decoration of export porcelain, came into being. A further step was the division of a scroll into smaller sheets which could be framed in the Western manner. This division often occurred in Canton, for sets of twelve 'Whampoa to Canton' views survive, each one about 18 x 30 inches, in Cantonese frames.[3]

By about 1800 'export' scrolls had been superseded by individual views, pairs or sets of four. Considering only the views of Canton, we are bound to be impressed by their variety – not only a variety of style, suggesting that a number of hands and studios were involved in their production, but small differences of architectural detail, indicating that the artists were quick to incorporate any changes in the appearance of the Factories. Fires (and bouts of rebuilding) were frequent, enabling us to date some Canton views with precision. Other elements, such as the junks and sampans in the river, were much less subject to change, and indeed certain groups of river craft recur in many hundreds of views.

No doubt we are generally given a sanitised impression of the site, but unappealing features do sometimes appear. After the great fire at Canton of 1822 piles of debris accumulated in front of the Factories; there were partial clearances, during one of which '3 or 4 corpses were found'. A gouache on paper watermarked 1827 (see page 255, upper), apparently shows (to the left of centre) this heap in about 1830, which is described in the East India Company Factory records as '…an obnoxious mound of rubbish in front of the Factories… within [whose] precincts a village of Hovels has grown up'. This 'nuisance' was finally removed, by hundreds of small boats, in January 1831.[4]

It is worth noting that, whereas Cantonese

'export' studios were adept in copying almost every kind of Western picture, in the case of topographical scenes of Chinese locations, Western artists frequently copied the Cantonese. It is an open question whether the spectacular oils of the Canton Factories by Thomas and William Daniell utilised Chinese views, at least in part; but there can be no disputing that some of the Daniells' aquatints in their book *Picturesque Voyage by the Way of China* (1810) are based on 'export' scenes. The drawings of Thomas Allom (1804-1872) were used to illustrate a book entitled *China …in a Series of Views*, with text by the Rev. G.N. Wright (1843); this proved the most popular work on China to be published in the nineteenth century. Allom never visited China, however, despite the Rev. Wright's implications to the contrary, and all his illustrations are re-drawn from the work of others, including a number which are evidently based on Chinese 'export' paintings, although not acknowledged as such. So high was Allom's reputation as a sinologist that for many years a detailed watercolour of Canton in the Victoria & Albert Museum was attributed to him. However an engraving dated 1838 exists, clearly taken from this watercolour, and its inscription sets the record straight: the watercolour was painted by Henry Melville, 'after a native artist', i.e. a Cantonese 'export' painter.

There is even a case of a European artist's attempting to sell a Chinese 'export' view of the Canton Factories as being a work painted by himself on his travels. The German-born Sigismund Bacstrom served as a surgeon in the Dutch navy from 1763 to 1770 and then settled in England, working for Sir Joseph Banks from 1772 to 1775, and for Captain William Kent until 1779, before returning to sea. A number of Bacstrom's drawings survive from his later journeys, including eleven taken in Canton and Macau in 1793-4.[5] Back in London in 1800 he offered a group of his pictures for sale, including (as his catalogue records) a:

View of that part of the Suburbs of Canton in China which faces the River, with the

Factories of the different European Nations… 30 Inches by 18… £52. 10.[6]

A painting which is surely the one in question has recently come to light, with the inscription in ink (similar to that on Bacstrom's drawings): 'Sigismund Bacstrom del. 1794 &1796'. The picture is a characteristic Cantonese 'export' gouache. No doubt Bacstrom owned the picture, inscribed his name on it, and tried to pass it off as his own work.

Macau

The Chinese 'export' paintings of Macau survive in some numbers, most of them from the nineteenth century. Since Macau enjoyed such a long and continuous period of association with Europe, having been settled by the Portuguese in the middle of the sixteenth century, we might expect that it would not be difficult to trace the origins of these paintings, and to find European prototypes for them. Yet their genesis is even more obscure than that of 'export' views of Canton.

We might also expect that prospects of Macau from the sea would often have been drawn by visitors. For a merchant vessel making its way eastward from Europe, Macau was one of the first cities to be encountered on the China coast. It presented to passing ships a spectacle of baroque churches, hilltop forts and (fronting the principal bay) imposing houses in a style reminiscent less of China than of European colonial mansions in India and the East Indies.

Yet the body of Western depictions of Macau, from its inception as a settlement until the arrival of George Chinnery in 1825, is surprisingly meagre. Early Portuguese views give a basic notion of a hilly peninsula with a scattering of dwellings and towers. The Dutch embassy to China in 1655 gave rise to an illustrated volume which was soon translated and widely read in the West; but the view of Macau published in this account is little more than fantasy, consisting of indeterminate architecture and imaginary topography. Most of the original drawings for this book were executed by its author, Jan Nieuhof, the embassy's steward; but many of the details were added in Europe by the engravers. In his text Nieuhof writes that the embassy's ship caught sight of Macau but, as he admitted, 'we came not near her'[7] – leaving the engravers (it would seem) to invent a substitute.

Several able draughtsmen visited Macau in the last quarter of the eighteenth century, among them John Webber (accompanying Captain James Cook), Thomas and William Daniell (on their circuitous voyage to India in 1785, and on their return journey in 1793), and William Alexander (accompanying Lord Macartney's embassy, as it was about to return home in January 1794). Yet between them they appear to have left no more than a handful of drawings of Macau, despite its plethora of temples and churches, its picturesque bays and rocky hillsides. For detailed visual records of Macau at this period we must turn to the work of the Cantonese export artists.

Whereas Chinese scroll paintings seem to have played a part in the creation of early 'export' scenes of the Canton river, the shape of Macau – a peninsula three miles long and a mile across at its widest point – did not lend itself to this treatment. Two eighteenth-century paintings of Macau (below and right) can be regarded as interesting early essays in 'export' art.

The one below does not fulfil Western ideals of topographical accuracy, as its mountains and islands play a largely decorative role; but the location is recognisably Macau, seen from the Inner Harbour. Church façades and baroque gateways are indicated by spiky finials, and just to the left of centre can be seen its most celebrated building – the church and convent of S. Paulo, raised above a broad flight of steps. In 1835 this church was to be reduced to little more than the great granite façade which survives today, with its four columned tiers (six are shown in this version) and its mixture of occidental and oriental motifs.

On the right is another view of Macau from the Inner Harbour which appears closer to Western artistic conventions in all respects but one: the bay itself, which Western viewers

Chinese artist, c1800, Macao from the 'Praya Piquena' (Inner Harbour), oils on canvas, 17 by 23 inches,
Courtesy of the Martin Gregory Gallery, London

Chinese artist, Macao: the Inner Harbour, oils on canvas, 16 by 22 inches.

would expect to see on or below the horizon, projects dramatically above it. One can assume that this notion was too bizarre for Western tastes, and that this composition had a brief existence.

Another early formula is represented by a painting which shows the Praya Grande from the south-east. This was perhaps conceived as a counterpart to a contemporary view of Canton, although the surrounding hills mitigate the diagrammatic effect. The curve of the bay has been in effect straightened out, so that the structures at the right-hand end (such as the decorated gateway to the convent of Santa Clara), which would be seen at an angle or indeed hidden by the curve of the bay, are shown here full-face.

Most views of Macau fall into one of four categories: the Inner Harbour, the Praya Grande from the northern end, the Praya Grande from the southern end, and the view along the peninsula from Penha Hill.[8] All these, and the last three categories in particular, were painted in many versions, with many small variations, from the late eighteenth century onwards. Yet I can discover only one case, before the arrival of George Chinnery in 1825, in which an 'export' view of Macau seems to have been derived from a European original. The Hong Kong Museum of Art holds an elaborate topographical drawing of the Praya Grande, which is signed by Captain Robert Elliot, R.N. and dated October 1824 (see page 254). This correlates closely with a painting in gouache of the same scene, in the Macau Museum of Art, (see page 255, lower) which may well have been taken directly from it.[9] Otherwise we must conclude that 'export' views of Macau, like those of the Factories at Canton, developed to a large extent as through a locally-generated momentum.

Notes and references

1   Kee Il Choi, 'Carl Gustav Ekeberg and the invention of Chinese export painting', *Antiques*, (March 1998), 426-437.
2   This handscroll is noted on an inventory of 1777: see Bo Gyllensvärd, 'Two Chinese Topographic

Paintings in the Chinese Pavilion at Drottningholm', *Museum of Far Eastern Antiquities Bulletin*, 50, (1978), 144ff.

3   See Martyn Gregory Gallery, London, *Catalogue 43*, (1986), no.13

4   See Hosea B. Morse, *The Chronicles of the East India Company Trading to China*, (Oxford, 1926-29), 5 Vols, Vol IV, 175-6, 278, 291. See also William Shang, 'Pearl River Landmarks – a method of dating paintings', *Arts of Asia* 31 no.5, (Sept.- Oct. 2001), 104.

5   Bacstrom's neat drawings of Hawaii, Tierra del Fuego, the north west coast of North America, and the south China coast are held in the archives of British Columbia and in the collection of the late Paul Mellon; the latter includes eleven drawn in Macau and Canton, two of them dated 'Dec. 1793' and '1794'

6   MS catalogue dated June 1800, formerly in the Paul Mellon Collection and now in the Beinecke Library at Yale. It lists 'some accurate and characteristic Original Drawings and Sketches made after nature during a late Voyage round the World in 1791, 92, 93, 94 and 95 by S. Bacstrom M.D. and Surgeon'. See also Douglas Cole, 'Sigismund Bacstrom's Northwest Coast Drawings and an Account of his Curious Career', *BC Studies* 46, (summer 1980), 61-86; and for his later career, Adam McLean, 'Bacstrom's Rosicrucian Society', *Hermetic Journal* 6, (1979).

7   Jan Nieuhof, *An Embassy from the East India Company of the United Provinces to the Grand Tartar Cham Emperor of China*, tr. John Ogilby, (London, 1669) 31. [1st ed., *Het Gezantschap...*, Amsterdam, 1665].

8   See P. Conner, 'Images of Macau', *Antiques* CLV no.3. 432-441.

9   For other detailed pencil drawings by Robert Elliott of Indian subjects see Martyn Gregory Gallery, London, *Catalogue 77*, (2001). The possibility that Elliott copied a Chinese 'export' work, rather than vice versa, cannot be ruled out.

Captain Robert Elliot, RN, 1824. Praya Grande from the south west, Macau, pencil, 16 x 35 inches.

Hong Kong Museum of Art.

Chinese artist, Canton, 'The Hongs'. Gouache on paper.

Chinese artist, mid-1820s. The Praya Grande from the south west, Water-colour and gouache, 19 x 32 inches.